Islamic Reform

Studies in Middle Eastern History

General Editors: Bernard Lewis of the Annenberg Research Institute and Cleveland E. Dodge, Professor of Near Eastern Studies Emeritus, Princeton University; Itamar Rabinovich of Tel Aviv University; and Roger M. Savory of the University of Toronto.

The Turban for the Crown
The Islamic Revolution in Iran
SAID AMIR ARJOMAND

Language and Change in the Arab Middle East
The Evolution of Modern Arabic Political Discourse
AMI AYALON

Islamic Reform
Politics and Social Change in Late Ottoman Syria
DAVID DEAN COMMINS

King Hussein and the Challenge of Arab Radicalism
Jordan, 1955–1967
URIEL DANN

Egypt, Islam, and the Arabs
The Search for Egyptian Nationhood, 1900–1930
ISRAEL GERSHONI AND JAMES JANKOWSKI

East Encounters West
France and the Ottoman Empire in the Eighteenth Century
FATMA MÜGE GÖÇEK

The Fertile Crescent, 1800–1914
A Documentary Economic History
EDITED BY CHARLES ISSAWI

Other Volumes are in Preparation

Islamic Reform

Politics and Social Change in Late Ottoman Syria

David Dean Commins

New York Oxford
OXFORD UNIVERSITY PRESS
1990

Oxford University Press

Oxford New York Toronto
Delhi Bombay Calcutta Madras Karachi
Petaling Jaya Singapore Hong Kong Tokyo
Nairobi Dar es Salaam Cape Town
Melbourne Auckland

and associated companies in
Berlin Ibadan

Published by Oxford University Press, Inc.,
200 Madison Avenue, New York, New York 10016

Library of Congress Cataloging-in-Publication Data
Commins, David Dean
Islamic reform : politics and social change in late Ottoman Syria
David Dean Commins.
p. cm.—(Studies in Middle Eastern history)
Includes bibliographical references.
ISBN 0-19-506103-9
1. Islam—Syria—History—19th century. 2. Islam—Syria—
History—20th century. I. Title. II. Series: Studies in Middle
Eastern history (New York, N.Y.)
BP63.S95C66 1990 89-16211
956.91'03—dc20 CIP

9 8 7 6 5 4 3 2 1

Printed in the United States of America
on acid-free paper

For Mona

PREFACE

In the autumn of 1979 Professor Richard P. Mitchell returned from the Middle East with a handwritten manifesto by a proponent of Islamic reform in Syria. Entitled "Our Call," it outlined the agenda of religious reformers:

> Return to the Quran and the Sunnah, and understand them as the pious forefathers had.
> Call Muslims to act according to their religion's teachings.
> Warn Muslims against polytheism in its various forms.
> Revive free Islamic thought within the bounds of Islamic principles.
> Set up an Islamic society and implement God's law on earth.

The anonymous author then listed the leading thinkers of the Islamic reform movement: Aḥmad ibn Taymiyyah (d. 1328), Jamāl al-Dīn al-Qāsimī (d. 1914), ʿAbd al-Razzāq al-Bīṭār (d. 1917), and later figures.

The following summer in Beirut I met the late Ẓāfir al-Qāsimī, the son of Jamāl al-Dīn al-Qāsimī, the foremost advocate of religious reform in turn-of-the-century Damascus. When I returned to the Middle East in 1981, I met again with Mr. Qāsimī, and he put me in touch with his nephews in Damascus, Muḥammad Saʿīd al-Qāsimī and Samīḥ al-Ghabrah. The former holds the Qāsimī library in his home, and he graciously allowed me to study the manuscripts and papers of his grandfather Jamāl al-Dīn. I also benefited from Mr. Ghabrah's interest in the history of Damascus and familiarity with his grandfather's life and work. To each of these members of the Qāsimī family I am deeply grateful for their kindness and hospitality during my stay in Damascus.

A. U.S. Department of Education Fulbright-Hays Research Abroad award made possible my research in Damascus. I would like to thank Mr. Jonathan Owen of the U.S. Information Agency in Damascus for his help in obtaining the necessary permits to conduct research at the Ẓāhiriyyah Library and the Center for Historical Documents, and for smoothing over the rough edges of daily life in Damascus. At the Center for Historical Documents, Ms. Daʿd Ḥakīm and her staff provided a most congenial atmosphere for research. Dr. Muṭīʿ al-Ḥāfiẓ of the Arabic Language Academy was helpful in tracking down a number of articles and books.

On returning to the United States I was assisted by a grant from the Joint Committee of the International Doctoral Research Fellowship Program for the Near and Middle East of the Social Science Research Council and the American Council of Learned Societies with funds provided by the Ford Foundation and the National Endowment for the Humanities. I would also like to thank Juan Cole, Rudi Lindner, Paul Dresch, and John Voll, whose comments and suggestions sharpened the perspective and improved the execution of this work.

I thank my parents for their generous financial support during my years at Michigan and for always encouraging me to pursue my interest in the history of the Middle East. My wife, Mona, with her good humor and patience, helped see me through the last stages of research in Damascus. Finally, I am most grateful to my late mentor and friend, Richard P. Mitchell, for his encouragement and for his inspiring, humane approach to the study of Muslims and their endeavors to shape their lives according to their highest ideals.

Carlisle, Pa. D.C.

CONTENTS

Islamic Reform

INTRODUCTION

A slice of the history of modern Islamic reform in Syria lies in the living room of a modest apartment in Damascus. Books, journals, manuscripts, and loose papers packed together on tall shelves line three walls. Hanging above the books on one wall are three portrait photographs that depict the heritage of a family central to the reform movement. On the left side is Muḥammad Saʿīd al-Qāsimī, a bearded, white-turbaned shaykh of some 50 years, pictured with a book open before him. In the middle stands his eldest son, Jamāl al-Dīn, another bearded shaykh wearing a robe and white turban, perhaps in his early 30s. On the right, Muḥammad Saʿīd's youngest son, Ṣalāḥ al-Dīn, presents a different aspect: a young man with a thin mustache, dressed in European-style coat and trousers, starched white shirt, bow tie, and topped with a fez.

Three portraits, three generations, three ways of seeing the world. The father (1843–1900), a religious scholar, spent most of his life holding customary Islamic beliefs. In his later years he embraced the reformist vision that the eldest son (1866–1914), also a religious scholar, elaborated in the name of a return to the sources of religion. The youngest son (1887–1916) left behind the religious vocation, became a medical doctor, and strove for an Arab national revival. Each of these outlooks—a customary interpretation of Islam, scripturalist reform, and Arabism—had its partisans among *ʿulamāʾ* (religious scholars) and young intellectuals in Ottoman Syria between 1885 and 1914. Scriptural reform in Damascus developed in the historical context of Ottoman bureaucratic reform and calls to purify Islamic practices and beliefs.

During the nineteenth century, Ottoman rulers adopted measures that displaced religious personnel and religious principles from their customary roles in administrative, legal, and educational institutions. These secularizing measures, when finally enforced in the provinces in the second half of the century, transformed the notable stratum in Arab cities. For centuries this group had included many ulama, but within a few decades they were almost totally displaced. Concomitant with their fall in status, secular law codes and public schools whose curricula derived from European models spread and broke the monopoly Islamic discourse had exercised over law and education. The turn to scripturalism represented the response of some ulama to these secular trends.

Scripturalism, which stresses the exclusive authority of the Quran and the Sunnah in determining what constitutes Islamic beliefs and practices, had been spreading in learned circles since the eighteenth century, most widely among Sufi orders, although the Wahhābī movement in Arabia is the best known instance. During the nineteenth century two developments reinforced the scripturalist trend. First, the secularist reforms signified to some Muslims that customary interpretations of Islam could no longer provide a foundation for Muslim vitality. For those who remained convinced of Islam's truth, Muslims' weakness vis-à-vis Europe made sense if one believed that they had strayed from "true" Islam. Hence, it was necessary to return to the sources for a guide to rediscovering "true" Islam. Second, Europe presented a military threat to Muslim lands. To counter that threat, Muslims had to unite, which required that they transcend their differences. It became common to argue that such differences had arisen in the course of Islamic history and coalesced as variant ways of performing ritual, attaining mystical union with God, and interpreting law. By returning to scripture as the sole criterion for religious beliefs and practices, Muslims could overcome their divisions.

The modern Islamic reform movement in late Ottoman Syria was part of a wider movement known as the *salafiyyah,* which had adherents in other Arab lands. The advocates of this trend called for a return to the practices of the pious ancestors, *al-salaf al-ṣāliḥ* in Arabic, hence the term "salafiyyah" for the movement and "salafi" for its partisans. It is important to distinguish between "salaf," which refers to the first generations of Muslims, and "salafi," which denotes modern advocates of a return to the first generation's practices and methods.

Throughout the reformist circle's development it was related to wider political currents, first with the Young Turks, then the Committee for Union and Progress, and finally young Syrians interested in reviving Arab culture and elevating the Arabs' status in the empire. The shaykhs became involved in incidents and trends that indicate the development of new forms of political action in Arab urban centers: elections, political parties, partisan press, and proto-nationalist societies.

This study approaches religious reform in Damascus from the perspective of the social history of intellectuals: the experiences and outlooks of groups of intellectuals, and their complex interactions with their social, political, and economic contexts. In setting out the context for Islamic reform, I start with a description of Damascene ulama's place in society and of stratification within the ulama corps. The central historical developments in nineteenth-century Syria and their impact on the ulama complete our picture of the general context from which advocates of religious reform emerged. Moving to a more specific level, I discuss intellectual trends in the wider Muslim world that may have fostered religious reform in Damascus. Then I narrow the focus further with a close examination of the social origins of the reformist ulama faction in Damascus.

Having established the contexts of religious reform, I turn to the initial emergence of the reformist circle and the reaction of conservative ulama against it, in particular their inciting Ottoman officials to persecute the reformers and thereby silence them. This informal censorship stifled the salafis in Damascus, and they reached out to sympathetic minds by corresponding with reformers in Egypt, Beirut, Iraq, and Morocco, constructing a network of contacts in Arab urban centers. To understand why the reformers so offended most ulama requires an analysis of the salafis' distinctive ideas, especially their critique of practices and beliefs then prevalent among the ulama and Muslims in general. The antisalafi reaction also demands an investigation of the conservative ulama's social identity and their defense of their vision of Islam.

Finally, I probe the relationship between the salafis and other reformist groups in

Damascus: the Young Turks and Arabists. The manifold social and political ties between the salafi ulama and the much younger, secularly educated Arabists deserve close scrutiny because of the tension between Islam and nationalism as poles of political identity, a tension that is a recurring theme of twentieth-century history in the Arab world.

Having laid out the structure and concerns of this work, let me briefly state my hypothesis regarding the origins and significance of the salafi trend in late Ottoman Damascus. Salafism represented a response of middle-status ulama to secularist tendencies in Ottoman educational and legal institutions on the one hand, and to the projection of European power in the Middle East on the other. The salafis assimilated current ideas about reason, progress, science, and technology to a vision of Islam that held out to Muslims the promise of remaining true to their religious and cultural identity at the same time that they were borrowing technology and scientific learning from the West. This vision of Islam clashed with the beliefs and practices of most ulama who had adjusted to the juxtaposition of religious and civil schools, courts, and law codes in the belief that they could best preserve Islam by guarding its remaining bastions—the religious law court, the religious school, and the mosque.

Certain ulama "newcomers," either by immigration or coming from families that recently attained ulama status, followed the customary pattern of striving for higher prestige and influence by setting their sights on posts in the Ottoman religious administration.[1] This traditional game of ulama politics was complicated by ideological developments in the nineteenth century and the perception of the ulama's waning influence. Upstart ulama accused the religious establishment of failing the Muslim community at large by clinging to beliefs and practices that had no scriptural basis, that were not truly Islamic. Because the ulama had so utterly failed to preserve true Islam, which would have never allowed Muslims to fall behind the West, Muslim rulers turned to the expedient of borrowing European laws and institutions. With no end to the process of Westernization in sight, the reformers blamed official ulama for perpetuating a false, conservative version of Islam, and clamored for their replacement by competent ulama (such as themselves).

This reformist critique directly hit the bases of official ulama's practices and therefore provoked a hostile, sometimes violent response. The one educated group that the salafis attracted was the corps of recent graduates of the Ottoman high school in Damascus. In addition to links of kinship in a few instances, the salafis appealed to state-educated Syrian youths by formulating Islam in a manner that permitted the budding stratum of professionals to harmonize their Muslim Arab identity with their concern to master sciences and techniques of Western provenance. Furthermore, just as the salafis' ideology and career aspirations were blocked by the high ulama, so the younger men were frustrated in launching their careers by first the existing urban elite (which was not competent in their eyes), and later by Turkish bureaucrats sent to administer the province in the constitutional period, 1908–1914. Intellectual elitism, an ethic of professionalism, blocked careers, and frustrated ambitions drew salafis and high school graduates together in common political endeavors, first in supporting the restoration of the Ottoman constitution, then in asserting Arab rights at a time when the dominant political force, the Committee of Urban and Progress, appeared bent on "turkifying" the empire.

1

Damascene Ulama and Social Change in Nineteenth-Century Syria

Between 1830 and 1880 the ulama of Damascus suffered a decline in status and material fortunes. That decline came as an effect of the Ottoman Empire's administrative reform movement and changes in cultural life. Political developments in the Ottoman Empire combined with social and economic change to further exacerbate the ulama's sensitivity to decline. To comprehend their predicament requires an account of their place in Damascene society and the impact of political events and economic trends on Damascus.

The Ulama of Damascus

A profile of Damascene ulama shows a social group sharing a distinct status, but stratified according to degrees of wealth. Max Weber's category of a status group fits the ulama. He defined a status situation as one "determined by a specific, positive or negative, social estimation of honor."[1] A social group's status is marked by its style of life, which can include special dress, marriage within the status group, and conventions to guarantee status distinctions. Damascene ulama enjoyed a highly positive social estimation of honor; they wore a special costume; they married the sisters and daughters of fellow ulama; and the conventions surrounding religious knowledge and its attainment regulated access to ulama status. The possession of religious knowledge constituted the basis of the ulama's status honor; therefore, their status depended on the value other social groups accorded to religious knowledge.

The practical expression of the ulama's religious knowledge lay in their preeminent roles in worship, education, and law. In 1890, Damascus had over 200 mosques, nearly 200 saints' tombs and holy places, and 14 Sufi lodges. At the mosques, ulama led prayers, preached sermons, and gave lessons on subjects in religion and Arabic grammar. At the Sufi lodges, holy places, and some mosques, ulama conducted the rituals of Sufi orders and gave instruction in mystical beliefs and practices. Some ulama achieved recognition for their qualities as teachers. At religious primary schools (sing. *kuttāb*) ulama taught young boys to memorize portions of the Quran and rudimentary skills of literacy. Damascus's mosques and 39 religious schools (sing. *madrasah*) provided settings for higher learning.[2]

In 1850, Damascus had six religious law courts. The ulama working in those courts included a jurisconsult (*muftī*), his deputies (sing. *amīn al-fatwā*), deputies (sing. *nā'ib*) to the Ottoman magistrate (*qāḍī*), and court secretaries (sing. *kātib*). A handful of families dominated these posts, which conferred prestige and influence with Ottoman officials. Nearly all ulama holding court posts belonged to the Ḥanafī school of jurisprudence, one of four Sunni legal schools (*madhāhib*) and the official school of the Ottoman Empire. Before Damascus came under Ottoman rule, the majority of ulama followed the Shāfiʿī school. During the eighteenth century many ulama switched from the Shāfiʿī to the Ḥanafī school, probably to strengthen ties with the Ottoman religious hierarchy, whereas most ulama without posts in the courts continued to adhere to the Shāfiʿī school throughout the nineteenth century. A third school, the Ḥanbalī, had an ancient presence in Damascus, but by the nineteenth century few ulama belonged to it. The Mālikī school had few followers in Damascus before the middle of the nineteenth century, when Algerians fleeing the French conquest of their land settled in Syria. Ḥanafī ulama obtained court posts more easily than ulama of other schools; otherwise, legal school differences had little significance, and ulama of different schools customarily studied with each other.[3]

The legal schools represented a recognized range of practices in worship (*ʿibādāt*) and such interpersonal transactions (*muʿāmalāt*) as contracts, inheritance, marriage, and divorce. Each school had authoritative collections of rulings to which most legal opinions (*fatāwā*) and court verdicts referred. The schools' rulings rested largely on the principle of *taqlīd,* accepting the rulings of earlier authorities without inquiring into their reasoning, which spared ulama the effort of searching scripture for rulings in commonly occurring cases. In the last decade of the nineteenth century the validity of taqlīd became a controversial issue among Damascene ulama.

Within the bounds of their common status, the ulama included men of wealth, modest means, and poverty. Inheritance documents provide information about the ulama's stratification according to wealth.[4] Of 106 such documents registered between 1890 and 1910, 13 show ulama whose wealth exceeded 50,000 piasters. These wealthy ulama included two jurisconsults, two members of *sharīf* families (descendants of the Prophet), four ulama from families of renowned teachers, one from a family of preachers at the Umayyad mosque (the most prominent one in the city), and the leader of a Sufi order.[5] Three ulama left their heirs between 30,000 and 50,000 piasters; they included the sharīf and a man from a family of court officials.[6] This upper stratum of well-to-do and wealthy ulama comprised about 15 percent of the total sample.

Fifteen ulama left between 12,000 and 30,000 piasters. These middle ulama included teachers, shaykhs of Sufi orders, a deputy jurisconsult, and sharīfs. Twenty-two ulama bequeathed between 5,000 and 12,000 piasters. Few of these men appear in the biographical dictionaries, and those who did were Sufi shaykhs and teachers.[7] These middle and lower middle ulama comprised over one-third of the sample.

Thirty ulama left between 1,000 and 5,000 piasters. Members of families known for preaching, teaching, and Sufism appear in this stratum.[8] The 22 poorest ulama left less than 1,000 piasters; none of these men appear in biographical dictionaries.[9] Ulama whose assets amounted to less than 5,000 piasters made up half of the total sample.

The wealthiest ulama filled the most influential religious posts: jurisconsult, law court officials, preacher at the Umayyad mosque, teachers of oral reports (*aḥādīth*) at the Umayyad mosque's Nasr Dome and at the Sulaymāniyyah Sufi lodge, and head of the descendants of the Prophet (*naqīb al-ashrāf*). The families that dominated these and other prestigious positions belonged to the local elite of absentee landowners of rural lands, owners of urban property, and merchants. These more mundane activities formed the basis of the high ulama's wealth, while their positions in courts and mosques augmented their status and influence.[10]

Wealthy ulama played an important role in articulating the religious and moral ideals of society, both in everyday life and on ceremonial occasions. A vivid example of how they functioned as the "voice of the community" was the reading of a famous collection of oral reports, al-Bukhārī's *al-Ṣaḥīḥ,* at the Umayyad mosque's Nasr Dome during the Muslim months of Rajab, Shaʿban, and Ramadan. These daily lessons combined the prestige of the city's foremost scholar of oral reports, the most authoritative collection of oral reports, and the high holy season of the Muslim year. Attended by large crowds, inaugurated and concluded with great fanfare, and endowed with a generous stipend, these ceremonial lessons were laden with symbols of piety and power. Virtually void of instructive content, they affirmed the integral union of learning and authority, the binding of sultanic power and ulama as symbols of the Muslim community before and during Islam's longest rite, the month of fasting.[11]

The middle ulama occupied lesser posts in the religious courts, worked in mosques and religious schools, and led branches of the Sufi orders. The middle ulama seldom associated with high Ottoman officials, but their acquaintances often included wealthy ulama and lay notables. Middle ulama sometimes engaged in trade.[12] The lower strata of ulama possessed little wealth and lived in close contact with the city's artisans, petty traders, and laborers. This large pool of poor ulama mostly worked at the local shrines, where they conducted popular rituals.

Three salient features of Damascus's ulama require emphasis to understand their responses to social, economic, cultural, and administrative changes in the nineteenth century. First, the ulama's status depended on the value attached to religious knowledge. Second, before 1860 the high ulama formed part of the city's political and economic elite. Third, the ulama included men of various means, ranging from the very wealthy to the destitute.

Changing Communal Relations

During the nineteenth century changes took place in relations between Syria's Muslims and non-Muslims to the latter's advantage. Political developments between 1830 and 1860 helped raise the status of non-Muslims, while economic trends favored their interests, and the Ottoman reform movement's measures further benefited them.

Political Developments, 1830–1860

The first shift in relations between Damascus's Muslims and non-Muslims occurred in 1832 when Syria came under Egyptian rule, which lasted for eight years. The commander of the occupying Egyptian army, Ibrāhīm Pasha, allowed the Christian soldiers of his Lebanese ally to ride their horses into Damascus, thus violating an ancient taboo that symbolized and perpetuated Muslims' dominion.[13] Ibrāhīm Pasha further annoyed Muslims by appointing a Christian to head the provincial administrative council and by allowing Christians to openly buy and sell alcohol. Communal tensions became manifest when several Muslims attacked Christians and looted Christian-owned shops. The Christian victims complained to the Egyptians, who beat the assailants and jailed them for several days.

As a result of the Egyptian's apparent partiality to Christians, Muslims would celebrate on hearing of revolts against Egyptian rule and threatened Christians with retribution should the Egyptians ever withdraw. Indeed, when Ottoman rule returned to Syria at the end of 1840, Muslims beat up Christians who persisted in exercising the "privileges" they enjoyed under the Egyptians, such as wearing a white turban. To the Muslims' dismay, however, the Ottoman authorities gave notice that they intended to guarantee Christians the same rights they had grown accustomed to under the Egyptians.

In 1839, the Ottoman sultan proclaimed legal equality for all his subjects, regardless of religion, in the Gulhane Rescript. This proclamation had different meanings for different groups. While Syrian Muslims thought it reinforced the rising status of non-Muslims, Ottoman reformers regarded it as a way to remove pretexts for European intervention on behalf of religious minorities at the same time it dampened separatist aspirations among Christians in the Balkans.[14] Because Ottoman control over Syria was tenuous between 1840 and 1860, the proclamation barely affected Damascus.

The European consulates that were established in the 1830s and 1840s also promoted non-Muslims' interests. One Muslim chronicler lamented that whenever a dispute arose between a Christian and a Muslim, the authorities sided with the Christian because he or one of his relatives enjoyed European consular protection.[15] In the light of this situation, Muslims interpreted the 1856 Reform Edict, which reaffirmed the legal equality of Muslims and non-Muslims, as evidence that European powers dictated policy to the sultan.[16]

Economic Trends, 1830–1860

During the same 30-year period, changes in the Syrian economy bolstered the effect of political developments on communal relations. In the 1830s, the Egyptians encouraged the growth of trade with Europe, from which would accrue customs revenues to help pay the costs of maintaining a large army in Syria. To increase the export of agricultural products, the Egyptians extended the margins of cultivation, introduced new crops, and provided loans and equipment to peasants. The Egyptians facilitated the growth of trade with Europe by allowing a British consulate to open in Damascus and by providing security for non-Muslims, the chief agents of European trade. In 1835, a fortuitous boost to trade came from the advent of steamship navigation to the eastern Mediterranean.[17]

Yet a web of internal tariffs, duties, and local monopolies obstructed the growth of trade with Europe. In 1838, an Anglo–Ottoman commercial treaty lowered and unified import duties and eliminated monopolies. Syrian Christians and Jews benefited because they could obtain consular protection and immunity from Ottoman taxes under the terms of capitulatory treaties between the Ottoman Empire and the European powers. Christian traders imported cheap English cotton goods, and Christian weavers purchased English yarns without paying the onerous duties exacted from their Muslim competitors. The 1838 treaty hurt Muslim artisans because it left intact internal duties on local manufacturers, so their wares competed with inexpensive, machine-made imports, which faced lower duties than local products.[18]

In 1850, the Ottoman Empire enacted a new commercial code based on French law and administered by courts composed of European and Ottoman judges. The European consuls favored the new code and courts because they expected them to facilitate trade. Preponderant European influence in the courts ensured that they operated in the interest of European and Ottoman non-Muslim traders.[19]

In the late 1840s, European shipping companies, merchants, and banks funneled capital into Syria to sustain the growing import-export trade. The role of European capital increased to the point that European currencies, most often in the hands of non-Muslims, began to replace Ottoman money in local moneylending activities. By 1850, many Damascene Muslim traders were relying on Christian financiers in Beirut for credit.[20]

In contrast to the non-Muslims' new prosperity, Muslims tended to suffer as the local economy became tied into the orbit of the European economy. The 1838 treaty's low import duties opened the Syrian market to European goods, which outcompeted the products of Muslim artisans. Furthermore, a shortage of raw materials developed as European buyers siphoned off agricultural products used in manufacturing, such as silk, which Damascene weavers had customarily obtained from Lebanon. In the 1850s, Lyon silk goods manufacturers began purchasing large volumes of Lebanese raw silk, driving up the price and cutting into the supply. Although gradual in its effect, by the 1870s this trend had reduced the formerly flourishing silk manufactures of Damascus to a moribund state.[21]

On the other hand, changes in the rural economy offered profitable opportunities to some Muslims. Cultivating crops for export, which the Egyptians encouraged in the 1830s, accelerated after 1846 when Britain abolished the Corn Laws, which had inhibited the import of grains into Britain. Foreign demand for Syrian grain increased over the next few years, then rose sharply during the Crimean War (1854–1856) as world market prices soared.[22]

Further change in the rural economy followed the promulgation in 1858 of the Ottoman Land Code, which mandated land registration. Peasants feared that registering their lands would enhance the government's ability to tax and conscript them, and therefore many registered their lands in the names of urban notables. Likewise, peasants indebted to urban moneylenders gave their creditors the titles to their lands. As a result, some Damascene Muslims accumulated extensive rural landholdings.[23]

Political Developments, 1860–1880

Muslim resentment of non-Muslims' economic gains and improved status smoldered until July 1860, when sectarian conflict in Lebanon between Druzes and Maronite Christians ignited an explosion of violence against Christians in Damascus. For several days Muslim rioters massacred Christians, looted their homes, and burned their quarter. The destruction of 3,000 Christian-owned looms underscored Muslims' bitter anger at Christians' economic gains.

Soon after the outbreak, a large Ottoman force occupied Damascus, and French troops landed near Beirut. The reformist foreign minister Fuad Pasha directed an investigation of the uprising in Lebanon and Damascus and meted out severe punishment to Muslim notables, Ottoman officials, and officers for failing to prevent the atrocities. Fuad's actions established Istanbul's authority more firmly, placated European demands for retribution, and assuaged Christians' anxieties. As for Damascus's Muslims, the events of 1860 reinforced their perception that the Ottoman reform movement, of which Fuad Pasha was a leading figure, represented European influence in the imperial center.[24]

Political instability between 1876 and 1878 further vexed Syrian Muslims, who feared that a European power would soon invade and occupy Syria. In 1876, Ottoman subjects saw two sultans deposed and a third sultan ascend the throne with the help of the same men who had done away with his two predecessors. Meanwhile, in the Balkans a crisis brewed that ultimately led to war between the empire and Russia in April 1877. Though waged in the Balkans, the war had severe repercussions in Syria as its people bore exceptionally high taxes levied to pay for the war effort, and the dispatch of all Syrian conscripts to the front deprived many families of manpower.[25]

In response to the political crisis created by the Ottoman army's poor showing in the war, a number of notables in Sidon, Beirut, and Damascus organized a clandestine political movement. In the event of the empire's collapse, they planned to set up an independent Syrian kingdom under the hero of Algeria's resistance to the French conquest, ʿAbd al-Qādir al-Jazāʾirī, who had resided in Damascus since 1855. The empire survived the war, which ended in January 1878, and the notables retired from their activity.[26]

Tanzimat and the Ulama

During the period of Ottoman reforms known as the Tanzimat (1839–1876), administrative, legal, and educational reforms implemented in Damascus reduced the ulama's influence in two ways. First, the reforms diminished their power by consolidating central control over Damascus and by increasing lay representation on the various new provincial councils. Second, the reforms' underlying assumptions and explicit ideas challenged the ulama's authority by putting in doubt the relevance of their expertise. The bureaucrats and officials who devised the reforms represented an emerging social group with its own outlook and interests that clashed with those of the ulama.[27]

The first blow to the ulama's power fell before the Tanzimat when the Egyptians lowered the proportion of ulama on the provincial council and restricted the purview of the religious courts to matters of personal status, but the ulama recovered their former status in 1840 when the Egyptians withdrew. Between 1840 and 1860 the ulama used their influence in the newly instituted provincial council to implement reform measures in a way congruent with their interests. For instance, high ulama and lay notables manipulated the application of conscription and new fiscal measures so as to burden poor Muslims, while exempting the wealthy from conscription and minimizing their taxes.[28] Because Ottoman officials depended on Muslim notables to administer the province and to finance the budget, the latter were able to block moves to reduce the number of Muslim councillors and increase non-Muslim representation on provincial councils. In 1850, Ottoman reformers did establish mixed courts to administer the new commercial code. The mixed court was the first of a series of law courts that gradually removed jurisdiction of commercial, criminal, and civil cases from the ulama's purview. Except for the commercial court, though, the ulama and their notable allies diluted the impact of reforms until 1860.[29]

In the wake of the massacre of Christians, Fuad Pasha exiled prominent ulama and selected lesser ulama to sit on the provincial council. This step indicated the reformers' determination to overcome the ulama's obstructive tactics. Fuad also pushed for improved communications and transportation to tighten Istanbul's hold on Syria. A telegraph linked Damascus to Istanbul in June 1861, and in January 1863, a French-built carriage road between Damascus and Beirut cut travel time from 3 days to 12 hours.[30] More effective control enabled Istanbul to proceed with judicial and administrative reforms.

The ulama maintained their prominence during the 1860s by obtaining seats on provincial judicial councils, the fiscal council, and a supreme provincial council convened in Beirut in December 1867. But their influence declined as statutory courts proliferated in the 1870s and 1880s, and the provincial council excluded ulama altogether between 1870 and 1900. Meanwhile Damascus's urban notable elite had reconsolidated itself on the basis of landholding and bureaucratic posts by shifting resources into the rural economy and obtaining posts in new government institutions. A few ulama families belonged to this new elite, but the proportion of ulama among Damascus's leading figures had sharply decreased.[31]

Just as the Tanzimat reduced the ulama's influence, it also diminished their authority in elite circles. Their authority rested on the value attached to religious knowledge, but the Tanzimat imputed value to nonreligious knowledge. The early Tanzimat reformers worked in the Ottoman foreign ministry's translation bureau and embassies in Europe. Their acquaintance with Europe influenced their ideas about how to strengthen the Ottoman Empire. For instance, the reformer Muṣṭafā Sāmī (d. 1855) toured Europe extensively and came to believe that the West's strength stemmed from the advanced state of its sciences, from religious tolerance, and a harmonious blending of innovations with heritage. Sāmī wrote that the Ottoman

Empire could achieve progress and parity with Europe if the empire improved the education of its subjects, thus articulating the view widespread in reformist circles that Ottomans had to master the sciences that gave Europe a technological advantage in the economic and military spheres.[32]

In keeping with the views of men like Muṣṭafā Sāmī, Tanzimat bureaucrats set up schools to teach the sciences and techniques deemed necessary to better manage the empire's affairs and defend its frontiers.[33] Those schools instructed young men in Western medicine, European military strategy and techniques, and law codes adopted from European prototypes. The Tanzimat reformers' assumptions about what kinds of knowledge and expertise were relevant to governing the empire implicitly discounted the value of the ulama's knowledge and expertise, and reformers' drive to establish schools and courts outside the ulama's domain reflected the belief that religious knowledge and law could not provide the bases of progress.

The Tanzimat era was so damaging to the ulama because it marked the arrival, at the center of imperial power, of men who believed it necessary to borrow from Europe and who regarded the ulama as a hindrance to the project of reviving the empire. The Tanzimat bureaucrats advanced their interests and attitudes in several ways, among them designing the empire's first public schools to impart skills and knowledge characteristic of modern professionals, be they bureaucrats, lawyers, doctors, or army officers. With these schools in place, the number of educated Ottomans holding Tanzimat values proliferated, and they advanced their interests and outlook, often to the detriment of the ulama.

Cultural Change in Damascus

Changes in cultural life reinforced the deterioration in the ulama's status wrought by the Tanzimat. In fact, the extension of public schools to Damascus and the appearance of the printing press there sprang from the transfer of Tanzimat institutions to Syria. The schools and printed matter conveyed new ideas to Syrian pupils and literate adults, while the authors of school primers and newspaper articles groped for simpler forms of expression. Changes in the media and agents of culture deepened a subtle process of secularization, wherein religious beliefs and symbols lost ground to ideas referring strictly to nature and society.

Education

Before the introduction of state schools to Damascus, the ulama provided the sole means of education for Muslim children. Instruction began at Quranic schools and continued in religious schools and at the public lessons of ulama in mosques. The most accomplished students and the sons of ulama attended the private salons of prominent scholars, who gave certificates (sing. *ijāzah*) attesting to students' competence in certain texts.

Damascus had long been an important center of higher learning in the Muslim world. Itinerant scholars from as far away as Morocco and India would spend months and years in Damascus, studying with prominent ulama and teaching subjects and books outside the specialization of local ulama. Propertied migrants from nearby villages would also come to Damascus to pursue learning and sometimes entered the ranks of the elite teachers.[34] Damascene ulama frequently traveled to Egypt, the Hijaz (Medina and Mecca), Baghdad, and Istanbul to study with those cities' famous scholars. Religious learning in Damascus, then, partook in a circulation of scholars throughout the Near East and the Muslim world.

Within Damascus there existed a hierarchy of mosques and schools ranked according to the prestige of their teachers. The most famous ulama held endowed teaching posts at the Umayyad mosque, which represented the pinnacle of Islamic learning in Damascus, the Sulaymāniyyah Sufi lodge, the ʿAbd Allah al-ʿAẓm school, and the Jaqmaqiyyah school. Endowments stipulated these institutions' curricula, usually oral reports, jurisprudence, Quranic recitation, and other religious subjects. A number of ulama specialized in the so-called rational (*maʿqūl*) sciences, such as logic, astronomy, arithmetic, and philosophy, but these subjects were considered ancillary to the central curriculum of traditional transmitted (*manqūl*) sciences. The qualifying examination for entering the religious institution reinforced the stress on religious subjects because it tested students' knowledge of a prescribed set of texts, which therefore formed the core of religious education. Other subjects received less attention.[35]

In 1755, French Lazarist monks established the first mission school in Damascus. The monks taught French, Latin, history, geography, and Arabic. During the 1830s, the Egyptians allowed other missionaries to open schools. The Egyptians also established the first state school in Damascus, a military secondary school, and they sent a number of Syrians to the new medical school in Egypt. With their withdrawal in 1840, the military school closed, and mission schools remained the only means for acquiring knowledge of European languages and sciences for several decades.[36]

In 1869, Ottoman reformers promulgated an education law to establish a uniform system of primary, intermediate, secondary, and high schools, but this law had little immediate effect in Damascus. Though a few public schools opened in the 1860s and 1870s, Damascenes held them in low regard compared to mission schools.[37]

The impetus to an educational reform movement came in January 1879 when controversy erupted over a British Protestant school for Muslim girls. The Ottoman governor at the time, the famous reformer Midḥat Pasha (1822–1883), exploited the issue to persuade Muslim ulama and notables to form a private association, the Islamic Benevolent Society, to direct the establishment of primary schools for Muslim children. The Society collected donations from wealthy Muslims and prepared rooms in mosques and religious schools to serve as classrooms. In the first half of 1879, the Society opened eight schools for boys and two girls' schools. Two years later the Society was dissolved and its supervisory function transferred to a provincial board of education, which included several former members of the Society. At that time, its schools became public.[38]

Besides Muslims' opposition to mission schools on religious grounds, Ottoman officials feared the schools might instill sympathy for the European nations that the missionaries represented. Throughout the 1880s and 1890s, the government promoted the establishment of state schools to attract Muslim children and to minimize the influence of the mission schools, which graduated Westernized (*mutafarnij*) students. For a time, Ottoman policy mandated fines on Muslims who sent their children to mission schools, and authorities in Istanbul ordered them to shut down temporarily.[39]

During the last decades of Ottoman rule, the options for a Muslim child's education widened. One could attend religious schools, state primary and secondary schools, or foreign mission schools. By 1890, state schools had the largest share of students, nearly double the number of students in religious schools.[40] The complexity of education in Damascus becomes clear when one considers that a Muslim child could pass through a Quranic school or attend lessons given by ulama in their homes, spend some years in a state school, and go to a mission school to master French.[41]

The significance of the state schools lay in their connection with and continuation of the Tanzimat movement even after it had lost its political momentum. The schools embodied the assumption that Muslims needed to learn "modern" sciences and European languages, and therefore implied that religious education alone no longer sufficed. The new judicial, administrative, and military institutions required men trained in a fashion different from that of men who worked in the religious courts, mosques, and religious schools. The new schools' curricula stressed subjects that would qualify students to serve in new institutions, and although those schools did not explicitly devalue religion, their implicit thrust lay in a secular direction by teaching primarily subjects unconnected with religion.

Printing

Before printing raised new possibilities for the mass reproduction and wide distribution of books, journals, and essays, literature existed in manuscript form. The manuscript "industry" involved a number of specialized functions, such as papermaking, fashioning writing implements, employing scribes, and proofreading sessions among ulama. As in other cultural spheres, the ulama dominated the production of manuscripts and the selection of texts for copying. The holdings of the Ẓāhiriyyah Library in 1896 show a preponderance of religious texts in the manuscript collection. There were 1,892 manuscripts on religious subjects and only 315 manuscripts on literature, history, and science.[42]

The Egyptians set up the first printing press in Damascus to issue military commands, regulations, and decrees. They also imported books printed at Cairo's Bulaq press on mathematics, medicine, literature, and histories of Western countries. Following the return of Ottoman rule, 15 years passed before Damascus had another press, and only in 1864 did the government set up the first permanent press. In the meantime, books from Egypt and newspapers from Beirut and Istanbul made the printed medium familiar to Damascenes.[43]

In 1865, the provincial printing press began publishing Damascus's first newspaper, *Sūriyā,* in Arabic and Turkish. The provincial press also published a few religious essays by local ulama, and the authorities announced that individuals could use the press to publish works, but at their own expense. The paucity of readers dampened whatever incentive existed for potential publishers to use the official press.[44]

In the years 1880–1908, five private presses appeared that published essays on religious subjects, especially Ḥanafī jurisprudence, as well as poetry collections and scientific works. A list of works published in Damascus between 1870 and 1908 shows 54 books and essays on religious subjects and 75 on nonreligious subjects, including literature (31), science (16), history and society (13), and school texts (12). A similar edge for nonreligious works in print appears in the list of the Ẓāhiriyyah Library's printed holdings in 1896. They included 460 on nonreligious subjects and 414 on religious subjects. A comparison of the proportion of religious and nonreligious works in manuscript to their proportion in print shows the growth of a secular trend.[45]

Printing caused the decline of manuscript production, temporarily centralized the production of texts, and made possible a new literary form, the newspaper. The aforementioned *Sūriyā* published laws and regulations, so its audience consisted mostly of Ottoman officials. *Sūriyā* had four pages divided into Turkish and Arabic sections, and the editors of the Arabic pages included men who played a seminal role in developing Damascus's Arabic journalism. The Arabic in the official section often reproduced colloquial expressions of the local dialect and grammatical errors, perhaps because Turkish officials wrote it. By contrast, articles on health, new inventions, and the means for developing agriculture and manufacturing showed the hand of educated Syrians. *Sūriyā* did not publish articles about Arabic literature; perhaps the authorities forbade such writing. In spite of a large dose of scientific articles, readers complained of the virtual absence of news about Istanbul and Europe. As a result, Damascus's small literate population avidly read newspapers smuggled from Egypt and Europe.[46]

The first privately owned newspaper in Damascus came out in August 1879. An ambitious young Damascene, Aḥmad ʿIzzat al-ʿĀbid (1855–1924), had worked on *Sūriyā* when he was chief of the provincial Turkish and Arabic correspondence bureau. ʿĀbid used his influence in official circles to obtain a license to publish his own weekly newspaper, *Dimashq,* in Turkish and Arabic. His venture lasted until 1887. After that, *Sūriyā* remained the only newspaper until 1896, when the first exclusively Arabic newspaper, *al-Shām,* came out.[47]

The manager of the provincial press, Muṣṭafā Wāṣif, published *al-Shām,* in which he printed political news, always casting the sultan in a favorable light. He reported on the disturbances in Crete, the government's military expeditions in Jabal Druze (in southern Syria), and developments in Egypt. *Al-Shām* also contained bits of local news, reports from Istanbul, and literary pieces.[48]

All three newspapers published before 1908 were printed at the official provincial press, and their editors worked in the provincial bureaucracy, so they expressed views in accord with those of the government. The journals had a dual secular effect in that they formed a cultural medium outside the domain of the ulama, who had dominated written production when it was restricted to manuscripts, and the newspapers' articles on new inventions and the means of progress coincided with state schools' implicit secular impact.

New Ideas

Although printing brought a new literary form, its chief significance lay in conveying the ideas of authors from distant cultural, historical, and geographical settings. Such ideas could contradict those held by men receiving them and provide a foil for contrasting local elites' ideas.

Egyptian newspapers carried articles about Europe and Arabic translations of works in European languages, thus giving Syrians access to ideas from culturally distant societies. Cairo's Bulaq press printed many classics of the Arab-Islamic literary tradition, thus presenting historically distant alternative views. The histories of Europe published by Bulaq offered ideas from societies removed in historical, cultural, and geographical senses.[49] In nineteenth-century Syria, European ideas about society and politics possessed an intrinsic authority because of Europe's military and economic superiority, which Syrians wanted to understand by discovering the causes of Europe's progress through reading European history.[50]

Political and cultural circumstances conditioned the Syrians' selective reception of European ideas. Among the various currents of nineteenth-century European thought, rationalist and scientific ideas made the greatest impression on Syrians, not romanticism or socialism. The interest in streamlining government and acquiring technical knowledge disposed Tanzimat reformers to accept positivist assumptions regarding the nature of progress and its reliance on developing modern science; many Syrians concerned with the problems that occupied the Tanzimat reformers made similar selections from European thought.

Language

Besides the more formal aspects of cultural change in schools and newspapers, the very medium of culture, language, also underwent transformation. A movement to change literary expression emerged in Istanbul among Tanzimat bureaucrats who wanted to abandon the prolix, dense chancery prose of the eighteenth century and to use simpler, more concise expression. The drive to assimilate European sciences provided further impetus to linguistic reform as Turks translated European works and scientific terms.[51]

State schools also contributed to the trend toward new forms of expression. The ornate, rhymed prose esteemed by the ulama as a sign of erudition had to be abandoned if the Arabs wished to assimilate European sciences. The state schools, with their new curricula, required textbooks in simple language to facilitate instruction. Journalism also provided an important laboratory for experimenting with new forms of expression.[52]

Many ulama remained attached to the old literary style in which one demonstrated one's command of language by oblique expression. They ridiculed simple texts in which language served an instrumental purpose, as though straightforward expression belied deficient intellectual attainment. On the other hand, the proponents of simpler expression criticized the old style. The clash over language was apparent in the differences between the subculture of religious schools with their commentaries on medieval texts (sing. *sharḥ, ḥāshiyah*) and state schools with their simple textbooks.[53]

Secularism

Secularization in Damascus involved something other than a clear separation of religion from politics, which did not occur. If secularization describes a period "when the habit of referring all practices, finally, to some central faith . . . is loosening or has been lost," we can say that late Ottoman Syria went through such a period, with the proviso that we are speaking of a habit loosened, not lost.[54]

The new understanding of nature provided by modern science contributed to secularism's advance by replacing religious explanations of natural phenomena and of the constraints nature imposes on human life.[55] Public schools instilled a scientific and technical outlook in students by teaching them sciences. That does not mean that all those students held only new values and ideas, because they had also assimilated traditional values and ideas through their upbringings. Nonetheless, state schools sowed the seeds of new attitudes, and the same conditions that nurtured their flowering in Istanbul during the Tanzimat era prevailed in Damascus in the late nineteenth century: economic weakness, military inferiority, and growing doubts about the relevance of prevalent (religious) values and ideas.

A more subtle aspect of secularization resides in new conceptions of cultural practices. Hitherto, the ulama had dominated literate culture. Journalism gave birth to a new type of author, one who wrote on scientific inventions, discussed the causes of progress, and reported political news. The act of reading also took on new meaning. Reading the Quran was an act of pious devotion, and its recitation could be ritual, a spiritual encounter, or didactic instruction. Reading a newspaper constituted an act of acquiring knowledge about the everyday world, and therefore it implied an orientation to society and nature rather than to religion.

Conclusion

The effects of political, legal, educational, and cultural changes in Ottoman Syria converged in diminishing the value of religious knowledge. Because the ulama's social status depended on how much importance other social groups attached to religious knowledge, the ulama's status declined with the devaluation of their distinctive possession. A vivid manifestation of the ulama's distress lay in the emergence of a new urban elite in which they played a subordinate role after they had comprised a prominent component of the old elite. The new elite grew rich and powerful by taking advantage of changes in the economy and provincial administration; the same changes put the ulama at a disadvantage and detached most of them from Damascus's wealthy, powerful stratum.

In the last decades of the nineteenth century, a faction of Damascene ulama broke with the beliefs and practices of their colleagues. This faction put forth an interpretation of Islam that met the ideological challenge of new Ottoman intellectuals and the social and political challenges posed by the ulama's detachment from the urban elite.

2

Sources and Agents of Religious Reform

Changes in Damascene ulama's status constituted one stimulus for subjecting prevailing religious beliefs and practices to reexamination. An additional stimulus came from their interaction with Islamic intellectual trends originating outside Damascus. In the eighteenth and nineteenth centuries religious reform movements that sprang up throughout the Muslim world appeared to represent a ubiquitous urge to revive "true" Islamic beliefs and practices.[1] The "Wahhābī" movement in Arabia is the best-known example of the early modern religious reform movements (its first phase lasted from 1744 until 1818). Scholars have traced the roots of reform movements from West Africa to India to the Wahhābīs' influence on ulama from those lands who visited Medina and Mecca and returned home imbued with Wahhābī ideas.[2] The question of whether the Arabian reform movement influenced Damascene ulama arises because of the Wahhābīs' proximity to Syria and because Syrian opponents of religious reform accused the salafis of propagating Wahhabism.

Another possible source of influence on Damascene salafis lay to the east in Baghdad, where the Alūsī family of ulama led a reform movement in the nineteenth century. In fact, the Alūsīs and the Damascene salafis shared a common program for reforming religious practices, and they cooperated in reviving the works of a thirteenth-century Damascene scholar, Aḥmad ibn Taymiyyah.

Another agent of reformism came from the west to reside in Damascus from 1855 until 1883. ʿAbd al-Qādir al-Jazāʾirī is famous for leading resistance to the French conquest of Algeria between 1832 and 1847. In his Syrian exile, he contributed to the emergence of religious reform and brought together Egyptian reformers and his followers among the ulama of Damascus.

The Wahhābīs

The term "Wahhābī" stems from the name of Muḥammad ibn ʿAbd al-Wahhāb (1703–1792), but his followers called themselves *muwaḥḥidūn,* professors of the unity of God, not Wahhābīs.[3] Ibn ʿAbd al-Wahhāb came from a family of Ḥanbalī ulama residing in the central Arabian region called Najd. In his youth he studied with his father, then with ulama in Mecca, Medina, and Basra, a city in southern Iraq. He returned to Najd around 1740 and began to call for the reform of religious practice. In 1745, Ibn ʿAbd al-Wahhāb transformed his mission into a powerful religious-political movement by allying with Muḥammad ibn Saʿūd, the ruler of a Najdi town. During the next 30 years, the Saudi–Wahhābī alliance gradually extended its dominion over all of central Arabia, and when Ibn ʿAbd al-Wahhāb died in 1792, Saudi forces controlled Najd, threatened the Hijaz, and raided towns in Iraq.

Muḥammad ibn ʿAbd al-Wahhāb's religious reformism consisted of attacking such popular worship customs as visiting saints' tombs to obtain their intercession with God. He held that any practice that implied worshiping anyone other than God constituted polytheism (*shirk*), and therefore its perpetrator was not a Muslim. Ibn ʿAbd al-Wahhāb followed the Ḥanbalī school of jurisprudence but did not insist on emulating only one school. Rather, he held that the other Sunni schools sometimes provided sounder rulings than those of the Ḥanbalī school, and in those cases he followed the rulings of other schools.

The rise of Saudi–Wahhābī power in Arabia had economic and political consequences for Syria. Beginning in the 1790s, Wahhābī raids on villages south of Damascus disrupted trade between Syria and the Hijaz. In 1803, the Wahhābīs seized Mecca and turned back the pilgrim caravan from Damascus, thereby diminishing the Ottomans' stature as defenders of Islam's holy places and ruining Damascus's annual trade with the Hijaz. Customarily, many Damascene merchants and laborers profited by catering to the needs of hundreds of pilgrims from Turkey, Iraq, and Iran who gathered in Damascus for the journey to Mecca. The pilgrim caravan also provided the occasion for heavy trading between Syria and the Hijaz because the armed escort offered protection from predatory bedouin raids.[4]

Between 1803 and 1813, the Wahhābīs restricted access to Mecca. In 1806 and 1807, they signaled their rejection of Ottoman authority by refusing to allow the governor of Syria and the caravan's armed escort to enter Mecca. The pilgrims who proceeded without the governor traveled under the Wahhābīs' protection, and the Wahhābīs dictated their performance of the pilgrimage rites. The Wahhābīs reached the peak of their power in 1810 when tribes near Aleppo and Baghdad paid allegiance to them. The next year the Ottomans turned to the powerful new governor of Egypt, Muḥammad ʿAlī, for help in their struggle with the Wahhābīs. Muḥammad ʿAlī's army wrested Mecca from the Wahhābīs in 1813, thereby restoring Ottoman control over the pilgrimage and reopening trade between the Hijaz and Damascus. In 1818, his army overcame the last Wahhābī stronghold in Najd.

Any attempt to gauge the reaction of Damascene ulama to the Wahhābīs in the early 1800s must reckon with a political element, namely, that sympathy for Wahhābī views implied disloyalty to the Ottoman sultans. The Wahhābīs rejected the Ottoman sultans' claims to the caliphate, which symbolized legitimate political authority, and they asserted that the Arabs were the caliphate's rightful claimants because they observed religious duties more strictly than Turks.[5] The Wahhābīs held that the third caliph, ʿUthmān, had converted the ruling institution of the Muslims from a caliphate into a kingdom, that is, from legitimate to illegitimate authority. That issue became controversial during the last three decades of Ottoman rule in Syria when tensions grew between Turks and Arabs.

The Wahhābīs' ideas about reforming religious practice evoked a hostile response from Damascene ulama. The Wahhābīs took an uncompromising stand against the practices of raising edifices over saints' tombs and of supplicating the prophets and saints for whom the tombs were built. The Wahhābīs considered such practices idolatry, and wherever they held sway they razed tombs, thereby arousing the animosity of Muslims who considered the sites sacred. Furthermore, the Arabian reformers regarded as an unbeliever (*kāfir*) anyone who rejected the Wahhābī creed. Their practice of *takfīr,* accusing Muslims of disbelief, justified their killing Muslims and plundering their wealth. The Wahhābīs' atrocities against Shī'ī Muslims in Iraq raised the specter of Khārijī fanaticism and sullied the Wahhābīs' name throughout much of the Muslim world.[6]

An "official" response from Damascene ulama to the Wahhābīs came in August 1810, when the Saudi ruler and a Wahhābī scholar wrote to the Ottoman governor of Syria calling on him to reject idolatry, to pray only to God, and to perform the duties enjoined by religion.[7] An unidentified Damascene scholar replied on the governor's behalf, stating that the Wahhābīs should address such a letter to unbelievers and idolaters, not to Muslims. The scholar called the Wahhābīs "Arabs of the desert, the group of Musaylima (i.e., followers of a false prophet)," and a tribe ignorant of Islam's principles. He told the Wahhābīs they should fight the enemies of religion, not Muslims, and he added that nothing is worse than killing Muslims, looting their wealth, burning their homes, and despoiling their honor, as the Wahhābīs did.

Since the Wahhābīs belonged to the Ḥanbalī school, one might expect to detect a more favorable response to their ideas among Ḥanbalī ulama in Damascus, but such was not the case because they had long coexisted harmoniously with ulama of other legal schools. Whereas the Wahhābīs condemned such popular practices as making amulets, working miracles, visiting tombs to obtain spiritual grace, and Sufi rituals, Damascene Ḥanbalīs accepted and engaged in these practices.[8] The leading Ḥanbalī scholar of Damascus, Ḥasan al- Shaṭṭī (1790–1858), commented on essays that Wahhābī ulama sent him. He wrote that the Wahhābīs practice takfīr without just cause, that their interpretations of scripture demonstrate ignorance, and that whoever regards Muslims as unbelievers is himself an unbeliever.[9] On the other hand, certain Wahhābī ideas did resonate in Shaṭṭī's works, in particular his discussion of two issues on which the Wahhābīs differed from most Muslims: tomb visits and emulation (taqlīd) in religious law.

Shaṭṭī composed an essay elucidating the correct performance of pilgrimage rites, perhaps responding to the Wahhābīs' challenge to prevalent practices. He stated that Muslims must address all prayers and supplications for mercy to God, not to the Prophet or the saints. Pilgrims must not circumambulate the Prophet's tomb or rub it for spiritual blessing; at the nearby tombs of Abū Bakr and 'Umar, the first two caliphs, one may greet them but not seek their intercession. In a passage on emulation, Shaṭṭī noted that Ḥanbalī jurisprudents fell into two camps: one side claimed that emulation is mandatory, the other held that it is permissible, but not mandatory.[10] Shaṭṭī recommended the latter view, thus agreeing with the Wahhābīs.

Shaṭṭī's anti-Wahhābī comments and his agreement with them on emulation and supplicatory prayers do not constitute a contradiction. On the latter two issues he merely took positions commonly held by Ḥanbalī ulama. His essays indicate his legal school, not sympathy for the Wahhābīs. Indeed, to the extent that they broke with Ḥanbalī beliefs and practices, Shaṭṭī disagreed with them, as he clearly indicated by criticizing the Wahhābīs.

In addition to the desire to defend customary religious practices, Damascene ulama rejected the Wahhābīs' ideas because the latter remorselessly killed Muslims and disrupted trade between Syria and the Hijaz. Further, the urban ulama of Damascus probably scoffed at the political claims of Najdi tribesmen, whom Damascenes feared and despised. The only Damascene shaykh known to have sympathized with Wahhābī views, Muḥammad al-ʿAṭṭār (1763/4–1827), lived in seclusion and had few students because people shunned him.[11]

The Alūsīs of Baghdad

A more likely source for Damascene religious reformers lay in Baghdad's renowned Alūsī family. Abū Thināʾ Shihāb al-Dīn al-Alūsī (1802–1854) was the first of several members of the Alūsī family of ulama to attain prominence in the nineteenth century. According to his biographers, Shihāb al-Dīn al-Alūsī imbibed Wahhabism from his teacher, ʿAlī al-Suwaydī, but what that meant precisely is unclear. Did Alūsī agree with the Wahhābīs' interpretation of takfīr? That appears to be quite unlikely because Alūsī had cordial relations with Shīʿīs and Bābīs in Baghdad. Did he sympathize with the Wahhābīs' rejection of Ottoman sovereignty? That appears to be more likely because he supported the autonomy of Baghdad's Mamluk rulers in the 1820s and the 1831 rebellion of the Mamluk Dāʾūd Pasha against the Ottomans. If Alūsī's Wahhabism consisted of an independent attitude toward the Ottomans, he abandoned it hastily when the Ottomans reasserted control over Baghdad in 1831. He made amends with the city's new masters, and in 1833 he became jurisconsult of Baghdad.[12]

Shihāb al-Dīn's stature in Muslim intellectual history stands on his nine-volume exegesis of the Quran. In it he cited many passages from the exegesis of Fakhr al-Dīn-al-Rāzī, a twelfth-century thinker who related Quranic verses to the natural sciences. Alūsī juxtaposed Rāzī's exegesis with selections from the exegetical works of Sufis and dialectical theologians (*mutakallimūn*). In sum, Alūsī's work shows eclecticism more than religious reform. However his son Nuʿmān Khayr al-Dīn (1836–1899) did embrace and propagate reformist ideas. Moreover, he presents a clear example of how nineteenth-century reformist trends of diverse origins interacted.[13]

Born in Baghdad in 1836, Khayr al-Dīn al-Alūsī spent his early adulthood in various parts of Iraq working as a religious magistrate. In 1878, he undertook a journey to do the pilgrimage, and on the way he passed through Egypt, where he had his father's exegesis printed. While in Cairo he saw the exegesis of a contemporary Indian Muslim reformer, Ṣiddīq Ḥasan Khān (d. 1889), which made a strong impression on him, especially the passages relating verses of the Quran to science and reform. When Alūsī reached Mecca, he asked ulama about Ḥasan Khān (who had been there on pilgrimage in 1868) and looked for other works of his. Khayr al-Dīn became acquainted with Shaykh Aḥmad ibn ʿĪsā al-Najdī, who knew about

Ḥasan Khān and gave Alūsī a number of the Indian reformer's works. Alūsī then began to correspond with Ḥasan Khān, who was an early figure in the Indian Ahl-i Ḥadīth movement.[14]

Ṣiddīq Ḥasan Khān derived many of his ideas from the works of a Yemeni scholar, Muḥammad ibn ʿAlī al-Shawkānī (1760–1835), and those of the eighteenth-century Delhi reformer, Shāh Walī Allah (1702–1762). Both Shawkānī and Shāh Walī Allah influenced later reformers in Damascus. The concerns of Shawkānī, the Indian Ahl-i Ḥadīth, and Khayr al-Dīn al-Alūsī converged in their interest in the works of Ibn Taymiyyah.[15]

Taqī al-Dīn Aḥmad ibn Taymiyyah (1263–1328), a remarkably prolific writer and independent thinker, came to hold the status of the intellectual ancestor of salafism. Religious reformers in Syria, Iraq, Yemen, and India accorded him the greatest respect, avidly sought his works, and strove to have them published.[16] Ibn Taymiyyah's positions on *ijtihād*, emulation, reason and revelation, and myriad other issues provided elaborate arguments, which the salafis appropriated. In late nineteenth- and early twentieth-century Baghdad and Damascus, religious reformers combed the manuscript collections of mosques, religious schools, and individual ulama for his missing works, about which the reformers knew from references in available works.

Khayr al-Dīn al-Alūsī helped launch the revival of Ibn Taymiyyah's legacy when he returned to Baghdad from Mecca. In March 1880, Alūsī completed a lengthy work defending Ibn Taymiyyah against his detractors. Alūsī's work, *A Clear View of the Trial of Two Aḥmads,* begins with a preface that includes Alūsī's license (ijāzah) from Ṣiddīq Ḥasan Khān and a sample of their correspondence. On the margins Alūsī inserted a biography of Ibn Taymiyyah that he obtained from a manuscript in Ḥasan Khān's hand. Alūsī mentioned Ibn Taymiyyah's most famous followers, including ʿAlī al-Suwaydī (Shihāb al-Dīn al-Alūsī's teacher), Khayr al-Dīn's father, Muḥammad al-Shawkānī, and Ṣiddīq Ḥasan Khān. In *A Clear View* Alūsī foreshadowed the Damascene salafis' treatment of ijtihād, emulation, and ritual innovations like using tombs for places of worship. His work played a key role in recovering Ibn Taymiyyah for Arab ulama.[17]

Ijtihād had the utmost importance for religious reformers. Literally, it means expending all one's effort to perform a difficult task. In religious legal theory, ijtihād means making an exhaustive attempt to obtain a ruling on a matter for which no unambiguous, definitive text exists in scripture. By contrast, most ulama engaged in applying religious law emulated the rulings of classical jurisconsults, whose authority was considered unassailable. Religious reformers denied the validity of emulation as a principle of jurisprudence and called on ulama to give legal rulings only on the basis of scripture and ijtihād.

Khayr al-Dīn al-Alūsī strengthened the Baghdad–India connection by sending his son ʿAlī ʿAlā' al-Dīn (1860–1921) to India to study with Ḥasan Khān. ʿAlī ʿAlā' al-Dīn later became an Ottoman magistrate and worked in various parts of the empire, including Baalbak, Lebanon, where he met Damascene reformers. Khayr al-Dīn had two other sons who also contributed to the religious reform movement. His nephew Maḥmūd Shukrī al-Alūsī (1857–1924) led the reformist trend in Baghdad after Khayr al-Dīn's death in 1899, and he corresponded with fellow admirers of Ibn Taymiyyah in Damascus, Kuwait, Jiddah, Najd, Qatar, and Istanbul.[18]

The Alūsīs did not propagate Wahhābī ideas, although both Iraqi and Najdi reformers agreed on the necessity of wiping out ritual innovations. Their emergence as religious reformers came at the same time as the salafis' appearance in Damascus. Therefore, though the Alūsīs were not a seminal influence on Damascene reformers, they affirmed their beliefs and offered textual support (Ibn Taymiyyah's works) for a reinterpretation of Islam.

ʿAbd al-Qādir al-Jazāʾirī in Damascus

The amīr ʿAbd al-Qādir al-Jazāʾirī (1807–1883) led Algerian resistance to French rule and headed an independent state from 1832 until 1847. Numerous scholarly and popular works recount the course of his military campaigns against the French, his endeavor to set up political mechanisms in the Algerian hinterland, and his final defeat. Yet few historians have studied Jazāʾirī's exile in Damascus and his influence on Damascus's social and intellectual life.[19]

Three features of Jazāʾirī's career before his exile clarify why he wound up in Damascus and became the catalyst in forging religious reform there. First, he traveled with his father, Muḥyi al-Dīn, to the eastern Arab lands in 1825 to perform the pilgrimage and to visit major centers of learning. On their way east, they visited Egypt, where the political and military achievements of Muḥammad ʿAlī impressed ʿAbd al-Qādir, who later tried to duplicate them in Algeria.[20] After completing the pilgrimage, Jazāʾirī and his father joined the pilgrim caravan bound for Damascus, and on the way they met the famous itinerant Sufi Shaykh Khālid al-Naqshbandī (1780–1827). In Damascus the Jazāʾirīs took up residence at one of the mosques Shaykh Khālid used for propagating the Naqshbandī-Khālidī Sufi order. They spent four months there practicing the Naqshbandī rituals and learning its prayers with one of Shaykh Khālid's deputies, Shaykh Muḥammad ibn ʿAbd Allah al-Khānī (1798–1862). When ʿAbd al-Qādir returned to Damascus in 1855, his friendship with Muḥammad al-Khānī revived, and in later years Jazāʾirī patronized Khānī's son and grandson.[21]

Second, Jazāʾirī's early education included not only Islamic sciences, but astronomy, mathematics, and geography. He studied the latter sciences with "one of the best-educated men in Algeria," Ṭāhir ibn Aḥmad, a magistrate at the port town of Arzew.[22] The magistrate had frequent contacts with European mariners who stopped at the port, and from them he learned of European developments in sciences relevant to navigation. It seems that the magistrate of Arzew contributed to the sympathy for scientific learning that Jazāʾirī later showed.

Third, Jazāʾirī's battles with the French gave him bitter firsthand experience of Europe's superior power. During his 15-year struggle, he, like Muḥammad ʿAlī and Ottoman rulers, introduced innovations designed to strengthen his country. Jazāʾirī based his novel undertakings on what he perceived to be the underpinnings of European power, such as arms factories and a standing organized military force. His war against the French alerted him to the imperative for Muslims to achieve progress to fend off European aggression.[23]

ʿAbd al-Qādir surrendered to the French in December 1847, and for the next five years they kept him captive in France. About a year after Louis Napoleon III consolidated his power late in 1851, he ordered Jazāʾirī's release. ʿAbd al-Qādir went to Istanbul, where he met with Sultan Abdülmecīd, and then settled in Bursa, in western Anatolia. Following a destructive earthquake in 1855, Jazāʾirī traveled to Istanbul and Paris to seek permission to reside in an Arab country, and the Ottomans and French agreed to allow him to emigrate to Damascus.[24]

Some months before Jazāʾirī moved to Syria, members of the Asiatic Society in Paris registered him as a fellow scholar and requested a sample of his work. In response, Jazāʾirī wrote an essay entitled *Reminding the Rational Man and Alerting the Neglectful Man,* in which he discussed the relationship between reason and revelation, emulation, and Christian–Muslim relations.[25]

At the beginning of this essay, Jazāʾirī cited a proverb that implies that men should ascertain the truth by exercising reason, not by accepting the opinion of an authority. The proverb states that, for the rational man, truth is the measure of men; men are not the measure of truth. Elaborating on this proverb, Jazāʾirī observed that people frequently believe what someone says because they like and respect him (they take men as the measure of truth). The scholar (*ʿālim*) benefits society by recognizing truth on the basis of evidence, not on the basis of what an "authority" claims to be true (he takes truth as the measure of men). Anyone who claims to be a scholar, yet emulates his forefathers' beliefs and prejudices and does not exercise the rational faculty, harms society. Jazāʾirī added that emulating books does even worse harm. With respect to jurisprudence, he noted that because ulama often disagree, one must select the ruling that most closely conforms to scripture.

Jazāʾirī described knowledge as the human trait by which man may attain perfection. He wrote that the sciences are the fruits of reason, and that God endowed man with reason to enable him to detect the existence of the unseen world. Therefore reason allows man to learn about both the mundane and the transcendental, and on that point Jazāʾirī based his discussion of the harmony of religion with rational knowledge. He asserted that revealed knowledge conveys truths beyond the reach of rational knowledge, but man comprehends revealed knowledge by exercising reason; therefore, the two forms of knowledge are complementary. Everything the prophets revealed harmonizes with sound reason because their revelations dealt with transcendent truths, not with the material world, which is accessible to reason.

On the relation of Islam to Judaism and Christianity, ʿAbd al-Qādir wrote that Muhammad complemented and perfected God's revelations to earlier prophets like Moses and Jesus. Jazāʾirī called on Muslims to therefore regard Christians as brothers. His ideas on Muslim–Christian relations reflect his experiences in Algeria, where his decent treatment of French prisoners won him a humanitarian reputation.[26]

The ideas Jazāʾirī expressed on reason and revelation represented a minority position in the history of Islamic thought, one held by rationalist philosophers and which was gaining strength as the nineteenth century progressed. That tradition's elevation of reason was appositive to Muslims' search for indigenous sources to affirm the principles of science that seemed to lie at the basis of progress.[27] ʿAbd al-Qādir's stress on reason and its consonance with religion and his critique of emulation formed a core of themes that the salafis later adopted.

By 1855, Jazā'irī enjoyed entree to the highest political circles in Europe and the Ottoman Empire. He had met with the French emperor three times, the Ottoman sultan twice, and with high military and civilian officials in both France and the Ottoman Empire. Accordingly, when he arrived in Damascus in November 1855, the Ottoman governor of Syria, the military commander, local notables, ulama, and townspeople gathered to greet the Algerian hero. During his first years there, he purchased several homes in town and rural lands in southern Syria, northern Palestine, and Damascus's environs. Using money from the enormous pension Napoleon III provided him, the amīr became one of the largest landholders in the province.[28]

Soon after ʿAbd al-Qādir arrived in Damascus, a number of ulama invited him to teach at the Umayyad mosque, where he gave daily lessons on the Quran and the Sunnah. Over the years, Jazā'irī lent his prestige and wealth to a circle of ulama who frequented his lessons and his home. He patronized a number of ulama with monthly stipends, bought a home for a shaykh, and dispensed rewards to ulama for composing verse in his honor.[29] The ulama of Damascus divided over Jazā'irī: some admired him, while others considered him an interloper.[30] With his large retinue of Algerians, huge wealth, scholarly status, and international standing, Jazā'irī established himself as a center of power in his own right.

In 1860, ʿAbd al-Qādir tried to use his influence to prevent the spread of sectarian violence from Lebanon to Damascus. He met with Druzes in nearby villages, wrote to Druze leaders in Lebanon and the Hawran (southern Syria), and tried to persuade the Ottoman governor and local Muslim notables to prevent an outbreak of violence in Damascus. Accounts of his motives differ. Most likely, he feared that an attack on Christians would provoke European intervention and an occupation of Syria, much as less serious affronts to European sensibilities had led to the French conquest of Algeria. He accurately warned Muslim notables that they would lose their power in the event of anti-Christian riots. During the days of violence, a mob threatened to attack his home, where he was sheltering Christians. With his retinue of armed Algerians, he stood up to the mob and warned them that if they did not stop, the French would come and convert the mosques into churches. In addition to saving the lives of Syrian Christians, Jazā'irī protected French Lazarist monks and nuns, the French consul, and the British consul.[31]

Jazā'irī's heroism won him the gratitude of European rulers, who showered him with awards, gifts, and medals. On the other hand, his defense of Christians alienated Muslims who suspected him of acting on behalf of French interests. As for the Turks, they resented his meddling and his immunity from Ottoman measures, which Jazā'irī owed to French influence. For instance, when the Turks ordered a general disarmament in Damascus, the French consul intervened to gain exemption for Jazā'irī's Algerian followers. Rumors that France sought to make him ruler of an independent Arab kingdom further aroused the Turks' suspicions. In fact, Napoleon III pondered that possibility and the alternative of persuading the sultan to name Jazā'irī governor of Syria. The French ruler believed that ʿAbd al-Qādir would facilitate French endeavors to construct the Suez Canal and thereby obviate the need to wrest permission from the reluctant Ottomans.[32]

While European newspapers speculated about plans to empower Jazā'irī, he decided to spend two pilgrimage seasons in the Hijaz. He and some ulama companions left Damascus in August 1862, and he spent most of the next 18 months in Mecca, where he devoted himself to worship and to following a Sufi shaykh of the Shādhilī order. When ʿAbd al-Qādir traveled back to Syria in June 1864, he stopped in Alexandria, where he attended a meeting of the Masons' lodge.[33]

Using the Masons' documents, a French historian has shown that Jazā'irī joined the Masons at the Alexandria meeting.[34] ʿAbd al-Qādir's first contact with them came in November 1860 when members of a Parisian lodge wrote to him expressing their admiration for his heroic deeds during the July riots. The Masons explained that they based their society on three principles: the existence of God, the immortality of the soul, and the brotherhood of all men. In the same letter, they invited him to join the Masons, and Jazā'irī replied by expressing interest in the secret society. The Masons wanted him because they thought it would be easier to spread freemasonry in the Arab lands with the support of so influential a figure. All they asked was that he accept the Masons' fundamental principles, which could be interpreted to accord with his beliefs. What motivated Jazā'irī to join the Masons? Perhaps he thought it politic to cultivate good relations with a group which included powerful figures in the French government, including Emperor Napoleon III's cousin Lucien Murat and high military officers.[35] Moreover, in the 1860s, the Masons had a reputation for spirituality and devotion to morality, their adoption of atheistic, anticlerical ideas not coming until 1871.

On a visit to France in the summer of 1865, Jazā'irī met with Masons in Paris and told them that Muslims considered the Masons atheists and troublemakers; indeed, he himself used to believe that. When the Masons asked Jazā'irī if he could help spread freemasonry in the Arab lands, he replied that it would be impossible to establish a Masonic lodge because the government would forbid it and the people were not ready for it. He told them that while he sympathized with the Masons, they erred in believing that he could propagate freemasonry.

Jazā'irī's association with the Masons, which apparently ended after his 1865 visit to Paris, exemplified his liberal ideas and European connections. In later years he remained such a prominent figure that the Syrian notables who organized the 1877–78 political movement nominated him ruler of a projected Syrian kingdom. His local and international prestige, the favor he enjoyed in European capitals, and his experience in heading an independent state in Algeria, made him a natural choice for the plotters. Jazā'irī stipulated that if the notables' plan came to fruition, Syria would remain in religious union with the Ottoman Empire and recognize the sultan as caliph. He also told the notables that he would rule only after receiving an oath of allegiance (*bayʿah*) from the people to consecrate his authority. The movement came to nought when the empire's fortunes revived.[36]

Although ʿAbd al-Qādir's early writings emphasized reason, his later work, composed after the 1862–64 sojourn in the Hijaz, expressed the outlook of a sharīʿah-minded, or scripturalist, Sufi. This union of scripturalism and reason later became a hallmark of salafi Islamic reform. Perhaps his encounter in Syria with the Naqshbandī Shaykh Khālid influenced him to embrace a scripturalist vision of religion. Jazā'irī's sharīʿah-mindedness may also have stemmed from his efforts to unify the fractious tribes of Algeria in order to resist French advances. Ahmed Nader, who has written on Algerian Sufi orders for the period 1830–1850, argues that political and military imperatives drove ʿAbd al-Qādir to base his authority on strict adherence to the Quran, to pose as *amīr al-mu'minīn,* commander of the believers, not just head of a local branch of the Qādiriyyah order. As Pessah Shinar has observed, Jazā'irī tried to enforce religious sanctions against alcohol, gambling, and smoking. The amīr's son and biographer, Muhammad Saʿīd, related that he also tried to force men to pray five times a day in mosques, and those found in their shops at prayer time were beaten.[37]

The greatest testimony to Jazā'irī's sharīʿah-minded Sufism is his lengthy *Book of Stations,* in which he expounded on the esoteric meanings of Quranic verses and Prophetic oral reports.[38] ʿAbd al-Qādir wrote that true Sufis neither invalidate the apparent meanings of scripture nor claim to possess the only true understanding of scripture. Rather, they affirm the literal meanings and claim to uncover hidden meanings in addition. Jazā'irī supported this argument by stating that the Companions of the Prophet also sought hidden meanings of scripture.[39]

In several passages ʿAbd al-Qādir reiterated the point that Sufis must adhere to scripture no matter how profound their esoteric knowledge. In fact, the true Sufi is he who adheres more strictly to the commands and prohibitions of scripture as he draws closer to God. Anyone who claims to follow the Sufi way and fails to observe religious law is a liar. He noted that some ignorant shaykhs commanded their disciples to fast at times not stipulated by the sharīʿah, presumably as a sign of devotion. Jazā'irī advised believers that following the commands and prohibitions of the Sunnah in word, deed, and intention required the greatest effort, and therefore supererogatory fasting is an unnecessary burden.[40]

Another broad theme running through *The Book of Stations* concerns the limits of reason. In this respect ʿAbd al-Qādir repeatedly criticized dialectical theologians for trying to understand the nature of God and His attributes by employing reason. He wrote that whoever tried to know God's essence through reason would become perplexed: Such were the theologians, who reach conflicting views of God's nature because of their reliance on reason. They are bound to fail because reason is limited and tied by its own rules, whereas God is above reason. Reason has a limit, and the nobility of reason lies in accepting the prophets' revelations.[41] These strictures on the limits of reason do not represent an abandonment of Jazā'irī's earlier essays, for they too drew a boundary between knowledge attainable by reason and knowledge accessible only through prophecy.

After ʿAbd al-Qādir died in May 1883, his ulama supporters perpetuated his legacy, which laid the basis for a religious reform movement stressing adherence to scripture, learning natural sciences, and rejecting emulation. Furthermore, Jazā'irī corresponded with the renowned Egyptian reformer, Muḥammad ʿAbduh (1849–1905), thus bringing his Damascene ulama followers into contact with Egyptian reformers.[42]

ʿAbduh and Afghānī

In the last year of Jazā'irī's life, a group of Egyptians arrived in Beirut, exiled by British authorities for their role in backing the ʿUrābī rebellion. The exiled Egyptians included Muhammad ʿAbduh, and Jazāʾirī immediately sent his son Muḥyi al-Dīn to meet him. Two ulama from Jazāʾirī's circle developed a rapport with ʿAbduh. ʿAbd al-Majīd al-Khānī (1847–1900), a young litterateur who sometimes composed panegyric verse to the amīr, began to correspond with ʿAbduh in the spring of 1883. ʿAbd al-Razzāq al-Bīṭār (1837–1917), another shaykh in Jazāʾirī's entourage, corresponded with ʿAbduh in 1885 and met him in April 1886. About that time Bīṭār is said to have embraced the reformist creed of relying on the Quran and the Sunnah instead of books of jurisprudence, and accepting rulings without a scriptural reference only when buttressed by evidence.[43]

The published letters from Khānī and Bīṭār to ʿAbduh bespeak their admiration for ʿAbduh but give no indication of their reformist beliefs. Those beliefs can only be inferred from ʿAbduh's writings in *The Firmest Bond* and his *Essay on the Unicity of God,* which contains portions of lessons he gave in Beirut.[44] Numerous studies of nineteenth-century Arab intellectual history have treated the themes of both works, but an indication of their bearing on political and cultural trends in Syria is in order here.

ʿAbduh cooperated with his mentor, Jamāl al-Dīn al-Afghānī, in publishing 17 issues of *The Firmest Bond* in Paris between March and October 1884. The journal consistently promoted the cause of Islamic unity to oppose European domination. ʿAbduh and Afghānī painted the political situation as a confrontation between Christian and Islamic civilizations. Therefore, Muslims had to unify on the basis of their common faith, "the firmest bond," to achieve the strength necessary to repel European encroachment. ʿAbduh wrote that Muslims could unite only by adhering to Islam's true principles and by abandoning innovations generally considered part of religion. ʿAbduh and Afghānī called on the ulama to get rid of fabricated oral reports (*aḥādīth mawḍūʿah*), which justified corruptions of religion, and to discredit fatalistic attitudes among Muslims, which obstructed the voluntarist outlook necessary to revival.[45]

Afghānī disseminated *The Firmest Bond* to rulers and ulama throughout the Muslim world. In Damascus, the journal's recipients included ʿAbd al-Majīd al-Khānī, the jurisconsult (Maḥmūd al-Ḥamzāwī), Ottoman officials, ulama, notables, and ʿAbd al-Qādir al-Jazāʾirī's two oldest sons.[46] Afghānī's and ʿAbduh's journal strengthened the lines of communication between Damascene ulama and the broader reform trend.

After *The Firmest Bond* ceased publication, ʿAbduh returned to Beirut and resumed teaching. The lessons that formed the basis of *Essay on the Unicity of God* addressed secular trends more than the politics of the Eastern Question. ʿAbduh asserted that Islam occupied a unique place among the monotheistic religions because it harmoniously joined reason and revelation.[47] Like ʿAbd al-Qādir al-Jazāʾirī, ʿAbduh adopted this position from a long line of Muslim thinkers who tried to solve the problem of reconciling philosophical knowledge with religion. Jazāʾirī and ʿAbduh revived a minority intellectual tradition to combat proponents of secularism, who wielded terms like "rational" and "modern" as a club against religion. ʿAbduh stressed Islam's rationality to defend religion not only against Europeans' critical remarks but also against local secularists such as Faraḥ Anṭūn, who debated ʿAbduh in the pages of Egyptian newspapers.[48]

Two more themes from the essay, again not original, but significant in late nineteenth-century Syria, rang clearly in salafi works for the next 30 years. First, ʿAbduh blamed Islam's decline on non-Arab neophytes who introduced beliefs and practices alien to Islam. That opinion eventually assumed a political dimension because it expressed a concern with completely mastering Arabic and, potentially, a growing sense of Arabness. Second, ʿAbduh condemned emulation and enjoined the free exercise of reason in worldly affairs.[49] This was an important stand at a time when new schools and new law codes were eroding the ulama's social position, for the promotion of reason's standing in religion could serve to restore the ulama in a cultural and ideological climate dominated by slogans of reason, science, modernity, and progress.

Conclusion

The interaction of Damascene ulama with intellectual trends in the Muslim world displayed a certain logic. Their hostility toward Wahhabism owed as much to that movement's association with Arabian tribesmen as to its peculiar ideas about the illegitimacy of Ottoman rule and the religious status of tomb visits. Damascenes feared predatory bedouin raids on the pilgrim caravan and on villages in the Hawran, an important source of grain lying to the city's south, and they held bedouins in contempt for their backwardness and ignorance. The Wahhābīs' wanton violence against Muslims conformed to Damascenes' perception of bedouins' behavior. The remarks of both Ḥasan al-Shaṭṭī and the anonymous shaykh show that Damascene ulama considered the Wahhābīs renegades and dismissed them as presumptuous upstarts.

On the other hand, the Alūsīs were urban ulama like those of Damascus, and therefore commanded respect as peers. Moreover, the Alūsīs represented a different strain of religious reform from that of the Wahhābīs. Khayr al-Dīn al-Alūsī concurred with them on the need to eliminate customs that had polytheistic implications, but he favored neither excommunicating Muslims who followed such customs nor rejecting Ottoman rule. His contribution to the reform trend lay in reviving Ibn Taymiyyah's legacy. But his work came at roughly the same time as the emergence of salafism in Damascus and should be regarded as a parallel, not a cause, of the latter.

The inspiration for Damascene religious reform came from ʿAbd al-Qādir al-Jazā'irī, whose wealth, scholarship, and status as a hero of Muslim resistance to European aggression endowed his views with authority. His ideas about reason, knowledge, and communal relations neatly tied in with the concerns of Damascene ulama witnessing disturbing economic trends and administrative reforms dictated by Istanbul. Jazā'irī presented a way to confront European power by adopting new technologies while remaining true to Islam. At the end of his life he served as the point of contact between ulama in his entourage and Egyptian reformers led by Muḥammad ʿAbduh.

Damascene ulama became familiar with the ideas of ʿAbduh and Afghānī through their short-lived journal, which articulated Muslims' resentment of European aggression and called on ulama to purify Islam of innovations. ʿAbduh himself met several ulama from Jazāʾirī's circle during his two years in Beirut and impressed them with his reformist ideas, which maintained the stress on reason characteristic of Jazāʾirī and added a commitment to reforming the ulama's practices. Damascene ulama influenced by Jazāʾirī and ʿAbduh eventually elaborated an interpretation of Islam that emphasized reason, spelled out the proper conduct of ulama, and revived the legacy of Ibn Taymiyyah.

3

The Social Roots of Salafism

Studies of Islamic reform have tended to dwell on ideas rather than spelling out their social import or reformers' motivations.[1] A more complete account would scrutinize the reformers' place in society rather than analyzing the ideas of Islamic reform alone. Some authors have suggested that nineteenth-century religious reform trends represented the outlook of particular social groups. In a work on late nineteenth- and early twentieth-century intellectual trends in Syria, Munīr Mūsā asserted that Islamic reform represented the outlook of "the bourgeoisie and the lesser aristocracy" and of "middle shaykhs." A Russian author, Z. I. Livin, proposed that an Arab bourgeoisie was forming in the nineteenth century and that it interpreted Islam to suit its needs. Livin held that Islamic reform showed its "bourgeois essence" by viewing the human personality as an active force expressing man's free will. Livin's identification of religious reform with the bourgeoisie rests on the application of Marxist categories without demonstrating their suitability to his subject, whereas Mūsā's work shows greater sensitivity to the social backgrounds of religious reformers and the specific nature of Syrian society. Though Mūsā employed Marxist categories of social class, he noted that families, not social classes, were the basis of social and political struggles in late Ottoman Syria.[2] Moreover, he accurately identified middle shaykhs as the agents of religious reform, but he did not explain why middle ulama would pursue religious reform. The task at hand is to firmly establish the social background of religious reform and to explain how religious reform provided solutions for the predicament of its advocates.

In the second half of the nineteenth century a social and cultural gap opened between Damascene ulama and both local notables and the imperial elite in Istanbul. At the same time, the ulama encountered the eclectic Islamic vision of ʿAbd al-Qādir al-Jazāʾirī. His international status, huge wealth, and liberal views attracted a number of ulama who enjoyed his patronage and gradually coalesced into a distinct group. Because the Damascene religious reform movement emerged from Jazāʾirī's circle, a close examination of its members would disclose whether or not salafism represented the outlook and interests of a particular social group.

The Khānī Family and the Khālidiyyah–Naqshbandiyyah Order

The Khānī family of Naqshbandī shaykhs typified the relationship between ʿAbd al-Qādir al-Jazāʾirī's ulama circle and the religious reform movement. Jazāʾirī's acquaintance with the Khānīs spanned three generations, beginning in 1826 with Muḥammad ibn ʿAbd Allah al-Khānī, and continuing after 1855 when Jazā'irī befriended Khānī's son and grandson.

The Khānīs owed their prominence in Damascus to their leadership of a local branch of the Khālidī-Naqshbandī Sufi order. It has been suggested that the Naqshbandī order contributed to the religious reform movement with its strict adherence to religious law, and the Khānīs' association with the Damascene circle of reformers would seem to affirm that idea.[3] However a rival Naqshbandī shaykh harassed the religious reformers in the early 1900s, so the Naqshbandiyyah and Islamic reform did not always converge.

The Sufi order named after Bahā' al-Dīn al-Naqshband (1318–1389) actually took shape in Central Asia during the century preceding his life. An important development in the order occurred in northern India in the sixteenth century, when Aḥmad Sirhindī (1563–1624) injected a dose of intolerance. Following Sirhindī's nickname "al-Mujaddid," the renewer, the Naqshbandī branches that he and his disciples established became known as the Mujaddidiyyah-Naqshbandiyyah. Murād al-Bukhārī (1640–1720) studied with Sirhindī's son, traveled in the Ottoman Empire founding branches of the Mujaddidiyyah-Naqshbandiyyah, and settled in Damascus, where his descendants became leading ulama, including six jurisconsults.[4] Around 1822, Mufti Ḥusayn ibn ʿAlī al-Murādī (d. 1850) invited Abū al-Bahā' Ḍiyā' al-Dīn Khālid al-Shahrazūrī, a Kurdish Naqshbandī shaykh, to settle in Damascus. Shaykh Khālid had studied under the order's leading shaykhs in India, where the order had undergone further change since Murād al-Bukhārī's arrival in Damascus. In the early nineteenth century, the Mujaddidiyyah-Naqshbandiyyah developed a stern insistence on Sunnism that expressed Sunnis' resentment of the growing power of the Sikhs, the Hindus, and the British. Indian Naqshbandīs' "bigoted" Sunnism appeared in a prayer that Shaykh Khālid taught, which cursed Christians, Jews, and Twelver Shīʿīs.[5]

The early nineteenth-century Indian Naqshbandiyyah, which influenced Shaykh Khālid, called for returning to religion's scriptural sources and scrupulously obeying religious law. The eighteenth-century Delhi reformer Shāh Walī Allah had incorporated this call into the Indian Naqshbandiyyah. His son Shāh ʿAbd al-ʿAzīz instructed Shaykh Khālid in the order's practices and beliefs, including its new scripturalist emphasis, and that could be taken to suggest that the Mujaddidiyyah-Naqshbandiyyah and Shaykh Khālid were precursors of modern Islamic reform. However the salafi Jamāl al-Dīn al-Qāsimī wrote that Shaykh Khālid's professed adherence to the Quran and Sunnah did not mean that he practiced ijtihād, the hallmark of modern reform; in fact, the Naqshbandī shaykh always followed the Shāfiʿī school.[6]

In 1826, Shaykh Khālid convinced a young shaykh from Hamah to move to Damascus and work in a mosque Khālid used as a site to propagate his order.[7] The young shaykh, Muḥammad ibn ʿAbd Allah al-Khānī, belonged to the Qādirī order and had a reputation for avoiding innovations in ritual and for coercing people to attend mosque prayers that may have attracted Shaykh Khālid's attention. Soon after Khānī came to Damascus, Khālid made him a deputy shaykh at the Murādiyyah mosque. After Shaykh Khālid died in 1827, Khānī became shaykh of the order's Damascene branch. Shaykh Muḥammad enjoyed paramount status in the local branch until 1843, when Khālid's brother, Maḥmūd al-Ṣāḥib, came to Damascus and secured an appointment from the Ottomans as shaykh of the Sulaymāniyyah lodge, thereby establishing a rival branch. Then, three years later, yet another branch appeared, located at Shaykh Khālid's tomb.[8]

The Khālidiyyah-Naqshbandiyyah (named thus after Shaykh Khālid) of Damascus enjoyed the patronage of Ottoman dignitaries in Istanbul. Shakyh Khālid had sent emissaries to the Ottoman capital in the 1820s to propagate the order among influential bureaucrats and ulama. Perhaps as a result of the order's success in attracting Ottoman dignitaries, Muḥammad al-Khānī received a monthly stipend of 1,500 piasters, most likely through Mūsā Safvetī, an Ottoman bureaucrat and devotee of the order. Safvetī came to Syria as governor in 1845, and the next year, when he led the pilgrimage caravan, he paid homage to Khānī by following his particular instructions in performing the pilgrim's ritual. When Khānī visited Istanbul in 1853, Safvetī and other Ottoman followers of the Khālidiyyah-Naqshbandiyyah celebrated his arrival, and Safvetī hosted Khānī during his four-month stay.[9]

Khānī gave an exposition of the Khālidiyyah-Naqshbandiyyah's beliefs and practices in a work he composed in 1837.[10] He stated that whereas the Quran and Sunnah suffice to instruct Muslims in law, exoteric knowledge alone cannot teach man to worship God fully but requires esoteric knowledge to complement it. Only a special guide can lead believers to that knowledge, and Sufi orders fulfill the need for a guide. Khānī's essay indicates that his order emphasized scripturalist (exoteric) aspects of religion while remaining committed to two fundamental Sufi beliefs that the salafis later rejected. First, Khānī wrote that a Muslim needs a shaykh to show the path to God. The salafis would reply that belief in the ability or power of shaykhs to guide believers to God imposes an intermediary between man and God and therefore approaches polytheism. Second, Khānī proclaimed that believers need esoteric knowledge to truly worship God. The salafis would argue that comprehensive knowledge of scripture suffices, although their emphasis on the "secrets" and "wisdom" (*asrār* and *ḥikmah*) of scripture indicates that the reformers retained traces of the esoteric paradigm.

Muḥammad ibn ʿAbd Allah groomed his eldest son, Muḥammad (1832–1898), to succeed him as shaykh of the Khānīs' branch of the Naqshbandī order. The elder Khānī initiated his boy into the order, taught him its rituals and prayers, and passed on his knowledge of Shaykh Khālid's customs. In 1846, Muḥammad the younger married the daughter of one of Shaykh Khālid's deputies, thus bolstering his status in the order. In 1859, he traveled to Istanbul and renewed his acquaintance with Mūsā Safvetī. Three years later, he went to Egypt in the company of Muḥammad al-Ṭanṭāwī, another shaykh from ʿAbd al-Qādir al-Jazāʾirī's entourage.[11]

Shortly after Khānī returned to Damascus his father died, and for the next 30 years Muḥammad the younger headed the Khānīs' Khālidiyyah-Naqshbandiyyah Damascene branch. In 1864, he strengthened his position in the order by marrying a daughter of Shaykh Khālid. That same year he began to frequent ʿAbd al-Qādir's circle and to study Sufism with the amīr, who provided Khānī with a monthly stipend, named him guardian for two of his daughters, and later bequeathed him 10,000 piasters. Khānī already owned two homes in Damascus and a farm he had inherited from his father. In 1898, his rural holdings produced Hawrani wheat, indicating a stake in Syria's grain export trade.[12]

Muḥammad's brother Aḥmad (1836–1900) also worked in the Naqshbandī order, but financial problems drove him to switch from the Shāfiʿī to the Ḥanafī legal school in order to obtain work in the provincial judicial administration. After several years he quit working in the courts and tried to live off his rural holdings, but, according to Biṭār, a taste for luxury lured him back to judicial posts. The precise nature of Aḥmad al-Khānī's financial distress is not clear, but he seems to have suffered such losses that when he died he left a rather paltry sum, less than 7,000 piasters, to his heirs.[13]

Muḥammad the younger's son, ʿAbd al-Majīd (1847–1901), represented the third generation of Khānīs to occupy a prominent place in Damascus's cultural scene. ʿAbd al-Majīd grew up in an intellectual atmosphere dominated by his grandfather, father, and Jazā'irī, as his early life centered on his father's salons at the Murādiyyah mosque, the family home in the Qanawat quarter, and Jazā'irī's villa in Dummar, a hamlet outside Damascus. In the 1870s, ʿAbd al-Majīd emerged as one of Damascus's finest literary talents. Like other members of Jazā'irī's circle, he corresponded with Muḥammad ʿAbduh and sympathized with the local group of salafis. Yet he was circumspect enough to observe the convention of lauding high Ottoman officials in his verse and to praise an essay composed in 1900 that criticized the Wahhābīs.[14]

The same financial distress that afflicted Aḥmad al-Khānī vexed his nephew ʿAbd al-Majīd. For a brief time the nephew worked in a religious court as a deputy to the Turkish magistrate, a fellow Naqshbandī. When the magistrate transferred to another post, ʿAbd al-Majīd resigned from the court and turned to managing his father's affairs. In 1896, ʿAbd al-Majīd went to Istanbul to seek an increase in his father's monthly stipend from 950 piasters to 1,500 piasters, which Muḥammad al-Khānī the elder used to receive. After nearly two years in Istanbul, he succeeded in securing a 300-piaster monthly increase.[15]

When Muḥammad al-Khānī the younger died in 1898, ʿAbd al-Majīd made a bid to succeed his father as head of the Naqshbandī order. But his uncle Shaykh Aḥmad contested his bid and obtained the post. When Aḥmad al-Khānī died the following year, yet another uncle, ʿAbd Allah, thwarted ʿAbd al-Majīd's ambitions, and the litterateur passed away a year later.[16]

Newcomers to the ulama corps of Damascus, the Khānīs did not penetrate the ranks of official ulama until the new secular institutions were already beginning to outstrip religious posts as sources of prestige and wealth. Muḥammad al-Khānī the younger sat on the provincial conscription council in the 1860s, ʿAbd al-Majīd briefly held a post in a religious court, and Aḥmad worked in the religious law courts for many years.[17] At midcentury Naqshbandī dignitaries in the capital patronized the Khānīs. Muḥammad ibn ʿAbd Allah benefited from his ties with Mūsā Safvetī, who may have had a hand in granting the Naqshbandī shaykh rural property and a monthly stipend. ʿAbd al-Majīd's journey to Istanbul to seek an increase in his father's stipend, the feuds over succession to leadership of the Naqshbandī order, and Aḥmad's pursuit of judicial posts suggest that by the 1890s the Khānīs had fallen on hard times. Perhaps the order's constituency, the elites of Istanbul and Damascus, had abandoned patronizing the Sufi order as their culture became more secular. On the other hand, the family disputes may have reflected ulama competition for shares of a shrinking pie.

Aḥmad al-Jazā'irī

Aḥmad al-Jazā'irī (1833–1902) lived 20 years longer than his brother ʿAbd al-Qādir, and belonged to the network of ulama reformers. Aḥmad attained neither the wealth nor the prestige of his older brother, but he did enjoy French consular protection in addition to drawing stipends from both French and Ottoman treasuries.[18] Aḥmad al-Jazā'irī espoused Sufism in the sober, rational vein taught by his older brother and the Khānīs. He taught at the ʿAnnābah mosque near his home in the Bab al-Sarijah quarter, and conducted *dhikr* sessions, or Sufi rituals, of the Qādirī order at his home.

In 1884/85, Aḥmad al-Jazā'irī wrote an essay defending the Sufi concept of the unity of the cosmos in being (*waḥdat al-wujūd*) and explaining "true" Sufism.[19] In much the same way that ʿAbd al-Qādir had argued in *The Book of Stations,* Aḥmad held that the true Sufi scrupulously observes divine commands and prohibitions as the pious forefathers (al-salaf al-ṣāliḥ) had done. He sharply denounced those who claimed to possess divine gifts (*al-karāmāt*) that supposedly permitted them to violate the dictates of revealed law, and those who said they had reached a state of proximity to God and were therefore above observing religious law. Such men knew nothing more than how to dress as Sufis in order to exploit the gullibility of the popular classes. Aḥmad al-Jazā'irī's defense of waḥdat al-wujūd set him apart from the Naqshbandī Khānīs, who held that the true unity of existence lay in the perception, not the reality, of unity (*waḥdat al-shuhūd*). Notwithstanding this difference, Jazā'irī and the Khānīs belonged to the same ulama faction.

The common ground Jazā'irī shared with the reformers appears in Jamāl al-Dīn al-Qāsimī's observation that Aḥmad conducted Sufi rituals "void of the blemishes of innovation." Further, Qāsimī wrote that "his school is the oral report, acting according to it, and calling to adhering to it."[20]

The Bīṭār Family

Rashīd Riḍā called ʿAbd al-Razzāq al-Bīṭār "the reviver of the salafi school in Damascus."[21] Bīṭār belonged to ʿAbd al-Qādir's circle of ulama; in fact, his constant attendance at Jazā'irī's home and lessons earned him the sobriquet, "the amīr's second."[22] ʿAbd al-Razzāq came from a renowned ulama family that attained prominence in the nineteenth century at roughly the same time that Muḥammad al-Khānī came to Damascus.

Bīṭār's grandfather, Ibrāhīm al-Bīṭār (1738–1813), was a wealthy merchant who lost his fortune to the rapacious governor of late eighteenth- and early nineteenth-century Syria, Aḥmad Jazzār Pasha.[23] Ibrāhīm's son Ḥasan (1791–1856) studied with the major ulama of Damascus and for five years closely followed the instruction of the Egyptian scholar Ḥasan al-ʿAṭṭār, who resided in Damascus from 1810 to 1815.[24]

Around 1820, the notables of the Maydan, a large quarter on the southern edge of Damascus, invited Ḥasan al-Bīṭār to live in their quarter to serve as prayer leader, teacher, and preacher at the Karīm al-Dīn, or "the Daqqāq," mosque. Ḥasan al-Bīṭār acquired such influence in his newly adopted quarter that in 1846 the Ottoman magistrate became angry with him for allegedly interfering with the government's business. The magistrate probably resented Shaykh Ḥasan's intercession with Ottoman officials on behalf of his Maydani clients, or the magistrate may have objected to Bīṭār's authority in the quarter, where he resolved disputes and problems rather than referring them to Ottoman authorities.[25] When the magistrate summoned Bīṭār and upbraided him, news of the confrontation spread, and an angry, well-armed crowd of Maydanis formed to demonstrate in Bīṭār's support. The judge retreated and apologized to Bīṭār before an assembled group of ulama and notables. The incident indicates not only the popular following some ulama had but the tenuous nature of Ottoman authority in Damascus at that time.

In 1847, Sultan Abdülmecīd invited Bīṭār to attend the ceremonial circumcision of his sons. As a guest of the imperial court, Bīṭār received a large sum to cover the expenses of travel to Istanbul, where Bīṭār met the empire's leading religious authority, Shaykh al-Islam ʿĀrif Ḥikmet Pasha, another former student of the Egyptian Shaykh Ḥasan al-ʿAṭṭār.[26] Sultan Abdülmecīd granted Bīṭār an audience and awarded him a monthly stipend.

This royal reception elevated Bīṭār's status, and though he never parlayed his prestige into an official post, he firmly established the Bīṭār name in Damascus's ulama circles by acquiring a following in the Maydan and patronage in Istanbul. Shaykh Ḥasan's four sons, all of whom he tutored, perpetuated the family's celebrity. The eldest son, Muḥammad (1816–1895), ascended to the ranks of the official ulama, a move requiring that he switch from the Shāfiʿī to the Ḥanafī school. Around 1865, the chief jurisconsult selected Muḥammad al-Bīṭār to serve as one of his deputies, and he remained in the post for 30 years until he died. Apparently he did not or could not use it to augment his personal wealth, as he bequeathed to his children a modest sum, 19,660 piasters, most of which came from the sale of his large private library.[27]

Shaykh Ḥasan's second son, ʿAbd al-Ghanī (1824–1897), became a scholar and teacher of such Sufi texts as Ibn ʿArabī's *The Meccon Revelations*. ʿAbd al-Ghanī's son Bahā' al-Dīn (1849–1910) also devoted his life to Sufism, and in a magnanimous gesture of piety he gave away the considerable property he had inherited from his mother, thereby becoming known as Abū Fuqarā', "father of the poor." Both Shaykh Ḥasan's youngest son, Salīm (d. 1923), and ʿAbd al-Razzāq taught and preached at the Daqqāq mosque.[28]

During the anti-Christian outburst in 1860, ʿAbd al-Razzāq publicly condemned the rioters in a sermon at the Daqqāq mosque. Only 23 years old at the time, Bīṭār followed the lead of the Maydan's other prominent ulama and notables who protected the Christian residents of the quarter. The Maydani notables may have acted thus because of their involvement in exporting grain to Europe, and Maydani Christians may have helped the notables cultivate ties with European importers. Furthermore, Maydani Christians did not manufacture textiles and so did not compete with Muslim weavers, unlike the residents of the old Christian quarter, Bab Tuma.[29] It seems that social and economic ties between Maydani Christians and Muslims lay behind the protection the latter afforded to the quarter's Christians in July 1860.

In his account of the riots, Bīṭār reproached the perpetrators of the atrocities and vividly described the terrified state of surviving Christians who took refuge in the homes of Maydani notables. On the other hand, Bīṭār disapproved of Fuad Pasha's stern measures against the city's Muslim leadership, including heavy taxes on Muslims to indemnify Christians.[30]

Of the next 25 years of Bīṭār's life, little is known other than that he became Jazā'irī's close companion and that he hosted salons at which ulama met for literary discussions, singing, and chanting Sufi verse. Bīṭār probably first corresponded with Muḥammad ʿAbduh in the spring of 1885, after Muḥammad ʿAbd al-Jawād al-Qāyātī's visit to Damascus. In April 1886, he went to Beirut, where he stayed with Qāyātī, who introduced him to ʿAbduh. These contacts corroborate his grandson's observation that Bīṭār embraced salafism when he was about 50 years old, which was in 1887. In a letter to Qāyātī, Bīṭār wrote that as soon as he returned to Damascus he described Qāyātī and the other Egyptians to his friends and conveyed Qāyātī's greetings to Muḥyi al-Dīn al-Jazā'irī (ʿAbd al-Qādir's son) and others.[31]

Bīṭār's one published work, a massive yet incomplete three-volume biographical dictionary of the thirteenth Muslim century, contains ambiguous evidence of his views. He composed much of the work before his conversion to salafism, and consequently many passages evoke a world of supernatural forces, spells, amulets, and miracles performed by Sufi shaykhs. Moreover, Bīṭār highly praised men who later became his bitter enemies.[32] The original manuscript contains more such passages than the published work edited by ʿAbd al-Razzāq's grandson, Muḥammad Bahjat al-Bīṭār, who deleted many portions approving practices and beliefs that ʿAbd al-Razzāq later rejected.[33] Sections of the work that Bīṭār probably wrote later in his life reflect his new scripturalist convictions. Examples of such passages include his praise of Nuʿmān al-Alūsī's tribute to Ibn Taymiyyah, *A Clear View,* condemnation of Sufis who openly flouted religious precepts, criticism of inheriting religious posts, a biography of Ṣiddīq Ḥasan Khān and his father Ḥasan al-Qanawjī, and a biography of Jamāl al-Dīn al-Afghānī that Bīṭār obtained from Muḥammad ʿAbduh.[34]

The Bīṭārs became prominent around the same time that the Khānīs did, and both families' fortunes rose while the ulama's status as a group was declining. Like the Khānīs, the Bīṭārs ascended by establishing a local base and cementing it with ties to Istanbul. The two ulama families also resembled each other in standing just outside the ranks of Damascus's high ulama, men of wealthier families holding more prestigious posts.

ʿAbd al-Ghanī al-Ghunaymī

ʿAbd al-Ghanī al-Ghunaymī al-Maydānī (1807–1881) had a reputation as a liberal thinker and contributed to the intellectual formation of Damascus's foremost advocate of educational reform, Ṭāhir al-Jazā'irī. Ghunaymī was a well-to-do man who attained fame more through his qualities as a scholar than as a notable. Though he held no official post, he was one of the Maydan's most influential ulama along with the Bīṭārs. In fact Ghunaymī developed close, friendly ties with Ḥasan al-Bīṭār, whose move to the Maydan he commemorated in verse. During the 1860 riot, he joined other Maydani ulama and notables in protecting Christians fleeing their burning quarter.[35]

By 1862, Ghunaymī had begun to frequent ʿAbd al-Qādir's circle, and that year he traveled with the amīr to the Hijaz. On the way to Mecca, they stopped in Alexandria, where foreign consuls and Egyptian officials received them, and in Cairo, where Viceroy Ismāʿīl invited them to a banquet honoring the French architect of the Suez Canal, which was under construction.[36]

Ṭāhir al-Jazā'irī

In 1847, an Algerian shaykh fled the French conquerors of his land and emigrated to Damascus. The emigrant, Ṣāliḥ al-Jazā'irī (d. 1868), became a leading scholar among the city's handful of Mālikī ulama and earned a reputation for his expertise in astronomy and other rational sciences. Along with Shaykh Ghunaymī, Shaykh Ṣāliḥ instilled in his son, Ṭāhir al-Jazā'irī (1852–1920), an aptitude for studying rational sciences. Ṭāhir credited Ghunaymī with opposing rigid thinking and scorning those superstitions and popular religious practices that masqueraded as Islam.[37]

By the time Ṭāhir came under Ghunaymī's tutelage, he had attended a government secondary school that introduced him to natural sciences, history, archaeology, Persian, and Turkish. Before the early 1860s, a shaykh like Ṣāliḥ al-Jazā'irī would have simply passed on his own store of knowledge to his son in much the same way he had learned it. The first government schools established in the 1860s made it possible to study subjects outside the religious curriculum without exposure to the cultural influence of foreign mission schools. Ṣāliḥ al-Jazā'irī's interest in subjects like astronomy may have disposed him to send Ṭāhir to a government school to supplement his religious education. In addition, Ṭāhir's innate intellectual curiosity led him to seek out students attending mission schools.[38]

Ṭāhir al-Jazā'irī could have followed in his father's footsteps by working in the religious institution as a teacher, but his particular upbringing, which involved far more contact with Turks than other sons of ulama experienced, steered him down a different path. Most biographical sources state that Ṭāhir's contacts with Turks and his command of Turkish influenced his intellectual formation, but none of the sources spell out their significance.[39] Perhaps his Turkish teachers imparted an appreciation of science and European technological advances.

Although the effect of Ṭāhir's Turkish teachers and associates on his thinking is not clear, their role in launching his career is discernible. When the renowned Ottoman reformer Midḥat Pasha arrived in Damascus as governor in 1878, Ṭāhir was teaching at a government primary school located in the mausoleum of Sultan Ẓāhir Baybars. Midḥat's ideas for administrative reform included the improvement of education for Muslim children. One of Ṭāhir's Turkish friends in the provincial administration recommended him to Midḥat to work on the project of setting up new schools, and in the first half of 1879, Jazā'irī joined the Benevolent Society that was founded at Midḥat's behest and helped convert rooms in mosques and schools into classrooms for primary schools. Later that year Midḥat appointed him superintendent of schools in the province, and Ṭāhir designed curricula and composed textbooks in the clear style characteristic of the Ottoman reform movement and the salafis. Two years later, when a provincial board of education supplanted the Benevolent Society, Ṭāhir al-Jazā'irī played a seminal role in founding Syria's first public library. He collaborated with other board members, mostly ulama, in gathering books endowed for religious schools and placing them in a repository built in the mausoleum of Sultan Ẓāhir Baybars, thus founding the Ẓāhiriyyah Library.[40]

In the early 1880s, Ṭāhir al-Jazā'irī worked for educational reform by composing school primers to teach grammar, religious doctrine, arithmetic, and anatomy, as well as by organizing the new book collection at the Ẓāhiriyyah Library. The provincial press published his textbooks, in which he endeavored to combine sound education in religion with a grounding in "rational sciences," a principal goal of the salafis.[41] Through his work at the Ẓāhiriyyah Library, Ṭāhir acquired a unique grasp of long-forgotten texts, including works by the thirteenth-century thinker Ibn Taymiyyah.[42] Ṭāhir's wide reading in the manuscripts made him a central figure in the nascent movement to revive elements of the Arab-Islamic heritage supportive of the salafi interpretation of Islam.[43]

The Qāsimī Family

While Jazā'irī worked for reform from his post in the provincial education institution, a promising young religious student was attracting the attention of Damascus's outstanding religious teachers. This student, Jamāl al-Dīn al-Qāsimī (1866–1914), hailed from a recently established family of ulama and became in due course the foremost proponent of religious reform in Damascus from 1896 until 1914.[44]

Qāsimī's grandfather Qāsim al-Ḥallāq (1806–1867) worked as a barber in his youth, but in 1825 quit his trade to pursue a religious education. Qāsim's first teacher was a *sayyid* (descendant of the Prophet) of Egyptian origin, Ṣāliḥ al-Dasūqī (1785–1831/2), who did not belong to the elite corps of notable ulama. In 1824, Dasūqī added the imamate at the prestigious Sināniyyah mosque to his tenure as teacher and preacher at the Ḥassān mosque. After Dasūqī's death, Qāsim studied with a number of elite ulama and developed friendly ties with the city's foremost scholar of oral reports and scion of a high ulama family, ʿAbd al-Raḥmān al-Kuzbarī (1771–1846).[45]

In 1840, Kuzbarī gave Qāsim's career a boost when he invited other high ulama to attend the closing lesson on a famous collection of oral reports that Qāsim had been teaching at a minor mosque. Kuzbarī suggested to Qāsim that he hold the closing lesson at the Sināniyyah mosque, the second most important one in Damascus.[46] Soon after the episode, Qāsim al-Ḥallāq moved to the Ḥassān mosque, where he served as prayer leader, preacher, and teacher for 20 years, a move that confirmed his higher status.

In the next two decades Qāsim achieved the distinctions of a middle shaykh. In

1842, he married the niece of his former teacher, Ṣāliḥ al-Dasūqī, thus improving his social status with this match. He acquired multiple affiliations to Sufi orders and traveled to Egypt to study with ulama at al-Azhar. In 1862, Qāsim reached the peak of his career when he succeeded the late Shāfiʿī prayer leader of the Sināniyyah mosque and began giving lessons on oral reports and jurisprudence there. His promotion to the Sināniyyah mosque probably gave him the means to purchase a large home in the Qanawat quarter in 1863. When Qāsim died in December 1867, his prominence merited the publication of some of his poems by the official provincial printing press.[47]

An improvement in Qāsim's material fortunes accompanied his rise in status. A number of anecdotes from the early 1840s show a man of poor means struggling to make ends meet, whereas in later years he had acquired a fair amount of wealth, enabling him to engage in moneylending and to bequeath 11,000 piasters and a spacious house to his heirs.[48]

Qāsim al-Ḥallāq's career illustrates how someone from an artisan background could enter the ranks of the ulama. He left a trade to become a scholar, and scholarship, like other trades, had a hierarchy through which one ascended by learning the craft's lore and techniques and by conforming to its cultural norms. As an apprentice needs a master, Qāsim the religious student needed the patronage of a master scholar to promote his fortunes. With the support of Ṣāliḥ al-Dasūqī and ʿAbd al-Raḥmān al-Kuzbarī, Qāsim secured a place in the ulama corps by the time he was 35 years old.

The status and means Qāsim attained after years of study passed by birthright to his first son, Muḥammad Saʿīd al-Qāsimī (1843–1900). Muḥammad Saʿīd's upbringing followed the pattern of education of scholars' sons, so that, as in any other trade, the father imparted his knowledge and skills to his son. After memorizing the Quran, he attended his father's lessons on Arabic and religious subjects as well as studying with other ulama. When Muḥammad Saʿīd was 19 he began to assist his father's lessons at the Sināniyyah mosque and serve as preacher at the Ḥassān mosque. When Qāsim died in 1867, Muḥammad Saʿīd, just 24 years old, succeeded him as prayer leader, teacher, and preacher at the Sināniyyah mosque.[49]

Besides the post at the mosque, Muḥammad Saʿīd al-Qāsimī inherited about 1,800 piasters and a share in the family home. Some time later he bought his brothers' shares in the house to make it his sole property. How he managed that is unclear, as his stipend for working at the mosque was a mere 200 piasters per month; perhaps he prospered when he traded in kitchen utensils and drinking glasses imported from Europe. Muḥammad Saʿīd somehow did well enough to dispense with the preacher's post at the Ḥassān mosque in 1882, which he passed on to his brother Muḥammad.[50]

The biographies of Muḥammad Saʿīd al-Qāsimī note that he avoided the company of wealthy and powerful men. For instance, when Ottoman officials and local notables invited him to such formal occasions as Ramadan banquets he rarely attended, because he considered it unworthy of scholars to associate with rulers and thought that only ulama seeking official posts attended such occasions.[51] While he may have believed that such distance was necessary to preserve his virtue, his independent religious post enabled him to keep aloof from the elite.

Muḥammad Saʿīd al-Qāsimī composed poetry that expressed his bitter resentment toward Damascus's wealthy elite.[52] In one poem Qāsimī ranted against the greed, miserliness, immorality, and impiety of Damascus's wealthy class, especially their failure to pay the obligatory tax on wealth (*al-zakāt*) enjoined by Islamic law. He gave a derogatory description of a rich man's demise: the gathering of the town rabble at his home to receive alms; the hypocritical prayers recited for the deceased; the heirs' quarrelling over the estate; their irreverent behavior and squandering of their patrimony on prostitutes and wine-soaked parties. In another poem, he heaped scorn on men who pretended to be scholars but were nothing but arrogant swindlers hypocritically preaching to people while they themselves acted greedily and insulted true scholars.

Muḥammad Saʿīd al-Qāsimī composed these scathing poems in his later years, between 1896 and 1900, and they articulate the growing gap between the wealthy elite and middle ulama, and, among the ulama, between those devoted to scholarship and those who pursued posts for power and prestige. The roots of that split lay in the local elite's willingness to work in the new secular institutions of the Tanzimat. Moreover, as the ulama's political importance and social status dwindled, the cultural and moral standards they upheld lost ground among the local elite. The new urban elite, which based its power on large rural property holdings and bureaucratic posts, may have emulated cultural trends emanating from Istanbul and Europe. Perhaps even more galling to men like Qāsimī were ulama holding official posts in the new order, men who in his view lacked both adequate training and moral fiber.

Muḥammad Saʿīd al-Qāsimī may have been only a second-generation shaykh, but he identified strongly with the values, norms, and manners attaching to the status of the ulama, perhaps more so than men from long-established families who might have been less self-conscious about upholding the same values because their status was assured. Younger members of those families were tending to study at public schools and to pursue careers in the lay bureaucracy.[53] Qāsimī expressed deep repugnance at Damascus's wealthy elite, both civilian and religious, a sensibility absent in the writings of his father, who died before the rearrangement of social relations wrought by mid-nineteenth-century economic and political changes.

Muḥammad Saʿīd al-Qāsimī inherited his status as a shaykh, but he also possessed the requisite intellectual gifts to gain fame for a wide knowledge of history, literature, and poetry. His evening salons, noted for singing and recitation of verse, attracted leading religious scholars and literati.[54] In such a rich intellectual atmosphere and comfortable, though not opulent, home, Muḥammad Saʿīd raised his eldest son, Jamāl al-Dīn.

The early upbringing and education of Jamāl al-Dīn al-Qāsimī followed the usual course for the children of ulama. He memorized the Quran, learned to read and write, and then studied medieval glosses and commentaries on classical texts concerning language and the religious sciences. Jamāl al-Dīn deviated from the traditional course at the age of 12 when he attended the government school at the mausoleum of Ẓāhir Baybars. Aside from his formal education, Jamāl al-Dīn noted in his autobiographical writings that as a boy he loved to copy books, compose essays, and read works of history and literature in the family library.[55]

In 1880, Jamāl al-Dīn began assisting his father's lessons, much as Saʿīd had done when he was young, and giving evening lessons of his own on jurisprudence.

Meanwhile, he pursued advanced studies with leading ulama, from whom he received certificates (*ijāzāt*) attesting his mastery of prescribed texts. That same year he began studying with Muḥammad al-Khānī, who had long attended Muḥammad Saʿid's salons and who became Qāsimī's companion for the next 14 years and encouraged his pupil to compose essays. For seven years (1885–1892) Khānī gave Jamāl al-Dīn instruction in Sufism, grammar, jurisprudence, and oral reports. Soon after they first met, Khānī initiated Qāsimī into the Naqshbandī order, but Jamāl al-Dīn attended its rituals for only a short time before quitting the order.[56]

In January 1886, Qāsimī, not yet 20 years old, began his career in local religious posts when people from the nearby Bab al-Sarijah quarter asked him to serve as Shāfiʿī prayer leader at the ʿAnnābah mosque. Aḥmad al-Jazāʾirī headed the party from Bab al-Sarijah because he was a leading notable, the Mālikī prayer leader, and teacher at the mosque. Jamāl al-Dīn's move to the ʿAnnābah mosque marked the beginning of a close relationship with Aḥmad al-Jazāʾirī, who, along with Khānī and ʿAbd al-Razzāq al-Bīṭār, was a major intellectual influence on Qāsimī, according to the latter's autobiographical notes. Over 20 years earlier Aḥmad al-Jazāʾirī had studied oral reports and Quranic exegesis with Qāsim al-Ḥallāq and received from him a certificate, which he passed on to Jamāl al-Dīn in the 1880s. Though 30 years Qāsimī's senior, Aḥmad became his good friend and a source of information on the Algerian resistance to France's invasion and political relations between Europe and Muslim countries.[57]

Through Jamāl al-Dīn's studies with Muḥammad al-Khānī he met ʿAbd al-Majīd, who had recently become acquainted with Muḥammad ʿAbduh. ʿAbd al-Razzāq al-Bīṭār rounded out the circle of reformist scholars who influenced Qāsimī. Among Damascus's ulama, Qāsimī most respected Bīṭār, who became his close friend for nearly three decades until Jamāl al-Dīn's death in 1914.[58] It appears odd, therefore, that nowhere did Qāsimī or his biographers mention the circumstances of their acquaintance. They probably first met through either Aḥmad al-Jazāʾirī or Muḥammad al-Khānī, both of whom Bīṭār had known for years.

Muḥammad Saʿid al-Qāsimī imparted to Jamāl al-Dīn his antipathy toward wealthy folk who neglected religious and social obligations to take care of the poor. Jamāl al-Dīn once wrote that the poor of Damascus resorted to beggary because the wealthy greedily hoarded their fortunes. Qāsimī blamed corrupt jurists for concocting legal fictions (*ḥiyal*) to relieve the rich of their divinely ordained duty to ease the misery of the poor. He observed that whereas artisans, middling merchants, and poor folk regularly attended mosque prayers, the wealthy came only for the Friday prayer and holy days.[59]

Jamāl al-Dīn's early writings provide few clues that he would later challenge prevailing conceptions of Islam. In his first composition, a commentary on a text about reciting the Quran, he broke no new ground. He did state the classic Ḥanbalī position on the nature of God's attributes, namely, that knowledge of God's essence surpasses human reason, and that man can know of God only what the Quran revealed of Him.[60] In the field of dialectical theology (*kalām*) that position is known as *madhhab al-salaf* (school of the forefathers), implying that the first generations of Muslims held that belief and that later theological views were innovations.

However the word *salaf* in this expression did not have the connotations that Qāsimī later attributed to it when he referred his interpretations of jurisprudence and worship to the way of the salaf.

In 1888, Qāsimī wrote a text for recital on the Prophet's birthday (*mawlid al-nabī*), and he based his text on a work that excluded customary anecdotes of miracles and superstitions usually affirmed at the popular ceremony. Qāsimī never denied the reality of miracles as such, but he and the other salafis believed that many miracle stories about the Prophet had no scriptural basis, and therefore constituted accretions that discredited religion before a growing number of skeptics.[61]

Qāsimī's essay on the Prophet's birthday may have signified a step toward salafism, not as an existent body of thought but as a tendency to purify religion of accretions, but the colophon on the essay indicates he had not yet broken with certain customs. He signed his name to the manuscript as Muḥammad Jamāl al-Dīn Abī al-Faraj al-Qāsimī al-Ashʿarī al-Dimashqī al-Naqshbandī al-Khālidī al-Shāfiʿī. He thereby proclaimed partisan sentiments for the Shāfiʿī legal school, Ashʿarī dialectical theology, and the Naqshbandiyyah-Khālidiyyah Sufi order, sentiments he later renounced. Qāsimī signed his name to a manuscript thusly for the last time a year later, in 1889, after which he signed as Muḥammad Jamāl al-Dīn al-Qāsimī al-Dimashqī, omitting all references to legal schools, Sufi orders, and theological schools.[62]

In the early 1890s, the Syrian provincial council nominated Jamāl al-Dīn for four consecutive years to undertake teaching tours in Damascus's outlying districts during Ramadan. He wrote an account of his first tour in 1892, listing the villages he visited in Wadi al-Ajam, which lies to Damascus's southwest, describing the countryside, and naming the ulama and officials he met along the way. Of his instruction, he wrote only that he led prayers and gave lessons.[63] The following year Qāsimī toured the Nabak district north of Damascus, and in 1894 and 1895 he gave lessons in Baalbak district, a mostly Twelver Shīʿī region in eastern Lebanon.

Qāsimī's April 1895 tour in Baalbak was his last Ramadan teaching tour. The provincial administration stopped appointing ulama for such educational and religious missions. Moreover, even if they had continued, the provincial council probably would not have appointed Qāsimī because of a controversy that swirled around him a few months later.

Other Reformers

Five other ulama belonged to the reformist faction but did not come from such renowned families as the Khānīs, Biṭārs, Jazā'irīs, or Qāsimīs. Salīm al-Bukhārī (1851–1927), the son of a low-ranking army officer of Anatolian origin, became a religious scholar by dint of his own efforts. Bukhārī studied with various ulama in Damascus, then traveled to Mecca to continue his studies. On returning to Damascus, he landed a post as jurisconsult of an artillery battalion in the Ottoman army stationed in Damascus. His proficiency in Turkish, which he probably acquired from his father, his education in a state school, and his religious training most likely got him the post. For 40 years Salīm al-Bukhārī was an important figure in the salafi movement.[64]

ʿAbd al-Ḥakīm al-Afghānī (1834/35–1908) was born in Qandahar, Afghanistan. He traveled to India, the Hijaz, and Jerusalem before settling in Damascus, where he resided at the Oral Reports College (*Dār al-Ḥadīth al-Nawawiyyah*), which ʿAbd al-Qādir al-Jazāʾirī had restored to prominence in 1856. Afghānī never married, did not hold a post, and lived ascetically on a small income from his work as a potter. He opposed such innovations as using charms and amulets to cure illnesses, and he favored ijtihād, even though he followed the rulings of the Ḥanafī school. He apparently favored the application of ijtihād within a legal school, a limited definition of ijtihād that the salafis transcended.[65]

Another reformist shaykh from Afghanistan, ʿAbd al-Bāqī al-Afghānī (d. 1905), was born in Kabul, grew up in Peshawar, and migrated to Rampur in India, where he taught for 25 years and where the reformist Ahl-i Ḥadīth movement may have influenced him. He then traveled to the Hijaz and Syria, where he spent the last 20 years of his life. He swelled in Damascus but briefly, preferring to travel as an itinerant teacher throughout Syria until he settled in Homs in 1902.[66]

ʿAbd al-Qādir ibn Badrān (1848–1927) was yet another outsider who became a Damascene reformer. Born in th nearby village of Duma to a local ulama family, Ibn Badrān studied with prominent Damascene ulama and attended the lessons of ʿAbd al-Qādir al-Jazāʾirī. Ibn Badrān first belonged to the Shāfiʿī school, but after studying the four Sunni schools he converted to the Ḥanbalī school as a result of the impression made on him by Ibn Taymiyyah and Ibn Qayyim al-Jawziyyah. For a time Ibn Badrān taught at the Umayyad mosque, then at the ʿAbd Allah al-ʿAẓm religious school.[67]

A similarly peripheral figure, Aḥmad al-Nuwaylātī (ca. 1868–1938), came from a family of artisans, and, like Ibn Badrān, never rose above the standing of religious teacher. Nuwaylātī taught illiterate artisans and workers at the Umayyad mosque, using language comprehensible to his audience, unlike the high ulama's practice. He expressed the views of middle ulama like Muḥammad Saʿīd al-Qāsimī when he castigated the wealthy of the city and impostor ulama; he also strove to eliminate ritual innovations.[68]

Conclusion: Salafism and Middle Ulama

The ulama discussed above—the Bīṭārs, the Khānīs, Aḥmad al-Jazāʾirī, ʿAbd al-Ghanī al-Ghunaymī—shared more than a common association with ʿAbd al-Qādir al-Jazāʾirī. They also shared a common position in the ranks of the ulama, namely, middling status, modest wealth, and local posts, but not official posts or the most prestigious local posts. These men stood a cut below the high ulama who monopolized the most important religious posts and accumulated great wealth. Members of ʿAbd al-Qādir's circle possessed influence in their respective quarters (Bīṭār and Ghunaymī in the Maydan) and Sufi orders (Khānī in the Naqshbandiyyah, Aḥmad al-Jazāʾirī in the Qādiriyyah). Each of them had enough wealth to do without official posts, yet their status entitled them to frequent the circles of official ulama and Ottoman administrators.

Besides sharing a common position in the ulama corps, most of the reformers were newcomers to the ranks of Damascus's ulama. The Khānīs, the Afghānī shaykhs, Ibn Badrān, and both Jazā'irī clans had recently settled in Damascus, while the Bīṭārs and the Qāsimīs had attained ulama status fairly recently. Families like the Ḥamzāwīs, ʿAjlānīs, ʿAṭṭārs, Ghazzīs, Kuzbarīs, Kaylānīs, and Usṭuwānīs had produced prominent ulama for over a century, and they controlled the key religious posts of Damascus.[69] ʿAbd al-Qādir al-Jazā'irī himself accumulated more wealth than the notable ulama families, but he never overcame the stigma of an outsider in the eyes of most Damascene Muslims.

We can further distinguish between the high ulama and Jazā'irī's circle by considering their roles in the 1860 massacre of Christians and its aftermath. At the time of the upheaval, six elite ulama held seats on the provincial council, and though they may not have had a hand in instigating the riots, Fuad Pasha exiled all of them. On the other hand, most of Jazā'irī's ulama associates actively opposed the riots, and all of them emerged from Fuad Pasha's investigations unscathed. Bīṭār and Ghunaymī acted out of solidarity with other Maydani ulama and notables; Muḥammad al-Khānī the elder was an immigrant shaykh who stood apart from the city's high ulama and enjoyed patronage in Istanbul.

The ulama in ʿAbd al-Qādir's camp escaped the punishment dealt to more prominent ulama; however, they suffered the effects of the malaise that afflicted Syrian ulama as a result of the Tanzimat. The Bīṭārs, the Khānīs, and the Qāsimīs' family histories showed an upward trajectory in a status group declining in relation to new local elites and ruling groups in the imperial capital. Propertied ulama families continued to prosper in the new economic and social order by investing in rural lands and preparing sons for careers in both religious posts and the growing secular bureaucracy. Middle ulama did not possess the means to compete for religious posts, and their limited wealth hampered their chances of joining the bonanza in rural estates. Their precarious social position made them more sensitive to the ulama's marginalization. Faced with the bleak prospect of further deterioration in their status, some middle ulama attempted to arrest their group's decline by redefining the role of the ulama and reinterpreting Islam.

The agent of that reinterpretation was ʿAbd al-Razzāq al-Bīṭār, whose relationships with ʿAbd al-Qādir al-Jazā'irī and Muḥammad ʿAbduh made a profound impression on him. In his turn Bīṭār imparted the reformist creed to younger ulama like Jamāl al-Dīn al-Qāsimī, who developed an elaborate vision of religious practice on the basis of general principles espoused by Bīṭār.

The salafi interpretation of Islam, then, represented an assertion of the relevance of "true" ulama's stock of knowledge. Specifically, the salafis reconciled current ideas about reason, science, and progress with religion to disprove an assumption embedded in the Tanzimat and later Ottoman reforms, namely that the ulama lacked the knowledge and skills necessary to guide the empire to prosperity. The salafis meant to show that the ulama (religious intellectuals) were quite capable, on both technical and moral grounds, of guiding society. At the same time the salafis criticized the practices of Damascus's official ulama and implied that they themselves possessed the intellectual and moral qualifications for high posts. Therefore, within the boundaries of the ulama status group, salafism represented the outlook of some middle ulama, while in the context of the empire, salafism expressed the ulama's desire to recover their former stature.

4

The Emergence of Salafism in Damascus: Early Vicissitudes, 1896–1904

Damascene ulama coped with the challenges posed by the new social and cultural order in various ways. Some wealthy ulama joined the emergent landholding-bureaucratic elite by acquiring rural landholdings and obtaining posts in the expanding bureaucracy. Those ulama who obtained choice religious posts adhered to established practices in jurisprudence and education. Middle ulama, who lacked the means to join either the urban elite or to secure high religious posts, had two motives to formulate a critique of more fortunate ulama. First, incumbent ulama stood between middle ulama and the greater influence afforded by higher posts. Second, middle ulama could hold the incumbents accountable for the general decline of the ulama's status. Salafism, then, represented both a critique of official ulama's practices and an assertion that the ulama should play a leading role in governing the empire.

Salafism's central concept, ijtihād, had a critical edge in that it discredited the basis of current religious jurisprudence: emulation of the legal schools' authorities. Ulama incumbents of the religious court posts referred their decisions to precedents codified in the legal schools' compendia of precepts. The salafis argued that true Islam forbids qualified ulama to practice emulation, which is proper only for ordinary Muslims incapable of deriving legal rulings. Ijtihād challenged the official ulama's customary authority because it clashed with emulation. The official ulama quickly perceived that salafism threatened their authority, which they may have been more zealous to protect in view of the inroads made by civil courts and public schools on the ulama's traditional domains.

The hostility that the salafis encountered from other ulama drove them to seek consolation in contacts with reformers outside Damascus. By correspondence and travel, the Damascene salafis cultivated a network of religious reformers holding similar goals, and these outside contacts enabled the salafis to break out of their local isolation and to participate in an intellectual movement encompassing much of the Muslim world.

The Mujtahids Incident

The salafis appeared as a distinct group for the first time in January 1896, when rival ulama embroiled them in a controversy that led to the reformers' trial. The "mujtahids incident" (*ḥādithat al-mujtahidīn*), as the controversy became known, partly backfired on its plotters, who sought to intimidate the salafis into silence but wound up bringing them a measure of celebrity instead.[1]

Events leading to the incident began in December 1895, when Aḥmad al-Jazā'irī visited Jamāl al-Dīn al-Qāsimī and asked him if he would like to visit ʿAbd al-Razzāq al-Bīṭār and Salīm Samārah, both of whom resided in the Maydan, across town from the ʿAnnābah mosque, where Jazā'irī and Qāsimī worked.[2] The four ulama had known each other for years, so the social call had no apparent significance beyond that of a customary visit. During their conversation they complained that the distance between their homes made opportunities to see one another infrequent. To remedy the situation, they agreed to meet once a week and to take turns hosting one another.

Qāsimī held the first meeting in his room at the ʿAnnābah mosque on Wednesday morning, December 19. Bīṭār, Jazā'irī, Samārah, Qāsimī's cousin Muṣṭafā al-Ḥallāq, and some of Qāsimī's students attended a few hours of scholarly discussion.[3] A week later Muṣṭafā al-Ḥallāq held the next meeting, at which Muḥammad Saʿīd al-Qāsimī and other ulama joined the core group. Aḥmad al-Jazā'irī took his turn as host next, and again the group's number grew. At the fourth meeting two notables hostile to Qāsimī showed up and argued with members of the group. Qāsimī became upset with the intruders, whom he deemed incompetent to discuss scholarly issues.

At the group's fifth meeting the doyen of Damascus's ulama, Bakrī al-ʿAṭṭār, attended, thereby conferring more prestige on the group, for the ʿAṭṭār family had produced eminent ulama for over a century. Shaykh Bakrī himself held a well-endowed teaching post at the Sulaymāniyyah Sufi shrine and had a reputation for his erudition and teaching.[4] ʿAṭṭār's presence may have riled Qāsimī's enemies and contributed indirectly to the mujtahids incident, for though Shaykh Bakrī did not espouse reformist views, he had tacitly endorsed Qāsimī's study group when he attended.

The fifth meeting marked a step toward a sharper definition of the group's purpose. The members decided to select a book to study together, and after brief discussion, they agreed on ʿAbd al-Wahhāb al-Shaʿrānī's *Removing the Affliction from the Entire Community*, a sixteenth-century work that compiled Prophetic oral reports setting forth the precepts of rituals and transactions. Shaʿrānī had embraced the same position as the salafis in opposing legal school partisanship and claiming the right to examine the proofs of legal schools' precepts. He tried to base rulings on Prophetic oral reports, which he placed above those decisions of the legal schools that were based on jurists' opinions. Qāsimī undertook to compose a gloss on the work, annotating its oral reports and explaining difficult passages.[5]

ʿAbd al-Razzāq al-Bīṭār invited the group, his brother ʿAbd al-Ghanī, and other friends to his home for the next session toward the end of January 1896. Qāsimī noted that in discussing matters such as the impurity of wine "only precision pleases them [the discussion group], and only clear proof with exactness convinces them." Qāsimī added that at the same meeting "a man attended who by his attire belongs to the ulama, but who spreads slanderous rumors." After the session this shaykh joined the two notables who had come to the meeting two weeks before. Together they spread such rumors about Qāsimī's group that it became known as the mujtahids' club (*jamʿiyyat al-mujtahidīn*), and it became identified with Qāsimī, so people called it "the Jamālī school." More ominously, people began to speak darkly of an alleged secret agenda. To allay growing suspicions about the group's motives, one of its members, Amīn al-Safarjalānī, invited Bakrī al-ʿAṭṭār to meet with its leaders. Shaykh Bakrī told them that they had a reputation for practicing ijtihād (something most ulama considered forbidden for their generation).[6] The alleged mujtahids defended their discussions, and ʿAṭṭār admitted they had done nothing wrong; in fact, he had a positive impression of the group. At the conclusion of their meeting with ʿAṭṭār the members probably felt relieved, but right after that the controversy grew sharper and the Ottoman authorities entered the picture.

A few men, whom Qāsimī refrained from naming in his account of the incident, approached the Ottoman governor and accused the group of conspiring with another shaykh, Badr al-Dīn al-Ḥasanī, to undermine Ottoman authority.[7] According to the charges, Ḥasanī had called for the prohibition of cigarette smoking, censured the trend to stop wearing turbans, and, most seriously, announced in a public lesson at the Umayyad mosque that the Ottoman sultans had converted the caliphate into unjust, oppressive rule. Furthermore, the group's practice of gathering to study oral reports and to search for proofs of venerated jurists' decisions was said to be tantamount to ijtihād. The plotters deceived the Ottoman governor into believing that the mujtahids' club and Ḥasanī shared a secret political scheme, thus instigating a confrontation between the salafis and the Ottoman authorities.

At a meeting of the provincial administrative council the governor asked the jurisconsult, Muḥammad al-Manīnī (1835–1898), what he knew about the group.[8] Manīnī is reported to have displayed anger at the group in order to placate the governor and to secure his post. The administrative council decided to appoint an investigative council headed by the magistrate and including the jurisconsult and his deputies. Then the magistrate ordered the police to summon the "mujtahids" to the central religious court. The magistrate summoned eight ulama for interrogation, but Bīṭār and Ḥasanī stayed away: Bīṭār feigned illness, and Ḥasanī claimed to be busy. Aḥmad al-Jazāʾirī's French protection gave him immunity from the inquisition, so the magistrate did not try to summon him.

On January 27, 1896, Qāsimī and five other ulama appeared before the special investigative committee, which had assigned Manīnī the task of interrogation (perhaps because the magistrate did not speak Arabic).[9] First, the court called on Qāsimī, the group's youngest member. A scribe of the court read the charges that he and the others met to interpret the Quran and oral reports according to their opinions, and that they rejected the opinions of the authoritative imams of the legal schools. Qāsimī tersely replied that they were innocent of the charges. When asked of the group's purpose, Qāsimī explained their principle and method. Manīnī grew impatient and charged Qāsimī with proclaiming the ritual purity of wine, whereupon Jamāl al-Dīn responded, "We studied the legal proof of wine's ritual impurity once.

I wrote an essay called 'Warning the Gullible by Refuting Specious Arguments for Ritual Wine's Purity.' Here is a copy."[10] The jurisconsult perused it quickly and then asked what exactly the group discussed. Qāsimī replied, "Either the meaning of an oral report . . . or Quranic verse, or legal issue, or literary issue, in order to increase understanding, as is the custom of scholars' salons."

Manīnī then asked why the group studied Shaʿrānī's *Removing the Affliction* and why Qāsimī wrote a gloss on it. Qāsimī stated that the group simply chose a book famous for its oral reports and still used by scholars; as for the gloss, he merely wanted to define precisely a few obscure terms. The jurisconsult retorted that the group had no business studying oral reports or Quranic exegesis, and that it should restrict its study to books of jurisprudence. Manīnī then put on a glowering expression and said, "It has become known in Damascus that you said in answering a [legal] issue, 'Take it [the decision] according to the Jamālī school.' " Qāsimī denied the charge, and after the jurisconsult berated him, he ordered that Qāsimī be detained at the police station.

Of the other men interrogated, Qāsimī's cousin Muṣṭafā al-Ḥallāq made light of the proceedings, Salīm Samārah and Amīn al-Safarjalānī defended the propriety of the group's meetings, Tawfīq al-Ayyūbī managed to get acquitted because his cousin worked in the court, and another man begged the council's forgiveness, swearing he never differed with the legal schools. Samārah asked Manīnī what harm ulama could do by meeting to discuss various issues and why Manīnī took offense at Qāsimī's writing a gloss to clarify difficult sentences. Safarjalānī stated that Bakrī al-ʿAṭṭār had attended a meeting and found nothing wrong with the group. Manīnī ordered him to refrain from mentioning ʿAṭṭār, probably to avoid the appearance of clashing with the prestigious shaykh.

After the interrogation the council deliberated and decided to let the matter end with a reprimand. That evening Manīnī let all but Qāsimī go free on condition they discontinue their meetings. When the council members left the court building they found a large crowd outside, curious, if not anxious, about the hearing's outcome. Qāsimī's brother Muḥammad ʿĪd had gathered some commoners from the Qanawat and, with their backing, intimidated the jurisconsult. Later that night, Muḥammad Saʿīd al-Qāsimī appeared at Manīnī's home and made the jurisconsult promise to release Jamāl al-Dīn the next day.

Meanwhile the magistrate had gone to the governor to inform him that the rumors about the mujtahids' club amounted to nothing. Whereas the governor had believed that the group harbored secret political plans, the magistrate told him the group met to discuss scholarly issues of no political import. The governor asked the magistrate to rectify the situation, so the next day he went to the police station, spoke some kind words to Qāsimī (through an interpreter), and had him set free. Muḥammad Saʿīd al-Qāsimī and a number of friends escorted Jamāl al-Dīn home, where Muḥammad al-Khānī told him the incident had boosted his status, and another shaykh congratulated him on his triumph.

The outcome of the mujtahids incident vindicated Qāsimī and humbled Mufti Manīnī, whom many blamed for mishandling the interrogation. Qāsimī made clear his resentment toward Manīnī, but he never identified the men who plotted the incident and apparently manipulated Manīnī. Jamāl al-Dīn wrote that before the trial people had taunted Manīnī by suggesting that no one would have dared to claim to practice ijtihād when Mufti Maḥmūd al-Ḥamzāwī was alive. Perhaps Manīnī reacted hastily to such provocative talk because of the controversy over his accession to the post of jurisconsult in 1887 following Ḥamzāwī's death when a party of ulama had backed the candidacy of the late jurisconsult's brother Asʿad and expected him to obtain the post. Manīnī's selection caused an uproar among Asʿad al-Ḥamzāwī's backers, and it seems that the new jurisconsult never achieved the status of his illustrious predecessor.[11]

After the mujtahids incident Qāsimī joined the ranks of ulama who bore Manīnī a grudge. In Qāsimī's eyes, Manīnī personified the impostor religious scholar who gave religion and religious knowledge a bad reputation. Qāsimī accused Manīnī of abusing his trust as administrator of the ancient ʿAdliyyah religious school by treating it as his own property. He allegedly constructed a large salon and furnished it with expensive chairs, tables, and divans; knocked in part of the school's wall to make an entrance for his carriage and animals; and converted classrooms into smoking and coffee-drinking chambers. Qāsimī remarked that his adversary had purchased his post rather than attaining it by merit, however less biased accounts depict Manīnī sympathetically.[12]

Manīnī belonged to a venerable ulama family that had come into wealth and posts. His great-grandfather Shihāb Aḥmad al-Manīnī had come to Damascus from a nearby village and become a leading shaykh in the first half of the eighteenth century. Shaykh Aḥmad obtained well-endowed, prestigious teaching posts and the custodianship of three schools, and his sons inherited these posts. Muḥammad al-Manīnī came to prominence in 1860 when the Ottomans exiled Shaykh ʿAbd Allah al-Ḥalabī to Rhodes. Ḥalabī had been the most influential shaykh in Damascus and taught the famous oral reports collection of al-Bukhārī at the Nasr Dome in the Umayyad mosque. When Fuad Pasha sent Ḥalabī into exile Manīnī assumed that teaching post, and later headed the civil court for 15 years before becoming jurisconsult.[13]

A month after the trial the magistrate invited members of the mujtahids' group to a special Ramadan banquet, where they snubbed Manīnī, who was seeking a conciliation with them. They further demonstrated their disdain for him by continuing to meet regularly in spite of his order banning their meetings. Early in 1897, Manīnī invited Bīṭār to come visit him, but Bīṭār refused. So the jurisconsult swallowed his pride, and, in a reversal of protocol, visited Bīṭār. When Bīṭār returned the visit two weeks later, the jurisconsult apologized for his role in the incident and told Bīṭār that a number of men had goaded him into persecuting the group. Although Bīṭār had accepted Manīnī's apology, Qāsimī refrained from visiting the jurisconsult until January 1898, when Manīnī sent engraved invitations to Jamāl al-Dīn and his father asking them to dinner. The Qāsimīs relented and accepted the invitation, thus ending the feud only months before Manīnī died. Jamāl al-Dīn noted that the jurisconsult's reconciliation with the mujtahids' group sullied the status of the men who had instigated the controversy in the first place.[14]

Qāsimī's account of the mujtahids incident contains several signs of a salafi trend. First, some people thought that Qāsimī wanted to establish a new legal school in his own name, a preposterous charge because the salafis opposed the institutionalization of any man's authority or learning. Yet inasmuch as Qāsimī wanted to undermine the four legal schools, he stood for a novel "school" in the sense of a method or principle, which the Arabic term *madhhab* encompasses in its field of meaning. Second, Qāsimī declared the group's commitment to adducing clear proofs and to a close study of all issues. Third, the group focused its attention on oral reports and the Quran, an agenda to which Manīnī and his deputies objected. Manīnī told Qāsimī that the group should not study books on oral reports or exegesis directly. Emphasis on the Quran and the Sunnah is a trademark of salafis, who base their understanding of religion on scripture without reference to the vast corpus of medieval, late medieval, and early modern texts. Fourth, the group's composition indicates its salafi orientation. Qāsimī and Bīṭār became Damascus's leading salafis, Aḥmad al-Jazā'irī was their close associate, and Muṣṭafā al-Ḥallāq had salafi tendencies. Finally, in the incident's aftermath, Qāsimī composed a short poem clarifying his views:

> People claim that
> My school is called al-Jamālī
> To which, when men ask me for a legal opinion,
> I ascribe my decision.
> No! The truth is that I
> Am of the salafi creed.
> My school is what is in the book of God,
> My Sublime Lord,
> Then that which is sound of the oral reports,
> Not disputable opinions.
> I follow the truth and I am not
> Satisfied with men's opinions.
> I consider emulation ignorance
> And blindness in all instances.[15]

Notwithstanding the salafi imprint on so many aspects of the episode it is ironic that the Ottomans did not interrogate Qāsimī and his group because of their views but on account of suspicions of a political plot. Concern with ijtihād and the authority of the legal schools reflected the outlook and interests of official ulama such as Mufti Manīnī. Who concocted the episode and what exactly motivated them remains a mystery. They successfully played on Manīnī's insecurity and persuaded him that the group challenged his status, an affront he took seriously. They spread rumors to give the Ottoman governor a false idea about the group; he thought that it was in league with Badr al-Dīn al-Ḥasanī, who had allegedly denounced Ottoman authority at the Umayyad mosque. Manīnī failed to realize that the Ottoman governor wanted to get to the bottom of a possible political plot and did not care a whit if some ulama practiced ijtihād or not. From the governor's perspective, the jurisconsult's line of questioning missed the point.

Yet the plotters succeeded to the extent that they instigated official action against the salafis. Qāsimī's son and biographer has suggested that the incident disposed Jamāl al-Dīn to compose his works by citing scripture and classical authorities rather than expressing his views in his own words.[16] Through his remarkably wide reading in classical works and scripture, he discovered passages, Quranic verses, and oral reports that informed his commitment to reforming religious practice and inspired his formulation of salafism. As an example of his appetite for reading, in the summer of 1898 he read three major collections of oral reports in less than three months. When Jamāl al-Dīn wrote, he marshaled his profound knowledge of scripture and classical works to select passages that conveyed the principles of salafism.[17] By speaking from behind the masks of the legal schools' eponymous founders, the Sufi masters, and the great scholars of the Islamic tradition, Qāsimī conferred authority on principles and methods that few would have accepted from a young shaykh like himself.

Restrictions on the salafis' ability to propagate their views amounted to informal censorship enforced by persecution and the threat of further persecution. This informal censorship operated effectively in Damascus as long as its agents could mobilize the coercive power of the government to punish those who transgressed the boundaries of acceptable discourse. With Sultan Abdülḥamīd on the throne, the ulama opposed to salafism found little difficulty in provoking government action to mute the call to religious reform. The sultan's Islamic policy and his principal adviser on religious affairs, Abū al-Hudā al-Ṣayyādī, favored prevalent religious beliefs and practices, which the salafis regarded as invalid.[18] For instance, Abdülḥamīd and Abū al-Hudā patronized popular Sufi orders to buttress the sultan's pose as caliph, supreme ruler of the Muslims. Under such a regime the salafis could not hope to make much progress in spreading their views, let alone obtain the government's backing. When someone did openly espouse religious reform, he drew a swift response resulting in his expulsion from Syria.

ʿAbd al-Ḥamīd al-Zahrāwī: *Jurisprudence and Sufism*

ʿAbd al-Ḥamīd al-Zahrāwī (1871–1916) published an essay in 1901 in which he contemptuously disparaged the heritage of jurisprudence and Sufism for diverting Muslims from true religious practice. Because of the prominence Zahrāwī achieved in both the religious reform and the Arab autonomy movements, his background deserves consideration.[19]

Zahrāwī came from a sayyid family of ulama in Homs, a medium-sized town some 125 miles north of Damascus. ʿAbd al-Ḥamīd attended and excelled at government primary and secondary schools; studied Turkish with a Turkish shaykh; and learned religion and language from local ulama. Zahrāwī's only noteworthy teacher was the salafi ʿAbd al-Bāqī al-Afghānī, who instructed him in theology and "rational" subjects. In 1890, ʿAbd al-Ḥamīd visited Istanbul and Egypt, where he frequented intellectuals' circles and stayed in Cairo with the doyen of Egyptian sharīfs, Tawfīq al-Bakrī.

These few details of Zahrāwī's youth show the son of a provincial religious notable in touch with ulama in more cosmopolitan centers. His father's decision to educate him in the new state schools and to teach him Turkish exhibited a desire to avail ʿAbd al-Ḥamīd of cultural equipment surpassing that possessed by more narrowly trained ulama. Other than his studies with ʿAbd al-Bāqī al-Afghānī, however, nothing in his formation suggests the making of a reformer.

Around 1891, Zahrāwī published a newspaper, *al-Munīr,* in which he criticized despotic government, alluding to Sultan Abdülḥamīd's regime. Rashīd Riḍā, a fellow salafi and friend of Zahrāwī, later asserted that Zahrāwī supported the Young Turks by espousing reformist ideas in his newspaper, which Ottoman authorities suppressed after publication of the first few issues.[20]

In 1895, Zahrāwī traveled to Istanbul to start a warehousing business, but he quickly lost interest in the venture and turned to studying history and jurisprudence at the public library. Two years later Zahrāwī took up work for a Turkish-Arabic newspaper as editor of the Arabic section. He wrote articles in which he called for reform and thereby attracted the favorable attention of Rashīd Riḍā and the less benevolent interest of Sultan Abdülḥamīd's agents. In order to remove Zahrāwī from Istanbul, the sultan offered him a provincial post, but the reformer refused it. Around the middle of 1900, Zahrāwī was expelled from Istanbul and exiled to Damascus, where he spent the next 18 months under house arrest and collected a modest pension.[21]

Even though the authorities kept Zahrāwī under surveillance, he continued to publish controversial articles, now in Egyptian journals and newspapers. In one article, "The Imamate and Its Conditions," he stated that for a ruler to have a legitimate claim to the caliphate, he must fulfill 22 conditions. Zahrāwī concluded that since Sultan Abdülḥamīd did not satisfy a single condition he must be deposed. The Ottoman authorities apparently did not ascertain Zahrāwī's authorship, as they took no action against him. About the same time, however, Zahrāwī published an article on divorce in an Egyptian newspaper. The article upset conservative ulama in Damascus, and they tried to persuade the governor to punish the irrepressible shaykh. The governor convened a meeting with the offended ulama, but when they failed to convince him of the article's importance, he dismissed the issue.[22]

At the end of 1901, a storm erupted over Zahrāwī's 60-page essay entitled *Jurisprudence and Sufism,* in which he recklessly shattered those two pillars of the Islamic heritage like so much worthless bric-a-brac. Conservative ulama publicly branded him an unbeliever (kāfir), and they enlisted the support of Bakrī al-ʿAṭṭār in directing the governor's attention yet again to Zahrāwī's allegedly misguided and harmful ideas. The governor, Ḥusayn Nāẓim Pasha, summoned Zahrāwī for a showdown with ʿAṭṭār, a Naqshbandī shaykh named Asʿad al-Ṣāḥib, and others. The confrontation left Nāẓim Pasha uncertain as to a proper course of action, so he referred the matter to Istanbul. He confided to British Consul Richards that he thought Zahrāwī was crazy and should be exiled, even though the matter had no political significance. From other quarters Richards heard that Zahrāwī was quite sane and, in fact, an intelligent, well-educated man.[23]

The governor had Zahrāwī arrested and sent him to Istanbul for final disposition of the case. In Damascus the police confiscated several dozen copies of the essay, including one in Jamāl al-Dīn al-Qāsimī's possession. Jamāl al-Dīn wrote in a letter to Rashīd Riḍā eight years later that the headman of his quarter and the police came to his home, and they demanded he turn over Zahrāwī's essay. Qāsimī anxiously waited for the issue's outcome and was relieved when tension over the incident subsided. Accounts of the incident do not refer to ʿAbd al-Razzāq al-Bīṭār in connection with the controversy over *Jurisprudence and Sufism,* but Bīṭār's grandson stated that Zahrāwī and Bīṭār were well acquainted. Another salafi shaykh, Salīm al-

Bukhārī, had also become acquainted with Zahrāwī during the latter's sojourn in Damascus, and some people suspected Bukhārī of collaborating with Zahrāwī in composing the essay.[24]

Jurisprudence and Sufism was the first publication by a salafi to stir up a controversy in Damascus. Although Zahrāwī clearly sided with the salafis in their project to reform religious practice, he differed with them in important respects. He stated familiar salafi themes in his essay when he attacked emulation and dogmatic adherence to the legal schools, asserted ijtihād as an indispensable method for understanding and practicing religion, and denounced the exploitation of fabricated oral reports for the sake of personal interests. Yet his introductory explanation of why Muslims were disunited differed with other reformers' interpretation of the same phenomenon.[25]

Zahrāwī held that Muslims had differed on political, religious, and other issues since the first century of Islam. At that early date, Muslims excommunicated each other, battled each other, and converted the original call to religion into a quest for dominion by restricting power to a dynasty. By the end of Islam's first century, conflicting parties had developed different readings of the Quran, certified different collections of oral reports, and embraced divergent doctrines. Ever since the murder of ʿUmar, the second caliph, Muslims had divided into factions that cursed and fought each other, and as a result political sects and legal schools arose that embodied these divisions. Furthermore, during the second century, disciples of renowned ulama recorded their teachers' opinions, and schools coalesced around these ulama. The schools mutiplied until rulers began to implement the legal decisions of some while ignoring others, thus restricting legitimate legal authority to a handful of schools and closing the door of ijtihād. Today each country follows the schools that rulers favored centuries ago.

After this explanation of the Muslims' past and present divisions, Zahrāwī condemned the use of fabricated oral reports, and he lamented their sanctification in emulation. He explained emulation as an aspect of people's tendency to attribute sanctity to things ancient, and argued that it signifies the surrender of legislative authority to famous men, an authority God granted to no man.

Zahrāwī then turned to the heart of his essay, a critique of Islamic jurisprudence as practiced in his day. He asserted that Islamic legal theory amounted to nothing more than a few technical terms and methods for extracting rulings from authoritative sources rather than a coherent set of principles for deriving such rulings. In particular he struck at two bases of Sunni jurisprudence, analogy and consensus, claiming that no warrant (*ḥujjah*) existed to make them sources of legal rulings. As for oral reports, they comprise a basis of jurisprudence, but Zahrāwī added that one must seek information about their soundness from scholars of oral reports, not from jurists (*al-fuqahā'*). He asserted that throughout Islamic history religious scholars had used false oral reports to legitimize men's fancies, and that even the greatest scholars did so, if not intentionally, then from ignorance of the oral reports' status. With regard to the Quran, Zahrāwī asserted that anyone who knows Arabic can understand it, for it addresses all believers from the time of its revelation to the present.

When Zahrāwī turned to the "branches of jurisprudence," or specific legal precepts, he sought to demonstrate the utter confusion that arose from the jumble of opinions and various collections of precepts. He conceded that some precepts stemmed from Quranic verses and oral reports, but he added that most arose from considered opinion. To make matters worse, excessive veneration of early scholars had frozen the development of law, thereby precluding independent thought on "settled" issues.

Zahrāwī concluded his assault on contemporary jurisprudence with a call to reform it by practicing ijtihād. Muslims should take religious law (*al-sharīʿah*) as a constitution (*al-niẓām*), but few remnants of that law survived after essays and books had distorted it for centuries. Zahrāwī claimed that the Prophet's Companions (contemporaries who met the Prophet and embraced Islam) had applied religious law by exercising independent reasoning and following the Quran and sound oral reports. He then echoed ʿAbd al-Qādir al-Jazāʾirī's use of the proverb "Know men by the truth, not the truth by men" and related it specifically to ulama who practiced emulation. The advocates of emulation justified their position, according to Zahrāwī, by claiming to follow the practice of their fathers and by rejecting the authority of anyone who dared to refute the great imam. Zahrāwī responded that God enjoined rational men to understand religion and its laws in all their aspects, so there was no justification for restricting competence in jurisprudence to ancient predecessors, let alone four famous men (the imams of the Sunni legal schools). Zahrāwī noted that someone might argue that God blessed the four imams with superior intellectual powers, that imitating them guaranteed sound practice, and that to abandon them would lead to innovations. He wrote that such a person could do as he pleased, but he himself would practice ijtihād.

In his "protestant" vision of jurisprudence, Zahrāwī wished to rely only on the Quran and the Sunnah, and to use reason, which he called a divine blessing that man was duty bound (*mukallaf*) to exercise. He took a parting shot at emulation and legal school partisanship, challenging their advocates to produce a textual proof for their practices.

Zahrāwī then took aim at Sufism, which he condemned without reserve, unlike the Damascene salafis' qualified criticism.[26] He called it a jumble of theosophy, Greek metaphysics, and bits from the Quran and the Sunnah. Sufi authors had coined terms that distorted words' proper meanings, and they had concocted customs and practices that they sanctified by claiming an Islamic origin for them. Zahrāwī attacked asceticism as a pretext for laziness and social parasitism and stated that genuine Sufism had no connection with asceticism. He admitted that all societies had ascetics, but impostors seeking commoners' admiration and money outnumbered real ascetics. Moreover, Muslims should not practice asceticism because the Prophet himself had rejected it and partook in earthly pleasures. The true Sufi abandons working for a living and patiently waits for donations; if none are forthcoming, he keeps his patience. By contrast, impostors have no shame. When someone gives them something, they ask for more; if no one gives them anything, they raise a commotion. Throughout this section Zahrāwī adopted an extreme position on Sufis, denouncing them as idle and corrupt, and arguing that man attains perfection by partaking of the world, not by rejecting it.

Jurisprudence and Sufism achieved neither rigor nor coherence, but then

Zahrāwī may not have sought either in his bid to eradicate nonscriptural and irrational practices and beliefs from religion. What Zahrāwī gained in rhetorical effect he lost in logical balance, but given the ideology of conservative ulama, he had little chance to convince them, no matter how eloquent his rhetoric or logical his arguments. A measure of the difference between Zahrāwī and the Damascene salafis appeared in Bīṭār's observation that the essay had some merits but should not have been published because it only stirred up fanatics, who called Zahrāwī an infidel and a heretic, and who clamored for his execution. Rashīd Riḍā, writing a few weeks after Zahrāwī's arrest and transfer to Istanbul, agreed with Bīṭār's assessment. Riḍā commended him for his courage and freedom of thought, even if he did go too far in criticizing jurists and Sufis.[27]

By embroiling Zahrāwī in trouble the conservative ulama affirmed their authority to decide what constituted correct religious practices and beliefs in Damascus. Their protests brought about Zahrāwī's deportation and the confiscation of a few dozen copies of the essay. Completing their work as censors, they intimidated the salafis by making an example of Zahrāwī.

Reaching Beyond Damascus: Correspondence and Travel

Between 1896 and the end of 1902, Jamāl al-Dīn al-Qāsimī composed 20 works, most of them brief essays. But he published only three works: a slim collection of literary riddles and their solutions (1898), a small compilation of supplicatory prayers (1901), and a collection of prayers from the Sunnah (1902).[28] The second of these three works was Qāsimī's first published work on a religious subject, and in it he gave hints of salafism. Qāsimī wrote in the introduction to *Selected Supplicatory Prayers* that he had gleaned all the prayers from the Quran and sound oral reports. In a passage on supplication, he cited Ibn Qayyim al-Jawziyyah, an important fourteenth-century writer whose works influenced the salafis.[29] The rest of the booklet contains supplicatory prayers with no additional comments, no mention of reform, and no call to the salafi way.

Qāsimī's reference to Ibn Qayyim suggests that he had become acquainted with Ibn Qayyim's mentor, the famous thirteenth-century reformer Taqī al-Dīn ibn Taymiyyah. Precisely when Qāsimī first encountered Ibn Taymiyyah's legacy he did not mention anywhere in his writings. In his autobiographical notes, he listed dozens of texts that he studied in the 1880s, and Ibn Taymiyyah's absence from the list suggests that Qāsimī became acquainted with him only after 1888, the last year of his studies. The Qāsimī library contains a copy in Jamāl al-Dīn's hand of Ibn Taymiyyah's *Lifting the Blame from the Eminent Imams,* and the colophon shows that Qāsimī finished copying the manuscript on August 23, 1896.[30]

From whom did Qāsimī obtain Ibn Taymiyyah's essay? Perhaps from a member of the Jazā'irī clan. Qāsimī wrote in his autobiography that he borrowed a collection of essays by Ibn Taymiyyah from Muḥammad Abū Ṭālib al-Jazā'irī, who lived in Beirut. Unfortunately, when Qāsimī copied a letter from Jazā'irī mentioning Ibn Taymiyyah, he omitted its date, unlike the many other letters that he recorded in his autobiography.[31] That Jazā'irī asked Jamāl al-Dī to convey his regards to the latter's father indicates the latest date would be early 1900; we may speculate the letter dates from 1896 when Qāsimī copied *Lifting the Blame*.

About the same time, Qāsimī began to contact reformist scholars elsewhere. In the spring of 1898, Jamāl al-Dīn wrote to the Iraqi reformer Khayr al-Dīn al-Alūsī, requesting a license connecting him to the Baghdad scholarly tradition and to Ṣiddīq Ḥasan Khān, the renowned Indian reformer. In his letter, Qāsimī expressed admiration for Alūsī's *A Clear View* and mentioned that he had met Alūsī's son ʿAlā' al-Dīn in Baalbak during Qāsimī's Ramadan teaching tour (probably in 1894) when the younger Alūsī was serving in Baalbak's district religious court. In a letter to Qāsimī, Khayr al-Dīn al-Alūsī lamented that so many Muslims had completely forgotten the salafi school with the exception of a few in Damascus, who had survived persecution three years before (a reference to the mujtahids incident).[32] Alūsī's letter expresses the salafis' belief that they were reviving practices and beliefs that had existed long ago and not inventing anything new, although their adversaries considered them mischievous innovators.

Qāsimī's correspondence with Alūsī in Baghdad and Muḥammad al-Jazā'irī in Beirut encouraged him to believe that the reform movement could grow in spite of locally adverse conditions. As the network of reformers gradually extended from Morocco to the Sudan to Java, his sense of isolation diminished. Publishing articles in the Arabic press of Beirut and Cairo likewise served to spread his reputation and put him in touch with reformers elsewhere.[33]

Meanwhile, in Damascus Jamāl al-Dīn attained greater prestige when he became prayer leader at the Sināniyyah mosque upon his father's sudden death in February 1900. Two days after the elder Qāsimī's demise, ʿAbd al-Razzāq al-Bīṭār, Ṭāhir al-Jazā'irī, and other ulama accompanied Jamāl al-Dīn to see the chief judge at the central religious court. There the group of notables and ulama recommended Jamāl al-Dīn for his late father's posts. Qāsimī presented the sultanic decree that had appointed his father Shāfiʿī prayer leader of the mosque. The judge examined the papers and gave the order for Qāsimī to assume his father's post.[34] Jamāl al-Dīn left his post at the ʿAnnābah mosque to become prayer leader, preacher, and teacher at the Sināniyyah mosque, where he had a wider audience than before.

Syria's stifling intellectual atmosphere under Sultan Abdülḥamīd affected not only the salafis but all writers wishing to express ideas other than adulation of the sultan. Studies of newspaper censorship during Abdülḥamīd's reign have uncovered lists of words forbidden to appear in print. The lists included revolution, anarchy, socialism, dynamite, madness, constitution, freedom, and equality. In the late 1880s, censorship impelled a flock of Lebanese and Syrian writers to emigrate to Egypt, which offered greater freedom of expression.[35]

Cairo emerged as the intellectual center of the Arab east, partly because it functioned as a refuge for dissident political figures and intellectuals of the Ottoman Empire. ʿAbd al-Ḥamīd al-Zahrāwī, who wound up in Homs after the incident of 1901, fled to Egypt in 1902. Ṭāhir al-Jazā'irī emigrated to Cairo in 1907; Rashīd Riḍā, ʿAbd al-Raḥmān al-Kawākibī, and other critics of Sultan Abdülḥamīd settled in Egypt. The rapprochement between Muḥammad ʿAbduh and the British made Cairo even more attractive to religious reformers.[36] In the British, ʿAbduh found a powerful patron to support his programs for reforming Egypt's religious institutions. Qāsimī and Bīṭār could only dream of such a fortunate situation. Egypt's material progress also won the admiration of Syrians and gave them hope that Muslims everywhere could achieve progress. As a beacon of intellectual freedom and a symbol of progress, Egypt drew Syrian writers of various stripes, among them religious reformers. In this light Jamāl al-Dīn al-Qāsimī's and ʿAbd al-Razzāq al-Bīṭār's journey to Egypt in 1903–1904 looks like another way of breaking out of their isolation in Damascus to breathe freer in Cairo's more tolerant atmosphere.

During a visit to a village outside Damascus in the fall of 1903, Qāsimī and Bīṭār discussed the idea of traveling to Egypt "to become acquainted with its ancient monuments, to get to know the state of its progress, and to visit our good friends."[37] In December 1903, the two salafi scholars embarked from Beirut on a French steamer bound for Port Said. Jamāl al-Dīn recorded his impressions of the city's sights—the wide streets, the fine architecture, the abundance of goods available in the stores, the electric lights, and the multitude of strollers. Likewise, when Qāsimī arrived in Cairo, the grandeur of the train station and the broad, busy square outside delighted him. Throughout his diarylike account of the journey, he expressed appreciation of Cairo's broad, tree-lined streets, its large buildings, luxuriant gardens, and modern conveniences, such as the telephone and the tramway.[38]

On arriving in Cairo, Qāsimī and Bīṭār went to a hotel to drop off their luggage and then rushed to al-Azhar to visit Muḥammad ʿAbduh, whom Bīṭār had met nearly 20 years before in Beirut. During their four-week stay in Cairo, Qāsimī and Bīṭār saw ʿAbduh frequently and attended a number of his lessons on Quranic exegesis.[39] On their first day in the city, ʿAbduh invited them to his home. As they rode a carriage through the city, the Egyptian reformer spoke on ijtihād, stating that all ulama had an obligation to practice it and to scrutinize oral reports for their soundness. They continued their discussion at ʿAbduh's splendid home, and though Qāsimī did not record details of their conversations, he wrote that he thoroughly enjoyed them and that the three men agreed on everything. One should not take that first impression to mean that Qāsimī came under ʿAbduh's spell, for the Damascene noted his differences with him on a number of issues, especially regarding Quranic exegesis. Nonetheless, Qāsimī held ʿAbduh in high esteem and relished his hospitality and attention.

A week after Bīṭār and Qāsimī arrived they met Rashīd Riḍā, whom they frequently saw thereafter. Qāsimī divulged practically nothing of his discussions with Riḍā, merely noting that they enjoyed long evening conversations. Qāsimī also became acquainted with another prominent Egyptian, Aḥmad al-Ḥusaynī, a wealthy lawyer and writer who twice invited Qāsimī and Bīṭār to his villa in the suburb of Halwan.

Qāsimī and Bīṭār stayed in Cairo with a friend from Damascus who had settled in Egypt and become a well-known author and journalist, Rafīq al-ʿAẓm, who will show up again later because he was an important figure in his own right.[40] Suffice it to say here that he accompanied them frequently on their rounds in Cairo. Occasionally, Qāsimī and Bīṭār would stay at al-Azhar in a room that ʿAbduh had reserved for them, but in general they spent little time at the most famous center of learning in the Muslim world. For centuries Damascene ulama, such as Jamāl al-Dīn's grandfather Qāsim al-Ḥallāq, traveled to study at al-Azhar. In Qāsimī's time, it was a center of opposition to religious reformers such as ʿAbduh, so Jamāl al-Dīn's friendship with the jurisconsult marked him as someone unsympathetic to al-Azhar's mostly conservative ulama.[41] Qāsimī and Bīṭār gravitated more to progressives like the Syrian editors of *al-Muqtaṭaf,* a popular scientific magazine.

At the end of the Cairo sojourn, ʿAbduh met Qāsimī and Bīṭār at the train station the morning of their departure. At their brief parting, Qāsimī asked ʿAbduh what book he would recommend for giving Muslims instruction in religion. ʿAbduh suggested the works of al-Ghazālī, on condition they be edited to omit weak oral reports and spurious stories. Qāsimī followed up on the suggestion and composed one of his most popular works, an edited version of al-Ghazālī's *Reviving the Religious Sciences.*[42]

Qāsimī and Bīṭār traveled to Alexandria, where they spent five days, and then took a French steamer to Beirut. There they met with Muslim reformers and spent an evening at the home of Muḥammad Abū Ṭālib al-Jazā'irī, from whom Qāsimī had borrowed works of Ibn Taymiyyah some years before. Jamāl al-Dīn recorded some details of their discussion of al-Shāṭibī's *The Book of Harmonies* (a famous treatise on legal theory), specifically the passages on emulation and ijtihād.[43] Bīṭār tarried several days in Beirut while Qāsimī returned to Damascus, where Jamāl al-Dīn's brother told him that news of his stay in Egypt and the men he met had preceded him and surprised many ulama.

Qāsimī's Egyptian journey raised his prestige in Damascus. Furthermore, his acquaintance with Riḍā bore fruit when the latter printed a short biography of the Prophet that Qāsimī had composed during his stay in Cairo. Riḍā praised it in a review in *al-Manār* a few months later.[44] Access to the pages of Riḍā's journal broadened Qāsimī's audience beyond the confines of Damascus and Beirut to the larger Egyptian readers' market and to the ends of the Muslim world. Yet while Qāsimī cultivated a growing network of contacts with salafis in Morocco, Iraq, Egypt, Lebanon, and Tunisia, his position in Damascus remained precarious.

Just six months after returning from Egypt, Qāsimī had another brush with the Ottoman authorities when Aḥmad al-Ḥusaynī came to Syria in July 1904.[45] As Ḥusaynī had so graciously entertained Jamāl al-Dīn in Cairo, the Damascene went to welcome the Egyptian visitor at his hotel. Soon after, the chief of police summoned Qāsimī and others who had gone to see Ḥusaynī. The police chief received Qāsimī politely and after some friendly chat began to inquire about Qāsimī's acquaintance with Ḥusaynī. The police official told Qāsimī the government viewed Ḥusaynī's visit with displeasure, and he advised Qāsimī not to meet again with the Egyptian, advice that Jamāl al-Dīn heeded.

The police chief then took Qāsimī and two other ulama who had visited Ḥusaynī to meet with the Ottoman governor, Nāẓim Pasha, who two years earlier had interrogated ʿAbd al-Ḥamīd al-Zahrāwī. Interpreting for the Turkish-speaking governor was Muḥammad Fawzī al-ʿAẓm, a wealthy and powerful notable.[46] Through ʿAẓm, Qāsimī and his companions understood that the governor had heard that they called for ijtihād. Nāẓim Pasha asked them about Ḥusaynī, how well they knew him, and whether he called to ijtihād. Qāsimī replied that Ḥusaynī was a Shāfiʿī jurist who wrote on religious law. One of the other interlocutors added that Ḥusaynī had written an essay in which he took issue with Ḥanafī scholars on a rather arcane topic, and the essay had angered certain Ḥanafī ulama of Damascus. Qāsimī wrote that Nāẓim Pasha threatened to exile him from Damascus should he visit Ḥusaynī again. Jamāl al-Dīn later learned that a slanderous spy report on Ḥusaynī had reached Nāẓim Pasha, and that a second report on Ḥusaynī's visitors stated that some of them had called to ijtihād. The governor thought Ḥusaynī might be in sympathy with them, so he had the Egyptian closely watched until he left Damascus.

Conclusion

The salafis suffered persecution at the hands of official ulama because religious reform threatened the latter's authority. The mujtahids' circle subjected legal rulings to close scrutiny and to the test of discussions governed by the force of better arguments. Only the Quran and sound oral reports had the status of unassailable authority in their discussions, whereas the opinions of men, be they great masters of jurisprudence or Sufi saints, counted only to the extent that they accorded with scripture. Qāsimī, Bīṭār, Jazā'irī, and the other participants established their study group outside the confines of the major mosques and religious schools in which convention restricted scholarly discussion. The mujtahids' search for the strongest proof would exceed the bounds of convention, so they met at peripheral mosques and at their homes.[47] The salafis' group soon attracted the hostility of other ulama, who pitted the mujtahids against the jurisconsult, who understood that ijtihād meant rejecting the legal schools' authority underpinning his own office.

While the mujtahids' circle implied a rejection of the ulama's practices, Zahrāwī's *Jurisprudence and Sufism* explicitly attacked two pillars of the ulama's authority. He launched a full-scale assault on contemporary jurisprudence, not merely its reliance on emulation to validate rulings but its underpinnings in legal theory (*uṣūl al-fiqh*) and its concrete manifestation in precepts (*furūʿ al-fiqh*). Likewise, Zahrāwī condemned current Sufi practices and held that genuine Sufis were rare. The thrust of his critique suggests that his animosity toward Sufism stemmed from his belief that Muslims had to shake off fatalistic attitudes that Sufism, in his opinion, encouraged. Like his polemic against jurisprudence, Zahrāwī's assault on Sufism signified a repudiation of established authority, for Sultan Abdülḥamīd's Islamic policy rested on cultivating the support of Sufi shaykhs and orders in the Arab lands.

The opposition to the mujtahids' circle and Zahrāwī overwhelmed the salafis and temporarily silenced them. The salafis responded by reaching beyond conservative Damascus to fellow reformers in Beirut, Cairo, Fez, and Baghdad. In the early 1900s, urban religious reformers gradually developed a network of correspondents that provided moral support to isolated figures like Qāsimī. It also served as a source of information about rare manuscripts and patrons willing to finance their publication. When Qāsimī and Bīṭār journeyed to Egypt they found religious reformers who could pursue their projects without fear of official persecution. Muḥammad ʿAbduh,

Rashīd Riḍā, and other reformers enjoyed freedom under British rule partly because their challenge to traditional religious authority did not impinge on Britain's authority in Egypt. In fact, the British believed that ʿAbduh could buttress their rule against the Viceroy, who enjoyed the support of ʿAbduh's conservative opponents. By contrast, the Syrian salafis' challenge to traditional religious authority collided with the sultan's claim to the caliphate.

5

Salafi Interpretations of Islam: Reason and Unity in Qāsimī

Controversial and commonplace ideas coexist in the salafis' interpretations of Islam. For instance, all Muslim jurists would agree with the following statement by Jamāl al-Dīn al-Qāsimī: "Know that the basis of every religious ruling is the Book [the Quran] because it is the fundamental principle and source. . . . Every religious ruling must refer to it and issue from it, such that even the Prophetic Sunnah's basis is the Book of God."[1]

However, Qāsimī's arguments against adhering to the legal schools stirred violent opposition. The present discussion of salafism will concentrate on its distinctive, controversial features and on the salafis' motives for espousing ideas that exposed them to persecution.

In embarking on a study of salafi thought in Damascus, an obstacle immediately arises, namely, the dearth of works by salafis other than Jamāl al-Dīn al-Qāsimī. Ṭāhir al-Jazā'irī wrote many textbooks for the new state schools, but he abstained from putting his reformist ideas into print, preferring to spread his ideas through private lessons. The senior salafi in Damascus, ʿAbd al-Razzāq al-Bīṭār, published nothing in his lifetime, while Salīm al-Bukhārī wrote very little. ʿAbd al-Qādir ibn Badrān's published works include an introduction to the Ḥanbalī legal school, a biography of a prominent notable, and a dictionary of Damascene religious schools, mosques, and Sufi lodges. Except for brief autobiographical passages, Ibn Badrān refrained from expressing his sympathy for salafism.[2] The lack of works by other Damascene salafis forces a nearly exclusive reliance on Qāsimī's oeuvre as the source of the salafis' ideas. However, his long, close friendship with Bīṭār and his briefer, yet profound interaction with Jazā'irī indicate that Qāsimī's works represented a consensus on fundamental issues.

The wide range of subjects that Qāsimī addressed in his nearly 90 essays and books afford ample evidence of how he viewed religious, political, and social issues. Most of his works deal with religious subjects, including Quranic exegesis, the methods of scholarship in oral reports, and legal theory. Qāsimī also wrote on history, divorce, genies, and photography. Some three dozen of his works have been published, one as recently as 1981.[3]

Qāsimī posited reason and unity as the fundamental principles of religious practices and beliefs. His program for reform included both critical and constructive aspects turning on the two pivotal principles of reason and unity. His critique of emulation (taqlīd) had an obverse, the call to ijtihād; the condemnation of ritual innovations (pl. *bidaʿ*) implied an insistence on correct performance of rituals; the desire to eliminate mutual excommunication (takfīr) accompanied a plea for tolerance among Muslims. Qāsimī related these matters and others to reason and unity. At times he suggested that the principles of reason and unity have their own relationship in which reason is a means for Muslims to attain unity. Indeed an instrumental conception of reason pervades Qāsimī's writings. That is to say, reason offers a tool for comprehending divine revelation, ordering society, and controlling nature.[4]

Qāsimī's vision of a rational, unifying religion had practical implications for the ulama because it redefined both the qualifications for attaining the status of religious scholar and the conduct of religious scholarship. Jamāl al-Dīn's formulations on ijtihād and emulation underlay the salafis' critique of contemporary ulama's practices and the assertion of their own competence to perform the tasks required of "true" ulama.

Reason and Unity

The relationship between rational knowledge and divinely revealed knowledge, between reason and revelation, has occupied Muslim thinkers since they became acquainted with the Greek philosophical tradition. Classical Muslim thinkers treated the issue by seeking to reconcile philosophy with religion.[5] In Qāsimī's day Muslim thinkers grappled with a new ideological challenge from the West: European science and technology accompanied by their occasional philosophical counterpart, positivism. Jamāl al-Dīn al-Qāsimī's thought shows how a Muslim thinker came to grips with the contemporary European stress on reason by reviving dormant elements of the Islamic intellectual heritage.

A clue to Qāsimī's motive for positing the centrality of reason in Islam appeared in a Beirut newspaper's review of his work, *The Proofs of Monotheism*. The review noted that the tendency of young men to turn away from Islam and to embrace European ideas necessitated a new critique of atheism. The reviewer praised Qāsimī for supplying such a critique by marshaling evidence from the natural sciences and philosophy to refute the materialists' arguments.[6]

Composed in 1908, *The Proofs of Monotheism* belongs to a genre of modern Muslim writing that revived traditional dialectical theology and Islamic neo-Platonic philosophy in order to controvert criticisms of Islam and ulama issuing from European and Middle Eastern intellectual circles. That Muslims from Java to North Africa greeted Qāsimī's work with enthusiasm attests to the popularity of this genre. A second edition came out in 1912. Qāsimī's timing in writing the work turned out to be ironically prescient: He completed it during the week of the Ottoman constitutional restoration, an event Qāsimī lauded in the book's afterword but which eventually promoted men holding the very secularist views he had intended to refute.[7]

In *The Proofs of Monotheism* Qāsimī set forth proofs of God's existence, refuted materialist ideas, and expounded the relationship between reason and revelation. Rather than elaborating a single, coherent argument for God's existence, Qāsimī enumerated a list of proofs gleaned from the works of Muslim philosophers and ulama, including Ibn Rushd, al-Ghazālī, Ibn Taymiyyah, Ibn Ḥazm, al-Fārābī, Mullā Ṣadrā, and Jamāl al-Dīn al-Afghānī. In all, he recited 25 proofs of God's existence, about half of which argue that features of the natural world suggest a creator, shaper, first mover, organizer, or sustainer. Other "proofs" include the existence of a word for God in all languages, an instinctive sense of God's existence, and the prophets' success in propagating religions.[8]

Jamāl al-Dīn tried to refute materialist ideas by denying that they had any connection with true philosophy and holding that materialist thinkers could put forth only hypotheses, not demonstrable proofs. For instance, materialists assert that the atom represents the smallest discrete particle, but no scientist can prove its existence; the materialists' notion that ether and matter are eternal cannot be proven; the idea that only matter is real is easily refused because matter cannot generate life and intelligence since it possesses neither, and therefore materialism cannot account for creation. Qāsimī's arguments indicate that he reacted against Arab admirers of Europe who had at best a superficial acquaintance with contemporary developments in Europe.[9]

Jamāl al-Dīn wrote that the materialists' call to abandon religion threatens society because man prospers best by adhering to religion. Islam safeguards against dissent and chaos and equips man for progress in this world and happiness in the afterlife. Atheists, by contrast, let their whims lead them astray into depravity; on a wider scale, the reign of human whim would cause the disintegration of society.[10] But Qāsimī did not explain how Europe had achieved progress and technological primacy without the sound religious basis he considered essential. When he traveled to Egypt and admired its relatively advanced state, he did not attribute it to the Egyptians' stricter adherence to Islam. In fact, he left the matter unexplained in his writings.

Qāsimī's utilitarian argument for religion in terms of mundane interests ties in with his formulations on reason. He observed that just as man possesses sensory faculties by which he hears, sees, and smells, his rational faculty allows him to distinguish between truth and falsehood. Man employs reason when he contemplates both material and spiritual realms.[11] This conception of reason as a human faculty, as an agency of perception, informed Qāsimī's position on the classic conundrum of reason and revelation.

Qāsimī posited the harmony of reason with revelation, and he stated that any apparent contradictions between them could be resolved by interpreting revealed texts with reason. Reason cannot contradict revelation because reason establishes, transmits, and preserves revelation. That is to say, reason functions for the good of religion. Furthermore, given their essential compatibility, greater knowledge of the natural sciences strengthens one's faith by raising awareness of the signs (*āyāt*) of God's existence. Modern discoveries in astronomy, physics, geology, and anatomy enhance man's faith rather than diminishing it. Qāsimī added that because science rests on observation and experiment and does not delve into intangible matters, it does not encroach on the domain of faith.[12] Thus he sometimes argued that science positively supports religion, while at other times he suggested they operate in different realms of reality, and therefore do not affect each other.

In other writings, Qāsimī's instrumental conception of reason emerged more clearly. He conceived of reason as a mental power man uses to understand texts, society, nature, and the cosmos. An instrumental conception of reason differs from rationalism, in which reason is the ultimate ground for all truths. Qāsimī and the other salafis never thought of removing the scriptures' authority or of subjecting them to the scrutiny of rational inspection to determine their truth. Rather, Qāsimī elaborated a critique of rationalism. He argued that rationalism was untenable because of the impossibility of precisely defining reason and of establishing criteria for choosing among competing rational arguments. What stands as truth today may be disproven tomorrow. In other words, rational knowledge is relative. For instance, conceptions from Greek science about the natural world had held sway for centuries as scientific certainties, but recent developments and discoveries proved Greek science to be mistaken. By analyzing matter and water, chemists discovered that they do not constitute basic elements but are composed of more fundamental elements such as oxygen, nitrogen, tin, and hydrogen. Likewise, man's knowledge of astronomy has advanced greatly over the ancient cosmological schemes, yet scientists remain puzzled by such unexplained phenomena as gravity.[13] Qāsimī interpreted scientific progress as signifying the limitations of reason, even in its most powerful and convincing applications.

In the realm of social relations the power of reason is even more circumscribed because it cannot provide organizing principles for society. Where reason falls short, revelation fills the gap because it guides man in his social affairs—prophets lay down laws to order society and teach morality. Qāsimī reckoned morality as important as knowledge in the formation of an individual's character, and in a collective sense, only by instilling in individuals both virtue and knowledge could society prosper. Qāsimī often remarked that knowledge in itself is amoral and does not suffice to guarantee upright morals: "Neither the sciences alone, nor teachers' licenses, nor school diplomas" impart morals.[14]

Reason's potency decreases further when man confronts the mysteries of God's nature. Muslims must accept the Quran's account of God's attributes without attempting to relate them to corresponding human features. Qāsimī espoused the Ḥanbalī doctrine of God's attributes, which holds that Muslims should believe in the Quran's account of divine attributes, without speculating about their nature. But he did not criticize the views of Ashʿarī and Muʿtazilī dialectical theologians, who sharply diverged in their interpretations of God's attributes.[15]

To recapitulate, Qāsimī conceived of reason as an instrument by which man understands revealed texts and applies them to his social relations. In studying the natural world and in developing technology, man could and should give his rational powers free reign. In this respect Qāsimī perpetuated ideas ʿAbd al-Qādir al-Jazāʾirī had expressed half a century earlier, and he endorsed the positivist idea that man had transcended the historical stage of childish thought and arrived at a phase of history in which human reason reigned.[16]

Like other Muslim reformers, Qāsimī believed that divisions along sectarian and *madhhabī*, or legal school, lines cause intra-Muslim strife, which leaves Muslims vulnerable to foreign domination. Moreover, he thought that factionalism violates one of Islam's cardinal principles—to unify mankind into a brotherhood of believers. Qāsimī expressed dismay at the ulama's unfortunate habit of accusing each other of misguiding Muslims (*al-taḍlīl*) and of spreading corruption (*al-tafsīq*), and he called on Muslims to put aside sectarian hostilities and to unite on the basis of the religion's most basic, universally accepted features. As long as one prayed to Mecca and followed religious law, one should be pardoned for mistakes on matters open to conjecture.[17]

Qāsimī sometimes used history as a device to strip away the Islamic veneer of certain beliefs and practices, and thereby discredit them. For example, he opposed the practice of excommunication (takfīr) without sufficient grounds when he wrote that the Khārijīs were the first group to inject extremism into the Muslim community by excommunicating all of their Muslim opponents. Therefore the sectarian practice of excluding Muslims from the community of believers had an historical origin and did not stem from revealed law. The practice of excommunication (al-takfīr) on the grounds of sectarian differences concerned Qāsimī, so he sprinkled his works with passages by classical authorities urging Muslims to refrain from that practice. In particular Qāsimī wanted to mitigate enmity between Sunnis and Shī'is, and to this end he devoted an essay to the oral reports scholars' practice of transmitting reports from members of all sects. He called on his contemporaries to follow the example of such scholars as al-Bukhārī, who accepted reports from Sunnis, Shī'is, Khārijīs, and Mu'tazilīs.[18]

Qāsimī addressed the problem of disunity in its more local manifestations when he criticized the practice of segregating worshipers according to legal schools. In correct practice, he wrote, the ruler appoints a prayer leader to each mosque with the congregation's consent. The prayer leader must conduct the prayer in the manner prescribed by the Quran and the Sunnah, instructing worshipers to form compact, even rows, in order to encourage a sense of unity. Straying from this practice causes confusion in the mosques and dissent among believers.[19]

By the turn of the twentieth century, Damascus had passed through 50 years of reform resulting in material improvements in transport, communications, hygiene, and new construction. The salafis had no quarrel with new roads and buildings, but they believed that the growing prevalence of secular courts and state schools, which damaged the ulama's material and status interests, would lead to cultural Westernization (*al-tafarnuj*).[20] The Tanzimat reforms carried the implication that the ulama could not contribute to the empire's quest to achieve progress, and the salafis responded by stressing Islam's rational and practical nature, which urges man to use his mind to manage and develop his material life.

At the same time, Syrian Muslims were apprehensive of European power and the possibility of occupation by the European army. A feeling of vulnerability triggered the call for Muslims to close ranks in the face of foreign threats. The principle of unity, then, assumed importance in Muslim circles and the salafis assimilated it to their reformulation of Islam.

Taqlīd and Ijtihād

Qāsimī's premise that Islam is rational and unites men underpins his critique of emulation, the unquestioning acceptance of earlier scholars' legal opinions. Whenever he denounced emulation, he attacked its institutional expression, partisan bias for the four Sunni legal schools (*al-taʿaṣṣub li al-madhāhib*). Qāsimī regarded emulation and legal school partisanship as irrational practices that perpetuated ritual innovations and stood in the way of progressive legal interpretations. His arguments against emulation encountered opposition because the majority of ulama in Damascus considered it a safeguard against misunderstanding the Quran and the Sunnah. Before treating Qāsimī's criticisms in detail let us consider a reasoned statement of the case for emulation.

Jurisconsult Maḥmūd al-Ḥamzāwī once gave a legal opinion (*fatwā*) on emulation when a fellow Damascene religious scholar asked him three related questions. Why is emulation restricted to the four imams of the legal schools? Why should people consistently emulate only one imam? What forbids people from taking the legal opinions of men other than the four imams?[21] After all, according to legal theory the rulings of the imams shared the same epistemological status as the rulings of other scholars; all fell short of certain knowledge into the category of considered opinion (*ẓannī*). Ḥamzāwī replied that Muslims had to emulate the four imams because only their schools had persisted to the present. However, one could give a ruling based on an oral report that the imams had not applied, even if that oral report differed with the legal school's ruling. Using such an oral report as a basis for practice did not mean one had abandoned one's legal school.

Ḥamzāwī also argued for emulation in a handbook he composed for jurisconsults and magistrates. In the preface he stated that he based his book on passages from authoritative works of the Ḥanafī school, a statement indicating his tendency to emulate. He wrote that whenever someone seeks a legal opinion on an issue and the school's authorities have agreed on a ruling for that issue, the jurisconsult must pronounce that ruling, even if his ijtihād leads him to a different ruling. That is because the authorities based their rulings on superior knowledge of the evidence and of the methods for deriving rulings. If the school's authorities disagreed, the jurisconsult must take the ruling that agrees with that of Abū Ḥanīfah, the school's imam. But if the disagreement stemmed from changes in circumstances occurring after the time of Abū Ḥanīfah, the jurisconsult should follow the ruling of more recent authorities. Ḥamzāwī did allow for ijtihād in cases when a clear text could not be found and the school's authorities disagreed. Whenever the jurisconsult lacks the ability to perform ijtihād, he should follow the ruling of someone more versed in law; that is, the jurisconsult should practice emulation.[22]

Two points in Ḥamzāwī's opinion on emulation converged with the salafis' position. First, he recognized the principle of the superiority of oral reports to imams' rulings that derived from their independent judgment. The salafis used this principle to attack emulation. Second, Ḥamzāwī allowed for ijtihād in certain circumstances. The salafis refused to restrict ijtihād as much as Ḥamzāwī had.

Maḥmud al-Ḥamzāwī was jurisconsult of Damascus for nearly 20 years (1868–1887), a prolific writer, and one of the city's last powerful ulama. His commitment to emulation was that of a "professional" scholar working in the religious courts, and his position on the subject stemmed from practical concerns. That Ḥamzāwī admitted ijtihād in certain instances indicates that the salafis' claims for it did not come out of the blue. Nevertheless, his defense of emulation clearly set him apart from the group of reformers who so trenchantly denounced it some years later.

Jamāl al-Dīn al-Qāsimī once wrote in a notebook he kept for jotting down ideas, "Taqlīd is a leprosy which has spread widely among the people. It has begun to wipe them out; indeed it is an infectious disease, a general paralysis, and a stupefying lunacy plunging man into apathy and indolence."[23] Qāsimī never composed a single, comprehensive critique of emulation, rather he dispersed comments on emulation throughout his books and essays. Depending on the subject at hand, he used emulation to mean either a deviation from the proper methodological principles of legal theory, a form of prejudice, or an intellectual shortcoming.

Qāsimī cited the imams of the Sunni legal schools to establish the principle of preferring sound oral reports to the imams' opinions. Al-Shāfiʿī said, "if an oral report is sound, then it is my school."[24] Aḥmad ibn Ḥanbal said, "Do not emulate me, or Mālik, or al-Awzāʿī, or al-Nakhaʿī, or anyone else; rather take rulings from whence they [the imams] took [rulings]."[25] In other words, Muslims must take scripture, not the imams' opinions, as the basis of rulings. Such nonsalafi ulama as Maḥmūd al-Ḥamzāwī had no qualms with this principle, but the salafis added that no imam had ever instructed Muslims to follow his rulings and to ignore those of other imams. Qāsimī cited Abū Ḥanīfah's statement, "It is not permitted to anyone to take our opinion when he does not know its source in the Book, the Sunnah, the community's consensus, or manifest analogy."[26] Qāsimī thereby used the objects of emulation, the imams, to invalidate emulation by showing that it contradicts the imams' explicit methods, principles, and statements. Against the majority of ulama of Damascus, Jamāl al-Dīn argued that the only correct way to follow the imams would be to apply their methods, not to reiterate their substantive rulings.

Qāsimī held that emulation had two harmful effects on the Muslim community: it sowed dissent among Muslims, and it obstructed the disinterested search for truth. With respect to the former, Qāsimī and the other salafis viewed emulation as the underlying principle of legal school prejudice (*al-taʿaṣṣub li al-madhhab*). To discredit legal school prejudice, Qāsimī depicted the schools as historical phenomena extraneous to Islam's essence. In support of this idea he included in two of his books passages by the eighteenth-century Indian reformer, Shāh Walī Allah.[27] The Indian scholar wrote that no legal schools had existed before the fourth Muslim century, at which time the quality of the ruling caliphs deteriorated and they could no longer distinguish between qualified and unqualified contenders for judicial posts. As incompetent men increasingly obtained such posts, more and more jurists could do no more than repeat what earlier authorities had written without understanding their reasoning. These developments led to the normalization of emulation and its institutionalization of the imams' rulings in legal schools. When ulama chose to follow one or another of the schools, they preferred the rulings of their respective schools without a reasoned consideration of the merits of each schools' rulings. "Madhhabī" prejudice became a ubiquitous feature of the jurists' discourse as they imparted their prejudices to pupils, and worshipers divided according to legal school by following different prayer leaders. Violent manifestations of madhhabī prejudice flared up when ulama of rival schools vied for rulers' favor and incited rulers against opposing ulama. In the most extreme cases of madhhabī prejudice, ulama excommunicated one another.[28]

Qāsimī believed that emulation divides Muslims into rival, sometimes hostile, schools because it disrupts rational discourse. In this regard he cited Ibn Taymiyyah's Ḥanbalī predecessor, Ibn al-Jawzī: "In emulation is the nullification of reason's useful purpose."[29] Madhhabī prejudice poses an obstacle between man and the truth because the partisans of legal schools believe only that which confirms their opinions. Qāsimī once lamented the spread of such prejudicial thinking to society at large:

> The hearts of most [people] are confused with the disease of imitation; they believe something, then seek a proof for it. They do not want anything but what agrees with what they believe. When someone comes with what differs with their belief, they reject it; they would oppose it even if that led to negating reason entirely. Most people believe and then reason; you rarely find one who reasons and then believes.[30]

Likewise the *muqallid* (one who practices emulation) accepts as sound those oral reports that accord with his school, while he concocts pretexts to reject oral reports that differ with his school's rulings.[31] In other words, the ultimate criterion of truth for the emulator is the imam of his school, not divine texts. The emulator recalls ʿAbd al-Qādir al-Jazāʾirī's comments on those who take men as the measure of truth. Qāsimī scorned the idea that people must refer all decisions to the imam as "scandalous ignorance and clear misguidance."[32]

As a result of the emulator's unthinking adherence to his school's rulings, any debate with him is bound to be fruitless, and therefore it is best to exclude him from rational discourse altogether. Qāsimī cited al-Ghazālī's dictum, "The basic condition of the emulator is that he be silent and not spoken of, because he is unable to follow the course of debate."[33] One should not debate an emulator because his perceptions fall short of the status of knowledge, which rests on proof, not on whim.[34] Qāsimī believed that divisions among Muslims largely stemmed from the presence of so many "muqallids" among the ulama, and he cited the proverb attributed to Socrates: "Were he who does not know to fall silent, then differences would be eliminated."[35] In other words, were discourse restricted to true scholars then many disagreements would disappear.

In addition to the general problems that emulation causes, it imposes hardship on believers because of its unbending application of rulings worked out in previous ages. Qāsimī gave the example of women whose husbands had emigrated to America without providing for their sustenance or appointing a legal guardian for them.[36] Jamāl al-Dīn often toured Damascus's environs and nearby district centers, where he met officials and notables who told him that many women suffered from such a situation. When they tried to annul their marriages after years with no word from their husbands, judges refused on the basis of the Ḥanafī school's ruling encoded in the Majallah, the Ottoman civil code.

Qāsimī proposed that a solution lay in a legal opinion (fatwā) by the Shaykh al-Islam in 1876, in which the high religious official allowed a Ḥanafī magistrate in a mostly Shāfiʿī region to give rulings according to the latter school. Jamāl al-Dīn cited two recent legal opinions that reinforced the earlier one. He concluded that Ḥanafī judges could issue rulings of other legal schools. Because the Shāfiʿī, Ḥanbalī, and Mālikī schools allow the annulment of marriage when it causes undue hardship on a woman, Ottoman judges had grounds for annulling the marriages of abandoned wives. Qāsimī demonstrated in this instance that emulation causes suffering because of its blindness to particular historical contexts. In late nineteenth-century Syria, large numbers of young men emigrated to North and South America, and some of them left behind wives who waited for years without any word from their men and without financial support. Qāsimī proposed that breaking with emulation would give these women the opportunity to remarry and allay their distress.

Qāsimī defined the terms of an ideal discourse in the obverse of his critique of emulation and madhhabī prejudice, the practice of ijtihād. The choice between emulation and ijtihād boiled down to a practical matter: how to derive and validate legal rulings. The partisans of emulation and the legal schools held that after a certain point in Islamic history, ulama could not equal the learning of the four imams, and that anyone claiming to be able to practice ijtihād was guilty of arrogance. Whereas changing circumstances in fact forced jurists to undertake ijtihād to arrive at rulings on new cases, such activity took place under the guise of following a school's methods and principles: jurists practiced ijtihād without calling it ijtihād.[37] The salafis objected to the conservatism of jurists who made a virtue of doggedly clinging to the legal schools, even if they occasionally violated that principle in deed.

Qāsimī explained ijtihād's utility in adapting to change in an essay on the legitimacy of using the telegraph to report that Ramadan has commenced and ended:

> The appearance of the telegraph is but a drop in an ocean of discoveries and inventions which will appear in the coming ages . . . including conveniences for people and benefits for them. It is a great blessing for the community of Muslims [*al-ummah*] that no age is devoid of men who stand up for God with proofs and explain problems with proof. Showing you that is the abundance in every country and town of muftis and legal opinions on that for which the two great sources [the Quran and the Sunnah] did not stipulate a ruling . . . the abundance of legal opinions and muftis is the token of the survival of ijtihād.[38]

Jamāl al-Dīn admitted that the ijtihād of several men on one issue could yield several plausible rulings. Because he held that it was impossible to establish criteria for choosing among competing rational arguments, an element of doubt always attached to rulings derived by ijtihād. To narrow the scope of dissent over competing arguments, he stipulated that mujtahids be well-versed in the Quranic verses and oral reports bearing on legal rulings and that they know the principles of legal theory. He also stressed that a mujtahid master the Arabic of the Quran in order to attain precise understanding of the revelation because faulty interpretation of texts leads to erroneous legal rulings.[39]

Qāsimī recommended reviving the art of disputation (*fann al-munāẓarah*) to promote a congenial atmosphere of cooperation among scholars in a search for the truth of complex issues. A few basic precepts informed Qāsimī's vision of the ideal scholarly discourse. The fundamental rule is to base conclusions on proofs and to set aside sectarian and legal school prejudices. Thought can wander freely only when it is not limited by the boundaries of the schools. Qāsimī cited al-Ghazālī to the effect that, in a truly free discussion, only mujtahids free of legal school biases should participate. Ulama with an interest in upholding the schools would refuse to admit the validity of positions at odds with their schools, thus allowing partisan interests to distort discourse. By contrast, the mujtahid discussant recognizes the truth no matter who speaks it and admits his own errors.[40]

Observing the rules of disputation would not only guarantee a disinterested search for truth, it would also minimize enmity arising from conflicting opinions. Qāsimī once noted that everyone seeks to convince others that their own ideas are correct. A discourse grounded in proofs offers the only way to amicably settle differences and to arrive at correct views. He called on Muslims to state their beliefs, present their arguments, and accept the most convincing proof, in essence to adopt the principle of subjecting views to a discourse ruled by the force of the better argument.[41] (Of course an important restraint remained, namely, that divine texts could not be abrogated).

Qāsimī tried to demonstrate how to abide by the principles of fair, unbiased discourse in several essays. For example, he composed one essay on the question of whether the practice of performing two prostrations (*rakʿatayn*) before the evening prayer is preferred (*mandūb*) or reprehensible (*makrūh*).[42] In this essay Jamāl al-Dīn intended to show how contemporary ulama could scrutinize accepted legal rulings and uncover errors arising from legal school prejudice. The bulk of the essay consists of a demonstration of the proper methods for weighing scriptural evidence. The gist of Qāsimī's argument lies in showing how an earlier Ḥanafī scholar, Kamāl al-Dīn ibn al-Humām, following his Ḥanafī bias, preferred the weaker of two Prophetic oral reports, thereby violating the rules of weighing oral reports' legal force (*qawāʿid al-tarjīḥ*).

In the essay's introduction, Qāsimī noted that later books on legal precepts (furūʿ al-fiqh) were of little value because their authors referred to the rulings of previous ulama, not to scripture, and therefore they fell into the low status of emulators. Ibn al-Humām began his treatise by citing two sets of oral reports, one allowing two prostrations before the evening prayer, and the other opposing the practice. Qāsimī adduced more oral reports allowing the practice, and concluded first, that it was permissible according to the Prophet's practice, and second, that the Companions had continued the practice as a preferred ritual act. Jamāl al-Dīn claimed that the transmitters of the pertinent oral reports were trustworthy and the texts of the oral reports sound.

As for Ibn al-Humām's evidence against the practice, Qāsimī admitted that some of the oral reports were sound and could not be rejected on the grounds of inferior status. The occurrence of two incompatible oral reports pertaining to the same issue sprang up frequently enough for Muslim legal theorists to devise procedures for evaluating and ranking the legal force of all the types of evidence. Qāsimī referred to a Ḥanafī work on legal theory because Ibn al-Humām was a Ḥanafī, as were all Damascene ulama working in the Ottoman religious institution. Applying Ḥanafī principles seemed an effective rhetorical device to refute Ibn al-Humām and to convince contemporary Ḥanafīs.

Qāsimī recapitulated Ḥanafī rules of weighing evidence, and on their basis he rated Ibn al-Humām's oral report weaker than the one permitting two prostrations. The former oral report came from Abū Dā'ūd's *Sunan,* whereas the latter came from al-Bukhārī's *al-Ṣaḥīḥ,* which, according to Qāsimī, possesses the greatest authority with respect to the soundness of oral reports. Moreover, the oral report from Abū Dā'ūd's work merely stated that its transmitter had never seen the practice under discussion, not that it was reprehensible. Because Ibn al-Humām allegedly violated the rules of legal theory, Qāsimī likened his argumentation to that of an emulator who adduces an oral report to buttress a ruling in accord with his legal school but rejects the same oral report if it contains another ruling conflicting with his school's position. But Qāsimī himself violated his own rules for discourse because he claimed to follow the methods of Ḥanafī legal theory, yet he asserted al-Bukhārī's priority in rating oral reports, and Ḥanafī ulama do not accord him the status of supreme authority on oral reports.

Qāsimī enumerated Ibn al-Humām's other "errors," such as denying the superiority of oral reports in the collections of al-Bukhārī and Muslim, claiming that both al-Bukhārī and Muslim related oral reports from unreliable transmitters, and resorting to the opinion *(ra'y)* of a Companion. Furthermore, Kamāl al-Dīn cited the rule that a weak oral report can rise to sound status with such ancillary evidences as other oral reports, and then he reasoned that a sound oral report can descend to weak status. Qāsimī wrote that the methods of scholars of oral reports did not allow for the latter point.

Qāsimī thought that his essay would suffice to convince Ḥanafī ulama of Ibn al-Humām's error on the issue. He wrote to a friend that two Ḥanafī scholars who read the essay had told Jamāl al-Dīn that he had presented a convincing argument.[43] Yet a Ḥanafī shaykh of Damascus rebutted Qāsimī point by point to vindicate Ibn al-Humām. The author, Muḥammad al-Ṭabbāʿ, reduced the issue to a squabble between two legal schools, pointing out that Qāsimī's position happened to match that of the Shāfiʿī school. Ṭabbāʿ stated that Qāsimī's real aim was to refute all Ḥanafī and Mālikī classical authorities (Mālikī jurists agreed with the Ḥanafīs on this issue).[44]

Ṭabbāʿ listed Qāsimī's mistakes: Ibn al-Humām did not transgress the rules of legal theory; the oral reports Qāsimī cited were of dubious value; Qāsimī misread Ibn al-Humām; the oral report Ibn al-Humām adduced is stronger than Qāsimī allowed; and the oral reports in al-Bukhārī and Muslim do not have the paramount value Qāsimī claimed for them.

In addition to a rather tedious redaction of Qāsimī's errors,[45] Ṭabbāʿ seized the opportunity to lampoon the salafi. He claimed that Qāsimī considered Muslims who do not properly esteem the collections of al-Bukhārī and Muslim to be unbelievers, a patently false charge. He also falsely accused Qāsimī of denigrating Abū Ḥanīfah and Mālik ibn Anas, the eponymous founders of two legal schools, and their illustrious successors. In another passage Ṭabbāʿ compared Qāsimī's reasoning to that of a contemporary scholar who by exercising ijtihād had ruled for wine's ritual purity. That was probably a veiled reference to Rashīd Riḍā's argument for the permissibility of using French perfumes with alcoholic content, an argument his adversaries seem to have intentionally misconstrued as permitting the consumption of alcoholic beverages.[46]

Ṭabbāʿ needled Qāsimī for stating that in judging the probity of transmitters of oral reports, one must follow the judgment of early oral reports scholars. Ṭabbāʿ professed surprise at that statement because Qāsimī usually scorned emulation. He then suggested that perhaps Qāsimī did not write that line, that someone else had "interpolated" it, a pun on Qāsimī's derogatory term for conservatives, *al-ḥashwiyyah,* those who insert things where they do not belong.[47]

Jamāl al-Dīn al-Qāsimī's criticisms of emulation and his claims for ijtihād constituted the methodological and epistemological bases of his vision of Islamic reform. He linked emulation and ijtihād to his core themes of reason and unity on the one hand, and he related a variety of religious and social issues to emulation and ijtihād on the other. The salafis argued that emulation and legal school partisanship, which most Muslims regarded as Islamic, were in fact irrational and un-Islamic. In step with ideas about reason and progress, the salafis claimed that divine scripture contains rational principles from which religious rulings derive. Legal theory's rational principle consisted in uncovering definitive proofs (sing. *al-dalīl al-qaṭʿī*) for a ruling in scripture. Because cases for which one could find definitive textual proofs were rare, Islam provided rational methods for arriving at rulings based on considered opinion (*ẓann*). Ijtihād is the act of exercising reason to derive rulings for such cases.

Ḥashwiyyah Ulama and Competence

A corollary of the mujtahid-emulator dichotomy is the distinction between competent ulama and incompetent men posing as ulama. Jamāl al-Dīn's harsh strictures against the latter recall the biting sarcasm of his father's verse deriding ulama impostors. That Qāsimī had partisan, ideological interests at stake is evident when we see that the target of his invective was always conservative ulama. He once wrote:

> How strange are the ultraconservatives [*al-jāmidīn*]! They see in their midst forbidden things violating [religious law] and traditional manners torn to shreds before their eyes; they see ritual innovations erase Prophetic customs, imitation of Europe inundate Muslim society, corruption gushing like a torrential flood, and Prophetic guidance oppressed. Yet not a vein of theirs beats, nor are they moved by sentiment, nor are they pushed to vindicate the truth with hand or tongue.[48]

Qāsimī's pet term of abuse for conservative ulama was al-ḥashwiyyah, a term that derived from either the verb *ḥashā,* which means to insert or interpolate (something where it does not belong), or from the noun *al-ḥashw,* which can mean nonsense. Qāsimī stated that the ḥashwiyyah ulama did not comprise a single group with a distinctive set of ideas; rather all schools of oral reports scholars, philosophers, jurists, and dialectical theologians included men who stubbornly employed sophistic argumentation. They concerned themselves only with emulating the sayings of prominent authorities rather than evaluating the relative strengths of oral reports and other evidence underlying precepts of rituals and transactions. The ḥashwiyyah had become a problem because so many ulama were incompetent pretenders who had no right to claim to be ulama.[49]

Qāsimī wrote that the debasement of knowledge largely stemmed from allowing teaching and judicial posts to pass from father to son. As he himself obtained his posts at the Sināniyyah mosque by a such procedure, he either objected to instances when the "heir" did not demonstrate the requisite qualifications or he failed to practice what he preached. He denounced the practice of inheriting teaching posts by which a few Damascene families had monopolized education. Only after the abolition of that custom would Damascus awaken from its long slumber and return to the ways of the early Muslim scholars, thus saving Muslims from an embarrassment to themselves and their religion.

To rectify the situation, Qāsimī proposed that the government remove unqualified men from endowed teaching posts. In making appointments to judicial posts, the ruler must consult with ulama to learn who is best qualified, but Qāsimī did not explain how a ruler should decide on which ulama to consult.[50] In several works he reiterated two points contained in his recommendation. First, rulers have a duty to consult ulama on certain matters. Second, rulers must appoint qualified men to posts. By emphasizing competence as the criterion for distributing positions of authority, both points express an intellectual's wish to lead society:

> In general, giving each man his due, putting things in their place, and entrusting tasks to those capable of them are obligatory to preserving rights, erecting the edifice of justice, keeping the order of affairs from imbalance, and curing the people of the nation of [their] ills. . . . All who follow the histories of nations . . . know that the glory of a throne has not been toppled except by entrusting tasks to him who cannot undertake them and placing things where they do not belong.[51]

The partisan nature of salafism stands out most strikingly in such passages, which Qāsimī included in several of his works.[52] The salafis considered themselves quite well qualified to fill the posts currently held by incompetent, ḥashwiyyah ulama. That does not mean that salafism was only a mask for realizing material interests, but merely that such interests helped shape salafism.[53]

Conclusion

Qāsimī wrote in his essay for using telegraph reports to verify the beginning and end of Ramadan:

> Many of our ulama and judges still think about applying many innovations in civilization to religious rulings and implementing them [innovations] in accordance with them [religious rulings], thereby verifying that Islam is a religion which supports civilization, helps its growth and progress, and eases the strengthening of its pillars in

> human society, as a mercy for it [society] and from concern for its well-being. . . . The magnanimous religious law [sharīʿah] is compatible with every age. If the age were taken into account in legal rulings on transactions, then the rulers would not be forced to use positive laws [*al-qawānīn al-waḍʿiyyah*].[54]

In other words, the ulama's failure to interpret religious rulings in accord with temporal circumstances disposed Muslim rulers to adopt European law codes. Qāsimī held that the rulers should turn instead to the "true" ulama, under whose guidance Muslim society would flourish. He argued for Islam's relevance to modern conditions and the ulama's central role in laying the ethical and legal foundations for a progressive, prosperous society.

Salafism in Damascus, then, had the markings of an ideology of and for intellectuals. Consider the substance of the salafis' arguments: Islam is intrinsically rational and it exhorts man to exercise reason. Only highly trained and qualified men should discuss issues in all their aspects without regard for earlier statements on the issues. These ulama should discuss matters in a spirit of fraternal cooperation and submit to the force of the better argument. Such assertions did not represent the position of disinterested observers but that of ulama who stood outside the religious judicial institutions and below the ranks of Damascus's wealthy ulama families. As ulama, the salafis had a stake in restoring the ulama to their former central place in society, a place that accorded them domination of the educational, legal, and cultural fields. But those ulama who still worked in the religious courts or taught in the manner by which they had themselves learned were not likely to sympathize with the salafis, who considered the practices and beliefs of those ulama deviations from Islam. Salafism implied more than changing methods; it sought a complete reevaluation of the religious heritage and a debunking of standard books and cherished customs that lacked a demonstrable basis in scripture. Only from outside the law courts and central mosque could come such a severe critique of what went on inside. Likewise, only from ulama of independent means could salafism issue in Damascus. The poorer strata of ulama, dependent on the largesse of wealthy patrons and intimately involved with the common people, would hardly appreciate a critique of such ritual practices as visits and donations to shrines, which helped them survive.

Salafism's critical face alienated fellow ulama of higher and lower status, while its positive content smacked of the ambitions of a specific social group, or more accurately, a faction within a status group. The salafis felt confident that they were qualified to practice ijtihād, that they were the true ulama. In their plan, discourse had to be restricted to competent men who displayed a command of language, texts, methods, and the discipline to observe rules of disputation. Only these mujtahids were fit to derive the legal rulings on which society should be based. All other men were "muqallids," incapable of understanding the process by which mujtahids derived evidence for rulings.

6

Salafi Interpretations of Islam: Society and Social Life in Qāsimī

In addition to redefining the qualifications and practices of the ulama, the salafis set out how ulama should relate to other social groups.[1] Qāsimī expressed his attitude toward the popular classes in his comments on innovations (bidaʿ) in ritual, on Sufi orders, and on visits to saints' tombs. He also partook in the debate that raged around 1900 in the Muslim world over the status of women. Apropos of the salafis' program for a reunited Muslim community, we have seen how they opposed legal school prejudice. An examination of Qāsimī's attempts to bridge differences between Sunnis and Shīʿīs complements the discussion of legal schools and raises the question of whether he achieved a disinterested position on issues at the root of Sunni-Shīʿī divisions or if he retained Sunni biases. We also consider how the salafis conceived of progress, their attitudes toward new inventions and imports from Europe, and the way they thought religion and progress buttressed each other.

Popular Religious Practices

Innovations

In one of Qāsimī's lengthier works, *Reforming the Mosques of Innovations and Customs,* he listed innovations and prescribed cures for the rash of nonscriptural practices plaguing Damascus's mosques. He stated the general definition for innovation, which has no specific status in religious law. Then he gave its technical meaning in religious law (*al-bidʿah al-sharʿiyyah*), which distinguishes between laudable and blameworthy innovations, according to their conformity with or violation of religious precepts and principles. For instance, building religious schools and minarets constitutes a laudable innovation because it contributes to the propagation of Islam. By contrast, any act of worship that lacks a scriptural reference is a blameworthy innovation. Instances of ritual innovations and customs include fasting during the month of Rajab, excessive decorations on mosques, placing elevated seats and balconies in mosques, and singing and dancing in mosques.[2]

Jamāl al-Dīn put forth a social explanation for the persistence of such customs and their resilience in the face of reformers' efforts to eliminate them. Most Muslims did not perceive innovative rituals as innovations but as genuine religious practices; therefore, when reformers attacked innovations, they appeared to be assaulting religion itself. In tune with Qāsimī's vision of the "true" ulama's guiding role in society, he suggested that innovations would vanish if ulama clearly distinguished between ritual obligations and supererogatory rites, and if ulama cited scripture when they taught people how to worship.[3]

Qāsimī indicated that the ulama's moral suasion alone would not suffice to rid the mosques of innovations. To be effective, the ulama need the support of political authorities, such as the Ottoman governor he commended for his efforts to forbid certain ritual innovations. Likewise, Qāsimī praised a jurisconsult who had persuaded a governor to send police to the Umayyad mosque in order to warn a group against performing a ritual innovation. Jamāl al-Dīn wished to see rulers consistently punish perpetrators of innovations, perhaps by jailing them so as to remove blemishes on religious practice altogether.[4] The irony of this line of thought escaped Qāsimī, who had suffered when rulers heeded the advice of his ulama adversaries to punish men they considered enemies of religion.

Sufi Orders and Sufism

Whereas Western scholars tend to think that religious reform and Sufism are diametrically opposed, the salafis took a more nuanced position than is sometimes supposed.[5] They made a distinction between the ecstatic rituals of popular Sufi orders and the "sober" Sufism characteristic of elite orders and individual, ascetic Muslims. Qāsimī recorded his only explicit statement on Sufism as a body of thought in an unpublished notebook.[6] The brief essay, entitled "Sufism: An Islamic Philosophy," stated that Sufi thought represents an attempt to formulate an Islamic philosophy distinct from Greek philosophy by combining religious doctrines, asceticism, and spiritual exercises to create a unique, Islamic philosophy (what Western writers call Sufi theosophy). Qāsimī regretted that non-Islamic ideas tainted the beliefs of many Sufis.

Following his usual bent for seeking a middle position on controversial issues, Qāsimī castigated both Sufism's detractors and its zealots. The former go too far when they forbid the study of Sufism and excommunicate Sufis for proclaiming union with and dissolution in God. First of all, no one can be excommunicated as long as he prays and believes as a Muslim. Second, Sufism's enemies understand references to union with God as literal expressions, whereas Sufis do not intend them that way. As for Sufi zealots, they exaggerate the importance of Sufism's masters and devote all their lives to studying Sufi texts.

Qāsimī's opinion of Sufi orders contrasted sharply with his tolerance of Sufi theosophy. He attacked fake Sufis who led Sufi orders, likening them to electric wires spreading madness among men, and reproaching them for feigning epilepsy and for ceaselessly repeating "Allah."[7] He scorned ignorant shaykhs for countenancing their followers' raucous behavior, such as eating fire and playing music in Sufi processions. Qāsimī found such spectacles not only repugnant but embarrassing: Sufi processions made Islam an object of foreigners' ridicule.[8] Furthermore, as one of Qāsimī's friends in Beirut wrote, Sufi shaykhs distorted religion by ascribing superstitions to it, and thereby alienated educated young people.[9]

Qāsimī held that true Sufism entails humility, sincerity, constant prayer, seclusion, and asceticism. In his biography of Aḥmad al-Jazā'irī, Qāsimī approved of Sufi practices that observed the bounds of permissible worship:

> He [Aḥmad al-Jazā'irī] had an appointed time between the evening prayers on Monday and Friday nights in his home; some adherents [of the Qādiriyyah order] would meet with him those nights and mention God, be He exalted, until the evening prayer, a dhikr [mention of God] devoid of innovative blemishes.[10]

On the one hand Qāsimī despised the outrageous practices of popular Sufi orders, on the other hand he respected ulama who practiced the more sober Sufism of intellectual elites. Notwithstanding his admiration of Aḥmad al-Jazā'irī (a Qādirī shaykh) and Muḥammad al-Khānī (for a time Jamāl al-Dīn's Naqshbandī shaykh), Qāsimī quit Sufism as a young man. In treating the salafis' ideas about Sufism, we should recall that ʿAbd al-Razzāq al-Bīṭār had studied and discussed Sufism for many years with ʿAbd al-Qādir al-Jazā'irī, who devoted his later years to studying and teaching the works of Muḥyi al-Dīn Ibn ʿArabī, the great thirteenth-century mystic. Other religious reformers, like ʿAbduh and Riḍā, had also had profound experiences with Sufism as young men, so the salafis' emergence from a cultural and intellectual milieu steeped in Sufi traditions should not surprise us; nor should Qāsimī's approval of sober Sufism appear strange.[11] The peculiar figure in the Syrian salafi camp was ʿAbd al-Ḥamīd al-Zahrāwī, who had launched an unconditional attack on Sufism in all of its manifestations. Perhaps enmity toward Abū al-Hudā al-Ṣayyādī, the patron of Sufi shaykhs in the Ottoman Empire, lay behind Zahrāwī's radical denunciation of Sufism; or some other experience of Zahrāwī's early years, of which we know little, disposed him to detest Sufism.

Tomb Visits

The salafis strongly objected to the popular custom of visiting saints' tombs and praying for saints' intercession with God to grant favors. That custom's status in religious law became a point of dispute between reformers and conservative ulama in Damascus and other Arab lands.[12] Qāsimī opposed popular customs that marred tomb visits and sarcastically nicknamed ulama who defended the practice "al-qubūriyyah," which we might loosely render as "tombsters." In *Reforming the Mosques of Innovations and Customs,* Jamāl al-Dīn counted supplicating saints among blameworthy innovations, and he held that constructing mosques at grave sites also constitutes such an innovation because worshiping at a grave amounts to polytheism. On the other hand he wrote that it was permissible for Muslims to visit the tombs of relatives and ancestors if one restricted oneself to greeting the deceased relative, praying to God, and seeking God's forgiveness. Muslims must neither seek intercession nor believe that visiting a tomb is better than prayer in a mosque. Muslims must not use the Prophet's tomb as a place of prayer, let alone the shrines of other prophets and saints.[13]

Qāsimī's criticisms of innovations, Sufi orders, and tomb visits stemmed from his scripturalist orientation and may have been related to a desire to remove any doubt about Islam's compatibility with reason. His belief that the bearers of reason, the ulama, could eliminate innovations by giving instruction to commoners indicates his faith in education as an instrument of reform. The same belief also suggests a paternalistic attitude toward the popular classes, whose practices need reform. Indeed Qāsimī wrote that ulama should avoid mixing with commoners except to teach them religious obligations and moral virtues. Similarly, he held that ulama should not spend much time with people of lesser intelligence.[14] Qāsimī's elitism also stands out in his discussions of Sufism and Sufi orders, for he had no qualms with the sober Sufism of urban elites, but he condemned the ecstatic ceremonies of Sufi orders of the urban and rural popular classes.

Status of Women

Qāsimī's views on the proper conduct of women reflect his beliefs about how Islamic legal rulings and moral injunctions would order society. He favored changes in women's status but stopped well short of the controversial ideas of Qāsim Amīn, an Egyptian writer whose two books on women in Muslim society made veiling, seclusion, and girls' education burning issues. Jamāl al-Dīn's positions on these issues indicate that he favored preserving social mores, whereas his critique of the ulama's and commoners' practices bespeak a desire to break with many customary religious practices and beliefs.

The debate that Qāsim Amīn sparked in Egypt when he called for an end to seclusion and veiling has become a standard topic in accounts of turn-of-the-century Egyptian intellectual life.[15] The debate's resonance in other Arab lands awaits consideration, but we can discern its echoes in Damascus. In 1899, a Damascene publisher issued Muḥammad Ṭalʿat Ḥarb's rejoinder to Amīn's first book, *The Emancipation of Women.* The following year the same publisher, al-Taraqqī press, put out an Arabic translation of a Turkish work refuting Amīn. In 1901, al-Taraqqī press published Ṭalʿat Ḥarb's critique of Amīn's second book, *The New Woman,* and the same year published a "Muslim" perspective on the issue by Farīd Wajdī, another Egyptian writer.[16]

No Damascene writer tackled the issue so hotly disputed in Egypt, probably because social conditions in Syria differed from those in Egypt. More conservative than Cairo and Alexandria, Damascus did not witness a sharp controversy over Amīn's work at the time (1899–1902) because traditional customs prevailed, except among the wives of a few Turkish officials.[17]

When Jamāl al-Dīn al-Qāsimī addressed the issues raised by Amīn, he adopted more conservative stances than the Egyptian. First, he upheld veiling, but not because of any scriptural command. Rather Qāsimī justified veiling as an application of an Islamic legal principle called *sadd al-dharāʾiʿ,* or blocking means of committing forbidden acts. With respect to polygyny, he disagreed with recent interpretations of scripture that forbade the practice. Qāsimī noted that the author of a magazine article had declared that religious law forbids polygyny because it stipulates that a man with more than one wife must treat them equally, in both emotional and material ways, which is impossible. Jamāl al-Dīn remarked that the article's author had made an egregious error because scripture clearly permits polygyny.[18]

Qāsimī joined Amīn in opposing seclusion, but did not want women to have the same degree of freedom that Amīn favored. In Jamāl al-Dīn's exegesis of the Quran he refuted exegetes who interpreted the word *al-sā'iḥāt* to mean silent instead of traveling. Such a misinterpretation arose from the idea that women should not travel because they are enjoined to don the veil, as though veiling meant "eternal captivity, or as though the breeze were a blessing given to all [mankind] but women, or as though God created women only for the prisons of their homes, which may be worse than the deepest prisons of lunatics, or as though the only thing for women in this hospitable world is a solitary house."[19] Against seclusion Qāsimī adduced oral reports that state that the Companions' wives often asked the Prophet questions in the company of men, and that when the Prophet visited his Companions their wives attended them. Other oral reports relate that women treated men wounded in battle and helped carry them home from the field of combat. Though Qāsimī opposed seclusion, he did advise married women and widows to stay home most of the time and to go out only with their husbands' permission.[20]

As for education, Qāsimī held that a father must teach his daughter the fundamentals of religion, such as the Quran, doctrine, and worship. He should also instruct his daughter in such social duties as obligations to parents, husband, and children, and such household skills as sewing, cooking, and managing a household budget. Qāsimī thought women should attend mosques to pray and take lessons in religion. The prevailing custom of forbidding women to attend religious lessons harmed society because it kept women ignorant and made them a source of innovation in ritual and belief. He also favored formal education for girls. Of his four daughters, two graduated from state primary school, while the other two attended but did not complete the same school, then the highest level of education for girls in Damascus. He agreed with Ṭāhir al-Jazā'irī that the government should open higher level schools for girls to allow them to pursue education beyond primary school.[21]

Qāsimī's allusion to the connection between ritual innovations and women, coupled with his insistence that married women go out only with their husbands' permission, bespeaks a patronizing attitude toward women. This attitude appeared even more clearly when he wrote that because women are vulnerable and weak, they need marriage more than men do. Furthermore, while he advised husbands to treat their wives kindly, he also held that men should protect their women and curb their whims, which usually corrupt morals. Qāsimī's remarks implied that women were less rational than men, more likely to indulge in immoral behavior, and a source of superstitions. In *The Dictionary of Damascene Crafts,* he wrote that only children, simpleminded men, and women fell for the tricks of quack doctors, fortune-tellers, and snake charmers.[22]

Qāsimī's positions on issues concerning women's status indicate his social conservatism. His advice for fathers and husbands to edify their daughters and wives recalls the way he urged ulama to instruct commoners in religious practices and beliefs. His patronizing attitudes toward women and the popular classes suggest a social elitism parallel to his intellectual elitism.

Sunni–Shīʿī Relations

Qāsimī's writings on Sunni–Shīʿī reconciliation resemble those against legal school prejudice in that both stemmed from the desire to unify Muslims, but important distinctions separate his treatments of sectarian disputes from his arguments against madhhabi prejudice.

A description of the Shīʿī presence in Damascus provides the context for understanding Jamāl al-Dīn's views on Sunni–Shīʿī differences. In 1890, Damascus had approximately 150,000 inhabitants, of whom 120,000 were Sunni Muslims and 7,000 Shīʿī Muslims, including 4,500 Twelver Shīʿīs and 2,500 Druzes and Alawis. The Shīʿīs of Damascus were concentrated in a quarter of the old city called the Kharab. Damascus apparently had no centers of Shīʿī learning and it is likely that Shīʿīs seeking religious education would have gone to Shīʿī centers in Lebanon, which provided religious leaders for Damascene Shīʿīs. In 1910, a Lebanese Shīʿī from Jabal Amil near Sidon came to Damascus to found a charitable association in the Kharab to help the poor, presumably poor Shīʿīs.[23]

Qāsimī appealed to Shīʿī sentiments in the context of general arguments against sectarianism. In his book on oral reports scholarship and an essay on evaluating the reliability of transmitters of oral reports, he argued for accepting reports of Shīʿīs as well as Khārijīs and Muʿtazilīs. He also praised Zaydī Shīʿīs for practicing ijtihād.[24] Otherwise Qāsimī argued against Shīʿī positions on substantial issues dividing Shīʿīs and Sunnis.

Qāsimī addressed Sunni–Shīʿī differences in 1909 when he received an essay from a Hadrami (south Yemeni) shaykh residing in Singapore. The shaykh, Muḥammad ibn ʿAqīl, had written an essay justifying the Shīʿī custom of cursing Muʿāwiyah, and he sent a copy to Qāsimī to solicit his comments. Qāsimī wrote comments on the margin of Ibn ʿAqīl's work, composed a draft from his notes, and sent copies to Ibn ʿAqīl and a friend in Jeddah. Unbeknownst to Qāsimī, his friend in Jeddah, a wealthy merchant, had the draft published. Jamāl al-Dīn then wrote an apologetic letter to Ibn ʿAqīl, explaining that he had not intended to denigrate him or to start a controversy.[25]

In the essay Qāsimī held that no scriptural evidence supports the Shīʿī view that Muslims had an obligation to pay allegiance to ʿAlī, the fourth caliph and the Prophet's kinsman. Rather than relying on the Quran and sound oral reports, he wrote, Shīʿīs use weak oral reports and the opinions of historians to buttress their positions. Furthermore, the Shīʿī custom of cursing Muʿāwiyah has no scriptural basis. Qāsimī claimed that since the Prophet had not named ʿAlī his successor, one could not blame Muʿāwiyah for not paying allegiance to him.[26]

In an essay on the science of evaluating the reliability of transmitters of oral reports (*ʿilm al-jarḥ wa al-taʿdīl*), Qāsimī provoked a Shīʿī response when he advocated accepting oral reports from Khārijī sources. Soon after the essay's appearance in *al-Manār,* a Shīʿī shaykh wrote to a Shīʿī journal published in Sidon to object to Qāsimī's allowing oral reports from Khārijīs.[27] The correspondent, Muḥammad al-Ḥusayn Āl Kāshif al-Ghiṭā', then published an essay to refute Qāsimī.

Kāshif al-Ghiṭā' (1877–1954) came from a prominent ulama family of Najaf, a Shīʿī shrine city in southern Iraq.[28] He composed his refutation in the same conciliatory tone as Qāsimī, yet he firmly asserted the Shīʿī position that Khārijīs cannot be a source for oral reports because they are infidels. Kāshif al-Ghiṭā''s reasoning went as follows: Only hypocrites (*munāfiqūn*) hated ʿAlī, and hypocrites are infidels; Khārijīs hated ʿAlī, therefore they were infidels. He put forward a second argument: Because loving the Prophet's family and descendants (*ahl al-bayt*) is a fundamental religious obligation, whoever hates the Prophet's family is neither a Muslim nor a trustworthy source of testimony and reports; Khārijīs hated the Prophet's kinsman ʿAlī and, therefore, are not Muslims.[29]

One of Qāsimī's most promising students, Muḥammad Bahjat al-Bīṭār, replied to Kāshif al-Ghiṭā''s critique. Bahjat al-Bīṭār, ʿAbd al-Razzāq's grandson, maintained the cordial tone of debate and acknowledged the virtues of the Shīʿī shaykh's essays. Bīṭār then demonstrated the weaknesses of the Shīʿī position: Loving the Prophet's family is indeed a religious obligation, but not a basic tenet of religion like praying, on which hinges one's status as a Muslim or a non-Muslim. Bīṭār countered Kāshif al-Ghiṭā''s claim that Khārijīs are hypocrites and infidels by distinguishing between various usages of the term "hypocrite." In the Quran, hypocrisy denotes the act of pretending to believe in God and the Prophet when one actually denies Islam. The oral report that states that no one hates ʿAlī but the hypocrite refers to someone who hated ʿAlī for being the Prophet's kinsman. The Khārijīs hated ʿAlī, but not because of his blood tie to the Prophet; therefore, they were not hypocrites.[30]

The debate between the Damascene salafis and the Shīʿī scholar and Qāsimī's critique of the Shīʿī custom of cursing Muʿāwiyah show that the salafis defended customary Sunni positions. Though they urged the amelioration of sectarian relations, they did little to resolve Sunni–Shīʿī differences on fundamental issues. Jamāl al-Dīn's ecumenical approach to evaluating the veracity of oral reports stopped short of any compromise on fundamental differences between Sunnis and Shīʿīs. Moreover, Qāsimī's view of Shīʿī commemorations of Ḥusayn ibn ʿAlī's martyrdom as an innovation typified his lack of sympathy for Shīʿī beliefs. When he criticized legal school prejudice, he used the sayings of the schools' imams to justify his arguments. He tried the same tactic to tone down Sunni–Shīʿī differences when he wrote that ʿAlī had never cursed his Syrian adversaries,[31] but in general Qāsimī did not use Shīʿī sources; rather he declared that Shīʿīs often cited dubious sources to support their opinions. He resorted to appeals for mutual tolerance ("do not excommunicate each other") to close the gap between the sects instead of setting forth principles that would transcend sectarianism altogether, as he attempted with respect to the legal schools. Over the years Qāsimī paid little attention to this issue compared to legal school prejudice, probably because he inhabited a mostly Sunni milieu in which the important divisions among ulama were those between legal schools.

The Means of Progress

The salafis believed in the compatibility of Islam and progress, yet they wrote far more to explain Islam's rationality than to set out what they meant by progress. Their few discussions of progress make it clear that the salafis intended material economic development. Qāsimī's thoughts on progress show how he envisioned Islam as a crucial factor in attaining prosperity.

Around 1891, Jamāl al-Dīn proposed to his father the idea of writing a work on the crafts and occupations of Damascus. Years before, Muḥammad Saʿīd al-Qāsimī had owned a retail shop in the old market and sold household utensils imported from Europe, so he had had experience in local commerce and firsthand knowledge of the role imported goods played in the local economy. Ḥāmid al-Taqī, a student and neighbor of the Qāsimīs, wrote that the senior Qāsimī would ride through the city's commercial and manufacturing quarters, write the names of trades in a notebook, and study those unfamiliar to him. When Muḥammad Saʿīd died in 1900, he had written on 140 crafts and occupations. Jamāl al-Dīn and his brother-in-law Khalīl al-ʿAẓm took another five years to complete the project, which was published in Paris in 1960.[32]

The Dictionary of Damascene Crafts stands alongside Jamāl al-Dīn's four-volume history of Damascus as witness to the salafis' interest in the everyday world of social, economic, and political affairs. Dominique Chevallier, a French social and economic historian of Syria, has speculated that the *Dictionary* reflects the anxious confrontation between the Islamic and European worlds.[33] Chevallier suggested that the Qāsimīs' project of surveying the city's economic and social survivals corresponded to their research into the religion's textual sources to demonstrate Islam's adaptability to modern conditions. Although aesthetically appealing, Chevallier's vision of a symmetry between the Qāsimīs' research in religious sources and their study of local economic life misconstrues the unity of their life projects. *The Dictionary of Damascene Crafts* fits into their general program of reform to strengthen Muslim society, but unlike rēligious reform, by which the salafis meant a return to true religious practice and belief, their vision of economic revival did not take the past as a model. The Qāsimīs applauded new technologies from Europe because they saw positive good in less painful remedies for illnesses and in machines that spared men toilsome labor.[34]

The salafis rejected the notion that technology alone suffices to bring prosperity. They emphasized the centrality of religious injunctions to a prosperous society, and they upheld the necessity of observing upright moral stands in economic transactions. The Qāsimīs deplored fraud, hoarding, and exploitation of peasants, and they warned of divine punishment for those who did not fear God in their economic transactions. In a later work on morals and manners, Jamāl al-Dīn wrote that fraud weakens society because it destroys mutual trust on which economic activities depend.[35] Technical knowledge of the means of progress had to be coupled with virtue for men's endeavors to be crowned with success.

Qāsimī once observed that, practically speaking, Damascus had to adjust to changes in trade patterns in order to attain lasting prosperity. He wrote that Damascus's status as an entrepôt of commerce had suffered successive blows beginning with Britain's circumventing the overland trade route by carrying on trade with India via the Cape of Good Hope. More recently, the opening of the Suez Canal had further diminished Damascus's role in trade. Qāsimī recognized that trade with Europe had become paramount in the Syrian economy, and he enumerated Syria's exports to Europe, mostly agricultural products and textiles. In order for Damascus to revive its trade, the government had to protect local manufactures from European competition, and rulers had to purchase locally made clothes and furnishings to influence people's taste.[36]

To increase agricultural production, Qāsimī advocated the adoption of modern farming techniques. The government should provide technical assistance to peasants to help them combat plant diseases and teach them how to use fertilizers to increase yields. Peasants should have easy access to credit, and the government should encourage extending the margins of cultivation. Qāsimī wrote that a major obstacle to advances in agriculture lay in the peasants' custom of adhering to their fathers' ways and rejecting modern agricultural techniques. Were they to apply new techniques and tools, they could double-crop their plots and reclaim unused lands.[37]

Qāsimī's interest in the means of economic development mirrored that of contemporary writers, professionals, and government officials throughout the Ottoman Empire. The salafis were not alone among the ulama in favoring the importation and use of European inventions, but by no means did all ulama adopt as benign an attitude toward them. The salafis' conservative adversaries also picked up the slogan of adopting the means of progress, but they opposed such inventions as photography, the phonograph, and certain uses of the telegraph.[38] By contrast, the salafis embraced all new inventions in the firm belief that Islam positively enjoins man to utilize reason to exploit nature in order to meet his needs and that Islam provides adequate ways of regulating inventions' social effects.

Conclusion

The salafis' condescending attitude toward the popular classes (who need the ulama's instruction to correct their misguided religious practices and superstitious beliefs) and towards women (who, like children and simpletons, must be protected from people who prey on their credulity) indicate that they perceived themselves as superior minds obliged to raise the level of society's benighted members. The intellectual elitism implicit in the salafis' restrictions on ijtihād and discourse corresponded to a social elitism. Never mind that the salafis were neither wealthy nor powerful; their independent means, relative comfort, and status as ulama raised them above the urban popular classes, materially, culturally, and spiritually. Likewise, Qāsimī's approval of sober Sufism and denunciation of popular Sufi orders bespeak a fundamental lack of sympathy for the popular classes' beliefs.

In addition to social elitism, Jamāl al-Dīn's opinions on women's status indicate a commitment to customary social relations and mores (he favored veiling and defended polygyny) and a favorable disposition to incremental social change (he opposed total seclusion and advocated girls' education).[39] With respect to the plight of the poor, Qāsimī repeated the platitude that the obligatory tax on wealth (al-zakāt) suffices to meet the needs of poor people, and at the same time it erases their resentment of the wealthy and awakens love in the wealthy for the poor.[40] He did not envision a way out of a society comprised largely of poor folk. Or if he did, he saw the solution in progress for society as a whole.

The salafis' formula for prosperity consisted of appropriating useful technology invented in Europe, laying down protective tariffs for local manufactures, and extending credit and technical assistance to peasants. Though critical of the wealthy for their greed, the salafis wished to see them behave better, not to witness a systematic redistribution of wealth. They believed in a technological solution to the Muslim world's backwardness, with a social order based on Islamic law. In this manner they assimilated the ideas of secular intellectuals to their religious and cultural heritage.

Finally, with respect to Shīʿīsm, Qāsimī's views reflect a communal orientation more than his social position as a middle-class intellectual. Because he inhabited a mostly Sunni city, he seldom met Shīʿī ulama who would debate him and force him to question the assumptions underlying the issues dividing Sunnis and Shīʿīs. The Shīʿī scholars to whom Qāsimī responded came from Iraq and Java, not from Syria. He reiterated standard Sunni positions, denied credence to Shīʿī sources, and called for greater mutual tolerance. Convinced that the Shīʿīs held many erroneous beliefs, Qāsimī nevertheless treated them in a more conciliatory fashion than he did Sunni partisans of the legal schools. His moderation vis-à-vis Shīʿīs stemmed from Damascus's overwhelmingly Sunni character. His views and situation sharply contrasted with those of his longtime correspondent and fellow salafi in Baghdad, Maḥmūd Shukrī al-Alūsī. Iraq had a large Shīʿī population and bordered on Shīʿī Iran. Consequently, Alūsī felt more threatened by Shīʿism than Qāsimī did. Whereas Qāsimī respected his Shīʿī opponent in debate, Muḥammad Ḥusayn Kāshif al-Ghiṭā', Alūsī vehemently denigrated him.[41] If Qāsimī's more benign attitude reflected his security in a Sunni city, his rejection of fundamental Shīʿī beliefs and texts signified a profound unwillingness to compromise with Shīʿʿism.

7

The Salafis and the Arabists

The salafis' incorporation of reason and progress into a scripturalist interpretation of Islam set them apart from their ulama colleagues, who rejected the reformers' ideas and persecuted them. But the salafis did find an audience receptive to their teaching in another quarter: the rising generation of secondary school graduates who became some of the first Arabists. The central figure in the salafi-Arabist relationship was Ṭāhir al-Jazā'irī, who besides espousing salafism figured prominently in movements for political and educational reform. Jazā'irī's story raises the possibility that the Young Ottomans influenced the reform movement in Damascus through his contacts with Ottoman reformers. The "senior circle," which formed around him in the early 1890s, embodied cooperation between Arabs and Turks who favored political reforms.

By 1902, a new generation of students had gathered around Jazā'irī and formed the "junior circle." The students' secondary school experiences had a formative impact on them, especially the school's curriculum, teachers, and the informal networks the students developed. The junior circle evolved from a loose association of friends sharing common literary and political interests into a more organized group, the Arab Renaissance Society. The salafis' student followers became advocates of first an Arab cultural revival, then greater political rights, and finally Arab autonomy, if not independence. Following the terminology rightly used by historians of Arab nationalism, we refer to the members of the senior and junior circles as Arabists, not as Arab nationalists, because few of them favored an independent Arab state before 1914.[1]

Ṭāhir al-Jazā'irī: Link Between Young Ottomans and Arabists

A career in the higher echelons of the Ottoman Empire's governing bodies bore the risk of internal exile whenever one fell out of favor with the sultan. When Sultan Abdülḥamīd vanquished the constitutionalist faction of Ottoman officials in 1877, he dismissed them from their posts and assigned them to provincial posts to remove them from the center of political life.[2] As the administrative center of Syria, Damascus received its share of demoted officials, including men who had worked for administrative reform and a constitution. Three particularly renowned reformers served as governors of Syria between 1877 and 1881.

The relationship between Syrian and Turkish reformers began during the brief tenure of Żiyā Pasha as governor of Syria in 1877. Żiyā Pasha (1825–1880) had already achieved fame as a leading voice of the Young Ottoman movement. The Young Ottomans were a group of Turkish intellectuals who had come together in 1865, united by discontent with the reigning clique of bureaucrats who came to power during the Tanzimat years and further developed Tanzimat policies. The Young Ottomans included liberal thinkers, disgruntled bureaucrats, and a member of the Egyptian ruling family. Their importance lies in launching the movement for constitutional government, opposing the Tanzimat reforms' promotion of non-Muslims' interests, arguing that the Tanzimat bureaucrats had gone too far in assimilating European ways, and insisting on preserving the empire's Islamic character. The Young Ottomans were also among the first to call for pan-Islamic unity to strengthen Muslims against Europe.[3]

The Young Ottomans' foremost writer was Nāmik Kemāl. He synthesized European and Islamic political concepts to propagate contemporary liberal ideas, like popular sovereignty, parliamentary government, and liberty. He and his compatriots also stressed that man should scientifically study the natural world because the resulting knowledge serves man's needs. With their desire to achieve political reform and technical progress, and to preserve the Islamic heritage, the Young Ottomans staked out positions the salafis later espoused.

After several years of exile in Europe, Żiyā Pasha returned to Istanbul in 1876 to sit on the commission that drafted the Ottoman constitution. Less than two months after the constitution's promulgation in December 1876, Sultan Abdülḥamīd got rid of the constitution's leading advocates, including Żiyā Pasha and Midḥat Pasha, by relegating them to provincial posts. Żiyā Pasha arrived in Damascus in February 1877 for his four-month term as governor during which his chief task was to organize elections for Parliament. Żiyā Pasha came to Damascus with a young protegé, Bahā' Bey, who served as secretary of official correspondence.[4] Bahā' Bey met Ṭāhir al-Jazā'irī, probably through the latter's Turkish acquaintances in the administration, and began to frequent the literary salons Jazā'irī hosted.

In April 1877, war broke out between the empire and Russia, and two months later Żiyā Pasha was transferred to another province. For the next 10 months the military commander, ʿIzzat Pasha, combined civil powers with his martial authority and ruled the province.[5] With the end of the war with Russia, civilian rule returned to Damascus in March 1878, when Aḥmed Cevdet Pasha came as governor. Cevdet was the most prominent religious scholar to work with the Tanzimat reformers. He arrived in Damascus shortly after capping a distinguished career by heading the commission that drafted the Majallah (Mecelle), a codification of Islamic laws on transactions. Just as Abdülḥamīd's consolidation of power led to the defeat of the constitutionalists, it resulted in ending Cevdet's work on the Majallah commission. The new sultan had allied with conservative ulama opposed to the code, and they convinced him to suspend the commission's work. As did some Tanzimat reformers, Cevdet strongly opposed the constitution, so it is ironic that he should have been dismissed along with the constitution's proponents.[6]

Cevdet Pasha governed Syria for only nine months in 1878, and details on his tenure are presently scarce; consequently it is difficult to comment on his impact on men like Jazā'irī. He knew Arabic well, unlike most later governors, so some interaction with Damascene ulama was likely. One local historian credited Aḥmed Cevdet with encouraging the establishment of new schools and enrolling more students.[7]

Midḥat Pasha replaced Cevdet and came to Syria ready to implement a broad spectrum of reforms, as he had in other provinces. A biographer of Ṭāhir al-Jazā'irī has claimed that Midḥat set up a Masonic lodge in Damascus, and that both Ṭāhir and ʿAbd al-Qādir al-Jazā'irī joined it. Although it is possible that a Masonic lodge functioned as a meeting place for reformist officials and Damascenes, it is more certain that Ṭāhir and Bahā' Bey went to Midḥat with the idea of forming a benevolent society to direct educational reforms.[8] Midḥat encouraged the project, and Jazā'irī persuaded several prominent ulama to participate in founding the Benevolent Society.

We have already discussed Jazā'irī's work for the Benevolent Society and its successor, the provincial education council, as well as the primers he wrote and his role in founding the Ẓāhiriyyah Library. Suffice it to say here that Ṭāhir's efforts to spread and raise the level of education and to organize the collection at the Ẓāhiriyyah Library earned him a reputation as a reformer. Shaykh Ṭāhir lost his position on the education council around 1886 and spent the next 12 years teaching in Damascus, researching at the Ẓāhiriyyah Library and traveling in Syria. He returned to the provincial administration in August 1898, when he became curator of the province's libraries.[9] Once again Ṭāhir's connections with Turkish officials proved instrumental: a former governor of Syria, himself a religious scholar, secured the appointment for Jazā'irī. To explore the possibilities for opening more libraries, Ṭāhir toured the province, and under his auspices, public libraries opened in Jerusalem, Homs, Hamah, and Tripoli.[10]

In Damascus, Jazā'irī purchased new books and collected manuscripts to place in the Ẓāhiriyyah Library. By virtue of his years in the library, he acquired a unique grasp of the location of manuscripts throughout the Arab world, printed Arabic works, and European works on Arabic literature. He served as a walking card catalog at a time when knowledge of the corpus of works belonging to the Arab-Islamic heritage was fragmented and scattered throughout the Arab world.[11]

Jazā'irī had few friends because of his eccentric personality. His longest association was with Salīm al-Bukhārī, another salafi shaykh. They knew each other from their youths when Bukhārī studied with Ṭāhir's father and Shaykh ʿAbd al-Ghanī al-Ghunaymī. They also shared the experience of working for the Benevolent Society to open new schools, and they avidly sought rare manuscripts, especially those of Ibn Taymiyyah and Ibn Qayyim.[12]

When Jazā'irī became acquainted with Jamāl al-Dīn al-Qāsimī is unclear. They certainly knew one another before 1900, for Qāsimī's father used to visit Ṭāhir. However, the two reformers only began to see each other frequently in 1906, when Jazā'irī would visit Qāsimī after the latter's evening lesson, which he gave at home. Qāsimī's diary entries of 1906 mention Jazā'irī's frequent visits, their discussions, and occasional excursions to the country villas of wealthier friends like ʿAlī al-ʿAẓm and ʿUmar al-Jazāʾirī, ʿAbd al-Qādir's son. They loaned each other manuscripts, discussed ways to advance the reform movement, and Jazāʾirī suggested revisions for Qāsimī's work on the methodology of oral reports scholars. When Qāsimī's enemies tried to stir up trouble against him in November 1906, Jazāʾirī came to his defense.[13]

Ṭāhir continued to visit Qāsimī regularly through the early months of 1907, while preparing to emigrate to Egypt. Since the previous summer, Jazāʾirī had been gradually selling his book and manuscript collection, and by March 1907 only three chests of books remained, which he left with his friend, ʿUthmān al-ʿAẓm. That month Ṭāhir quietly bade farewell to his friends and then went with Qāsimī to ʿUmar al-Jazāʾirī's home for his last night in Damascus. He then toured Lebanon and Palestine for several weeks before he left for Egypt from Beirut in the middle of April.[14]

Why did Jazāʾirī disguise his emigration as a tour of the outlying districts in his capacity as curator of the libraries? A firm answer can only come from a detailed study of Jazāʾirī's career. He may have been fed up with official harassment, such as the incident in November 1902 when the governor received orders from Istanbul to search Ṭāhir's home and his room at the ʿAbd Allah al-ʿAẓm religious school. At the same time police searched nearly 20 other homes for evidence of correspondence with members of the Young Turk movement residing in Europe. Qāsimī hinted that Jazāʾirī forsook Syria to seek respite in Egypt's more tolerant intellectual and political climate.[15]

The Senior Circle

Muḥibb al-Dīn al-Khaṭīb, a pupil of Jazāʾirī and later a leading literary figure in the salafi movement, wrote that when he was a youth he knew two types of reformer. One group consisted of Turks and Turkish-speaking Arabs working in the army and administration. They tended to join the Young Turks (see following) and read their publications issued from Paris and Cairo. The other group included Arab scholars of literature, history, and religion seeking to revive Arab culture. Jazāʾirī's salons brought together the two reform trends by providing an informal setting for the mingling of Turkish and Arab officials and officers, religious students, and students in state schools. Because of the importance some Arab historians have ascribed to these salons, a closer look at the individuals who attended them is warranted.[16]

The salons' older members included Jazāʾirī, Salīm al-Bukhārī, and Rafīq al-ʿAẓm. Bukhārī's post as prayer leader of an artillery brigade and examiner of religious students seeking exemption from conscription offered opportunities to meet young men ripe for recruitment to the reformist cause. Through his contacts with Turkish army officers, Bukhārī met members of the Young Turks, who were clandestinely organizing against Sultan Abdülḥamīd and seeking a restoration of constitutional government. Shaykh Salīm cooperated closely with the Young Turks in Damascus during Abdülḥamīd's reign, thus personifying the alliance between religious reformers and constitutional forces in Damascus.[17]

The senior circle also included Rafīq al-ʿAẓm (1867–1925), who became a prominent writer and activist in the movement for Arab autonomy. The ʿAẓms had been Damascus's leading notable family since the early eighteenth century when Ismāʿīl Pasha al-ʿAẓm became the first of several ʿAẓms to govern Syria between 1725 and 1783. In the nineteenth century, the ʿAẓms remained an influential and wealthy family. Rafīq al-ʿAẓm's father, Maḥmūd (1836–1875), was one of the few family members to develop literary interests.[18]

Rafīq al-ʿAẓm's education consisted of private tutoring from his father, attending a Quranic school, Arabic lessons with a religious scholar, and three years in a state secondary school. Thereafter, he studied history and literature on his own, and he frequented literary salons. In 1884, he traveled with a relative to Egypt to study, but he fell ill and returned to Damascus the following year. In the early 1890s, Rafīq began to frequent Ṭāhir al-Jazā'irī's salon, where he met an Arab officer named Asʿad Bey Darwīsh al-Ṭarābulsī.[19]

Asʿad Bey had formed the Constitution Society, a secret political group allied to Turkish officers active in the Young Turk movement. ʿAẓm joined the Society, but his participation in it and in Jazā'irī's circle ended abruptly when he emigrated to Cairo in 1894. His paternal aunt had left him a share of the family's endowed properties in Egypt, and her husband, a member of the Egyptian ruling house, encouraged him to come settle in Cairo.[20]

By the time of ʿAẓm's departure, the group attending Jazā'irī's salon included a trio of secondary school students who later became leaders of the Arabist movement: Shukrī al-ʿAsalī (1878–1916), ʿAbd al-Wahhāb al-Inklīzī (1878–1916), and Salīm al-Jazā'irī (1879–1916). Shukrī al-ʿAsalī came from a Maydani family with property in pious endowments in their ancestral village in the Ghutah, an agricultural district on the outskirts of Damascus. Both his father and grandfather had held seats on provincial and municipal councils. Young Shukrī attended state primary and secondary schools until 1896, when he moved to Istanbul to pursue higher education in preparation for a career in the Ottoman bureaucracy. In 1902, he graduated from the imperial civil college and began a career in the provincial bureaucracy. His close friend, ʿAbd al-Wahhāb al-Inklīzī, was born in a village in the Ghutah and attended school with ʿAsalī for 10 years, from around 1892 until 1902.[21]

Together with Salīm al-Jazā'irī, ʿAsalī and Inklīzī joined Asʿad Bey Darwīsh's Constitution Society. Other members of the Society included Fāris al-Khūrī, a Christian member of Ṭāhir al-Jazā'irī's group, Ḥusayn Avnī Bey, who later became the director of public instruction for Syria, and Rifʿat Bey and Badrī Bey, high-ranking Turkish army officers.[22]

The only account of a meeting of the senior circle describes a gathering to read a proconstitution newspaper at the country home of ʿUmar al-Jazā'irī. Shaykh Ṭāhir, Salīm al-Bukhārī, Asʿad Bey Darwīsh, and others attended, including a man who reported the meeting to Aḥmad al-Shamʿah, a wealthy notable and confidant of Abū al-Hudā al-Ṣayyādī. How Jazā'irī and his group managed to escape punishment is unclear. The account states that a former student of Jazā'irī's worked in the Aleppo telegraph bureau and intercepted the message reporting the group's subversive activity.[23] This incident suggests that for members of Jazā'irī's circle and the Constitution Society, secret activities included meeting to read newspapers and journals smuggled from Europe and discussing the merits of a liberal political system.

Another decade would pass before men like ʿAsalī, Inklīzī, and Salīm al-Jazā'irī carried reformist action beyond discussion groups and set up secret societies. In the meantime, these three young men departed for Istanbul to attend the imperial colleges, the incubators of the Young Turk movement.[24]

In the senior circle—a group of reformist ulama, Turkish liberals, and students—Ṭāhir al-Jazā'irī brought together three strands of progressive opinion in Damascus and thereby initiated the alliance between salafis, proconstitution Turks, and Arabists. The nature of the Young Turks' activities and organization in Damascus deserves attention because some of its partisans interacted with the Damascene reformers.

The Young Turks

Organized opposition to Sultan Abdülḥamīd's rule appeared in 1889 among students in Istanbul's Military Medical School. They formed the Society for Union and Progress, which recruited students and teachers in other government military and civilian schools. In the early 1890s, prominent officials dissatisfied with the sultan's reign joined the Society, and in 1895 members residing in Europe and Egypt began to publish newspapers calling for reform and criticizing the sultan. The Young Turks suffered a severe setback in August 1896 when the sultan's agents uncovered a plot to depose the sultan, thereby forcing the movement's leaders to flee the empire for safer confines in Paris, Geneva, and Cairo.[25]

In Damascus, though, the Young Turks continued their activities until July 1897. The clandestine group drew support from soldiers frustrated by arrears in their pay and a protracted campaign against the Druzes. Discontent in the military surfaced in September 1896, when a Turkish lieutenant interrupted a theater performance to deliver a speech denouncing the sultan, and officers in the audience prevented the police from arresting the lieutenant. The following March, the British consul reported discontent among the troops and rebellious talk among officers upset at the long delay in their pay. In July 1897, an official inquiry into the Young Turks' activities resulted in the expulsion from Damascus of 18 Egyptians who allegedly had ties with the Young Turks, the exile of the director of the Tobacco Regie, and the recall of governor Ḥasan Rafīq Pasha. That Young Turk activities increased after Ḥasan Pasha's arrival in Damascus and then subsided after his recall suggests that he countenanced, if not encouraged, them.[26]

The foregoing discussion of liberal Ottoman governors of Syria, Ṭāhir al-Jazā'irī's early years in provincial educational posts, the senior circle, and the Young Turks shows that the reformist trend in Damascus joined Turks and Arabs favoring the extension of public education and improving the province's administration. From the time of Ẓiyā Pasha's and Midḥat Pasha's terms as governor, Damascus had a handful of Turkish and Arab supporters of constitutional government. In the 1890s, Jazā'irī became the pole around which Damascus's reformist groups coalesced to form the senior circle. The circle's members shared a vision of reform that included constitutional government, education in natural and physical sciences, and the solidarity of the Ottoman Empire's several ethnic groups to fend off European aggression. The senior circle marked the beginning of a long association between the salafis and other proconstitution forces.

While the Syrian members of the senior circle studied the Arab-Islamic heritage, the Young Turks displayed a more secular bent, if not disrespect for Arabic and the Islamic tradition. This cultural difference became more sharply defined in the early years of the twentieth century when a new generation of Syrian students came of age and raised Arab consciousness to a new level of expression and organization.

The Junior Circle and the Arab Renaissance Society

Ṭāhir al-Jazā'irī continued to enjoy a following among students and through them made a lasting impression on Damascus's cultural and political life. Young men attending his circle between 1902 and 1905 formed their own clique and later on gave the first organized expression to Damascus's reformist trend. Their relationship with the salafis shows affinities and differences that informed the earliest formulations of Arabism.

In 1903, several secondary school students who frequented Ṭāhir al-Jazā'irī's salons formed the "junior circle." The members included Muḥibb al-Dīn al-Khaṭīb, Ṣalāḥ al-Dīn al-Qāsimī, ʿĀrif al-Shihābī, Luṭfī al-Ḥaffār, Ṣāliḥ Qanbāz, and ʿUthmān Mardam-Beg, all born between 1886 and 1892. The senior circle's student members had all been born before 1880, and by 1902 they had completed higher studies in Istanbul or begun careers in Damascus's bureaucracy.[27] The junior circle, then, represented a distinct generation. Most of its members attended Damascus's sole higher secondary school (*al-iʿdādiyyah*), Maktab ʿAnbar, where they met between 1902 and 1905. A younger classmate of theirs described the school in an account that indicates how their experiences at Maktab ʿAnbar contributed to their ideological formation.[28]

Maktab ʿAnbar, which opened in 1893, taught religious subjects, social studies, physical sciences, and languages. Classes on the Quran, Islamic doctrine, and law comprised the religious curriculum. Students took courses in economics, geography, and Ottoman and world history. Instruction included Arabic and Turkish language, Ottoman literature, and French and Persian grammar. Maktab ʿAnbar's pupils also studied chemistry, physics, algebra, and geometry. How well these courses were taught is a question requiring research into the history of education in Syria; however effectively teachers taught and pupils learned, the intention to combine religious instruction with courses on history, science, and foreign languages fit the salafis' formula of joining Islam and modernity.

As in all Ottoman state schools, Turkish was the language of instruction. The principal and all but two of the teachers were Turks, including the Arabic teacher. Syrian Arab pupils learned Arabic grammar from a Turkish textbook written for Turkish pupils in Anatolia and Rumelia. Though Syrian youths eagerly seized the opportunity to master Turkish and thereby enhance their prospects for a career in the Ottoman bureaucracy, they resented the fact that most of their teachers were Turks. Maktab ʿAnbar's pupils divided into cliques of Arabs and Turks, and in 1904 fights broke out. Meanwhile junior circle members had begun to smuggle banned Egyptian newspapers into the school and circulate them among trusted friends. Many of the school's graduates headed for Istanbul to study at the empire's civilian and military colleges in hopes of pursuing careers in the bureaucracy and the army.[29]

The junior circle members' school experiences and association with the senior circle suggest a blend of growing Arab consciousness with the assimilation of such values as competence, reason, and freedom of speech. The junior circle embraced the salafi program for reviving the Arab-Islamic heritage, borrowing Western technology, and pursuing representative government.[30]

The Arab Renaissance Society

In 1906, two members of the junior circle graduated from Maktab ʿAnbar and went to Istanbul for higher studies. There they were shocked to meet fellow Arab students unfamiliar with the Arab cultural heritage and anxious to adopt Turkish manners.[31] Muḥibb al-Dīn al-Khaṭīb, ʿĀrif al-Shihābī, and two other Arab students met in December to form a society dedicated to the revival of Arab culture and progress for the Arab people. They held weekly evening meetings in their rooms to read classic Arab works because they believed that language is among "the firmest bonds between men, that it is a great factor in revival and progress in nations' political, social, and scientific life."[32] The Society's numbers grew in the next few months, and its members donated small sums of money to a common fund. In June the Society held a banquet at a nearby resort area, at which Khaṭīb delivered a speech and Shihābī recited a poem.

That same month Khaṭīb wrote to Ṣalāḥ al-Dīn al-Qāsimī, Jamāl al-Dīn's younger brother, and to Luṭfī al-Ḥaffār, suggesting they form a branch of the Society in Damascus. Qāsimī and Ḥaffār responded to the idea with enthusiasm, and began to meet twice weekly with three other peers. In August the Istanbul members returned to Damascus during school vacation, and after a meeting of the two branches, the members decided to establish headquarters in Damascus. At a banquet that same month, members delivered lectures on religious reform, Arabic, education, and science—all subjects the salafis promoted.

The Arab Renaissance Society met secretly for the next year until the July 1908 Turkish "revolution," or constitutional restoration. In January 1908 the Society's central committee resolved to set up a small library of books and journals. ʿUthmān Mardam-Beg, who belonged to the junior circle, volunteered a room in his large home for the library. The Society also wanted to publish a number of "contemporary" works, but lacked adequate financial resources.

Family Ties

In a number of instances, the close ties binding the salafi ulama and the Arabist students involved more than a common interest in harnessing the Arab-Islamic heritage to modernity. In the cases of Ṭāhir al-Jazā'irī, Salīm al-Bukhārī, and Jamāl al-Dīn al-Qāsimī, the salafis instilled reformism in younger relatives, who in turn developed ideas along more secular, nationalist lines.

Ṭāhir al-Jazā'irī took charge of his nephew Salīm al-Jazā'irī's upbringing when the infant Salīm's father died. Ṭāhir sent Salīm to attend the government schools he had helped set up and taught the boy Islamic history in private lessons at home. Naturally, Salīm became part of the senior circle before going to Istanbul to attend the War College. Some time during his years in Istanbul, he joined the Committee for Union and Progress (CUP), and after the constitution's restoration, he became a leader of the CUP's Damascus branch. Between 1909 and 1914, Salīm participated in founding some of the public and secret Arab societies. At the same time he taught at the War College, where he gained renown for giving anecdotes from Muslim history in his lectures, whereas most instructors were said to refer to European history.[33]

Like Salīm al-Jazā'irī, Maḥmūd Jalāl al-Bukhārī (1882–1916) was raised by a prominent salafi, his father Salīm. Jalāl attended Maktab ʿAnbar, and in 1908 he went to Istanbul to study first at the civil, then the law college. He joined Arab societies, which flourished among Arab students in Istanbul, and was especially active in the Literary Club, which sponsored lectures and discussions on Arab history and culture.[34]

Ṣalāḥ al-Dīn al-Qāsimī (1887–1916) was 21 years younger than his brother Jamāl al-Dīn, so they represented different generations and upbringings.[35] Just as Ṭāhir al-Jazā'irī supervised Salīm's education, Jamāl al-Dīn took over Ṣalāḥ al-Dīn's when their father died in 1900. The salafi shaykh enrolled his younger brother at Maktab ʿAnbar in 1902, and encouraged him to master the sciences and foreign languages (French and Turkish) that he himself had not had the opportunity to study. Jamāl al-Dīn gave Ṣalāḥ al-Dīn lessons at home in religious subjects and Arabic, and urged him to explore his literary talent from an early age. When only 15 years old, Ṣalāḥ al-Dīn published a literary journal at his school. After graduating from Maktab ʿAnbar, he entered the medical college that had opened in Damascus in 1901, and he completed his studies in 1914.

Ṣalāḥ al-Dīn attended the literary salons of Ṭāhir al-Jazā'irī and those of Jamāl al-Dīn at home. In 1906, the Qāsimī home became a center for the meetings of the reformist group, so Ṣalāḥ al-Dīn became acquainted with senior circle members like ʿAsalī, Inklīzī, Salīm al-Jazā'irī, Muḥammad Kurd ʿAlī, and ʿAbd al-Raḥmān Shahbandar. The Qāsimī salon discussed classical Islamic works by al-Ghazālī and Ibn Khaldūn as well as current affairs and politics. Jamāl al-Dīn took the opportunity to learn from the young men versed in European languages, literature, and sciences.[36]

Ṣalāḥ al-Dīn al-Qāsimī still lived at home with his older brother in 1907, so we may assume that Jamāl al-Dīn encouraged or did not object to Ṣalāḥ al-Dīn's joining the Arab Renaissance Society. Even though none of the salafis joined the Society, that does not mean they disapproved of it. Their abstention reflected the fact that the Society resembled a club for young men who had formed friendships and common interests in school. When new members enrolled, they usually were younger relations or classmates of members.[37] The salafis were much older men, born between 1837 and 1866, so even the youngest among them, Jamāl al-Dīn al-Qāsimī, was 20 years older than the oldest member of the Society.

From this review of the junior circle and the founding of the Arab Renaissance Society the following observations can be made. First, the state secondary school in Damascus, Maktab ʿAnbar, provided a setting for bright, ambitious students to meet and form common interests. The school's curriculum and some of the students' relatives encouraged the young men to take an interest in subjects that led them into careers as doctors, lawyers, writers, and army officers. Their training for these professions differed from that imparted in Syria before the late nineteenth century. The junior circle members studied a curriculum inspired by the idea of achieving parity with Europe by learning "European" sciences. Syria had had doctors, legal specialists, writers, and military men before, but the training for those professions had changed, and a corresponding change occurred in the outlooks and values of those professionals. From their relations with the salafis and reactions against Turkish domination of Maktab ʿAnbar, the students developed an interest in their heritage as Arabs. The public school, then, contributed to the birth of a new type of Arab intellectual with new technical and ethnic interests.

Second, the salafis played a seminal role in fostering the combination of technical and ethnic interests by calling for the adoption of European technology, the acquisition of competence in science, and the revival of Muslims' true religious practices, which they claimed had a rational, pragmatic character. By declaring that Islam enjoins man to study nature and use reason, the salafis provided the younger generation with a palatable formula for studying what were perceived as European sciences. While by no means did all the junior circle members have older relatives who were salafis, all the young men came into contact with and admired the salafis for espousing progressive ideas.

Third, the Arab Renaissance Society marked the first organized expression of the local reformist trend. Hitherto the salafis comprised a circle of scholars meeting outside the mosques and religious schools, the loci of organized cultural life with fairly standard curricula, texts, and interpretations of Islam. The meetings of the mujtahids group and Jazā'irī's and Qāsimī's salons took place in private homes where discussants did not have to observe the conventions of the mosques and schools. Ulama had customarily held salons, so the salafis did not invent anything by holding their own; rather, they used an existing social custom to nurture their nascent intellectual movement, which stood for practices and beliefs in opposition to those prevailing in mosques and schools.

The Arab Renaissance Society represented an attempt to recruit new members, organize cultural activities, and propagate the emergent ideology of Arabism in a more conscious, orderly fashion than the salafis' ad hoc activities. In its first year and a half, the Society regularly held study meetings, started a fund to purchase books and periodicals, and set up a private reading room. That young Syrians launched their Society in Istanbul suggests that they emulated the nationalist cultural societies of such other groups as the Greeks and the Armenians.[38]

Finally, the junior circle's intellectual formation included doses of science, European history and languages, Arabic, and religious subjects. To be sure, the salafis made an impression on their student following, but the students' education and experiences gave them an orientation different from that of their mentors.

Arabism's Departures from Salafism

The salafis and the Arabists shared overlapping interests in social and political reform, Arab-Islamic history, and European inventions. Yet two different kinds of education—one specializing in religious subjects, the other more focused on science and foreign languages—produced divergent emphases in the reformist camp's two strands. Whereas the salafis stressed Muslim unity and subordinated reason to religion, regardless of what they may have claimed about their intrinsic harmony, the younger generation tended to emphasize their Arab identity and the qualities of intellectuals with a new kind of technical training. Ṣalāḥ al-Dīn al-Qāsimī's essays, lectures, and articles vividly portray how the Arabists both perpetuated and departed from the salafis' ideas.

Three central themes pervade Ṣalāḥ al-Dīn's writings and lectures: the means of achieving progress, social unity, and an Arab revival. Although in their general features these themes duplicate the salafis' concerns, Ṣalāḥ al-Dīn's writings significantly diverge from the paradigms of religious reform. Most notably, the salafis' fundamental issues—ijtihād, emulation, legal school prejudice, innovations in ritual, proper understanding of the Quran and the Sunnah, and the methods for extracting rulings from scripture—practically disappear in Ṣalāḥ al-Dīn's articles.

He came closest to reproducing his older brother's thinking in an article he wrote in 1909, entitled "The Ulama's Distress."[39] Like Jamāl al-Dīn, he denounced so-called ulama who pretended to stand for religion and the common people while actually pursuing selfish interests. Such men distorted religion, and, consequently, intelligent people regarded religion as a bundle of superstitions. Whenever true ulama challenged the impostors, the latter persecuted them and accused them of being infidels. Ṣalāḥ al-Dīn noted that Islamic history is rife with instances of oppression of men who practiced ijtihād. Great Muslim scholars like Mālik ibn Anas, Abū Ḥanīfah, Aḥmad ibn Ḥanbal, Ibn Taymiyyah, al-Ghazālī, and others suffered persecution. Likewise, current reformers in Syria, Iraq, and Egypt endure persecution, a thinly veiled reference to Jamāl al-Dīn's tribulations. Although the salafis also wrote along these lines, they addressed specific issues of religious belief and practice, whereas the younger generation dealt exclusively with the social manifestations of "incorrect" religious practice and belief: corrupt ulama, incompetent preachers, and intolerance.

Ṣalāḥ al-Dīn dealt with religious institutions in only one lecture, in which he discussed ways to reform the Friday sermon (*al-khuṭbah*) in the mosques.[40] He noted that most preachers addressed their audiences in an emotional manner, spoke in rhymed prose (*al-sajʿ*), used arcane words, and did nothing to benefit society. Whereas Jamāl al-Dīn had broached the same subject by publishing a collection of sermons from classical sources for various occasions, Ṣalāḥ al-Dīn stated that the language and content of sermons needed reform. A sermon should be coherent, logical, in accord with scientific facts, and it should promote the public interest by guiding the people to an economic and moral revival. Ṣalāḥ al-Dīn described how the sermons of the Prophet and ʿAlī guided and united Muslims, but more contemporary themes overshadowed this appeal to the Islamic heritage. As more recent exemplars of preachers (or more precisely, shapers of men's ideas), Ṣalāḥ al-Dīn mentioned Victor Hugo (*sic*), Voltaire, and Rousseau for promoting causes leading to the French Revolution.[41]

The salafis and the Arabists agreed that their society must adopt such European inventions as electricity, streetcars, and telegraphs. The salafis justified the borrowing of technology by stressing that Islam upholds man's ability to exercise reason in acquiring the means of life. The Arabists concerned themselves less with proving the harmony of religion and material progress, and more with mastering the keys to progress, a preference consonant with their schooling in science and European culture.

The salafis had argued that knowledge in itself is amoral, and that to benefit society, man must join knowledge to moral virtue. When Jamāl al-Dīn al-Qāsimī wrote on this matter, he referred to the need for the religious scholar to combine his knowledge with virtue. Ṣalāḥ al-Dīn discussed the theme of knowledge and virtue in relation to society, and he called for a division of labor between technical scientists (inventors, doctors, chemists) and humanist intellectuals (lawyers, economists, historians). According to Ṣalāḥ al-Dīn, scientists serve mankind by inventing the tools of economic development, while intellectuals alleviate social ills. Therefore, both scientists and intellectuals are indispensable to a prosperous, healthy society. Ṣalāḥ al-Dīn thought that men had to couple technical knowledge with virtue to achieve progress, and he concluded from that that ulama, teachers, scientists, and intellectuals should assume positions of leadership.[42]

Similarly, the salafis had asserted a leading role for the ulama, an ideal cherished by ulama for centuries. In addition to the ideal of an alliance between scholars and rulers (*al-ʿulamāʾ wa al-umarāʾ*) Ṣalāḥ al-Dīn's scheme resonated echoes of the St. Simonian vision of a society led by scientists. He wrote: "Those more endowed with intelligence and more virtue are the people most deserving respect and favor."[43] Also:

> The nation [al-ummah] has no prop on which to lean, no foundation stone on which to rise except for its active scholars and its enlightened men. On them depends its [the nation's] revival. . . . [T]hey are the cause of good fortune. Around such enlightened individuals would form literary societies and schools, and newspapers would be established. Talented doctors would appear, just lawyers, sincere journalists, honest merchants, industrious, knowledgeable farmers, and active artisans.[44]

This passage clearly expresses the Arabists' belief that only intellectuals could lead society to prosperity. The parallel to Jamāl al-Dīn's vision of a society guided by mujtahid ulama is striking. It suggests that both religious and lay intellectuals felt confident of their abilities to remedy the problems besetting the empire, and that both groups wished to assume leading positions in society.

Ṣalāḥ al-Dīn emphasized social unity as much as knowledge and virtue in his writings on how to achieve progress. But whereas the salafis made religion the unifying principle, Ṣalāḥ al-Dīn's group emphasized Arab unity. Even though he and other Arabists claimed to subordinate Arab unity to the cause of a wider Ottoman or Islamic unity, the call to an Arab revival inevitably led to growing friction with the Turks. Ṣalāḥ al-Dīn tried to minimize such friction by depicting the empire as a conglomeration of nationalities: Arabs, Turks, Kurds, Albanians, and Armenians. In his view the stronger each ethnic component, the stronger the empire would be as a whole. Ṣalāḥ al-Dīn argued that in history, nationalism had proved to be an element of progress. For instance, Europe and America attained a high level of civilization only when nationalism took hold in the minds of their peoples. The Ottoman Empire contained several nationalities, and Ṣalāḥ al-Dīn held that the empire as a whole could rejuvenate itself only to the extent that its constituent parts, its national groups, underwent revivals. His bias for intellectuals' interests showed up again when he wrote that the heroes of nationalism were scholars, writers, and poets who formulated nationalist ideals to inspire their people. Given the Arab Renaissance Society's fundamental goal of reviving Arab culture and Ṣalāḥ al-Dīn's sanguine view of nationalism, his call for Arabic to be the language of instruction in Syrian schools naturally followed.[45]

In addition to the Arabists' shift in emphasis from religion to nation as the ultimate object of loyalty and identity, Ṣalāḥ al-Dīn's articles and speeches show a mind impressed, though superficially familiar, with European history and culture. He and the other Arabists could read at least one European language. Whether the courses in French at Maktab ʿAnbar sufficed to impart fluency is uncertain, but even if they did not, they certainly gave a foundation on which motivated students could build. Ṣalāḥ al-Dīn sprinkled his articles with anecdotes from European history and often simply listed the great men of European culture. He devoted one lecture to the French Revolution's intellectual antecedents: John Locke on man's natural rights to freedom and property, Montesquieu, Voltaire, Rousseau, Diderot, the physiocrats, and Adam Smith.[46] In accord with Ṣalāḥ al-Dīn's intellectualist bias, he credited intellectuals with a leading role in the French Revolution, and he asserted that a political revolution bears fruit only if a revolution in ideas precedes it.

In contrast to his frequent references to Europeans, Ṣalāḥ al-Dīn seldom referred to Islamic history and famous Muslims. In fact, the dominant metaphor in his writings came from Darwinian ideas about evolution and survival of the fittest and their Comtean conversion into principles of historical sociology. Qāsimī stated that the Arab Renaissance Society followed the law of evolution in its modest beginnings and progress, starting as a live, dynamic atom and striving to gather Arabs around it. In other essays, Ṣalāḥ al-Dīn wrote of "the stages of gradual evolution," "the law of evolution and progress," and "the law of the survival of the fittest."[47] Like late nineteenth-century European Social Darwinists, Ṣalāḥ al-Dīn believed that just as the scientific study of nature yielded natural laws, the study of society yielded social laws: "Our knowledge of natural laws is equivalent to our knowledge of the laws of nations [*al-umam*]."[48] He also subscribed to the positivist belief that in the past, "scientific issues were closer to intuition and estimation than to investigation based on experience and experiment."[49]

The differences between salafis and Arabists should not be exaggerated. Ṣalāḥ al-Dīn wrote an article on the ḥashwiyyah and the Wahhābīs in which he denigrated Damascus's conservative ulama for their prejudices. He observed that the ḥashwiyyah had come to view the liberal Egyptian newspapers *al-Ahrām* and *al-Muqaṭṭam* as Wahhābī newspapers. In a reference to Jamāl al-Dīn, he remarked that "any teacher or preacher who recited oral reports on polytheism, explicitly or implicitly, happens to be called a Wahhābī."[50] Ṣalāḥ al-Dīn then described the Wahhābīs: they are a Ḥanbalī group who avoid polytheism and ritual innovations; they generally behave uprightly and observe the pillars of religion; and Muḥammad ibn ʿAbd al-

Wahhāb brought nothing new, but followed great mujtahid scholars. Ṣalāḥ al-Dīn closed this article with some of his brother's favorite slogans against legal school prejudice and for fairness in debate.[51]

Ṣalāḥ al-Dīn al-Qāsimī's frequent references to European philosophers, European history, and positivist ideas are perhaps the most striking contrast to his older brother's writings, which are steeped in an Islamic intellectual heritage. Also, the Arab element of the Arab-Islamic heritage outweighed Islam in his thought and the Arab Renaissance Society's program. But the divergent emphases on religious versus secular knowledge mattered little compared to the common features of the salafis' and the Arabists' outlooks. In particular their insistence on giving intellectuals a central role in society constituted a strong bond between the two groups. Their enthusiasm for European technology also set them apart from other Damascenes. Finally, Ṣalāḥ al-Dīn's criticisms of conservative ulama indicates the perception of a common enemy both to religious reform and to an Arab cultural revival. In a letter his older brother expressed his satisfaction with Ṣalāḥ al-Dīn's generation precisely because they supported the salafis against the conservative ulama:

> You ask about those [graduates of public schools]: do they know the salafi madhhab? My brother! No one knows the salafi madhhab but he who devotes himself to it. . . . Be content for now with the fact that they are supporters of the truth and adversaries of the tombsters [*al-qubūriyyīn*]. If a matter comes to light with its proof, they accept it; if not, they reject it. They are an enlightened group, discerning, intelligent.[52]

Ideological differences between the salafis and the Arabists were not so substantial as to generate controversy or strife between them, but the youths clearly transcended the stage of tutelage and departed from the salafis' concerns to reform religious practices. Ultimately, the differences arose from the specific contrast between the ulama's religious education on one hand, and the schooling of bureaucrats, lawyers, doctors, and army officers on the other. The latter represented a new group in Syria that appeared between 1890 and 1910, a new type of professional. That does not mean that Syria previously lacked administrators, legal specialists, doctors, and military men, but their training changed radically with the introduction of state schools, especially the secondary schools preparing youths for higher education in Istanbul, and after 1901, in Damascus's medical college.[53]

Conclusion

The genealogy of reformism in Damascus reaches back to the Young Ottomans, and proceeds through the salafis, Young Turks, and Arabists. Perhaps through direct contact with the Young Ottomans, and certainly under the influence of more diffuse cultural and social trends, a faction of Damascene ulama adopted the call for reform. These ulama performed a double legitimation: They proclaimed Islam's rationality and its compatibility with progress in order to shore up the ulama's declining status; and they reconciled new ideas and ways of education with Islam, thereby making them more acceptable to Syrian Muslims. Having fused Islam with ideas about reason, technology, and progress, the salafis passed this synthesis on to young men studying in state schools that gave instruction in sciences.

The critical shift from salafism to Arabism involved more than a move from religious to ethnic identity. That move stemmed from the changes in forms of education, not only because one form belonged to a venerable religious tradition while the other had a more recent, foreign pedigree; more importantly, religious education prepared young men for careers as ulama, as men with prescribed places in the social and political orders, whereas the graduates of state schools in Syria were bound for careers as state bureaucrats and army officers, social and political actors with confidence in their roles, but with less certain destinies. The salafis as religious intellectuals held a recognized place as representatives of cultural traditions; the Arabists as lay intellectuals felt they deserved a similar place and recognition of their qualities, but as a new social group they cast about for a role. The Arab Renaissance Society embodied their aspirations for themselves and on behalf of their people.

8

Conservative Ulama and Antisalafi Action

The stiffest opposition to the salafis came from ulama who defended customary practices and beliefs. These ulama constituted a distinct faction of religious scholars who shared a common interpretation of Islam, loyalty to Sultan Abdülḥamīd, and a strong aversion to European manners and ideas. They may also have shared a common social identity anchored in wealth and status in the Damascene ulama corps.

The conservatives were able to persuade Ottoman officials to see the salafis as a potential threat to Sultan Abdülḥamīd's reign because of the political climate, in which genuine and illusory dangers to the ruler combined to cast doubt on the loyalty of religious reformers. Although the salafis suffered occasional persecution, they survived each episode unscathed. Why they did so requires an explanation that considers the salafis' and the conservatives' respective relationships with local and imperial authorities.

The Conservative Ulama and Society

An analysis of the social origins of ulama opposed to the salafis shows two distinct groups and several individuals whose relationships with other conservatives do not form a pattern. One group included members of ulama families that customarily held high religious posts. The other group centered on Badr al-Dīn al-Ḥasanī, a popular teacher of oral reports. The other conservative ulama included a Naqshbandī shaykh, a Tunisian shaykh, a member of a leading notable family, and the uncle of Jamāl al-Dīn al-Qāsimī.

The conservative camp included five ulama whose families had been preachers at the Umayyad mosque, doyens of the Prophet's descendants (sing. naqīb al-ashrāf), and prayer leaders at the Umayyad mosque. Four of these ulama became closely associated with Damascus's mouthpiece of antisalafism, the monthly journal *al-Ḥaqā'iq*.

That journal's founder, ʿAbd al-Qādir al-Iskandarānī, came from one of the Fertile Crescent's most celebrated ulama families, the Kaylānīs, who derived their fame from their illustrious ancestor, the venerated Sufi master, ʿAbd al-Qādir Gīlānī (1077–1166). A popular Sufi order named after Shaykh ʿAbd al-Qādir spread widely in the Muslim world and his descendants occupied a privileged place in the order. By the eighteenth century, the Kaylānīs had established branches of their family in Hamah, Damascus, Istanbul, Tripoli, and Baghdad. Early in that century they obtained administrative posts and tax farms around Hamah, while relatives in Istanbul arranged religious posts for family members in Damascus. In the early years of the twentieth century, Sultan Abdülḥamīd's pan-Islamic policy and claims to the caliphate drew support from the popular Sufi orders, and in Syria the Kaylānīs' Qādiriyyah order backed the sultan. Details on ʿAbd al-Qādir al-Iskandarānī's life are scarce at present; however, his writings in *al-Ḥaqā'iq* and a trio of anti-Wahhābī tracts show that he opposed the salafis.[1]

The Shāfiʿī prayer leader at the Umayyad mosque, ʿĀrif al-Munayyir, contributed to Iskandarānī's journal and wrote several essays that refuted works by Jamāl al-Dīn al-Qāsimī, with whom he had carried on a friendly correspondence during a stay in Istanbul in the 1890s. Later on, Munayyir became a leader in the Rifāʿiyyah Sufi order, which flourished during Sultan Abdülḥamīd's reign. The sultan's Syrian adviser, Abū al-Hudā al-Ṣayyādī, headed the Rifāʿiyyah order, and through its many branches in Syria and Iraq, he cultivated a vast network of clients. Munayyir's association with this order suggests loyalty to the sultan, which he expressed more explicitly in an essay comprising 40 oral reports enjoining Muslims to obey the commander of the faithful (the sultan) and forbidding them to rebel.[2] The essay's conservative thrust appeared when Munayyir wrote, "Obeying the imam [the sultan] is the same as obeying the Prophet; and rebelling against him [the imam] is the same as rebelling against him [the Prophet]." He denounced Ottoman subjects who opposed the sultan and fled to foreign countries, whence they plotted against Muslims, probably a reference to the Young Turks, the salafis' constitutionalist allies.[3]

Three other conservative ulama came from families that had dominated the post of Friday preacher at the Umayyad mosque for a century. ʿAbd al-Qādir al-Khaṭīb incited mobs against the salafis in 1908 and 1909, and his relative Hāshim al-Khaṭīb wrote articles against the salafis in *al-Ḥaqā'iq*. The preacher at the Umayyad mosque during the constitutional period, Ḥasan al-Usṭuwānī, occasionally wrote in *al-Ḥaqā'iq* and criticized the salafis in his sermons.[4]

A second group of conservatives centered on Shaykh Badr al-Dīn al-Ḥasanī (1851–1936), who headed a circle of religious students and young shaykhs, some of whom also published in *al-Ḥaqā'iq*.[5] Shaykh Badr al-Dīn had been implicated in the mujtahids incident of 1896, when his alleged denunciation of Ottoman rule led the governor to suspect local ulama of conspiring against the sultan. Ḥasanī's father, Shaykh Yūsuf al-Maghribī, had settled in Damascus in 1857 after ʿAbd al-Qādir al-Jazā'irī helped him restore the city's ancient Oral Reports College (*Dār'al-Ḥadīth*) and made it a family pious endowment for the benefit of Shaykh Yūsuf and his descendants.[6]

Shaykh Yūsuf died in 1862 when Badr al-Dīn was still a youth, and the young boy's education was entrusted to a prominent shaykh. Whereas most shaykhs' sons attended the lessons of various ulama, Badr al-Dīn studied on his own. In 1881, he began teaching oral reports at the Sināniyyah mosque, and he soon acquired a reputation for his prodigious memory, which allowed him to teach famous collections of oral reports without notes or books.[7] In the early years of the twentieth century, Ḥasanī began to develop an aura of special status and attracted a circle of disciples.

Four outspoken adversaries of the salafis fit into neither Ḥasanī's circle nor the category of official ulama families. The first of these, Shaykh Asʿad al-Ṣāḥib (1855–1926), joined the ulama who objected to ʿAbd al-Ḥamīd al-Zahrāwī's 1901 essay attacking jurisprudence and Sufism, and five years later he tried to convince the Ottoman governor to act against Bīṭār and Qāsimī. Ṣāḥib's uncle, Shaykh Khālid al-Naqshbandī, had established the Khālidiyyah-Naqshbandiyyah Sufi order in Damascus in 1825, and his father Maḥmūd had settled there in 1843 when he set up and became shaykh of Damascus's second Khālidiyyah center at the Sulaymāniyyah lodge. Shaykh Asʿad quarreled with the Khānīs after ʿAbd al-Majīd al-Khānī published a work (1890) on the Naqshbandiyyah's history and shaykhs, because ʿAbd al-Majīd did not mention Ṣāḥib's father. Until then, Ṣāḥib and the Khānīs had been on friendly terms, but thereafter the former stopped visiting them, and he denied that Shaykh Khālid had deputized Muḥammad al-Khānī the younger, ʿAbd al-Majīd's father. In 1900, Asʿad al-Ṣāḥib opposed ʿAbd al-Majīd's bid to become shaykh of the Khānīs' Khālidiyyah branch.[8]

Another antisalafi shaykh, Ṣāliḥ al-Sharīf al-Tūnisī (1869–1920), came from an old ulama family of Tunis.[9] He studied at the Zaytūnah mosque, the leading center of Islamic learning in the country, and taught there for 12 years before emigrating to Istanbul in 1906, by which time Shaykh Ṣāliḥ had emerged as a leading opponent of the religious reform trend in Tunis. He resisted efforts to include "scientific" subjects in Zaytūnah's curriculum, and in September 1903, he debated Muḥammad ʿAbduh, whom he accused of propagating Wahhabism.

Tūnisī moved to Damascus in 1908 and began to teach at the Umayyad mosque. In October of that year he incited a riot against the salafi Rashīd Riḍā and the Committee of Union and Progress.[10] Tūnisī later made his peace with the CUP and accompanied Enver Pasha (one of the party's leaders) to Libya to rally resistance to the Italian invasion of 1911. Back in Damascus in 1913, Shaykh Ṣāliḥ joined with notables loyal to the CUP in opposing the Arab Congress that convened in Paris to demand administrative autonomy for the Arab provinces.[11]

Muḥammad al-Qāsimī, Jamāl al-Dīn's uncle, did not let family ties keep him from disparaging the salafis in the pages of *al-Ḥaqā'iq*. Muḥammad al-Qāsimī was Muḥammad Saʿīd's younger brother, and he became prayer leader and preacher at the Ḥassān mosque some years after Saʿīd inherited their father's posts at the Sināniyyah mosque. His opposition to the salafis may have stemmed from jealousy of Jamāl al-Dīn's obtaining the posts at the Sināniyyah mosque, while he remained at the obscure Ḥassān mosque. Muḥammad al-Qāsimī opposed Ḥāmid al-Taqī, the disciple of both Muḥammad Saʿīd and Jamāl al-Dīn, when Taqī tried to become prayer leader at the Sādāt mosque, on the grounds that his nephew's follower advocated Wahhabism.[12]

Mukhtār al-Mu'ayyad al-ʿAẓm (d. 1921) came from Damascus's foremost notable family. He wrote essays and articles against the salafis of Damascus and Egypt, participated in plotting the riot against Rashīd Riḍā in 1908, denounced Qāsimī in the pages of *al-Ḥaqā'iq,* and defended conservative positions on the legal schools and on supplicating saints.[13]

Of these 10 conservative ulama, three did not come from Damascene ulama families. Mukhtār al-Mu'ayyad al-ʿAẓm came from a notable family; Ṣāliḥ al-Tūnisī emigrated from Tunisia; and Badr al-Dīn al-Ḥasanī's father had settled in Damascus in the 1850s. Inheritance documents provide information about the wealth of six of the conservative Damascene ulama, all but Asʿad al-Ṣāḥib. ʿAbd al-Qādir al-Kaylānī, ʿĀrif al-Munayyir, and Ḥasan al-Usṭuwānī came from wealthy families; Muḥammad al-Qāsimī and ʿAbd al-Qādir and Hāshim al-Khaṭīb came from middle-class families.[14]

The foregoing review of the conservative camp accounts for 10 of its members. The names of other conservatives show up in the pages of *al-Ḥaqā'iq,* but until further information on them comes to light, this number must suffice for analysis. Though the conservative camp included men of diverse backgrounds, their attacks on the salafis did not lack specific social contexts. First of all, the conservatives included men from the ranks of the official ulama and their relatives. Official ulama had grounds for opposing the salafis, who denounced preachers for using rhymed prose and perpetuating superstitions, teachers for reducing pedagogy to the recitation of texts, commentaries, and glosses, and jurists for tenaciously clinging to the legal schools. Second, leaders of Sufi orders resented the salafis' critique of Sufi processions and beliefs associated with Sufi saints. Hence men like Iskandarānī (of the Qādiriyyah order) and Ṣāḥib (of the Khālidiyyah-Naqshbandiyyah order) strenuously opposed the salafis. Though most sources on Badr al-Dīn al-Ḥasanī stress his qualities as a scholar of oral reports, he also had a reputation as a Sufi master.[15]

Opposition to the salafis, then, came from the very quarters one would expect it: ulama whose practices and beliefs took the brunt of the salafis' criticisms. The conservative camp included well-to-do men (Munayyir, Usṭuwānī, Kaylānī) and ulama of more modest means (Qāsimī, Ṣāḥib, Khaṭīb). Besides their fidelity to customary religious practices, they also shared loyalty to Sultan Abdülḥamīd.

The Caliphate, Wahhābīs, and Salafis

Prior to 1908, the conservative ulama enjoyed qualified success in enlisting government support for their antisalafi actions because five aspects of regional politics combined to make Ottoman authorities suspicious of the salafis. First, Sultan Abdülḥamīd buttressed his rule by pursuing an "Islamic" policy that consisted of claiming the caliphate and patronizing popular Sufi orders. Second, the viceroy of Egypt countenanced challenges to the sultan's claim to the caliphate. Third, the religious reform camp in Egypt led by Muḥammad ʿAbduh did not denounce British rule, which Abdülḥamīd greatly resented. Fourth, the Wahhābīs recovered Najd in 1902, rejected Ottoman authority, and posed yet another Arab challenge to the sultan's claims to the caliphate. Fifth, the Zaydī imam of Yemen rebelled against the Ottomans in 1904 and declared himself caliph. The salafis' enemies exploited Ottoman sensitivity to these political situations by positing links between religious reformers and opposition to the Sultan.

Controversy over the caliphate stemmed from the Ottoman sultan's claim to represent the world's Muslims in his capacity as caliph. Before the late eighteenth century, the Ottoman sultans had not claimed to rule as caliphs, that is, as successors of the Prophet's religious and political authority. They put forth the claim as a diplomatic weapon beginning in 1774 at the conclusion of a war with Russia. In the anti-European climate of the last decades of the nineteenth century, Sultan Abdülḥamīd's claim on the caliphate served both his standing in diplomacy and before his Muslim subjects. He hoped that his stature as caliph would bolster his bargaining position against the European Powers, and at the same time give him a crucial advantage over dissident political elements, such as the Young Turks, whose lack of prestige and authority hampered their cause.[16]

Sultan Abdülḥamīd marshaled considerable resources to strengthen his claim to the caliphate, the supreme symbol of religious and political authority over Muslims. His chief agent for securing legitimacy in the Arab lands was Abū al-Hudā al-Ṣayyādī, a Sufi shaykh of humble rural origins from northern Syria. The sultan put at Ṣayyādī's disposal large sums of money from the imperial and provincial treasuries and from pious endowments.[17] With these funds Abū al-Hudā financed an expansion of Sufi orders in Syria and Iraq, especially the Rifāʿiyyah order, which he headed. He had Sufi lodges (sing. *zāwiyah*) constructed, appointed a deputy shaykh (*khalīfah*) to each lodge, paid the deputy a monthly salary, and provided funds for the lodges' expenses. Abū al-Hudā also dispensed money to repair existing lodges and to restore the tombs of locally revered saints. In 1886, Sultan Abdülḥamīd granted members of the Rifāʿī clan exemption from military service.

To extend this patronage network, Abū al-Hudā integrated into the Rifāʿiyyah order small Sufi orders of the popular classes in towns and villages by fabricating genealogies to incorporate the popular orders' shaykhs into the Rifāʿī clan. Since members of that clan had attained the status of sharīfs, the minor Sufi shaykhs acquired the privileges of the Prophet's descendants, such as exemption from conscription and taxation. These local shaykhs in intimate contact with the popular classes provided a bedrock of support for the sultan. Ṣayyādī also distributed posts, stipends, and medals to clients, had new mosques and religious schools constructed, and had old ones restored. Many mosque workers, from prayer leaders to muezzins to caretakers, depended on Ṣayyādī's patronage.[18]

Abū al-Hudā's books, and writings he commissioned to be published in his name, expressed the sort of Islamic ideology that underpinned Abdülḥamīd's reign. Like the essay by Ṣayyādī's fellow Rifāʿī shaykh, ʿĀrif al-Munayyir, these works endorsed the sultan's claim to the caliphate and called on Muslims to support him. Abū al-Hudā wrote that the Quran commands Muslims to unite by rallying to the caliph: Muslims could prove their faith by submitting to and praising their sultan, whose absolute rule conformed with the principles of Islamic government. He also made veiled criticisms of religious reformers.[19]

Abdülḥamīd's fear of a movement in Egypt to establish an Arab caliphate stemmed from a few obscure events that occurred between 1895 and 1902. The idea of setting up an Arab caliphate may have originated in the suggestion of Wilfrid Blunt, an English aristocrat and traveler, to select a member of the Quraysh (the Prophet's clan) to serve as a caliph possessing spiritual, but not political authority.

Blunt attracted ʿAbduh, the Egyptian Viceroy ʿAbbās Ḥilmī, and others to his idea, but it lacked credibility because it looked like a British plot.[20] The idea of an Arab caliphate, however, continued to crop up now and then in association with the activities of Viceroy ʿAbbās Ḥilmī. In the summer of 1895, he visited Istanbul and secretly met with Jamāl al-Dīn al-Afghānī, then a captive-guest of the sultan. The only report of their meeting came from Abdülḥamīd's spies, who claimed the two men had discussed how to consummate plans for an Arab caliphate. Rashīd Riḍā later observed that Abdülḥamīd was suspicious of Afghānī's dealings with ʿAbbās Ḥilmī.[21]

The Ottoman sultan's doubts about ʿAbbās Ḥilmī had a more substantial basis when it came to the latter's relations with the Young Turks gathered in Egypt, who enjoyed the viceroy's patronage. In 1896 the Young Turks' newspaper in Cairo concocted stories about a conspiracy to create an independent Arab caliphate. According to Rafīq al-ʿAẓm, who was in Cairo at the time and in touch with the Young Turks, the Arab caliphate story was just a ploy intended to frighten the sultan and force him to restore constitutional government.[22] A few years later a Syrian writer from Aleppo published a book calling for an Arab caliphate and rejecting Ottoman sultans' claims to the caliphate. ʿAbd al-Raḥmān al-Kawākibī's work heightened the sultan's suspicions of Syrian and Egyptian intrigues, and Rashīd Riḍā's serialization of the book in *al-Manār* reinforced the perception that religious reformers were participating in a conspiracy against the empire.[23]

After Jamāl al-Dīn al-Qāsimī and ʿAbd al-Razzāq al-Bīṭār returned from Egypt, the salafis' sympathies for and relationship with Muḥammad ʿAbduh became well known. Equally well known to Ottoman authorities was ʿAbduh's accommodation to British rule in Egypt. The British named him chief jurisprudent of Egypt in the belief he would reshape legal practices and religious instruction in a fashion amenable to Britain's interests. For his part, ʿAbduh saw in the British the means to attain the influence necessary for reforming Egyptian religious institutions and, by extension, Egyptian society. Therefore the view that ʿAbduh cooperated with British rule was warranted, but to leap from that premise to the conclusion that the Damascene salafis would welcome a British occupation required some imagination.[24]

From the Arabian peninsula came more substantial challenges to the sultan's claim to the caliphate. Throughout the nineteenth century, the Ottomans remained sensitive to signs of a renascence in the Wahhābīs' power. On four occasions in the 1870s and 1880s, the Ottomans deported from Mecca Indian Muslims suspected of propagating "Wahhābī" ideas. In 1902, Saudi-Wahhābī forces reconquered Riyad and displaced the loyalist Rashidi clan as rulers of Najd, causing Sultan Abdülḥamīd to fear the spread of Wahhabism. He hoped that Abū al-Hudā al-Ṣayyādī's cultivation of Arab ulama would nullify the Wahhābī threat. Baghdad's leading salafi of the time, Maḥmūd Shukrī al-Alūsī, had contacts with the Wahhābīs, and thereby attracted the suspicion of Ottoman authorities. Likewise in Syria the Ottomans could not blithely dismiss the possibility that the salafis sympathized with the Wahhābīs.[25]

In another quarter of Arabia, the Zaydī imam of Yemen raised a rebellion against Ottoman attempts to reassert control over that region.[26] Imam Yaḥyā demanded autonomy and pressed his own claim to the caliphate. Syrian troops in the Ottoman force sent to quell the revolt displayed an unwillingness to fight the Yemenis, and many Syrians deserted to the imam's side. The Syrians' treasonous behavior and the imam's claims heightened the sultan's fears of Arab plots against his throne.

The revolt in Yemen, the Wahhābīs' renascence, ʿAbbās Ḥilmī's flirtations with Afghānī and the Young Turks, and Kawākibī's book fueled Ottoman fears of a plot to establish an Arab caliphate. In view of these regional developments, a British/Wahhābī plot with Syrian religious reformers to detach Syria from the empire seemed credible, and conservative ulama exploited Ottoman fears to give credence to their spurious charges against the salafis.

Antisalafism in Action

The five instances of antisalafi persecution between 1905 and 1908 must be seen in the light of the political developments just outlined. On four occasions conservative ulama persuaded Ottoman authorities to investigate Jamāl al-Dīn al-Qāsimī and ʿAbd al-Razzāq al-Bīṭār for alleged subversive activities. In the other incident, the Ottomans suspected Muḥammad ʿAbduh and his followers in Syrian coastal towns of plotting a secessionist movement. Although this incident did not involve the Damascene salafis, it shows how the combination of political trends made religious reformers objects of suspicion.

In June 1905, Ottoman authorities arrested Muḥyi al-Dīn Ḥimādah, former mayor of Beirut and a close associate of Muḥammad ʿAbduh, who had resided near Ḥimādah's home during his exile in Lebanon and married into the Ḥimādah family. In the spring of 1905, Ḥimādah traveled to Egypt and spent several weeks there. Ottoman authorities suspected him of conspiring with ʿAbduh to launch a movement for Syrian independence, and they thought he intended to recruit Syrians to the cause and to raise funds for "an Anglo–Egyptian party." His position as agent of the British Khedivial Mail Steamship and Graving Dock Company stoked the Ottomans' doubts about him. Rashīd Riḍā wrote that Abdülḥamīd's spies in Egypt had reported that Ḥimādah was returning to Beirut armed with a legal decision (fatwā) by ʿAbduh proclaiming the deposition of the sultan, but when police searched Muḥyi al-Dīn's belongings they only found portions of ʿAbduh's Quranic exegesis. The British ambassador in Istanbul intervened to secure Ḥimādah's release.[27]

On the heels of Ḥimādah's arrest, Ottoman police in Beirut, Tripoli, Sidon, and Acre searched the homes of men suspected of complicity with the Beirut notable and ʿAbduh. Police seized books and private papers from Rashīd Riḍā's home and arrested his brother. A biographer of Riḍā related that Riḍā's father was suspected of conspiring with ʿAbduh to set up an Arab state. In the search for forbidden materials smuggled from Egypt, police in Beirut confiscated books from two printing presses. Both Riḍā and the British consul to Beirut attributed the searches to fears that Syria would follow Yemen's move to break away from the empire.[28]

This episode shows how apprehension of Syrian separatism, rebellion in Yemen, British intrigue, and religious reformers' complicity in a secret plot took shape as a bogey in the minds of loyalists to Abdülḥamīd. In the fall of 1906, conservative ulama manipulated a similar set of circumstances to harass the salafis in three interconnected incidents. First, a conservative shaykh accused ʿAbd al-

Razzāq al-Bīṭār of propagating Wahhabism in Damascus. Second, conservative ulama agitated against Jamāl al-Dīn al-Qāsimī for publishing excerpts of classical works that proclaimed ijtihād and attacked emulation. Third, the salafis' enemies charged Bīṭār with hatching a plot to annex Syria to British-ruled Egypt.

A feud between Badr al-Dīn al-Ḥasanī and ʿAbd al-Razzāq al-Bīṭār began in September 1906 when Bīṭār's younger brother Salīm paid Ḥasanī a visit in his room at the Oral Reports College.[29] According to Jamāl al-Dīn al-Qāsimī's account of the incident, Ḥasanī queried Bīṭār in an accusatory tone about the Bīṭārs' relations with a number of Najdi (i.e., Wahhābī) ulama staying in the Maydan. He then accused the Bīṭārs of proclaiming Wahhabism, and Salīm al-Bīṭār denied the charge. Ḥasanī summoned one of his students, who claimed that the Bīṭārs and several of their friends were propagating Wahhābī ideas. Before Shaykh Salīm left, Ḥasanī threatened to discuss the matter with the governor unless the Bīṭārs ceased spreading Wahhabism.

When Shaykh ʿAbd al-Razzāq heard from his brother what had happened, he resolved to see Ḥasanī, with whom he had hitherto maintained cordial relations. The next day the older Bīṭār passed by Jamāl al-Dīn al-Qāsimī's home to ask his friend to join him. Bīṭār informed Qāsimī that Ḥasanī had accused them, Jamāl al-Dīn's brother Qāsim, and Ṭāhir al-Jazā'irī of being Wahhābīs. Qāsimī told Bīṭār he should not bother with Ḥasanī because he held no official position and the exercise of power by ulama had ended with the exile of the powerful Shaykh ʿAbd Allah al-Ḥalabī after the 1860 massacre of Christians. Bīṭār went ahead anyway with his brother Salīm and Shaykh Salīm Samārah.

At the Oral Reports College Bīṭār told Ḥasanī how annoyed he was at the fabrications about his being a Wahhābī, and he urged Ḥasanī not to disturb their friendship. Ḥasanī, unwilling to back down, repeated the charge to Bīṭār, then summoned the student who alleged that he heard Bīṭār declare Wahhābī views. The student, Amīn al-Zabadānī, stated that Bīṭār had denied the efficacy of seeking the prophets' intercession. When Bīṭār denied that, Zabadānī called him a liar and accused him of denying the charge because he feared Ḥasanī. After more angry exchanges between Bīṭār and Zabadānī, the reformer turned to Ḥasanī and told him he did not care what nonsense the young student spoke, but he did hold Ḥasanī responsible for countenancing such insolent behavior. Ḥasanī claimed he wanted to reconcile Bīṭār with Zabadānī, thus placing the elderly shaykh and the young man on the same level while assuming a superior position as arbitrator. Bīṭār refused and left.

News of the confrontation spread, and people divided into two camps. Ḥasanī's backers suggested Bīṭār had become enamored with strange ideas (Wahhabism) in his old age, while Bīṭār's supporters held that Ḥasanī had no right to try to intimidate Shaykh ʿAbd al-Razzāq. Qāsimī observed that some people believed that Ḥasanī sought to dominate the city's ulama.[30]

A few days later one of Bīṭār's students, Muḥammad ʿAlī al-Maydānī, composed a poem ridiculing Badr al-Dīn and recited it at a number of salons.[31] Another one of Bīṭār's students sent a copy of the verse to Ḥasanī, perhaps with Bīṭār's approval. Naturally, this infuriated Ḥasanī and his students, and they responded by going to the governor, before whom they accused Bīṭār of advocating Wahhabism and of letting his students recite derogatory poetry insulting to Ḥasanī and the prophets. Governor Shukrī Pasha turned a copy of the poem over to the jurisconsult, Ṣāliḥ al-Qaṭanā, to decide the issue. Qaṭanā bore a grudge against Ḥasanī, yet harbored no sympathy for the reformers. He told the governor that the poem indeed mocked Ḥasanī, but far from insulting the prophets, it sought their intercession (*tawassala bi-him*). To settle the controversy, the magistrate and Qaṭanā decided to form an investigative council including themselves, a deputy jurisconsult, another prominent shaykh, and an influential notable.[32]

The council held a number of hearings at which Ḥasanī's students, Bīṭār's backers, Bīṭār, and Ḥasanī gave testimony. Zabadānī and another student of Ḥasanī's testified that they had asked Bīṭār about a number of religious issues and that he had replied that to pray to anyone but God is disbelief (*kufr*); that whether saints and martyrs are alive in their tombs cannot be ascertained; that men other than the Companions and the four imams may hold correct legal opinions; that the Wahhābīs are good Muslims; and that Muḥammad ibn ʿAbd al-Wahhāb was a righteous, pious man who guided the people of Najd.

Ḥasanī himself avoided attending the hearings because he felt his standing would suffer were he to submit to the council's authority. Ultimately, he had to attend, indeed at some cost to his dignity. First, Ṣāliḥ al-Qaṭanā arrived for Ḥasanī's session an hour late, probably to deflate his status. When Qaṭanā did show up, Ḥasanī's students entered with their shaykh, but were expelled and told they could attend only with the council's permission. After a desultory session with Ḥasanī, the council decided to drop the matter because Ramadan had commenced and the Ottoman authorities did not want to bother with the squabbles of Damascus's ulama.

In the month since Ḥasanī had tried to intimidate Bīṭār and his camp, Ottoman authorities had lost interest. But before the month of fasting ended, Jamāl al-Dīn al-Qāsimī would fire the next salvo in the battle over how to define Islamic practices and beliefs with an anonymous publication of four excerpts on legal theory by famous classical authorities.[33]

In a letter of September 1906 to Shaykh ʿAbd al-Raḥmān Nasīb, a former magistrate of Syria, Qāsimī wrote that he had recently visited ʿAbd al-Qādir al-Jazā'irī's villa outside Damascus. In the library there he looked through Ibn ʿArabī's *The Meccan Revelations,* and it occurred to him to excerpt for publication its chapter on legal theory. Qāsimī thought it important to publish the chapter because it would acquaint Ibn ʿArabī's many admirers among conservative ulama with his opinions on legal theory, specifically his critique of emulation, advocacy of ijtihād, and adherence to the Ẓāhirī school of jurisprudence.[34]

At the end of September, Qāsimī undertook his annual pre-Ramadan trip in the company of his brother Qāsim and Ṭāhir al-Jazā'irī.[35] While the Bīṭār-Ḥasanī feud approached its climax, Qāsimī and Jazā'irī toured Lebanon. They first visited Qāsimī's relatives in Baalbak, then went to Sofar at the invitation of Shakīb Arslān, the Druze notable who studied with the salafis and later became a leading voice of pan-Islamism after the world war. Arslān and Qāsimī had met several times in Damascus the previous summer.[36] Two days later the small band of Damascene reformers arrived in Beirut, where they stayed with Muḥammad Abū Ṭālib al-Jazā'irī, a fellow salafi.

In Beirut, Qāsimī and his friends left the essays on legal theory with Shaykh Muṣṭafā Najā, who was to supervise their printing. At the time, Najā was Beirut's director of education and jurisconsult of Baalbak, and he later became jurisconsult of Beirut. Qāsimī and his company then visited Sidon for a few days, and on returning to Beirut found the essays printed and ready for distribution. Jamāl al-Dīn had requested that his name not appear on the title page because he knew his enemies would make trouble for him if they knew that he was behind the essays.[37] While in Lebanon Qāsimī followed the latest developments in the Bīṭār-Ḥasanī controversy. Among other news, rumors reached Lebanon intimating that Qāsimī and Jazā'irī had fled Damascus because they feared the ramifications of an airing of the Wahhabism issue.

On returning to Damascus for the start of Ramadan in mid-October, Qāsimī gave five copies of the essays to the jurisconsult, Ṣāliḥ al-Qaṭanā, and attached to them a note explaining that a Beirut publisher had asked him to compile such a collection of classical essays. He added that the former magistrate ʿAbd al-Raḥmān Nasīb was one of many friends who had encouraged him to pursue the project. Qāsimī stated in his account of the ensuing incident that he intended by this message to apprise Qaṭanā of the essays' publication and the support of a former magistrate for them.[38] When some of Qāsimī's friends received batches of the essays, they guaranteed the essays' circulation by placing them in the book market in front of the Umayyad mosque, which was always busy during Ramadan. On discovering the essays, conservative ulama became upset, and one of them tried to prompt the magistrate to take action against Qāsimī, but the magistrate consulted with Qaṭanā, who said he saw no harm in the essays.

Qāsimī's publication disturbed the conservatives because the selections put forth principles that deviated from those of the four recognized legal schools. The excerpt from Ibn ʿArabī indicated its author's adherence to the Ẓāhirī school, thus scoring a point against the exclusive authority of the four Sunni schools.[39] Ibn ʿArabī was one of the most venerated figures in Damascus, especially among Sufis, and his tomb in a suburb of Damascus was an object of popular veneration. Essentially Qāsimī taunted the conservatives with the excerpt from Ibn ʿArabī's magnum opus. The collection's popularity among more progressive ulama delighted Qāsimī, and many religious students studied the essays and sought him out to discuss them.

Toward the end of Ramadan, Asʿad al-Ṣāḥib tried to convince the Ottoman governor to punish Qāsimī for publishing the essays. Ṣāḥib complained to Governor Shukrī Pasha that the essays did great harm, and he asked Shukrī Pasha if he knew that the last governor had threatened to exile Qāsimī for advocating ijtihād. It then happened that ʿAbd al-Raḥmān al-Yūsuf, one of Damascus's most wealthy and powerful notables, entered while Ṣāḥib was casting aspersions on Qāsimī. Though neither a reformer nor an intellectual himself, Yūsuf had friendly relations with the reformers, and he defended Qāsimī and the essays. He told the governor that he had looked over the essays, and he declared that he could not understand them because only true scholars comprehended such matters. He then took Shukrī Pasha aside and told him that Ṣāḥib was known for his envy of other ulama and his habit of slandering them. The governor either believed Yūsuf or chose to ignore yet another dispute among the ulama, because he took no action against Qāsimī. Shukrī Pasha may also have thought that because the essays had been printed and published in Beirut they fell outside his jurisdiction.[40]

The governor's reluctance to involve himself in the ulama's disputes did not dissuade Asʿad al-Ṣāḥib from trying once again to make trouble for the salafis. A month after his fruitless effort to incite the governor against Qāsimī, he accused Bīṭār of plotting Syria's secession from the empire.[41] Ṣāḥib reported to authorities in Istanbul that Bīṭār was corresponding with political figures in Egypt and that he used a relative or in-law named "Ṭayyār" as an intermediary. Shukrī Pasha received an order from Istanbul instructing him to investigate the allegation that Bīṭār was conspiring to annex Syria to Egypt and to deliver Najd to the British. He then summoned ʿAbd al-Raḥmān al-Yūsuf and another notable to ask them their opinions of the report, and they both affirmed Bīṭār's innocence.

Hungry for more information, the governor sent a Damascene officer of the gendarmerie, Aḥmad al-Quḍmānī, to inquire about Bīṭār. Quḍmānī happened to be one of Qāsimī's neighbors, so he went to the salafi to ask if Bīṭār had a relative by the name of "Ṭayyār." The officer found out from Qāsimī and others that no such relative existed, and Shukrī Pasha reported to Istanbul that Bīṭār was innocent. Before Bīṭār learned of his exoneration, he had asked ʿAbd al-Raḥmān al-Yūsuf to accompany him to see the governor. During their meeting Bīṭār ridiculed the notion that he could "deliver" Syria, and Shukrī Pasha reassured Bīṭār that the case was closed, as he had already written to the capital to dispel any lingering doubts.

Thus closed a distressing three-month period for the salafis. Qāsimī later wrote to Rashīd Riḍā that the ongoing controversy over the Bīṭār–Ḥasanī feud and his collection of essays had caused him much anxiety.[42] The salafis enjoyed a period of calm following the stormy fall of 1906, then Qāsimī endured one more instance of persecution before political changes allowed him to openly proclaim salafism.

On March 11, 1908, police entered Qāsimī's room in the Sināniyyah mosque and then his home to seize books and papers. After a thorough investigation of the impounded materials, the authorities returned them to him two months later. Qāsimī alluded in his diary to a stroke of luck: The police had not entered his private library where he kept many forbidden works printed in Egypt; instead they had taken books from a front sitting room. Qāsimī felt alarmed because at that time he was working on a book that he intended to publish without official authorization.[43]

When some conservative ulama heard that the authorities had found nothing incriminating in Qāsimī's books and papers, they objected that the books contained ijtihād that the government inspectors could not detect because only ulama understood such matters. A committee was formed that included the magistrate, the jurisconsult's deputy, a member of the education council, and four members of the administrative council. On reinspecting Qāsimī's books and papers they found no offensive materials, and the magistrate acquitted him. Just two months after Qāsimī got his books back, a military mutiny forced Sultan Abdülḥamīd to restore the constitution, thus marking the dawn of a new stage in the evolution of Ottoman politics and bringing fresh hope to the beleaguered salafis of Damascus.

Between 1896 and 1908, conservative ulama tried on seven occasions to persuade Ottoman authorities to punish the salafis. The conservatives succeeded in embroiling the salafis in controversy and in intimidating them, but none of the actions culminated in the exile or imprisonment of a Damascene salafi, with the minor exception of Qāsimī's one night of incarceration in the police station in 1896. Although the Ottomans worried about the Wahhābīs, the British, and the Egyptian viceroy's ambitions, the Ottoman governors of Syria apparently realized that the salafis posed no threat, even if their ideas bore a resemblance to certain Wahhābī tenets. The mujtahids' trial, the uproar over Zahrāwī's essay, the charges against Bīṭār, and the examination of Qāsimī's papers and books, all ended when Ottoman governors discovered the nature of the salafis' activities. Only in Zahrāwī's case did antisalafi action bear any fruit, his deportation from Syria, but that was because Zahrāwī had already acquired a troublesome reputation.

Conclusion

The conservative ulama represented a faction of religious intellectuals who held fast in the face of the changes wrought by the Tanzimat in Damascus. Professional interests in customary practices and beliefs operative in law courts, mosques, and shrines buttressed the comfortable option of upholding inherited interpretations of Islam. The salafis' critique of emulation and adhering to the legal schools alienated religious court officials. Religious teachers had a stake in perpetuating the curriculum of commentaries and glosses they had studied but which the salafis considered a hindrance to understanding divine scripture. Sufi shaykhs at the popular shrines would lose their livelihoods were Muslims to heed the salafis' call to abandon ritual innovations. Preachers resented the salafis' charge that their use of rhymed prose made sermons incomprehensible and that their sermons perpetuated innovations.

Sultan Abdülḥamīd's patronage of Sufi orders and shaykhs gave the conservatives a respite after the Tanzimat reforms had circumscribed the ulama's authority by establishing secular judicial and educational institutions. Emboldened by the sultan's patronage, conservative ulama took it upon themselves to act as ideological police upholding traditional religious beliefs and the sultan's authority. Though the conservatives could harass the salafis, they never convinced an Ottoman governor to exile or imprison a salafi because the ulama had lost much of their influence by the time the salafis appeared, and because governors of Syria under Abdülḥamīd were preoccupied with more pressing matters such as security, fiscal affairs, and foreign encroachment. To the extent that the conservative ulama could make a plausible case that the salafis represented a political threat to Ottoman rule, they succeeded in engaging the attention of various governors. On closer inspection, the governors found the salafis harmless, and, consequently, took no action against them.

9

Antisalafi Ulama's Interpretations of Islam

Although the constitutional restoration of 1908 did not end the salafis' difficulties with conservative ulama, it did change the political context of their rivalry. In the new balance of political forces, the salafis sided with the Committee of Union and Progress, the strongest constitutionalist party in Syria and the empire. Meanwhile, the conservative ulama remained loyal to Abdülḥamīd and joined with anticonstitution notables to attack the salafis and thereby challenge the CUP. Antisalafi incidents that took place between July 1908 and April 1909 resulted in the defeat of the anticonstitution forces, and thereafter the conservative ulama could no longer persecute the salafis.

On the other hand, the greater press freedom of the constitutional era offered a new medium for opposing salafism, and the conservatives seized the opportunity to use the press to continue their campaign against the salafis. Prior to 1908, conservative ulama of Damascus did not publish refutations of salafism per se. Two anti-Wahhābī essays appeared in 1900, but these did not address the central issues of the salafi agenda. Two works by Yūsuf al-Nabahānī, a Palestinian shaykh, give an idea of the flavor of antisalafi writing in the preconstitutional period.

Damascus's conservative ulama lapsed into political quiescence following their defeat in April 1909. A year later a monthly journal appeared, marking a new phase in the campaign against salafism and a novel development in the conservative interpretation of Islam. This journal, *al-Ḥaqā'iq,* articulated conservatives' objections to salafism and indicated their adjustment to ideas about progress.

Yūsuf al-Nabahānī: Antisalafi Polemist

Yūsuf al-Nabahānī (1849–1932) came from a small Palestinian village near Haifa. His father, a village shaykh, gave him a rudimentary religious education and then sent him to study at al-Azhar. Nabahānī spent seven years there (1865–1872) during which he met Jamāl al-Dīn al-Afghānī and Muḥammad ʿAbduh, then returned to Palestine where he taught in his home village and in nearby Acre. He began his career in the Ottoman religious and civil courts when he became deputy to a subdistrict magistrate in Palestine. In 1875, Nabahānī traveled to Istanbul and resided there for 2½ years. In the imperial capital he worked on the foremost Arabic periodical of the time, *al-Jawā'ib,* and acquired a reputation as a gifted poet. He then moved on to a judicial post in Kurdistan and returned to Istanbul around 1883 when he entered the ranks of Sultan Abdülḥamīd's ulama protegés, apparently after developing an acquaintance with Abū al-Hudā al-Ṣayyādī.[1]

Nabahānī parlayed his connections in Istanbul into higher and more lucrative judicial posts closer to his homeland: five years in Latakia and several months in Jerusalem as chief judge of the (secular) criminal court, then 20 years in Beirut as chief judge of its criminal court. His posts in Latakia and Jerusalem brought him 1,400 piasters per month, and the one in Beirut earned him 3,500 piasters until 1896, when his salary fell to 2,500 piasters as part of a general retrenchment in the budget.[2] After the constitutional restoration, Nabahānī lost his post and went to live in Medina, not to return to Syria until the British drove the Ottoman army out of Palestine.

Nabahānī's career bears a resemblance to that of his patron, Abū al-Hudā. Both men hailed from small villages; the fathers of both were village shaykhs; both men accumulated affiliations to several Sufi orders; both used their poetic talents to ingratiate themselves with powerful figures; both supported Abdülḥamīd's claims to the caliphate; and both firmly opposed the salafi trend. Yet their common backgrounds and sentiments did not keep Nabahānī from eventually deserting Ṣayyādī and attaching himself to the rising star of Aḥmad ʿIzzat al-ʿĀbid, Ṣayyādī's more urbane rival from Damascus.[3]

The spiteful, mocking tone of Nabahānī's writings clearly distinguishes them from the subdued tone of debate in Damascus. This contrast might have sprung from the difference between a dispute among members of a local status group, Damascene ulama, who observed certain limits on public statements because of a residual sense of cordiality, and an unrestricted war of words between figures sharing no such common bonds. Jamāl al-Dīn al-Qāsimī kept his enmity toward Nabahānī a private matter; even after July 1908 when Qāsimī could have publicly condemned Nabahānī with impunity, he never published a harsh word against him or any other adversary. But in private correspondence, Jamāl al-Dīn wrote of Nabahānī in May 1909, "As for 'al-Nabahānī,' let him die in his rage, may God fight such a superstitious man who does harm to many simpletons with his writings. . . . [A] sign of this age is rejecting writings such as his, barren of knowledge and culture."[4] A year later Qāsimī visited Medina and by chance met Nabahānī at a library where Jamāl al-Dīn was copying a manuscript. Qāsimī wrote in his account of his journey to Medina: "While I was writing, the famous Shaykh Yūsuf al-Nabahānī came in, shaykh of the ḥashwiyyah and the tombsters [al-qubūriyyah]. He greeted me and I returned the greeting. He sat down next to me while I was writing. With me was . . . a ḥashwī student who inclines to Nabahānī's opinions, and who does trade with visitors [to Medina] in superstitions and innovations which the true religion rejects."[5]

Nabahānī never attacked Qāsimī but stalked larger prey: Ibn Taymiyyah, the Wahhābīs, Jamāl al-Dīn al-Afghānī, Ṣiddīq Ḥasan Khān, Muḥammad ʿAbduh, Rashīd Riḍā, and Shukrī al-Alūsī. In *Testimonies of Truth on Supplicating the Lord of Creation* (1905), Nabahānī declared that the gate of ijtihād was closed, argued for the efficacy of praying to prophets for intercession, and defended tomb visits. Throughout the book he cited ulama more often than the Quran or oral reports to buttress his points. His central ideas are that no one could claim ijtihād after the tenth century, that contemporary Muslims could not understand the Quran and the Sunnah well enough to derive legal rulings from them, and that Khayr al-Dīn al-Alūsī's *A Clear View* contained many harmful notions.[6]

In Nabahānī's second antisalafi tract he vehemently attacked Afghānī, ʿAbduh, Riḍā, and Alūsī, claiming they falsely postured as religious reformers when they actually sought to destroy Islam and spread atheism. He reiterated his arguments against ijtihād and those for the legal schools, tomb visits, and supplicatory prayers. Both of Nabahānī's works occasioned responses from the reformist camp. Shukrī al-Alūsī wrote a long refutation of *Testimonies of Truth* to reiterate the case against worshiping at tombs and seeking the prophets' intercession; he also defended the Wahhābīs and the restoration of ijtihād. Nabahānī's second work drew a response from Wahhābī ulama and ʿAbd al-Razzāq al-Bīṭār's grandson, Bahjat al-Bīṭār.[7]

Nabahānī's *ad hominem* arguments and his reliance on the sayings of ulama and Sufi saints to defend popular Islam and the legal schools' authority underlines his rejection of the ideas and methods of the salafis and their reformist predecessors. To convince fellow ulama, the salafis had staked out the Quran and the Sunnah as the grounds of their interpretation of Islam. Their assimilation of reason, unity, and progress to a reformist vision of Islam served to persuade Muslims with a "modern" education that religion could provide the basis for reforming the empire. Nabahānī did not provide a conservative alternative to the salafis that addressed these pressing needs, but a group of ulama in Damascus formulated such an alternative in the journal *al-Ḥaqā'iq*.

Al-Ḥaqā'iq and Antisalafism

The publication of a monthly journal, *al-Ḥaqā'iq,* marked the conservative faction's coalescence around a mouthpiece for the expression and elaboration of antisalafism. The journal represented a shift from political harassment to an intellectual critique of the salafis as well as a more positive effort to formulate conservative positions that took account of the ubiquitous yearning for progress. In their arguments the conservatives assimilated slogans and themes that the salafis had used to validate reformist measures, thereby transcending the level of Yūsuf al-Nabahānī's polemics and confronting the salafis on the ground of reasoned argumentation. This discussion of *al-Ḥaqā'iq* focuses on the journal's appropriation of potent symbols wielded by the salafis, the points of divergence on which the conservatives held fast, and the journal's conflation of the salafis with Westernizers.

The first issue of *al-Ḥaqā'iq* came out in August 1910.[8] In the inaugural editorial, the journal's editor, ʿAbd al-Qādir al-Iskandarānī al-Kaylānī, listed five subjects that *al-Ḥaqā'iq* would address: religious sciences, Arabic language, ethics, history, and literature. Iskandarānī described the journal's major themes as researching the causes of decline and progress, refuting false arguments, serving knowledge, and encouraging unity.[9] For three years *al-Ḥaqā'iq* combated both salafi and westernizing (mutafarnij) reformers in Damascus and defended traditional religious practices and beliefs. As the leading organ of antisalafism in the city, *al-Ḥaqā'iq* attracted contributions from prominent opponents of salafism.

In April 1911, the leading Arabist newspaper of Beirut, *al-Mufīd,* published an article about *al-Ḥaqā'iq*. The article stated that the journal was a tool of Shaykh Ṣāliḥ al-Sharīf al-Tūnisī, who briefly led antisalafi forces in Damascus in 1908. In response, *al-Ḥaqā'iq* declared that it was proud that some of its contributors were indeed Tūnisī's disciples, but that the publishers issued the journal to serve religion and to resist European cultural influence, not just to reiterate Tūnisī's ideas. *Al-Ḥaqā'iq* did publish his legal opinions and speeches and called him a great reformer, but its contributors also included members of well-known ulama families, middle ulama, and students of Shaykh Badr al-Dīn al-Ḥasanī.[10]

During its three years of existence, *al-Ḥaqā'iq* published articles on diverse subjects. Of greater interest than the specific issues which the journal addressed is the manner in which it assimilated some of the salafis' slogans to a defense of prevalent religious practices and a critique of salafism. *Al-Ḥaqā'iq* called on Muslims to follow the way of the salaf by adhering to the Quran and the Sunnah. Like the salafis, the conservatives called on Muslims to achieve progress by borrowing European inventions, to unite in the face of European aggression, and to revive true Islamic learning. In the magazine's first issue, Iskandarānī concluded an article by calling Islam the religion of civilization and consultation [*shūrā*] and adding that Islam enjoins its believers to strive for solidarity. Likewise, the journal advocated building factories and borrowing technical means of progress from Europe. *Al-Ḥaqā'iq's* writers stressed that Islam's laws were applicable to modern conditions. For instance, the journal encouraged Muslims to take advantage of the city's new water system because it provided a more sanitary water supply. *Al-Ḥaqā'iq* added its voice to the chorus calling for large commercial ventures, reviving local manufactures to stem the tide of European imports, increasing exports, and improving agriculture by using machinery and introducing new methods of cultivation.[11]

On Islamic unity, *al-Ḥaqā'iq* agreed with the salafis that Muslims had to close ranks to confront an aggressive Europe, but they took opposing positions on how Muslims should unite. The conservatives invoked unity to buttress the sultan's claim on Muslims' loyalty. For instance, Ṣāliḥ al-Tūnisī urged recalcitrant Yemenis to give up their revolt and to rally to the Ottoman sultan-caliph. The ulama writing in *al-Ḥaqā'iq* paid their allegiance to a person, the sultan, who represented Islam, whereas the salafis made abstract beliefs and a set of practices the center of Muslim solidarity.[12]

Al-Ḥaqā'iq also agreed with the salafis that Islam had begun to decline when ignorant men entered the ranks of the ulama. Impostors posing as ulama swindled the masses and humored the whims of rulers by justifying their evil deeds with distortions of religious law. As property and wealth increasingly accrued to the ulama, greedy men pursued and obtained posts that genuine ulama should have held. Muslims could make great strides toward progress only if they would entrust posts to qualified ulama. A disastrous consequence of the ulama's degenerate state was that they had become objects of derision, which made it easier for Westernizing writers to denigrate religion and demand its separation from politics. *Al-Ḥaqā'iq* called on the true ulama to undertake reform by spreading knowledge and combating innovations, by which was meant European ways and manners, not ritual innovations.[13]

The journal's declarations of support for the constitution indicated the rapprochement that took place between the conservative ulama and the CUP around 1910. One article praised the constitution for bringing free speech and press freedom, and another remarked that the ulama could awaken Muslims from their slumber now that they enjoyed freedom of speech.[14]

Al-Ḥaqā'iq's use of the same slogans and positions as the salafis demonstrates, first, that those slogans and positions must have had some efficacy in winning adherents, and second, that a new ideological consensus had emerged that the salafis first articulated in the vocabulary of the ulama. That the conservative ulama called to the way of the salaf, the Quran, and the Sunnah merely tells us that the ground that the salafis occupied was available to all Muslims. The idea that Muslims had to borrow the technical means of progress indicated a wider ideological shift in Damascus. An ideology of progress, first expressed in Damascus in Islamic terms by ʿAbd al-Qādir al-Jazā'irī, had gained acceptance in most quarters by 1910. *Al-Ḥaqā'iq's* support of constitutional government reflected more a tactical political adjustment than an ideological shift. Following the CUP's definitive defeat of Abdülḥamīd in 1909, Damascus's anticonstitution faction accommodated itself to the new dominant political power. The salafis' alliance with the Arabists, whom the CUP came to distrust, facilitated a rapprochement between conservatives and the CUP.

Although conservative ulama incorporated the salafis' more persuasive positions, they staunchly defended practices and beliefs that the salafis attacked. The outstanding issues were the legal schools, emulation, and ijtihād. *Al-Ḥaqā'iq* asserted that Muslims must follow the four Sunni legal schools except in the most pressing circumstances. More than once the journal stated that it represented Sunni beliefs, and denied the label of emulator in preference for follower (*muttabiʿ*). One article defended jurists against their critics (such as ʿAbd al-Ḥamīd al-Zahrāwī), and declared that the books of jurisprudence contain laws suitable to modern circumstances, thus rebutting arguments for ijtihād as a necessary tool of adaptation to changing conditions.[15]

Al-Ḥaqā'iq held that opening the door of ijtihād means abandoning the four imams' rulings. Those imams thoroughly comprehended legal theory, legal precepts, and Arabic; they memorized the Quran and thousands of oral reports; and their learning far surpassed that of the present day's so-called mujtahids. The conservatives considered the salafis upstarts whose claims to practice ijtihād provided pretexts for neglecting religious injunctions. Advocates of ijtihād allegedly made forbidden things allowable (*mubāḥ*) and justified innovations. The conservatives asserted that so-called reformers allowed wine, pork, and European headwear, and the journal alleged that reformers traveled to Europe and Egypt rather than performing the pilgrimage to Mecca.[16]

Al-Ḥaqā'iq also defended practices that the salafis had labeled ritual innovations, including public recitation of oral reports from al-Bukhārī's *al-Ṣaḥīḥ* in order to ward off misfortune, and standing up at the mention of the Prophet's birth.[17]

Some of *al-Ḥaqā'iq's* sharpest attacks on the salafis came in passages describing the salafis as willing accomplices in a pernicious plot to implant Western culture and manners in Muslim society. The journal accused the salafis of sympathizing with Westernizers' efforts to unveil women and send children to schools directed by foreigners. The salafis, whom the journal referred to as spurious reformers [*muntaḥilū al-iṣlāḥ*], discredited Islam by accusing the ulama of rejecting progress and of looking after selfish interests.[18]

In a description of the reform party, *al-Ḥaqā'iq* lumped together men hankering for official posts, advocates of ijtihād, opponents of praying to the prophets, agents of foreign powers, imitators of European manners, and ethnic chauvinists (Arabists). At times *al-Ḥaqā'iq* zeroed in on Westernizers rather than the salafis, as in the inaugural editorial in which Iskandarānī announced his intention to avoid any praise for Western civilization. At another point, the journal attacked Westernizers for mocking the ulama and pressing for the separation of religion and politics. These Westernizers believed that Islam caused backwardness because they were infatuated with European ideas. They thought that Europe had achieved progress only after its people had abandoned religion. *Al-Ḥaqā'iq* discerned an intrinsic European enmity toward Islam and a European plot to invade the Ottoman Empire from within, a plot that consisted of sending teachers to the region to spread atheism. Once they infected a generation of Muslim graduates with the germ of atheism, Westernized "Muslims" would in turn spread the contagion by teaching the next generation of Muslims.[19]

Al-Ḥaqā'iq perceived the embodiment of counterfeit reform and Western cultural influence in Muḥammad Kurd ʿAlī and his publications, *al-Muqtabas* magazine and newspaper. The editors of *al-Ḥaqā'iq* singled out Kurd ʿAlī and his publications for criticism on at least three occasions. In April 1911 an article accused Kurd ʿAlī of denigrating ulama because of his sympathy for Western culture. Kurd ʿAlī had denounced an historical episode of sectarian intolerance, when Sunnis killed Shīʿīs for publicly cursing the first two caliphs, Abū Bakr and ʿUmar. *Al-Ḥaqā'iq* justified such persecution by stating that it was the only way to protect religion from heretics and atheists: How could Kurd ʿAlī label such zeal for religion "fanaticism?" Kurd ʿAlī asserted that waves of religious fanaticism hurt innocent people as well as the guilty. *Al-Ḥaqā'iq* replied that perhaps innocent people had suffered, but were the possibility of innocence to stand in the way of punishing suspected criminals, then chaos would reign, and all thieves, murderers, atheists, and slanderers would go free.[20]

To provide more insight into *al-Ḥaqā'iq's* critique of the salafis and Westernizers, let us examine the journal's treatment of two controversial issues: the proper use of the telegraph and the status in religious law of theatrical performances. In October 1910, Jamāl al-Dīn al-Qāsimī contributed an article to Kurd ʿAlī's daily *al-Muqtabas* in which he justified the practice of relying on telegraphic messages to declare the end of Ramadan. Qāsimī concluded from a recent instance of using the telegraph in this manner in Egypt that ulama and judges were implementing new inventions according to religious law, thus proving that Islam supports civilization.[21]

In response to Qāsimī's article, *al-Ḥaqā'iq* published a rebuttal enumerating the legal stipulations of testimony (*shahādah*) and of the witness (*shāhid*). Because a telegraphic report does not fulfill those stipulations, it cannot be the basis for declaring the end of Ramadan. To emphasize the telegraph's unreliability, *al-Ḥaqā'iq* cited instances of erroneous telegraphic messages. The journal then recounted Qāsimī's arguments for using the telegraph to inform people that Ramadan has begun or ended. Qāsimī could only establish that a telegraphic report was equivalent to the report of one man (*khabar al-āḥād*). According to religious law, such a report can neither establish the new moon of Ramadan nor that of the next month if the sky is clear. At most, one can use an isolated report to begin fasting if one finds it credible. In subsequent issues, *al-Ḥaqā'iq* published letters and articles by ulama rebutting Qāsimī.[22]

Qāsimī responded to the articles in *al-Ḥaqā'iq* with an essay entitled *Guiding Mankind to Acting According to the Telegraphic Report*. He argued that according to a Prophetic oral report the ruling for Ramadan's commencement and termination can be based on an isolated report and does not require testimony. He also used nontextual arguments, such as general welfare (*al-maṣāliḥ al-mursalah*) to justify using telegraphic reports.[23]

Some of *al-Ḥaqā'iq's* most biting criticisms of the salafis and Westernizers appeared in the wake of a theatrical performance by high school students depicting an Arab hero of Andalusia. The Umayyad mosque's preacher, Shaykh Ḥasan al-Usṭuwānī, gave a Friday sermon in which he censured the performance. *Al-Ḥaqā'iq* published several articles and letters by ulama who proclaimed that Islam forbids theatrical performances. Most of the ulama justified their ruling on the grounds that plays contain slander, lies, satire, and effeminate behavior by boys, in essence equating the fictional depiction of characters with intentional lies. One of the articles against theater named ʿAbd al-Razzāq al-Bīṭār, Jamāl al-Dīn al-Qāsimī, and four other ulama who attended the play, and insinuated that these men had to account for their tacit endorsement of theater.[24]

Why *al-Ḥaqā'iq* ceased publication after its third year is unclear, but its termination did not mark the end of antisalafism in Damascus. Rather, *al-Ḥaqā'iq* signaled the beginning of more elaborate arguments against salafism, and the continued strength of the conservative ulama manifested itself in an efflorescence of anti-Wahhābī tracts in the early 1920s. The authors of these tracts, including ʿAbd al-Qādir al-Iskandarānī, did not refrain from publishing them under their real names, whereas the new leader of the salafis, Muḥammad Bahjat al-Bīṭār, put out two essays defending the Wahhābīs under pseudonyms, a sign of the salafis' chronic weakness.[25]

Conclusion

Before 1908, the conservatives exploited the political situation to prompt Ottoman authorities to harass the salafis. The outcome of events in 1908–1909 heartened the salafis and dismayed the conservative ulama, who could no longer count on financial subsidies and the government's ideological antipathy toward religious reform. Unable to persecute the salafis after Abdülḥamīd's deposition in April 1909, the conservative ulama took up the pen to criticize their rivals.

By calling on Muslims to follow the way of the salaf and to refer to the Quran and the Sunnah as authoritative sources of how Muslims should worship and live, *al-Ḥaqā'iq* pulled the rug of Islamic legitimacy from under the salafis. That the salafis and the conservatives both claimed to stand for sacred principles shows that they shared a general outlook according to which Islam was the ultimate authority for right and wrong, true and false.

The conservative ulama's espousal of acquiring the technical means of progress demonstrated that a growing consensus overwhelmed resistance to European inventions. Once restricted to a faction of the empire's ruling elite, the ideology of progress had become generally accepted. The dominance of the Tanzimat reform party, the perpetuation of the campaign for material improvements under Sultan Abdülḥamīd, and the CUP's ascent to power created a political environment favorable to the anchoring of ideas about progress in Ottoman society.

A more detailed study of the conservative ulama would establish the timing of their adoption of the slogan of progress. The contrast between Nabahānī's *ad hominem* tracts and *al-Ḥaqā'iq's* adoption of more reasoned discourse suggests an important transition in the conservative faction's outlook. However, that transition did not signify a convergence of conservative and salafi streams of thought. Rather it indicated the conservatives' recognition of the efficacy of some of the salafis' arguments and an attempt to negate the salafis' rhetorical advantages. Substantial differences between the parties remained: *al-Ḥaqā'iq* did not yield on ijtihād, emulation, and adherence to the legal schools, and the journal defended popular religious practices and beliefs.

Furthermore, deep political divisions continued to characterize the salafi–conservative rivalry. The salafis' support for the CUP melted away in the fall of 1909, and they threw in their lot with the empire's decentralist faction, itself a loose coalition of ethnic minorities and CUP dissidents rather than a close-knit party. When the salafi-Arabist camp became alienated from the CUP, the city's conservative notables and ulama moved closer to the ruling party in order to bolster their local power and to obtain a powerful ally in their disputes with Damascus's reformers.[26]

10

Salafis and Arabists in Politics, 1908–1914

The constitutional restoration of 1908 heralded a new age of politics in the Ottoman Empire. Syrians witnessed a period of greater press freedom than before, the emergence of political parties contesting general and local elections, and the rise to influence of social groups hitherto excluded from political participation.[1] The salafis celebrated the new political order in the belief that it signaled the triumph of the forces of reform and progress, but they soon learned that their opponents would not relinquish power without a fight.

An overview of the salafis' and the Arabists' experiences during this dynamic period will shed light on two questions. First, what motivations lay behind their political behavior? For approximately 15 years before 1908, they cooperated with Turkish constitutionalists in opposing Sultan Abdülḥamīd's rule, but within 18 months of the constitutional restoration the former allies became adversaries, and the Syrians launched a movement for administrative decentralization. The motivations for their opposition to, first, Sultan Abdülḥamīd and, then, to the CUP resemble those described by western scholars concerned with explaining why western intellectuals engage in political activities. They observe that intellectuals become alienated from the dominant political order when they find career opportunities blocked and when they experience a sense of status disparity, the gap between their high self-esteem and their meager power and wealth.[2]

Second, what limited the salafis' and Arabists' political achievements? The ability of their conservative opponents to stir up crowds against them indicates the liberal camp's vulnerability. The CUP's willingness to abandon its erstwhile supporters stemmed from its assessment of the balance of political forces in Damascus, where the salafis and Arabists never attracted a mass base. In their relations with other social groups lay the roots of their political weakness.

Rallying to the Constitution

Since the 1890s, the salafis and the Arabists had favored the restoration of constitutional government, hence their enthusiasm for the news of July 24, 1908. The salafis showed their approval by attending private celebrations and elaborating arguments to justify constitutional government in Islamic terms. The Arab Renaissance Society organized public demonstrations, while members of the senior circle emerged as leaders in Damascus's branch of the CUP.

The announcement of the Ottoman constitution's restoration brought no immediate public response in Damascus; however, Jamāl al-Dīn al-Qāsimī expressed his delight in his diary on July 24, 1908:

> A telegraph [message] from Grand Vizier Said Pasha came to the provinces today in accordance with the issuing of the sultanic decree to implement the constitution and to elect members of Parliament. Thus have coincided the freedom of America on July 4, the freedom of France on July 14, and the freedom of the Ottoman Empire on July 24.[3]

Qāsimī wrote in the afterword to his book *The Proofs of Monotheism* that he completed his revisions,

> [i]n the week during which the Ottoman nation was granted constitutional practice based on the principles of justice, respect for consultation, spreading the sciences, and liberating the people from the chains of tyranny. Praise God for that week which toppled the monarchy, altered the country's condition, and transformed the land. The former life has been cast off, the life of lethargy and humiliation, captivity, weakness, and ignorance, and it has been replaced by the life of might, energy, power, knowledge, and solidarity. To you, our Lord, is praise for clearing away the hated clouds, for removing floods of sorrows, for making the sky rain down blessings, for making streams of dignity flow.[4]

Public manifestations of support for the constitution began July 31 and continued through the first two weeks of August. The British consul described popular demonstrations, street decorations, illuminations on public buildings, and rallies at public gardens. The attendance of the governor and military commanders at some of the rallies encouraged local partisans of the constitution to organize their own celebrations. On August 6, the Arab Renaissance Society held a public meeting at a theater at which several members delivered speeches. Salīm al-Jazā'irī, Asʿad Darwīsh, and ʿAbd al-Raḥmān Shahbandar, all of whom had belonged to the senior circle, attended and spoke. The only speech that has come down to us is one by Ṣalāḥ al-Dīn al-Qāsimī entitled "The Turkish Firmament," in which he lauded the new age of freedom, justice, and progress based on a constitutional government.[5]

The Arab Renaissance Society's gathering affirmed the younger Arabists' solidarity with the CUP. Meanwhile former senior circle members, both Turks and Arabs, emerged as leaders of the Committee's local branch. Ḥusayn Avnī, director of public instruction since 1897, became head of the branch and, according to a contemporary account, the most powerful figure in Damascus. Asʿad Darwīsh had belonged to the CUP before July 1908, and he became the chief of police. Salīm al-Jazā'irī, by then an officer in the Ottoman army, was another member of the local CUP branch who came from the senior circle.[6]

A few days after the Arab Renaissance Society's celebration, a private gathering took place bringing together an altogether different group. Salīm al-Kuzbarī, a prominent shaykh, invited leaders of the CUP and fellow ulama and notables to his home. The list of invitees reads like a directory of Damascene notables: ʿAbd al-Raḥmān al-Yūsuf, Aḥmad al-Shamʿah, ʿAbd Allah al-Jazāʾirī, and others. Kuzbarī also hosted such leading liberals as Rafīq al-ʿAẓm, Asʿad Bey Darwīsh, and Jamāl al-Dīn al-Qāsimī.[7] ʿAbd al-Raḥmān al-Yūsuf delivered an impromptu speech on the deeds of the army (which had mutinied to force the sultan to restore the constitution), and he asked the notables to swear allegiance to the army to uphold the constitution. After Rafīq al-ʿAẓm and Asʿad Darwīsh addressed the distinguished audience, Yūsuf stood to shake hands with the latter and declared his loyalty to the CUP. Then Qāsim al-Qāsimī read a speech his brother had composed entitled "The Status of the Constitution in Religion."

The setting for Jamāl al-Dīn's piece on constitutional government differed from Ṣalāḥ al-Dīn's speech to the Arab Renaissance Society's meeting where the audience was already committed to the new regime. By contrast, Jamāl al-Dīn addressed skeptical notables and ulama. Under Abdülḥamīd, conservative ulama had enjoyed a respite from the disquieting policies and measures of the Tanzimat period. They reacted to the July 24 coup by speaking out against the constitution on the grounds that it would abrogate divine laws and institute laws of human invention. Qāsimī responded to the conservatives' suggestion that constitutional government is un-Islamic with his speech, in which he argued that a constitution harmonizes with Islamic principles. Qāsimī began by stating that a constitution resembles precepts of jurisprudence in that both are derived by ijtihād and extracted from the Quran, the Sunnah, consensus, and analogy.[8] To support his position, he cited recent authorities who had written that religious precepts could underpin constitutional law. For the sake of ulama in the audience, Qāsimī referred to classical authorities who had distilled general principles from religious law: consider public welfare and avert harmful things (*iʿtibār al-maṣāliḥ wa dar' al-mafāsid*). A constitution provides a way to uphold these general Islamic principles.

Qāsimī also undertook to explain the meaning of freedom to his listeners, some of whom equated freedom with licentiousness:

> If the word freedom has nearly intoxicated the people . . . they have a right, for the joy of release after bondage and of freedom after enslavement is a joy surpassing description and definition. However, the rational one knows that freedom, if not circumscribed by religious manners and protected by a bulwark of effective morals, is not the long-sought goal. Therefore, it is obligatory to observe the manners of religion, to cling to the bonds of certainty, to be rightly led by the prophets' and the messengers' guidance, and to follow sincere, wise men.[9]

Jamāl al-Dīn took the opportunity to assert his conviction that education and knowledge are essential bases for progress:

> To covet knowledge, to dedicate oneself to acquiring it and striving night and day to obtain its general and specific truths. Knowledge! Knowledge! No nation has reigned except by knowledge, no nation has risen except by knowledge, no nation has become great except by knowledge. Therefore make it your ambition to

obtain knowledge, to increase knowledge, and to give all effort [*al-ijtihād fī*] to learning and teaching.[10]

After this encomium to knowledge, Qāsimī called on his listeners to adhere to their religion with resolve, "For by religion success is strengthened and salvation is completed."[11] He closed his speech by exhorting the notables and ulama to join in a common effort to strengthen and advance the homeland.

The rhetorical purpose of Qāsimī's speech is evident. He offered a legitimation of the constitution by claiming that rather than violating religious law, it fully accords with fundamental principles of Islam. He interpreted freedom in a fashion designed to allay conservatives' anxieties, explaining that genuine freedom keeps within the bounds of religion. Furthermore, the frequent references to classical jurists, religious manners, and prophets bespeak Qāsimī's ability to employ the ulama's idiom to validate the new political situation.

Qāsimī expanded his explanation of and justification for constitutional government in an unpublished essay entitled "The Basis of Laying Down the Constitution."[12] He wrote that a constitution consists of laws pertaining to transactional matters of jurisprudence, the military, leadership, education, and finances. The constitution protects individuals from the aggression and tyranny of rulers and restrains the hand of corrupt officials. Making government consultative under a sultan means that every town of a certain population elects qualified men with knowledge of civil laws. All of the representatives meet in an assembly headed by the sultan, and they contemplate ways to improve the administration of the empire.

Consultative government provides a way to end despotic rule, which oppressed Muslims ever since the end of the age of the rightly guided caliphs, and which weakened the Muslim nation after it had been mighty and prosperous. Current reformers installed a consultative government to allow the people to choose their rulers and to safeguard their rights against arbitrary violations, such as imprisonment and fines without just cause. At the same time a constitutional regime guarantees freedom, which Qasimi construed to mean freedom to practice one's religion. Christians and Jews can practice their religions without fear of molestation, while Muslims are free to follow any legal school as long as they professed the faith and performed the pillars of Islam. Freedom most certainly does not mean the license to commit acts forbidden by the Quran and the Sunnah.

The virtue of a constitution lies in its allowing for changing laws according to need and based on the principle of safeguarding the public welfare. Jamāl al-Dīn traced this principle to the writings of medieval jurists (Najm al-Dīn al-Ṭūfī, Ibn Qayyim, Ibn Taymiyyah) to attest its authenticity as an essential element of Islam. He closed his essay by claiming that a constitution supports religion and offers the firmest way to preserve rights.

Qāsimī's speech and essay on constitutional government contain both his justifications and expectations of the new regime. As with his claims for ijtihād and free exercise of reason, he couched his argument in Islamic principles extracted from scripture and classical texts. Jamāl al-Dīn favored constitutional government in part because he believed that under such a government he could propagate his views without fear of persecution; in fact, he first published his writings in Damascus soon after July 1908. Furthermore, the salafis and the Turkish constitutionalists had been allies since the 1890s, and that gave Qāsimī reason to believe that he and his party would enjoy not only freedom but influence under the new regime. Jamāl al-Dīn did gain a measure of freedom in the constitutional period, but he became disillusioned when it became clear that he and his fellow salafis would remain marginal figures in local religious and educational affairs.

On the other hand, Ṭāhir al-Jazā'irī held less sanguine views about the new regime. When his friends in Damascus heard that Ṭāhir distrusted the CUP, they dismissed him as an inveterate malcontent.[13] Yet Jazā'irī certainly had a better grasp of the currents in the ideologically mixed Turkish constitutionalist movement than his colleagues in Damascus. His contact with Turkish reformers stretched back 30 years, he spoke Turkish, and while in Cairo he met with representatives of the various Turkish factions. The Turkish constitutionalists fell into two camps, one for a strong central government to hold the empire together, the other advocating a decentralized structure of administration designed to satisfy the ethnic minorities' desires for greater autonomy while maintaining the empire's integrity. Ṭāhir probably knew that the CUP included men who represented the centralist tendency, and he feared their ascendance. At first glance, one might doubt the veracity of the account of Jazā'irī's skepticism of the new regime and regard it as an embellishment intended to impress readers with Ṭāhir's wisdom, but it would explain why Jazā'irī chose to stay in Cairo while Rafīq al-ʿAẓm and ʿAbd al-Ḥamīd al-Zahrāwī rushed back to Syria.[14]

The salafis and the Arabists took advantage of the favorable political climate to declare their allegiance to the constitutional regime. The Arabists joined with Turkish officers in organizing celebrations of the event, while the salafis endowed the constitution with legitimacy by proclaiming its harmony with Islamic principles. The conservative ulama, though, were neither convinced by Qāsimī's speech nor comforted by the prospect of their rivals' ascent on the coattails of the CUP. Sultan Abdülḥamīd remained on the throne, and his survival gave the antisalafis hope they could regain their former status if they took action.

The Conservative Reaction

Feroz Ahmad noted in his study of the Committee of Union and Progress that it took several years before the Committee consolidated its power in the empire. The CUP's bastion of strength lay in Macedonia among Turkish officers of the Third Army, while its hastily established provincial branches gave more an illusion of strength than a structured foundation of widespread support.[15] The CUP's trump card was its influence in the army, but even there the CUP would be challenged in the first year of the constitutional period. In Damascus conservative elements tested the CUP's staying power in October 1908 and again in April 1909, and on both occasions struck at the salafis, the most vulnerable group supporting the CUP.

During the first weeks of August, several societies appeared in Damascus to organize proconstitution forces. Army officers founded the largest one, the Liberty Society, which enrolled over 100 officers by August 12. Other societies included the

Medical, Commercial, and Free Ottomans societies. The salafis helped launch a society for advancing education. Qāsimī, Bīṭār, Salīm al-Bukhārī, and Rafīq al-ʿAẓm attended meetings headed by Ḥusayn Avnī, chief of the CUP branch and director of education.[16]

The new freedom to form societies provided conservatives with the opportunity to organize too. Ulama "anxious to conserve and uphold Islam against the liberal views of the Young Turks" set up an Ulama Society and agitated against allowing unveiled women to appear in public.[17] These ulama had good reason to oppose the new regime, for Abū al-Hudā al-Ṣayyādī, the conservative ulama's patron, had been arrested and removed to an island in the Bosphorus, and ʿIzzat al-ʿĀbid, the other patron of Damascene conservatives, also fell from power.

Furthermore, the CUP dismissed lower officials of the ancien régime in Damascus. By early October the ranks of former officials included six district heads, the secretary of the religious court, the head of the administrative council (Muḥammad Fawzī al-ʿAẓm), and 30 others. According to Rashīd Riḍā, disgruntled former officials combined with conservative ulama to oppose the CUP. In addition to protesting the appearance of unveiled women, the ulama denounced CUP members for their irreverent behavior, in particular their failure to observe the Ramadan fast. Riḍā wrote that a number of leading notables bitterly resented the prestige and influence accruing to Asʿad Darwīsh, Salīm al-Jazā'irī, and Ḥusayn Ḥaydar, prominent members of the CUP.[18]

The liberal party threw down the gauntlet in September when half a dozen well-known partisans of the CUP appeared on the list of candidates for parliamentary elections scheduled for November. The list featured Arabists (ʿAbd al-Wahhāb al-Inklīzī, Shukrī al-ʿAsalī), members of the CUP (Ḥusayn Ḥaydar, Asʿad Darwīsh), and the salafi shaykh Salīm al-Bukhārī.[19] In a daring attempt to thwart the CUP's chances for electoral success, the conservative opposition incited a riot against the Committee toward the end of October on the last night of Ramadan. The outburst represented not only an attack on the CUP, but an escalation of the campaign against the salafis as well.

The ostensible target of the riot was Rashīd Riḍā, who came to Damascus while touring Syria and Lebanon. Riḍā had already suffered an attack during his Syrian journey when a man struck him on the head with a club in Tripoli. On Thursday evening, October 22, Riḍā arrived at Damascus's train station, where Qāsimī, Bīṭār, ʿUthmān al-ʿAẓm (Rafīq's brother), and ʿAbd al-Raḥmān al-Yūsuf had gathered to greet him. Qāsimī rode with Riḍā in a carriage to ʿAẓm's home, where Riḍā stayed during his visit. The next day at the Umayyad mosque, Riḍā gave an impromptu lecture in which he urged his listeners to strive for progress by learning practical skills and sciences such as mathematics, economics, and the natural sciences. With a command of those fields of knowledge, Muslims would be able to manufacture arms to defend their land and construct railroads and trains to advance commerce. By combining religious teachings with new technology, Muslims could achieve strength. When Riḍā finished, the notables and ulama in attendance invited him to speak again the next day. He returned to ʿUthmān al-ʿAẓm's home where he spent the evening in conversation with Qāsimī, Bīṭār, Yūsuf, and others.[20]

Meanwhile, the enemies of the salafis and the CUP met to devise a way to disrupt Riḍā's next lesson. One of the conspirators approached Ṣāliḥ al-Tūnisī, who had recently arrived in Damascus. Five years before, Tūnisī had badgered Muḥammad ʿAbduh for his "Wahhabism" when ʿAbduh came to Tunis, so he suited the task the plotters had in mind. Riḍā later claimed that a client of Abū al-Hudā al-Ṣayyādī promised to compensate Tūnisī for a recently lost stipend if he cooperated.[21]

On October 24, Riḍā passed the afternoon at Qāsimī's home looking at manuscripts of Quranic exegeses in his host's library. Then they went to the Umayyad mosque where Riḍā gave a lesson before a large audience.[22] He reiterated his call to couple Islam with modern sciences (*al-ʿulūm al-ʿaṣriyyah*) in order to attain progress, and he suggested ways to simplify religious instruction for lay Muslims. When he explained the meaning of polytheist (*mushrik*) he stated that it denotes one who prays to intercessors rather than to God. At that point, Ṣāliḥ al-T ūnisī strode toward Riḍā and interrupted by calling for the congregation's attention, thus causing a commotion. Riḍā hushed the crowd, and T ūnisī proceeded to make two statements. First, he proclaimed the legitimacy of tomb visits and supplicating saints for God's blessings. He warned the people to avoid anyone who forbids those practices, such as the Wahhābīs, who led Muslims astray and rebelled against the sultan. Second, T ūnisī declared that Muslims have an obligation to emulate the imams of the legal schools, and he added that acting on the basis of jurisprudence texts is the same as following the Quran and the Sunnah. In a parting shot at Riḍā's aside on polytheists, T ūnisī asked if praying to the saints for intercession, belief in saints' miracles, and adhering to the legal schools were all polytheistic.

Riḍā replied that T ūnisī's objections missed the point of the lesson, in which Riḍā intended to explain how to simplify religious education. He tried to deflect the charge of Wahhabism by stating that he believed in visiting tombs for meditation, and by praising the imams of the legal schools. Before he could resume his lesson, however, Shaykh ʿAbd al-Qādir al-Khaṭīb rose to urge the people to follow the imams and to denounce the Wahhābīs, alluding to Riḍā. The crowd grew restive, and ʿUthmān al-ʿAẓm headed off further trouble by announcing that the lesson was over and inviting to his home anyone interested in discussing controversial matters with Riḍā. As Riḍā made his way out of the mosque, the din grew louder, and conservative ulama shouted insults at him.

When word of the incident reached the authorities, Police Chief Asʿad Darwīsh had T ūnisī arrested and interrogated for inciting a riot. This move by a representative of a party suspected of harboring antireligious sentiments could not have come at a less propitious time. After all, it was the last night of Ramadan, the eve of the breaking of the fast; an evening when the mosques and streets would be choked with thousands of the faithful; an evening when religious feeling would be intense, and police action against a shaykh could easily trigger a reaction by the crowds. One of Riḍā's friends, ʿAlī al-Jazā'irī, heard about T ūnisī's detention and realized it could kindle a disturbance. He went to the police station to release T ūnisī on his, Jazā'irī's, recognizance. But Asʿad Bey's misstep had already handed the plotters a pretext to oppose him and the CUP directly. The conservatives sent men to the Umayyad and other mosques to rally believers to protect the ulama from the CUP, which allegedly sought to get rid of the ulama and wipe out Islam. Paid agents aroused a mob to chant, "Down with Asʿad, down with the Committee, down with the constitution! Long live the governor!"[23]

Qāsimī described the mob action in his diary:

> After the *tarāwīḥ* prayers [evening devotions after breaking fast], the ḥashwiyyah turbaned ones in the Umayyad mosque called out; they announced to the worshipers the demise of religion, and they began to lament, cry, and shout. They roused them [the worshipers] to join together to go to the government building. Then they [the ḥashwiyyah ulama] led them [the worshipers] out, and large numbers followed them, for it was the eve of the feast [the last night of Ramadan before the breaking of the month of fasting] and it goes without saying how crowded the markets are [at that time]. The crowd went to the government building and asked for [Ṣāliḥ al-Tūnisī]. They were told that he had been released, but they did not believe it. They shouted and clapped until he was brought from the home of Amīr ʿAlī Pasha [al-Jazāʾirī]. When they saw him, they applauded, put him in a carriage, shouted abuse of al-Sayyid Rashīd, and called for killing him.[24]

Qāsimī did not mention that before ʿAlī al-Jazāʾirī arrived with Tūnisī, the crowd had stormed the government building hoping to liberate him. A number of men headed for Police Chief Asʿad Darwīsh's office, but they found it defended by a band of strongmen from the Qanawat quarter. The latter group held its ground, thereby saving three men inside, including Asʿad Bey and Ḥusayn Ḥaydar.[25] As for Rashīd Riḍā, he had learned from ʿUthmān al-ʿAẓm that the disturbance was part of a plot and that Tūnisī was not its author. Rather, the plotters were more powerful men who sought to influence the elections for Parliament. One of ʿAẓm's relatives, ʿAbd Allah al-Muʾayyad al-ʿAẓm, advised Riḍā to leave Damascus as soon as possible, and the next morning he departed by train.[26]

The riot also forced Asʿad Darwīsh's hasty flight to Beirut. He then went to Salonica and Istanbul, where he reported to the CUP's central councils on the October 24 outbreak. Asʿad Bey secured the dismissal of the governor of Syria for failing to head off the outbreak. According to some accounts, Governor Shukrī Pasha rode in a carriage with Tūnisī after the shaykh's release, and he advised the military commander against ordering troops to quell the uprising.[27]

While Riḍā and Asʿad Bey fled Damascus, Qāsimī and Bīṭār stayed to bear the brunt of the conservatives' wrath. The antisalafi ulama accused Qāsimī and Bīṭār of sharing Riḍā's Wahhābī views, and they instigated crowds against the two men. Qāsimī's enemies even tried to have him relieved of his posts at the Sinānīyyah mosque. In this intimidating atmosphere, both salafi shaykhs secluded themselves in their homes, and for three months Jamāl al-Dīn abandoned his posts. During that time he went out only for the Friday congregational prayer at a mosque near his home.[28] Ten days after the outbreak, Qāsimī wrote in his diary: "Since the day of al-Shaykh Rashīd Riḍā's story on 29 Sha'ban until today, my brothers and I are annoyed and distressed, staying at home because the townspeople plot against us and accuse my brother ʿĪd of causing the disturbance."[29] Three months passed before Jamāl al-Dīn ventured to return to his duties at the mosque, and Bīṭār kept to his house five weeks longer.[30]

The Ramadan incident marked a temporary setback for constitutional forces in Damascus. CUP leaders Asʿad Darwīsh and Ḥusayn Ḥaydar fled, the salafis were intimidated and isolated, and Rashīd Riḍā made a hurried exit. Even the wealthy, powerful ʿAbd al-Raḥmān al-Yūsuf suffered a browbeating from the conservative jurisconsult, Ṣāliḥ al-Qaṭanā, who insulted Yūsuf's liberal views. The CUP eventually recovered from its setback, although its list fared poorly in the November parliamentary elections.[31]

The constitutional forces broadcast their staying power on the occasion of the opening of the Ottoman parliament on December 17, 1908, when the CUP organized official celebrations to greet the resumption of parliamentary government.[32] Early in the morning students and professors of the medical college marched through the city singing freedom songs. The Ottoman military commander met them and thanked them for their demonstration of support. Then began an official parade that included the military commander, former Governor Shukrī Pasha, high-ranking officers and civilian officials, and European consuls. At 8:00, cannons were fired to mark the opening of parliament, and celebrations continued all day.

That evening the Arab Renaissance Society opened a new public reading room. At this inaugural meeting, Society members delivered speeches on the social benefits of public libraries and their history in Syria, the purpose and history of the Society, and educational reform. By early November the Society had changed its name to the Syrian Renaissance Society, in compliance with the law of associations that banned societies representing ethnic interests. The publication on December 17 of Muḥammad Kurd ʿAlī's *al-Muqtabas* daily newspaper signaled another gain for the Arabists and the Syrian Renaissance Society. In the first issue, Kurd ʿAlī included an article about the Society and announced the time and place of its library's opening.[33] In subsequent issues, *al-Muqtabas* reported on the Society's meetings and activities, and published articles by Society members, older Arabists, and salafis.

While Qāsimī and Bīṭār remained in seclusion, the Society used its reading room to offer night courses in Arabic for illiterate artisans and traders. A salafi shaykh, Aḥmad al-Nuwaylātī, taught the lessons. It seems the Society chose Nuwaylātī because he had attracted a following among the illiterate to his evening religion lessons at the Umayyad mosque. In March 1909, the Society formed a committee to draft a charter, and in early April the general membership ratified it. The Society then proceeded to elect its first board of officers.[34]

In the spring of 1909, the Syrian Renaissance Society was enjoying its new freedom to publish, teach, and organize, and the salafis emerged from seclusion, but at the same time conservative forces were flocking to a newly formed anti-CUP party. Officially founded in Istanbul on April 5, 1909, the Muḥammadan Union centered on the figure of Darvīsh Vaḥdetī and his newspaper, *Volkān.* Since he had begun publishing in November 1908, Vaḥdetī vehemently attacked the CUP for its members' affectation of European manners. He did not explicitly denounce the constitution, but he did advocate the introduction of religious law to the secular courts. Even before Vaḥdetī formally announced the Muḥammadan Union's formation, it spread to Damascus, where it attracted 1,000 signatures to a petition supporting the application of religious law. The Union's leaders in Damascus included antisalafis like Ṣāliḥ al-T ūnisī and ʿAbd al-Qādir al-Khaṭīb.[35]

In Istanbul on April 13, mutinous soldiers joined with religious students and preachers in an uprising to oust the CUP from the capital. When news of the Committee's defeat reached Damascus, partisans of the Muḥammadan Union rejoiced.[36] The Union's leaders in Damascus wanted to celebrate the April 13 coup with a procession, decorations, and illuminations to match the festivities attending the constitutional restoration, but the governor and the military commander forbade marches to the Umayyad mosque, the garrison, and the governor's residence. Instead, the Union posted declarations against promulgating any law contrary to Islamic principles.

Once again the conservative ulama put the heat on the salafis as the tide of imperial politics turned against the CUP and its allies. Reports reached Cairo that Tūnisī and Khaṭīb were urging mobs to kill the "Wahhābīs."[37] Before anything so drastic occurred, a pro-CUP army entered Istanbul on April 24 to cut short the conservatives' ascent, and on April 27, the National Assembly deposed Sultan Abdülḥamīd. Events in Istanbul caused the dissolution of the Muḥammadan Union in Damascus, and its partisans scurried into obscurity while leaders destroyed membership rolls. At the end of May, authorities arrested three of the Union's leaders and sent them to the capital to stand trial.[38] Some weeks later, the police apprehended Ṣāliḥ al-Tūnisī. Qāsimī wrote to a friend in Jeddah:

> As for [Ṣāliḥ al-Tūnisī] who incited the well-known riot against the owner of *al-Manār,* I now send you the good news that he has been accused of belonging to the corrupt Ḥamīdian society [the Muḥammadan Union], whose members the deposed sultan dispatched to overthrow the constitution and restore tyranny in the name of religion. About a week ago . . . he was arrested in the marketplace and thousands of childish folk followed him. At the police station he was interrogated. Then he was released while his answers were being inspected. Now the government is intensifying its search for him because he fled and hid. God disgrace him and his group.[39]

Qāsimī went on to describe his sufferings in the wake of the Ramadan riot, then he added:

> Now God has taken divine revenge on them [Jamāl al-Dīn's adversaries]. Every one who stood against us has been accused of belonging to the corrupt society [the Muḥammadan Union]. Some of them have been exiled, some interrogated by the government, some are in flight, some in hiding, some are terrified, and so on. Praise God for giving us victory over them. We will see more of His benevolence and favor, for God does not squander the wage of the patient.[40]

Having survived the last two eruptions of antisalafism, Qāsimī now reveled in his enemies' discomfiture. Moreover, the CUP's consolidation in Istanbul after Abdülḥamīd's deposition augured well for the salafis and their Arabist allies, who had thrown their lot in with the constitutionalist movement since the 1890s, rejoiced at the restoration of July 1908, rallied support for the new regime, and then weathered the conservatives' counterattacks in October 1908 and April 1909. In the summer of 1909, then, Damascus's liberal camp had good reason to believe that halcyon days had finally come. They had, but they were numbered.

Rupture with the CUP

The alienation of the salafis and the Arabists from the CUP comprised one of many episodes in the tale of sour relations between Arabs and Turks. Zeine Zeine located the origins of Arab nationalism as a political movement in the Arabs' resentment of the CUP's so-called turkification policies.[41] Whether turkification was a policy or a perception stemming from personal grievances and slights is moot. Our concern is the salafis and their experiences that shed light on the rupture between the CUP and its erstwhile Syrian allies.

The salafis invested high hopes in the eventuality of a constitutional regime. They not only thought that it would be good for the nation, but good for themselves, too. Ṭāhir al-Jazā'irī had held government posts, and he believed that the state needed more men like himself to reform the empire.[42] Jamāl al-Dīn al-Qāsimī also expected to find himself in a higher post under the new regime.

In a letter to Rashīd Riḍā, who was visiting Istanbul in the spring of 1909, Jamāl al-Dīn complained of the neglect he continued to endure even though he had suffered so much at the hands of the deposed sultan and his agents. Qāsimī wrote that immediately after the July revolution, Salīm al-Jazā'irī had recommended him for a teaching post with a stipend of 500 piasters per month (his post at the Sinānīyyah mosque carried a stipend of 200 piasters). Salīm and other members of the CUP wrote a petition on Qāsimī's behalf, but nothing came of it. Jamāl al-Dīn lamented that his influential, liberal brothers had disappointed him. It seemed to him that they favored only their close comrades, as though there were no liberal ulama worthy of promotion.[43] Qāsimī wrote in his letter to Riḍā:

> Were the Committee of Union and Progress to know what harm befell me, especially from the oppression of the deposed [sultan] and his evil helpers, then it [the CUP] would place us in a high position. By God! What happened to me would gray children and shake heroes. I mention to you some of it; perhaps you will mention it to people vigilant and zealous for their brothers.[44]

Jamāl al-Dīn then proceeded to describe the mujtahids incident, the uproar over Zahrāwī's essay, his interrogation for visiting Aḥmad al-Ḥusaynī, the incidents of 1906, the seizure of his books in 1908, and the Ramadan riot.[45] At the end of this litany of misfortunes, he concluded:

> I do not think this number [of incidents] has befallen anyone. . . . Somebody other than me would have taken departure as a way of escape and to comfort the mind. As for us, we are in the midst of the clamor. If the nation's liberals have been forgotten . . . God does not forget.[46]

Contrary to the impression given by the above letter, the salafis did not suffer total neglect. At an official celebration of the constitution's heroes held at the Sulaymāniyyah shrine, ʿAbd al-Razzāq al-Bīṭār recited a text of the Prophet's birthday (mawlid al-nabī), as was customary on special occasions. After Bīṭār's recitation, the assembled officials, notables, and ulama sat in the shade to eat ice cream and listen to speeches and poems eulogizing the martyrs of the constitution and praising freedom.[47] More than any other event that has come to light, this early summer gathering epitomized the brief rapport between the salafis and the CUP, when Bīṭār's reading of a religious text preceded lyrical acclaim for the champions of the constitution.

Later that month, a delegation from Damascus departed for Istanbul to congratulate the new sultan on his accession to the throne. Bīṭār represented the city's ulama, the salafis' friend ʿAbd al-Raḥmān al-Yūsuf went on behalf of the notables, and Ṣalāḥ al-Dīn al-Qāsimī accompanied the delegation as a correspondent for *al-Muqtabas*. At the audience with Sultan Meḥmed V, the new ruler expressed his wish to close the rift between Arabs and Turks, and to unite them in the name of Islam. Bīṭār closed the meeting with a prayer for the sultan and the constitution.[48]

The presence of a salafi shaykh and a young Arabist on an official delegation to the Ottoman court attests to the liberal camp's good fortune in the new political order. The conservatives had been defeated with the sultan's deposition and the suppression of the Muḥammadan Union. *Al-Muqtabas* published the views of the salafi-Arabist group, and the Syrian Renaissance Society freely pursued its activities. But the sultan's allusion to strains between Arabs and Turks indicated a new problem for the Syrian liberals, and in the fall of 1909 ethnic tensions irreparably damaged their relations with the CUP.

As early as February 1909, Ṣalāḥ al-Dīn al-Qāsimī registered Arabs' discontent with Turkish domination. In an article entitled "The Arab Question and Its Origin," he wrote that Turks abused Arabs with insulting language and that Arabs found Turkish teachers' and professors' disparaging remarks especially galling. The idea of an Arab caliphate held sway only among a few traitors aiming to foster misunderstanding between Arabs and Turks. Ṣalāḥ al-Dīn called on all the Ottoman peoples (*shuʿūb*) to unite in freedom and equality, yet he reserved a role for Arab nationalism, namely, to defend Arabs' rights within the empire.[49]

Ṣalāḥ al-Dīn frankly discussed the tensions in Arab–Turkish relations that became manifest when Muḥammad Kurd ʿAlī triggered a confrontation between the CUP and the Syrian liberals by publishing an inaccurate version of a declaration by the Shaykh al-Islam, the highest religious authority in the empire.[50] On September 14, 1909, Kurd ʿAlī misquoted him as stating that the Ottoman Empire was not a caliphate (that is to say, not a legitimate Islamic government), and that the caliphate had ended after the age of the first four caliphs (*al-rāshidūn*). Naturally, this report angered the authorities, and the following day Kurd ʿAlī printed an apology with the correct version of the Shaykh al-Islam's announcement. Nonetheless, the authorities shut down *al-Muqtabas* printing press and suspended the newspaper. Fearful of the consequences, Kurd ʿAlī fled to Beirut, and from there to Paris.

Kurd ʿAlī's recklessness exacerbated Arab–Turkish relations. By declaring that the caliphate had ended 1,200 years ago, he fueled the Turkish authorities' suspicions of a plot to establish an Arab caliphate. Moreover, Kurd ʿAlī already had many enemies because he incessantly criticized conservatives and carped about the government's shortcomings in the pages of his newspaper. In *al-Manār* Rashīd Riḍā observed that Ḥusayn Avnī Bey, the CUP director of education, bitterly resented Kurd ʿAlī's exposés of the education department and wanted to punish the outspoken journalist.[51] The article gave his adversaries a perfect opportunity to accuse him along with his salafi and Arabist friends of seeking an Arab caliphate, which meant secession from the empire.

Less than two weeks after Kurd ʿAlī's flight, Qāsimī and Bīṭār complied with an order to appear at the central court's interrogation bureau. Muṣṭafā al-Ghalāyīnī, a salafi journalist in Beirut, wrote that the public prosecutor had received a report alleging that Kurd ʿAlī, Qāsimī, Bīṭār, ʿAbd al-Raḥmān al-Yūsuf, Shukrī al-ʿAsalī, ʿAbd al-Wahhāb al-Inklīzī, and the Syrian Renaissance Society were conspiring to set up an Arab caliphate.[52] At the court, an investigator accused Qāsimī and Bīṭār of inspiring the Syrian Renaissance Society's formation and of guiding its actions. He alleged that the Society had branches in Yemen and Najd (rebellious provinces in Arabia), advocated administrative autonomy, and sought to create unrest by demanding an Arab government. The interrogator told Qāsimī and Bīṭār he had heard that they corresponded with the Wahhābīs and the rebellious ruler of Yemen. He then asked them about Wahhabism and the Wahhābīs' numbers in Damascus.

Qāsimī and Bīṭār denied the allegations. They disingenuously stated that they had no connection with the Syrian Renaissance Society and that it pursued strictly literary interests. More honestly, they denied having worked on behalf of ʿIzzat al-ʿĀbid, who financed opposition parties from his exile in France. The salafi shaykhs satisfied their interlocutor and left.

After the salafis acquitted themselves it was the Syrian Renaissance Society's turn to face the heat of official pressure. In early October, Rushdī al-Ḥakīm of the Society's Damascus branch wrote to Muḥibb al-Dīn al-Khaṭīb in Cairo:

> I believe you have heard the charge against the Society, namely that it is working for an Arab caliphate. But do not be alarmed, my brother, by this news, for it is of no importance. The Society is still persisting in its work, holding meetings, and discussing its affairs. It pays no attention to this obstacle placed before it by its enemies. The affair of Muḥammad Afandī Kurd ʿAlī is still unresolved because the Turkish members of the Committee of Union and Progress think very badly of him. They want to efface us from existence because we strive for reviving our language and our nation.[53]

Toward the end of October, the CUP exerted pressure on the Society to abandon its separate existence and to merge with the CUP. Ṣalāḥ al-Dīn al-Qāsimī and ʿĀrif al-Shihābī went on the Society's behalf to meet with Muḥrim Bey, a representative of the CUP. Muḥrim Bey complimented the Society for its sound aims, then he said he thought it unfortunate that the Society's enemies accused it of acting on behalf of ʿIzzat al-ʿĀbid, but such dark rumors about the Society seemed credible to CUP circles in Istanbul and Salonica. Finally, he suggested that Kurd ʿAlī's case and the charges against the Society could be resolved if the Society agreed to dissolve itself and join the CUP.

Qāsimī and Shihābī reported to the Society on their conversation with Muḥrim Bey. Initially, the members refused to merge with the CUP, but on considering the Committee's strength, their own vulnerability, and Kurd ʿAlī's predicament, they decided to join. Moreover they knew that notables and wealthy merchants would continue to harass them, so they took refuge in the arms of the CUP. The move paid off. In January 1910 the authorities cleared Kurd ʿAlī of any wrongdoing and quietly dropped the case against Qāsimī, Bīṭār, Yūsuf, and the Society.[54]

The CUP's heavyhanded tactics in dissolving the Syrian Renaissance Society aggravated the Arabs' gnawing sense of anger at the Turks. Yet that was not the end of the Society. It is not clear what happened, but the Society continued to meet clandestinely after its "dissolution." In January 1912, Ṣalāḥ al-Dīn al-Qāsimī wrote that when the Society had failed to attain legal status, it kept open its reading room, performed plays, and held parties. Finally the Society amended its charter in order to conform with the new law of associations and attained legal status. The Society then expanded the holdings of its reading room and raised funds from donations and theatrical performances.[55]

The Society's struggle to survive, the persecution of Kurd ʿAlī, and the salafis' interrogation belonged to a chain of events in the escalating battle between advocates of Arab interests and the dominant, centralist wing of the CUP. The trials of the salafis and the Arabists at the end of 1909 sundered the alliance between Syrian liberals and Turkish constitutionalists that had originated in Ṭāhir al-Jazā'irī's senior circle. The break appeared most starkly in the enmity between Ḥusayn Avnī Bey and Muḥammad Kurd ʿAlī, both of whom had belonged to the senior circle. The union of Turkish and Arab liberals arose from their common interests and goals during Abdülḥamīd's reign. The CUP's triumph in April 1909 weakened conservative forces in Damascus, but the deposition of the liberals' common enemy removed the raison d'être of their old alliance. Subsequently, the vigorous cultural assertion of the empire's various ethnic groups poisoned Turkish–Arab relations, as ethnic pride fused with political aspirations.

Political Realignments, 1910–1914

The salafi-Arabist camp passed through four phases during the first 18 months of the constitutional period. For the first three months, they rallied to the constitution by holding public celebrations, declaring its consonance with Islam, and running candidates for Parliament. Then from late October until late April 1909, they endured the conservatives' counterattacks, which ended when the CUP deposed Sultan Abdülḥamīd. During the third phase in the summer of 1909, the salafis and Arabists briefly enjoyed a sense of greater influence. Throughout the first three phases, the salafis relied on the CUP to squelch the conservatives' initiatives, and expected that the CUP would reward their service to the constitutional cause. Finally in the autumn of 1909, the salafis and Arabists collided with the CUP, which was bent on cementing its grip on the empire by centralizing administration. Irreconcilable differences between the CUP and the Syrian liberals took the shape of incompatible visions of reform: Whereas the Syrians took reform to mean a greater degree of self-rule, the CUP intended greater centralization.

The CUP and Damascene conservative forces apparently drew closer to each other after the summer of 1909. The timing of this rapprochement is difficult to trace yet was visible in the election of 1912. The CUP list included conservative notables with the backing of antisalafi ulama, whereas the opposition party, the Liberal Entente, attracted Arabist-salafi support.[56] Abdülḥamīd's deposition alienated the conservatives, but the CUP's persecution of the salafis and Arabists a few months later signaled an opportunity for the conservatives to make peace with the CUP, the empire's dominant power. A similar sense of pragmatism probably propelled the CUP to side with the conservatives, who commanded greater resources than their rivals and therefore made more useful allies.

After 1909 the salafis and the Arabists threw in their lot with the empire's decentralist forces. The Liberal Entente was founded in November 1911 to represent the empire's minorities and Turks sympathetic to the idea of decentralized administration.[57] If victorious, a decentralist regime would have brought a windfall of administrative and military posts to the Syrian graduates of state schools who filled the ranks of the Arabist movement. Prominent Arabists ran on the Liberal Entente ticket in Damascus in 1912, and the salafis supported the Entente. During the election campaign a provincial official pressured ʿAbd al-Razzāq al-Bīṭār and his salafi brother Salīm to cease their pro-Entente activities. After the election, which the CUP rigged, police searched the homes of Bīṭār, Inklīzī, and others.[58]

The Syrian decentralists' next initiative came from Cairo in January 1913 when a group including Syrian salafis founded the Party for Administrative Decentralization.[59] Some months later young Arabist students in Paris called on fellow advocates of decentralization to hold a conference, the Arab Congress of June 1913. Before the Congress met, sympathizers in Damascus sent a petition supporting the Congress's goals. The signatories included prominent Arabists, members of the Arab Renaissance Society, and salafis.[60] After six days of meetings and speeches the Congress issued a set of resolutions urging the CUP to satisfy the decentralists' demands. Meanwhile the CUP's supporters in Damascus, conservative notables and ulama, denounced the Congress.[61]

Arabist-salafi solidarity persisted into the years of the world war when both groups suffered under the harsh measures of Jamāl Pasha, a leading CUP figure who held military and civilian powers in Syria. Jamāl Pasha decided to decapitate the Arabist movement because he suspected its leaders of plotting with Britain (the empire's wartime adversary) to foment rebellion in Syria. He set up a court martial that found prominent Arabists guilty of treason, and he ordered their execution. In May 1916, ʿAsalī, Inklīzī, Salīm al-Jazā'irī, and ʿAbd al-Ḥamīd al-Zahrāwī were hung. Two salafi shaykhs, Salīm al-Bukhārī and Muḥammad Saʿīd al-Bānī, were exiled to Anatolia for the duration of the war. In Cairo, Ṭāhir al-Jazā'irī reacted to Jamāl's execution of his nephew and former pupils by throwing his support to the Arab Revolt led by Sharīf Ḥusayn of Mecca and backed by the British. The Turkish governor's punitive measures did not affect the two leading salafis because Jamāl al-Dīn al-Qāsimī had succumbed to typhoid fever several months before war broke out, and the elderly ʿAbd al-Razzāq al-Bīṭār, who died in 1917, did not arouse Jamāl Pasha's suspicion.[62]

Conclusion

From the early 1890s until July 1908, the salafis supported the constitutional movement. Only after July 1908 did they openly declare their political sympathies, both to counter the claims of conservative ulama and to position themselves for the spoils of the coup. The moment when competent men would take their rightful places, and posts, had arrived, or so they thought. Qāsimī's plaintive letter to Rashīd Riḍā expressed the salafis' disenchantment with the results of the CUP's success.

Jamāl Pasha described the Syrian reformers as "a few persons who were hankering after offices and dignities." Among scholars who deal with the political aspirations of intellectuals, Alvin Gouldner offers a less cynical perspective while retaining a connection between interests and politics.[63] He holds that a blockage of opportunities and status deprivation fuel intellectuals' alienation. Gouldner states that "blocked ascendence [*sic*] produces an increase in political activity . . . not only when the economic interests of intellectuals are restricted, but also when their opportunities to exercise political influence are blocked."[64] Qāsimī's letter to Rashīd Riḍā and Ṭāhir al-Jazā'irī's wish to hold an influential post betray their frustration not just with the state of society, but with the failure of its rulers to reward the salafis for their competence and virtue. The younger Arabists shared the same sense of blocked ascendance. The local landholding-bureaucratic elite and Turkish officials stood in the way of ambitious, educated Syrian youths, whose espousal of administrative decentralization masked the career interests underlying their political activities. In a manner parallel to nationalist movements against imperialism, the Arabists initiated "a struggle to preempt elite positions for native intellectuals and intelligentsia, by taking over and creating their own state apparatus."

Gouldner defined intellectuals' status disparity as one "between their great possession of culture and their correspondingly lesser enjoyment of incomes in power and wealth." Like Western intellectuals, the salafis and the Arabists believed that their "high culture represents . . . the deepest ancient wisdom and the most advanced modern scientific thought." Both groups believed "that the world should be governed by those possessing superior competence, wisdom, and science—that is, themselves." The unpleasant realities of political weakness and modest economic means yet high self-esteem informed the consciousness of salafis and Arabists and disposed them to a critical posture, if not alienation.

There remains yet another aspect of intellectuals' political behavior that Gouldner addressed in a fashion relevant to the salafis and the Arabists: the way they exert influence in political life. "The central mode of influence used by and characteristic of the New Class [of modern intellectuals] is communication—writing and talking. . . . The New Class gets what it wants, then, primarily by rhetoric, by persuasion and argument through publishing or speaking." From this perspective, Kurd ʿAlī's *al-Muqtabas,* the Arab Renaissance Society's public meetings, and Qāsimī's speech, sermons, and essays comprised the intellectuals' chief source of influence. Members of Damascus's landholding-bureaucratic elite wielded far greater power by virtue of their wealth, posts, and entree to high places, without publishing a single article or delivering any speeches. The conservative ulama's recourse to the printed word in *al-Ḥaqā'iq* signaled their diminished power after the overthrow of Abdülḥamīd. No longer able to persuade the authorities to intimidate the salafis into silence, the conservatives resorted to the intellectuals' weapon.

The efficacy of daily newspapers and monthly journals in a society with few literate members is limited, even assuming that illiterates used to gather to listen to readings of articles. The speech and the sermon remained the primary means of addressing large numbers. As long as the mosque remained the most important meeting place for Damascenes, religious preachers retained a greater measure of influence than Arabist journalists and orators. The conservative ulama's hold on the preacher's post at the Umayyad and most other mosques provided a resource that the salafis lacked. The efficacy of this source of power became manifest during the Ramadan incident.

On the other hand, the Arabist-salafi camp's superior position in the field of publications did have important political consequences, notwithstanding the low literacy rate. *Al-Muqtabas's* readership may have been limited, but the influence of its constituency was disproportionate to its numbers. Rashid Khalidi's studies of Damascene politics in the constitutional years have shown that the growing ranks of young literate, educated Syrians put their stamp on political life by leading popular demonstrations and articulating urban Syrians' distrust of Turkish authorities.[65] The Arabists' command of the printed medium, though, mainly served the struggle for Arab rights, and it carried little weight in the debate between salafis and conservatives over how to interpret Islam because that debate's locus lay in the mosques and religious schools.

The salafis and the Arabists tried to influence politics with the spoken and printed word. But whereas Western intellectuals acquired influence by allying with the bourgeoisie, the Syrian intellectuals had no such ally. Damascus's puny bourgeoisie consisted largely of Christians by the early 1900s, and unlike their wealthier and more numerous counterparts in Beirut, they stayed out of politics.[66] This explains the salafis' and Arabists' reliance on the CUP to stabilize Damascus after the conservative upheavals of 1908–1909, and their vulnerability to the CUP's repressive measures. Moreover, the CUP broke with the salafis and Arabists because they divided over the substance of their favorite slogan: reform. In addition, the CUP saw that the conservative notables would make more useful allies than the salafi-Arabist camp. The CUP's leaders did not esteem the salafis' expertise in religious law, and it could govern the empire without the Arabists. Thus did social, political, and ideological factors combine to limit the political influence of the salafis and the Arabists.

CONCLUSION

The salafi interpretation of Islam grappled with a dilemma that troubled Syrian Muslims, namely, how to be a Muslim and modern at the same time. Effective technologies and methods of organization had come to be associated with Europe, and therefore Muslims often believed that adopting them meant abandoning Islam. The salafis held that the association between Europe and modern techniques and inventions was not substantial, but incidental. In other words, the salafis removed the stigma of "European" from innovative practices and technologies, and claimed that Islam provides for adaptation to changing circumstances. Therefore, Muslims could adhere to their religion and attain progress.

The salafis' definition of "true" Islam involved a critique of their contemporary ulama for practicing emulation, rigidly adhering to the legal schools, and countenancing ritual innovations. Their denial of the ulama's legitimacy constituted a more direct challenge to Damascene ulama than did the Tanzimat, which undermined the ulama by bypassing them rather than confronting them directly. Consequently, conservative ulama tried to silence the salafis in order to keep their grip on religious life. The mujtahids incident and the uproar over ʿAbd al-Ḥamīd al-Zahrāwī's tract against Sufism and jurisprudence represented the conservative ulama's early response to the salafi critique.

The salafis also made positive assertions about what the ulama should do. They assimilated current ideas about reason and science to an interpretation of Islam in which ijtihād played two roles. First, ijtihād gave practical expression to Islam's rationality: ulama exercise their powers of reason to understand scripture; with that understanding, ulama discern general principles by which social affairs should be governed; and ulama derive specific precepts from those general principles. Second, ijtihād would replace the legal schools as the basis of juridical practice, divisions arising from legal school partisanship would disappear, and Muslims would attain unity.

At first glance, it would appear that opening the door of ijtihād would increase divisions because each religious scholar would be free to derive rulings according to his reasoning. But the salafis made the right to practice ijtihād contingent upon a scholar's qualifications. They believed that if ijtihād were restricted to competent ulama, their observance of rules of discourse would dispel disagreements stemming from the emulation of legal school authorities. Dissent would dwindle to such slight differences of opinion that enmity among Muslims would vanish.

The salafis also defined how the ulama should interact with other social groups. Their disdain for the practices and beliefs of the popular classes bespoke their patronizing attitude and their belief that they formed an elite by virtue of intellectual and moral superiority. They also asserted that society would benefit most from competent ulama practicing ijithād if rulers consulted with ulama when assigning judicial and teaching posts. In view of the salafis' elitism and belief that they were qualified to practice ijithād, their hopes for the ulama represented their own aspirations for influence.

Both the salafis and their conservative adversaries asserted the value of the ulama's religious knowledge against the tendency in Istanbul to entrust power to men with secular training. The two ulama factions faced a similar problem in their relations with the local elite. Before the Tanzimat period, the ulama comprised a large proportion of the city's elite. The landholding-bureaucratic elite that emerged after 1860 included a smaller proportion of ulama than before. Muḥammad Saʿīd al-Qāsimī's scathing poems against impious wealthy folk expressed the gap that grew between some ulama and the urban notables; and Jamāl al-Dīn al-Qāsimī once remarked that the upheaval of 1860 sealed the age of powerful ulama.[1] After that event the ulama still exerted influence, but they needed allies among the new elite to affect local politics. Thus the conservative ulama joined with disgruntled notables in the autumn of 1908 when the CUP seemed poised to divest the latter of power. Again in April 1909, conservative ulama and notables banded together to lead the Muḥammadan Union. The ease with which the Union was suppressed indicated that even though conservative ulama commanded a greater street following than the salafis, their power in the wider imperial context was slight. The salafis had a narrower social base than the conservatives because they had a limited following among religious students, few ulama converted to salafism, and the salafis came from less prominent ulama families. On the other hand, the conservatives' assimilation of salafi arguments and slogans constituted a backhanded acknowledgement of their appeal, which stemmed from salafism's blend of familiar Islamic terminology and symbols with the new esteem for rationality, technology, and progress.

Despite the appeal of salafi ideas, their authors fell short of achieving their goal of restoring the ulama and Islamic law to a central place in society and politics. The Tanzimat era had left its mark on the outlook of Ottoman rulers and bureaucrats even after the reaction against the Tanzimat's "European" aspect. No longer did the ulama's knowledge represent the pinnacle of learning. Graduates of Istanbul's colleges for military officers and bureaucrats possessed the skills and knowledge deemed beneficial to the empire. So even though the salafis argued that Islam is rational and progressive, and therefore relevant to the empire's needs, their marginal social position restricted the effect of their arguments. By contrast, the secular outlook, while not necessarily expressed in a more coherent fashion than salafism, had the advantage of the European example to "prove" its efficacy. Within the ulama corps, the conservatives benefited from Abdülḥamīd's patronage, which bolstered their version of Islam. The salafis could not effect their program of social and religious reform because they had a narrow social base and correspondingly weak backing for their ideas, not because their arguments may have lacked consistency, relevance, or rigor.

The salafis' biggest success lay in attracting public school students to their salons. Pupils in the senior and junior circles represented an emerging social group whose education entitled them to influential careers denied to the salafi ulama, and whose numbers were increasing. Compared to the salafis, the Arabists had a broader social base and better opportunities to achieve positions of power. Furthermore, the Arabists' espousal of Arab ethnic interests against centralist policies emanating from Istanbul had a more populist appeal than the salafis' vision of Islamic intellectual elitism. Certainly, the Arabists perpetuated the salafis' belief that society needs an intellectual elite to guide the masses and to guarantee prosperity, but the Arabists also seized on political issues that could mobilize large numbers, such as using Arabic in schools, courts, and government bureaus.

Fundamental differences between Arabists and salafis lay in their respective educations and professions. By training and vocation, the salafis were ulama, specialists in religious knowledge, whereas the Arabists attended schools imparting knowledge of worldly matters, including geography, physical sciences, and foreign languages. This training equipped young Syrians for careers that had taken on new forms during the Tanzimat era.[2] The Arabists' cultural lore and technical skills drew heavily on European sources, and they left behind the medical, legal, administrative, and martial practices of earlier generations in favor of practices borrowed from Europe. In this respect the Arabists realized the salafis' wish to import European techniques, skills, and inventions.

The tenor of Arabist writings is less systematic and coherent than that of the salafis. Perhaps the Arabists' passionate involvement in advancing ethnic interests nudged their intellectual pretensions to the periphery of their thought. By contrast, the salafis' intellectual qualifications as religious scholars were their main claim to leadership. Even so, the Arabists held values much like those of modern Western intellectuals in professing an ethic of intellectual merit and moral virtue and in validating their ambitions with their supposed merit and virtue.

The similarity between historical trends in late Ottoman Damascus and those that attended the appearance of modern intellectuals in western Europe suggests that an analogous group was emerging in Syria. Public schools were set up outside the realm of religious authority; a linguistic reform movement took place that aimed to bring literate discourse closer to everyday life; solidarity between the ruling elite and (religious) intellectuals broke down; and new means and media of cultural production (printing and newspapers) appeared.[3]

In both Ottoman Turkey and Syria, modern intellectuals appeared on the scene, but at different rates and among two different nationalities. The Turkish intellectuals appeared earlier at the imperial center among the people who ruled the empire. Syria's new intellectuals emerged later in a provincial center ruled from Istanbul. Therefore the Turkish intellectuals had both a headstart on their Syrian counterparts and greater proximity to the levers of power. During the 1890s and early 1900s, the two groups cooperated in the campaign for constitutional government. Once ensconced in power, Turkish intellectuals, represented by the CUP, asserted a monopolistic claim to the knowledge and virtue necessary to save the empire. After Abdülḥamīd's overthrow the CUP squelched Syrian (Arab) intellectuals' initiatives, which aimed at administrative reforms designed to obtain posts for graduates of public schools. Even though the Arabists had acquired the requisite skills for careers in the bureaucracy and the army, the Turkish "new class" blocked their path by filling posts to which Arabists aspired.

The salafis, then, heralded the adjustment of religious intellectuals to changing social and cultural conditions in late Ottoman Syria. Their redefinition of the qualifications and practices of the ulama evoked the hostility of fellow ulama who adhered to customary practices and beliefs. That the salafis hearkened to the practices of the first generations of Muslims does not gainsay the fact that salafism represented adaptation to, not a rejection of, social change. The salafis' "modern" aspect made possible their links with Syrians educated in state schools, a new group of intellectuals. And the salafis' interaction with these younger men contributed to the emergence of Arabism as a cultural and political movement directed and organized by religious and secular intellectuals sharing a vision of a prosperous society under their guidance.

NOTES

Introduction

1. The seminal essay on notable politics in Arab urban centers during the nineteenth century is Albert Hourani, "Ottoman Reform and the Politics of the Notables," in *The Beginnings of Modernization in the Middle East: The Nineteenth Century,* William R. Polk and Richard L. Chambers, eds. (Chicago: University of Chicago Press, 1968); a fine study of ulama newcomers and notable politics in late Ottoman Damascus is Ruth Roded, "Tradition and Change in Syria During the Last Decades of Ottoman Rule: The Urban Elite of Damascus, Aleppo, Homs, and Hama, 1876–1918" (Ph.D. dissertation, University of Denver, 1984).

Chapter 1

1. H. H. Gerth and and C. Wright Mills, eds., *From Max Weber: Essays in Sociology* (New York: Oxford University Press, 1946), pp. 187–191.

2. ʿAbd al-Raḥmān Sāmī, *al-Qawl al-ḥaqq fī bayrūt wa dimashq* (Beirut: Dār al-Rā'id al-ʿArabī, 1981), pp. 95, 97. Originally published as *Safar al-salām fī bilād al-shām* (Cairo: Al-Muqtaṭaf Press, 1892).

3. Linda Schatkowski Schilcher, *Families in Politics: Damascene Factions and Estates of the 18th and 19th Centuries* (Stuttgart: Franz Steiner Verlag Wiesbaden GMBH, 1985), pp. 116, 120; John Voll, "Old Ulama Families and Ottoman Influence in Eighteenth-Century Damascus," *American Journal of Arabic Studies* 3 (1971): 56–59; John Voll, "The Non-Wahhābī Ḥanbalīs of Eighteenth-Century Syria," *Der Islam* 49 (1972): 277–291.

4. The inheritance documents are at the Center of Historical Documents (Markaz al-wathā'iq al-tārīkhiyyah) in Damascus. The documents itemize belongings and property holdings, their value, and the estate's total value. The documents also record how the heirs divided the estate. In some instances, the documents underestimate the worth of estates because the value of property is not always mentioned. I examined the following registers for the period 1890–1910: Sijillāt 926, 960, 993, 1001, 1030, 1035, 1040, 1053, 1054, 1055, 1059, 1080, 1093, 1103, 1113, 1119, 1124, 1135, 1139, 1151, 1166, 1183, 1189, 1192, 1203, 1226, 1229, 1233, 1252, 1263, 1273, 1278, 1285, 1313, 1340, 1347, 1354, 1382, and 1533.

5. Jurisconsult Maḥmūd al-Ḥamzāwī left the largest bequest in this series of documents. The value of his heritable assets exceeded 260,000 piasters; sijill 878, no. 111, pp. 71–77. Jurisconsult Muḥammad al-Manīnī left 71,103 piasters to his heirs; sijill 1119, pp. 122–126 (not all documents are numbered, but the registers have been paginated). ʿAbd al-Qādir al-Kaylānī, a sharīf, left 121,724 piasters; sijill 1313, no. 5, pp. 120–123. Another sharīf, ʿAbd al-Bānī al-ʿAjlānī, left over 100,000 piasters; sijill 960, pp. 60–61. ʿUmar al-ʿAṭṭār, a renowned teacher, left 67,323 piasters; sijill 926, no. 173, pp. 177–179. Muḥammad ibn ʿAbd al-Raḥmān al-Mujtahid, another teacher, left 135,580 piasters; sijill 1103, pp. 12–16. Ṣāliḥ al-Munayyir, a prominent teacher, left 50,505 piasters; sijill 1203, pp. 84–88. Kamāl al-

Kuzbarī, whose family was famous for teaching oral reports at the Umayyad mosque's Nasr Dome, left 59,944 piasters; sijill 926, no. 109, pp. 104–106. Muḥammad Amīn al-Usṭuwānī belonged to a family famous for its preachers at the Umayyad mosque and for teachers; he left 60,140 piasters; sijill 1030, pp. 174–176. A prominent Sufi, Muḥammad ibn Muḥammad al-Khānī, left nearly 60,000 piasters; sijill 1151, pp. 180–182.

6. Muḥammad Saʿīd al-Usṭuwānī, preacher at the Umayyad mosque, left 42,392 piasters; sijill 1030, pp. 177–178. Darwīsh al-Ḥamzāwī was a sharīf who left 46,389 piasters; sijill 1080, pp. 181–184.

7. Deputy jurisconsult Muḥammad al-Bīṭār left 19,669 piasters; sijill 1040, pp. 38–43. Members of the Kaylānī family of sharīfs left 28,193 and 13,471 piasters; Muḥammad Saʿīd al-Kaylānī, sijill 1119, pp. 60–67; Fāris al-Kaylānī, sijill 1354, no. 94, pp. 21–23. Aḥmad ibn Muḥyi al-Dīn al-ʿĀnī belonged to a famous Sufi family and left 22,307 piasters; sijill 1151, pp. 90–96. Two members of another Sufi family fell into the lower middle ulama. Aḥmad al-Khānī left 6,893 piasters; sijill 1183, pp. 1–2. His brother Maḥmūd al-Khānī left 6,559 piasters; sijill 1192, pp. 34–36. Another Sufi left 15,549 piasters; sijill 1139, pp. 148–149. ʿAbd al-Mālik al-Kuzbarī belonged to a famous family of teachers and left 6,194 piasters to his heirs; sijill 1340, pp. 59–60. A former naqīb al-ashrāf, Muḥammad Ṣāliḥ Āl Taqī al-Dīn al-Ḥiṣnī, left 6,142 piasters; sijill 1001, no. 127, pp. 126–127.

8. Two members of the Āl Taqī al-Dīn al-Ḥiṣnī family of sharīfs left 3,477 and 4,293 piasters, respectively; sijill 1151, pp. 4–5; sijill 1166, no. 170, p. 36. Ṣāliḥ al-Ghazzī, whose ancestors were leading Shāfiʿī ulama, left 3,039 piasters; sijill 1382, p. 62.

9. For examples of ulama who left less than 1,000 piasters, see sijill 1192, pp. 128–129, 144; sijill 1166, no. 157, p. 22; no. 202, pp. 69–70.

10. The post for teaching al-Bukhārī's *al-Ṣaḥīḥ* at the Sulaymāniyyah lodge carried an annual stipend of 4,000 piasters for seven lessons during the months of Rajab and Shaʿban. In the eighteenth and nineteenth centuries, the ʿAṭṭār family held this post. Muḥammad Jamīl al-Shaṭṭī, *Aʿyān dimashq fī al-qarn al-thālith ʿashar wa niṣf al-qarn al-rābiʿ ʿashar* (Damascus: Al-Maktab al-Islāmī, 1972), pp. 44–48, 74–75, 338–340, 409–412.

11. Muḥammad Bahjat al-Bīṭār, "al-Mudarrisūn taḥt qubbat al-nasr," *Majallat al-majmaʿ al-ʿilmī al-ʿarabī* 24 (1949): 59–72.

12. For a time Muḥammad Saʿīd al-Qāsimī had a shop that sold household goods. Muḥammad Saʿīd al-Qāsimī, *Qāmūs al-ṣināʿāt al-shāmiyyah,* vol. 1 (Paris: Mouton & Co., 1960), p. 8.

13. On the Egyptian occupation and its impact on communal relations, see *Mudhakkirāt tārīkhiyyah ʿan ḥamlat Ibrāhīm Bāshā ʿala sūriyā,* Aḥmad Ghassān Sbānū, ed. (Damascus: Dār Qutaybah, n.d.), pp. 50, 60, 62, 68, 85, 88, 99, 137.

14. On Ottoman reformers' motives for proclaiming religious equality, see Roderic H. Davison, *Reform in the Ottoman Empire, 1856–1876* (Princeton: Princeton University Press, 1963), pp. 87–88; on Muslim opposition to the reforms, see Şerif Mardin, *The Genesis of Young Ottoman Thought* (Princeton: Princeton University Press, 1962), p. 18.

15. "Muntakhabāt min mudhakkirāt Muḥammad Abū al-Suʿūd al-Ḥasībī," in *Bilād al-shām fī al-qarn al-tāsiʿ ʿashar,* Suhayl Zukkār, ed. (Damascus: Dār Ḥassān, 1982), p. 285.

16. Anonymous, *Hasr al-lithām ʿan nakabāt al-shām* (Cairo: n.p., 1895), p. 223.

17. Introduction by Sbānū to *Mudhakkirāt tārīkhiyyah,* pp. 16–17; Schilcher, *Families in Politics,* p. 61.

18. Moshe Ma'oz, "Communal Conflict in Ottoman Syria during the Reform Era: The Role of Political and Economic Factors," in *Christians and Jews in the Ottoman Empire: The Arabic-Speaking Lands,* eds., Benjamin Braude and Bernard Lewis, 2 vols. (New York: Holmes & Meier, 1982), 1:96; E. Roger Owen, *The Middle East in the World Economy, 1800–1914* (London: Methuen, 1981), p. 99; Charles Issawi, ed., *The Economic History of the Middle East* (Chicago: University of Chicago Press, 1966), pp. 38–40, 208, 230, 242.

19. Charles Issawi, "British Consular Views on Syria's Economy in the 1850s–1860s," in *American University of Beirut Festival Book,* Fu'ad Sarruf and Suha Tamin, eds. (Beirut: American University of Beirut, 1967), pp. 109–110; Moshe Ma'oz, *Ottoman Reform in Syria and Palestine, 1840–1861* (Oxford: Clarendon Press, 1968), pp. 155, 174–175; Mardin, *The Genesis,* p. 16.

20. Schilcher, *Families in Politics,* pp. 70, 82–83; Owen, *The Middle East,* p. 98.

21. Nuʿmān Qasāṭilī, *al-Rawḍah al-ghannā' fī dimashq al-fayḥā'* (Beirut: n.p., 1879), p. 123; Owen, *The Middle East,* p. 92.

22. Schilcher, *Families in Politics,* pp. 75–78; Charles Issawi, "British Trade and the Rise of Beirut, 1830–1860," *International Journal of Middle East Studies* 8 (1977): 97.

23. Salah M. Dabbagh, "Agrarian Reform in Syria," *Middle East Economic Papers* (1962): 2.

24. On the July 1860 massacre and its aftermath, see Schilcher, *Families in Politics,* pp. 87–106; Philip S. Khoury, *Urban Notables and Arab Nationalism: The Politics of Damascus, 1860–1920* (Cambridge: Cambridge University Press, 1983), pp. 23–26; Kamal S. Salibi, "The 1860 Upheaval in Damascus as Seen by al-Sayyid Muḥammad Abū'l Suʿūd al-Ḥasībī, Notable and Later *Naqīb al-Ashrāf* of the City," in *The Beginnings of Modernization in the Middle East: The Nineteenth Century,* W. R. Polk and R. L. Chambers, eds. (Chicago: University of Chicago Press, 1968), pp. 185–201. Similar perceptions developed in the Hijaz in the aftermath of an anti-Christian riot in Jiddah in June 1858. See William Ochsenwald, *Religion, Society and the State in Arabia: The Hijaz Under Ottoman Control, 1840–1908* (Columbus: Ohio State University Press, 1984), pp. 137–151.

25. Bernard Lewis, *The Emergence of Modern Turkey* (New York: Oxford University Press, 1961), pp. 159–178; Max Gross, "Ottoman Rule in the Province of Damascus, 1860–1909" (Ph.D. dissertation, Georgetown University, 1979), pp. 231–239.

26. On the notables' movement, see ʿĀdil al-Ṣulḥ, *Suṭūr min al-risālah: Tārīkh ḥarakah istiqlāliyyah qāmat fī al-mashriq al-ʿarabī sanat 1877* (Beirut: Dār al-ʿIlm li al-Malāyīn, 1966).

27. During an earlier phase of administrative and military reform (1792–1839), certain elite ulama of Istanbul supported the measures taken by Sultans Selīm III and Maḥmūd II. At that time, however, the reforms did not appear to entail any encroachment on the place of Islam in the empire or on the central role of the high ulama in the governing elite. See Uriel Heyd, "The Ottoman ʿUlemā' and Westernization in the Time of Selīm III and Maḥmūd II," *Scripta Hierosolymitana* 9 (1961), pp. 63–96.

28. Moshe Ma'oz, "The Ulama and the Process of Modernization in Syria during the mid-nineteenth Century," *Asian and African Studies* 7 (1971): 80–83.

29. Schilcher, *Families in Politics,* pp. 53–55; Moshe Ma'oz, "Syrian Urban Politics in the Tanzimat Period Between 1840–1861," *Bulletin of the School of Oriental and African Studies* 29 (1966): 281, 291–292, 300; Ma'oz, *Ottoman Reform,* pp. 155, 174–175.

30. Kamāl Ṣalībī and ʿAbd Allah Abū Ḥabīb, "Lamaḥāt min tārīkh dimashq fī ʿahd al-tanẓīmat," *al-Abḥāth* 21 (1968): 59–60; Gross, "Ottoman Rule," pp. 58–60.

31. Ṣalībī and Abū Ḥabīb, "Lamaḥāt min tārīkh," 61–69; Khoury, *Urban Notables,* pp. 30–31.

32. Niyazi Berkes, *The Development of Secularism in Turkey* (Montreal: McGill University Press, 1964), pp. 129–130.

33. The 1869 education law proposed a curriculum emphasizing mathematics, history, and physical and natural sciences. ʿAbd al-ʿAzīz Muḥammad ʿAwaḍ, *al-Idārah al-ʿuthmāniyyah fī wilāyat sūriyah, 1864–1914* (Cairo: Dār al-Maʿārif, 1969), pp. 254–257.

34. The Kuzbarī family was a prominent ulama family in Safad in northern Palestine. ʿAbd al-Karīm al-Kuzbarī settled in Damascus in 1604. His descendant Muḥammad ibn ʿAbd al-Raḥmān al-Kuzbarī (1727–1806) established the family's fame in 1795 when he became

teacher of oral reports at the Nasr Dome. Muḥammad Adīb Āl Taqī al-Dīn al-Ḥiṣnī, *Muntakhabāt al-tawārīkh li dimashq,* 3 vols. (Damascus: Al-Ḥadīthah Press, 1928), 2:679; Shaṭṭī, *Aʿyān dimashq,* p. 258. Aḥmad al-Manīnī (1678–1759) came to Damascus from a village near Tripoli, Lebanon, and studied with leading Damascene ulama. He ascended to the highest ranks of the ulama when he became preacher and prayer leader at the Umayyad mosque. Ḥiṣnī, *Muntakhabāt,* 2:617.

35. On religious education in general, see Aḥmad al-Ṭarabayn, "al-Ḥayāt al-ʿilmiyyah fī bilād al-shām fī al-qarn al-thālith ʿashar al-hijrī min khilāl *Ḥilyat al-bashar fī tārīkh al-qarn al-thālith ʿashar* li al-shaykh ʿAbd al-Razzāq al-Bīṭār," in *al-Muʾtamar al-duwalī al-thānī li tārīkh bilād al-shām,* 1516–1939, 2 vols. (Damascus: Damascus University, 1978), 2:650–653, 671; ʿAwaḍ, *al-Idārah al-ʿuthmāniyyah,* p. 253; on the Ottoman examinations, see Ḥiṣnī, *Muntakhabāt,* 2:301; Voll, "The Non-Wahhābī Ḥanbalīs," p. 278.

36. On the Lazarist school, see ʿAwaḍ, *al-Idārah al-ʿuthmāniyyah,* pp. 265–266; on the Egyptian initiatives, see Asad Rustum, *al-Maḥfūẓāt al-malikiyyah al-miṣriyyah,* 4 vols. (Beirut: American University of Beirut Press, 1940–1943), 2:431, 488.

37. ʿAwaḍ, *al-Idārah al-ʿuthmāniyyah,* pp. 254–263.

38. On the controversy over the British school, see Great Britain, Public Record Office, Foreign Office 78/2985/4: Jago to Salisbury, 27 January 1879; on the Benevolent Society's schools, see FO 78/2985/10: Jago to Malet, 2 March 1879; ʿAdnān al-Khaṭīb, *al-Shaykh Ṭāhir al-Jazāʾirī, rāʾid al-nahḍah al-ʿilmiyyah fī bilād al-shām* (Cairo: Maʿhad al-Dirāsāt al-ʿArabiyyah, 1971), pp. 105–108.

39. Gross, "Ottoman Rule," pp. 378–380.

40. ʿAwaḍ, *al-Idārah al-ʿuthmāniyyah,* p. 363; Sāmī, *al-Qawl al-ḥaqq,* p. 101.

41. Muḥammad Kurd ʿAlī (1876–1953) studied at state primary and secondary schools, the lessons of ulama, and the French Lazarist school. Sāmī al-Dahhān, *Muḥammad Kurd ʿAlī: Ḥayātuhu wa ʿāthāruhu* (Damascus: Al-Majmaʿ al-ʿIlmī al-ʿArabī, 1955), pp. 16–20. Rafīq al-ʿAẓm (1867–1925) studied with his father, a litterateur, and then in a mission school to learn French. ʿAẓm later studied in a state school and with ulama. ʿAbd al-Razzāq al-Bīṭār, *Ḥilyat al-bashar fī tārīkh al-qarn al-thālith ʿashar,* 3 vols. (Damascus: Majmaʿ al-Lughah al-ʿArabiyyah, 1961–1963), 2:630–631.

42. On the production of manuscripts, see Usāmah ʿĀnūtī, *al-Ḥarakah al-adabiyyah fī al-shām fī al-qarn al-thāmin ʿashar* (Beirut: St. Joseph University Press, 1971), pp. 42–43; Philippe de Ṭarrāzī, *Khazāʾin al-kutub al-ʿarabiyyah fī al-khāfiqayn,* 3 vols. (Beirut: Dār al-Kutub, 1947–1951), 3:819–917; on the manuscripts in the Ẓāhiriyyah Library in 1896, see Ḥabīb al-Zayāt, *Khazāʾin al-kutub fī dimashq wa ḍawāḥīhā* (Damascus: Alif Bāʾ Press, 1982), pp. 17–19.

43. Khalīl Ṣābāt, *Tārīkh al-ṭibāʿah fī al-sharq al-ʿarabī* (Cairo: Dār al-Maʿārif, 1958), pp. 96–97; Shams al-Dīn al-Rifāʿī, *Tārīkh al-ṣiḥāfah al-sūriyyah* (Cairo: Dār al-Maʿārif, 1969), p. 31.

44. Ṣābāt, *Tārīkh al-ṭibāʿah,* p. 97.

45. Iskandar Lūqā, *al-Ḥarakah al-adabiyyah fī dimashq, 1800–1918* (Damascus: Alif Bāʾ Press, 1976), pp. 274–285; Zayāt, *Khazāʾin al-kutub,* pp. 17–19.

46. Jūsuf Ilyās, "Taṭawwur al-ṣiḥāfah al-sūriyyah fī al-ʿahd al-ʿuthmānī," (Master's thesis, Lebanese University, 1972), pp. 29, 59–61, 114–123.

47. Ibid., pp. 59–61.

48. Ibid., pp. 62–64.

49. The Egyptians sent to Damascus a catalog of books printed at Bulaq press. Those books included histories of Italy, America, Alexander the Great, ancient Egypt, and ancient Greek philosophy. Asad Rustum, *al-Maḥfūẓāt al-malikiyyah,* 3:176–177.

50. For a discussion of printing's cultural significance for conveying meanings from

distant societies, see Raymond Williams, *Culture* (Glasgow: Fontana, 1981), pp. 97–98, 110; Alvin W. Gouldner, *The Future of Intellectuals and the Rise of the New Class* (New York: Oxford University Press, 1979), pp. 3–4.

51. On the Turkish linguistic reform movement, see Şerif Mardin, "Some Notes on an Early Phase in the Modernization of Communication in Turkey," *Comparative Studies in Society and History* 3 (1961): 250–271; Berkes, *The Development of Secularism,* p. 197. On lexical developments for political terms in Arabic in the nineteenth century, see Ami Ayalon, *Language and Change in the Arab Middle East* (New York: Oxford University Press, 1987).

52. Muḥammad Saʿīd al-Bānī, *Tanwīr al-baṣā'ir bi sīrat al-shaykh Ṭāhir* (Damascus: Al-Ḥukūmah al-ʿArabiyyah al-Sūriyyah Press, 1920), pp. 15–23.

53. Ibid., pp. 22–23.

54. Williams, *Culture,* p. 130.

55. For a general statement of the relationship between religious and scientific explanations of nature, see Goran Therborn, *The Ideology of Power and the Power of Ideology* (London: Verso, 1980), p. 37.

Chapter 2

1. Fazlur Rahman, *Islam* (Garden City, NY: Doubleday & Co., 1966), pp. 237–260.

2. For speculation that the Wahhābīs influenced the northern Nigerian Islamic movement of Osman dan Fodio, see Mervyn Hiskett, "An Islamic Tradition of Reform in the Western Sudan from the Sixteenth to the Eighteenth Century," *Bulletin of the School of Oriental and African Studies* 25 (1962): 577–596; on the association of Wahhabism with Indian reform movements, see Muʿin al-Din Ahmad Khan, *History of the Fara'idi Movement in Bengal* (Karachi: Pakistan Historical Society, 1955), p. xxxv.

3. On the Wahhābī movement, see H. St. John Philby, *Saudi Arabia* (New York: Praeger, 1955), pp. 1–146; Ṣalāḥ al-Dīn al-ʿAqqād, "Daʿwah ḥarakat al-iṣlāḥ al-salafī," *al-Majallah al-tārīkhiyyah al-miṣriyyah* 7 (1958): 86–105. On the Wahhābīs' impact on Syria, see George Koury, "The Province of Damascus, 1783–1832," (Ph.D. dissertation, University of Michigan, 1970), pp. 4–5, 100–109, 114–150. On Muḥammad ibn ʿAbd al-Wahhāb's ideas, see Henri Laoust, *Essai sur les doctrines sociales et politiques de Takī-al-Dīn Aḥmad ibn Taimiya* (Cairo: L'Institut Francais d'Archéologie Orientale, 1939), pp. 506–541.

4. On the pilgrimage's importance for the economy of Damascus, see Karl L. Barbir, *Ottoman Rule in Damascus* (Princeton: Princeton University Press, 1980), pp. 109–113, 133–177; Abdul-Karim Rafeq, *Province of Damascus, 1723–1783* (Beirut: Khayats, 1970), pp. 52–76.

5. Mikhā'īl Mushāqa, *Mashhad al-ʿiyān bi ḥawādith sūriyah wa lubnān,* in *Bilād al-shām fī al-qarn al-tāsiʿ ʿashar,* ed., Suhayl Zukkār (Damascus: Dār Ḥassān, 1982), p. 108; ʿAqqād, "Daʿwah ḥarakat," p. 94; Albert Hourani, *Arabic Thought in the Liberal Age, 1798–1939* (London: Oxford University Press, 1970), p. 38.

6. The Khārijīs were a political group that appeared in the first century of Islam rejecting the legitimacy of the Umayyad caliphs; their name became synonomous with extremism in belief and action.

7. "Majmūʿah makhṭūṭah," *Majallat al-majmaʿ al-ʿilmī al-ʿarabī* 5 (1925): 61–69.

8. For the Ḥanbalīs of Damascus, see John Voll, "The Non-Wahhābī Ḥanbalīs of Eighteenth-Century Syria," *Der Islam* 49 (1972): 277–291.

9. On Ḥasan al-Shaṭṭī, see ʿAbd al-Razzāq al-Bīṭār, *Ḥilyat al-bashar fī tārīkh al-qarn al-thālith ʿashar,* 3 vols. (Damascus: Majmaʿ al-Lughah al-ʿArabiyyah, 1961–63), 1:478–480; Muḥammad Jamīl al-Shaṭṭī, *Aʿyān dimashq fī al-qarn al-thālith ʿashar wa niṣf al-qarn al-rābiʿ ʿashar* (Damascus: al-Maktab al-Islāmī, 1972), pp. 76–78. On Ḥasan al-Shaṭṭī's response to

the Wahhābī essays, see Muṣṭafā al-Shaṭṭī, *al-Nuqūl al-sharʿiyyah fī al-radd ʿala al-wahhābiyyah* (n.p., n.d.), pp. 10–11; Muḥammad Jamīl al-Shaṭṭī, *Mukhtaṣar ṭabaqāt al-ḥanābilah* (Damascus: Al-Taraqqī Press, 1921), p. 139.

10. Ḥasan al-Shaṭṭī, *Aqrab al-masālik li bayān al-manāsik* (Damascus: Al-Taraqqī Press, 1932), p. 35; Ḥasan al-Shaṭṭī, *Risālah fī al-taqlīd wa al-talfīq* (Damascus: Rawḍat al-Shām Press, 1910).

11. Aḥmad Taymūr, *Aʿlām al-fikr al-islāmī fī al-ʿaṣr al-ḥadīth* (Cairo: Lajnat Nashr al-Mu'allafāt al-Taymūriyyah, 1967), pp. 222–223.

12. On Abū Thinā' Shihāb al-Dīn al-Alūsī, see ʿAbbās al-ʿAzzāwī, *Dhikrā Abī Thinā' al-Alūsī* (Baghdad: Sharikat al-Tijārah wa al-Ṭibāʿah, 1958); on Alūsī's "Wahhabism", see ʿAzzāwī, pp. 35–39; ʿAbd al-ʿAzīz Nawwār, "Mawāqif siyāsiyyah li Abī Thinā' Maḥmūd al-Alūsī," *al-Majallah al-tārīkhiyyah al-miṣriyyah* 14 (1968): 143–168.

13. On Alūsī's exegesis of the Quran, *Rūḥ al-maʿānī fī tafsīr al-qurān wa sabʿ al-mathānī,* see Manīʿ ʿAbd al-Ḥalīm Maḥmūd, *Manāhij al-mufassirīn* (Cairo: Dār al-Kitāb al-Miṣrī, 1978), pp. 475–482; Muḥammad Bahjat al-Atharī, *Aʿlām al-ʿirāq* (Cairo: Al-Salafiyyah Press, 1926/27), p. 29; on Fakhr al-Dīn al-Rāzī's exegesis, see Maḥmūd, *Manāhij,* pp. 145–152; on Nuʿmān Khayr al-Dīn al-Alūsī, see Atharī, *Aʿlām al-ʿirāq,* pp. 57–68.

14. On Khayr al-Dīn al-Alūsī's journey and discovery of Ṣiddīq Ḥasan Khān, see Atharī, *Aʿlām al-ʿirāq,* p. 60. On Ṣiddīq Ḥasan Khān and the Indian Ahl-i Ḥadīth movement, see Barbara Daly Metcalf, *Islamic Revival in British India: Deoband, 1860–1900* (Princeton: Princeton University Press, 1982), pp. 264–296.

15. Muḥammad ibn ʿAlī al-Shawkānī (1760–1835) deserves mention because he was a source for the Damascene salafis' discovery of Ibn Taymiyyah. Shawkānī worked as a judge and wrote prolifically on ijtihād, taqlīd, and fabricated oral reports. He favored restricting the bases of religious practice to the Quran and the Sunnah, and he considered consensus and analogy fallible sources; on Shawkānī, see Muḥammad ibn Muḥammad Zabārah, *Nayl al-waṭar min tarājim rijāl al-yaman fī al-qarn al-thālith ʿashar* (Cairo: Al-Salafiyyah Press, 1929/30–1931/32), pp. 297–302; ʿAlī al-Muḥāfaẓah, *al-Ittijāhāt al-fikriyyah ʿinda al-ʿarab fī ʿaṣr al-nahḍah, 1798–1914* (Beirut: Al-Ahliyyah li al-Nashr wa al-Tawzīʿ, 1980), pp. 44–49. On Ibn Taymiyyah's life and works, see Laoust, *Essai sur les doctrines;* for an overview of trends in western scholarship on Ibn Taymiyyah and his Sufi affiliations, see George Makdisi, "Ibn Taymiya: A Sufi of the Qādiriya Order," *American Journal of Arabic Studies* 1 (1973): 118–130.

16. The Damascene salafi Jamāl al-Dīn al-Qāsimī corresponded with the Baghdadi salafi Maḥmūd Shukrī al-Alūsī in the early 1900s. Much of their correspondence consisted of information about recent discoveries of Ibn Taymiyyah's manuscripts in Damascus and Baghdad. Alūsī to Qāsimī, 25 December 1908, 18 March 1909, 30 March 1909, 22 April 1911, 28 July 1911, 17 October 1913. Photocopies of originals in author's possession. Qāsimī also corresponded with a Hijazi merchant of Jeddah, Muḥammad Naṣīf, to whom Jamāl al-Dīn expressed his desire to see Ibn Taymiyyah's works edited and published; Ẓāfir al-Qāsimī, *Jamāl al-Dīn al-Qāsimī wa ʿaṣruhu* (Damascus: Al-Hāshimiyyah Press, 1965), pp. 585–591, 620–621.

17. Nuʿmān Khayr al-Dīn al-Alūsī, *Jalā' al-ʿaynayn fī muḥākamat al-ahmadayn* (Cairo: Būlāq Press, 1881). The discussion of this work is based on the preface and pp. 20–30, 102–114, 269–327. On the encounter of Rashīd Riḍā with Alūsī's work, see Jamʿiyyat al-Shabbān al-Muslimīn, Baghdad, *Dhikrā ḥujjat al-islām ṣāḥib al-Manār* (Baghdad, 1935), p. 14; for Jamāl al-Din al-Qāsimī's appreciation of *Jalā' al-ʿaynayn,* see "Tārīkh al-ustādh Jamāl al-Dīn al-Qāsimī," manuscript, Qāsimī library, Damascus, p. 67.

18. Muḥammad Bahjat al-Atharī, *Maḥmūd Shukrī al-Alūsī wa ārā'uhu al-lughawiyyah*

(Cairo: Al-Kamāliyyah Press, 1958), p. 44. Other Alūsīs active in the reform movement included Khayr al-Dīn's sons Thābit and Ḥusām al-Dīn, ibid., p. 42. On Maḥmūd Shukrī al-Alūsī's wide contacts, see his correspondence with Jamāl al-Dīn al-Qāsimī.

19. On ʿAbd al-Qādir al-Jazā'irī's resistance to the French, see Raphael Danziger, *Abd al-Qadir and the Algerian Resistance to the French and Internal Consolidation* (New York: Holmes & Meier, 1977).

20. Ibid., p. 56.

21. On Jazā'irī's eastern journey, see Muḥammad ibn ʿAbd Allah al-Khānī, *Kitāb al-bahjah al-saniyah fī ādāb al-ṭarīqah al-ʿaliyah al-khālidiyyah al-naqshbandiyyah* (Cairo: Dhāt al-Taḥrīr Press, 1885/86), p. 2; ʿAbd al-Majīd al-Khānī, *al-Ḥadā'iq al-wardiyyah fī ḥaqā'iq ajillā' al-naqshbandiyyah* (Cairo: Dār al-Ṭibāʿah al-ʿĀmirah, 1890), p. 280.

22. Danziger, *Abd al-Qadir,* pp. 54–55.

23. Charles Henry Churchill, *Ḥayāt ʿAbd al-Qādir: al-Sulṭān al-sābiq li ʿarab al-jazā'ir* (Tunis: Dār al-Tūnisiyyah li al-Nashr, 1971), p. 23. Arabic translation of *The Life of Abdel Kader, Ex-Sultan of the Arabs of Algeria* (London: Chapman & Hall, 1867).

24. Khānī, *Ḥadā'iq,* p. 280; Bīṭār, *Ḥilyat al-bashar* 2:893–896.

25. ʿAbd al-Qādir al-Jazā'irī, *Dhikrā al-ʿāqil wa tanbīh al-ghāfil* (n.p., 1855). On the French scholars' request for an essay, see ibid., p. 3; and Philippe D'Estailleur-Chanteraine, *L'Emir magnanime Abd-El-Kader le croyant* (Paris: Librairie Arthème Fayard, 1959), p. 185. Churchill wrote that Jazā'irī based much of the essay on al-Ghazālī's famous work, *Iḥyā' ʿulūm al-dīn;* Churchill, *Ḥayāt ʿAbd al-Qādir,* p. 47. Jazā'irī first wrote on the relation between reason and revelation in 1848 in *al-Miqrāḍ al-ḥādd li-qaṭʿ lisān muntaqiṣ dīn al-islām bi al-bāṭil wa al-ilḥād* (Beirut: n.p., n.d.). That essay is summarized in Muḥammad ibn Abd al-Qādir al-Jazā'irī, *Tuḥfat al-zāhir fī tārīkh al-jazā'ir wa al-amīr ʿAbd al-Qādir* (Beirut: Dār al-Yaqẓah al-ʿArabiyya, 1964), pp. 543–550. The following discussion covers themes found in Jazā'irī, *Dhikrā,* pp. 5–7, 22–24, 35, 50–59, 76–78.

26. Jamil Abun-Nasr, *A History of the Maghrib* (Cambridge: Cambridge University Press, 1971), p. 244.

27. The Egyptian thinker Rifāʿa al-Ṭahṭāwī (1801–1873) similarly revived a dormant Islamic intellectual tradition in his work on practical philosophy. See Juan R. Cole, "Rifāʿa al-Ṭahṭāwī and the Revival of Practical Philosophy," *Muslim World* 70 (1980): 29–46.

28. Muḥammad al-Jazā'irī, *Tuḥfat al-zāhir,* pp. 596–597, 618, 622; on Jazā'irī's stipend from Napoleon III, see ibid., p. 726; Bīṭār, *Ḥilyat al-bashar,* 2:896, 903; Great Britain, Public Record Office, Foreign Office 195/1448/27: Block to Wyndham, 13 October 1883.

29. Jazā'irī paid Muḥammad al-Ṭanṭāwī 1,000 piasters per month; Jamāl al-Dīn al-Qāsimī, "Taʿṭīr al-mashām fī ma'āthīr dimashq al-shām," 4 vols. manuscript, Qāsimī library, Damascus, unrevised copy, 2:8. Jazā'irī also bought a home for Ṭanṭāwī; *Aʿyān dimashq,* p. 332. ʿAbd al-Qādir awarded ʿAbd al-Majīd al-Khānī for panegyric verse; Qāsimī, "Taʿṭīr al-mashām," unrevised copy, II, unnumbered pages, p. 7. Jazā'irī paid Muḥammad ibn Muḥammad al-Khānī a monthly stipend and bequeathed him 10,000 piasters; Qāsimī, "Taʿṭīr al-mashām," unrevised copy, 2:22.

30. On Jazā'irī's admirers, see Chapter 3, this book. On those who resented him, see FO 195/1448/14: Block to Wyndham, 30 May 1883.

31. Muḥammad al-Jazā'irī, *Tuḥfat al-zāhir,* p. 632; Mushāqa, *Mashhad al-ʿiyān,* pp. 246, 248, 260; Churchill, *Ḥayāt ʿAbd al-Qādir,* p. 285; "Muntakhabāt min riwāyah mārūniyyah ʿan ḥawādith 1860 bi qalam muʿāṣirihā Anṭūn Ḍāhir al-ʿAqīqī al-Kisrawānī," *Bilād al-Shām,* ed., Zukkār, p. 382; Charles-Robert Ageron, "Abd el-Kader souverain d'un royaume arabe d'orient," *Revue de l'Occident Musulman et de la Méditerranée,* Numéro Spécial, 1970, IIe Congrès International d'Études Nord-Africaines, 18. For speculation on Jazā'irī's moti-

vations in 1860, see Linda Schatkowski Schilcher, *Families in Politics: Damascene Factions and Estates of the 18th and 19th Centuries* (Stuttgart: Franz Steiner Verlag Wiesbaden GMBH, 1985), pp. 92, 94, 99.

32. Mushāqa, *Mashhad al-ʿiyān,* p. 260; Max Gross, "Ottoman Rule in the Province of Damascus, 1860–1909," (Ph.D. dissertation, Georgetown University, 1979), pp. 44, 364. On Napoleon III's schemes to set up an Arab kingdom, see John P. T. Bury, *Napoleon III and the Second Empire* (London: English Universities Press, 1964), pp. 128–129; William H. C. Smith, *Napoleon III* (London: Wayland Ltd., 1972), p. 191; Ageron, "Abd el-Kader Souverain," pp. 12–20, 22, 24, 27, 28; Marcel Émerit, "La crise syrienne et l'expansion économique française en 1860," *La Revue Historique* (1952): 221. In 1862, rumors spread in Damascus that Jazā'irī was considered a candidate for the Greek throne; "Risālah tārīkhiyyah min al-Shaykh Ṣāliḥ Qaṭanā ila al-Sayyid ʿAlā' al-Dīn al-ʿĀbidīn—1279," *Majallat al-majmaʿ al-ʿilmī al-ʿarabī* 15 (1937): 238.

33. On Jazā'irī's journey to and sojourn in the Hijaz, see Bīṭār, *Ḥilyat al-bashar,* 2:897.

34. The following information on Jazā'irī and the Masons comes from Xavier Yacono, "Abdelkader, franc-macon," *Humanisme* 57 (1966): 5–37. Much of ʿAbd al-Qādir's correspondence with the Masons has been published; ʿAbd al-Jalīl al-Tamīmī, "Wathā'iq jadīdah li al-amīr ʿAbd al-Qādir," *Revue d'Histoire Maghrebine* 6 (1979): 23–32. A local chronicler of Damascus related that the Masons came to Damascus during Meḥmed Reshīd Pasha's term as governor, 1866–1871, and that Meḥmed Reshīd was a Mason; Nuʿmān Qasāṭilī, *al-Rawḍah al-ghannā' fī dimashq al-fayḥā'* (Beirut: n.p., 1879), p. 92; the memoirs of a twentieth-century Syrian politician mention Jazā'irī as a leader of a Masonic lodge in Damascus; Fakhrī al-Bārūdī, *Mudhakkirāt al-Bārūdī,* 2 vols. (Beirut: Dār al-Ḥayāt Press, 1951), 1:63; another author claims that Jazā'irī joined a Masonic lodge established in Damascus around 1879 by governor Midḥat Pasha; ʿAdnān al-Khaṭīb, *al-Shaykh Ṭāhir al-Jazā'irī* (Cairo: Maʿhad al-Dirāsāt al-ʿArabiyyah, 1971), p. 137.

35. Yacono, "Abdelkader, franc-macon," pp. 8–9; Ernest d'Hauterive, ed., *The Second Empire and Its Downfall: The Correspondence of the Emperor Napoleon III and His Cousin Prince Napoleon,* (Freeport, NY: Books for Libraries Press, 1970), pp. 171–175.

36. ʿĀdil al-Ṣulḥ, *Suṭūr min al-risālah* (Beirut: Dār al-ʿIlm li al-Malāyīn, 1966), pp. 98, 100, 103.

37. Ahmad Nadir, "Les ordres religieux et la conquête française," *Revue Algerienne des Sciences Juridiques* 9 (1972): 838, 845–846; Pessah Shinar, "ʿAbd al-Qādir and ʿAbd al-Krim: Religious Influences on Their Thought and Action," *Asian and African Studies* 1 (1965): 150; Muḥammad al-Jazā'irī, *Tuḥfat al-zāhir,* p. 310.

38. ʿAbd al-Qādir al-Jazā'irī, *Kitāb al-mawāqif fī al-taṣawwuf wa al-waʿẓ wa al-irshād,* 3 vols. (Damascus, 1966).

39. Ibid., pp. 26–27.

40. Ibid., pp. 33–34, 61–62, 142.

41. Ibid., pp. 49–50, 383–384, 271–272.

42. Churchill, *Ḥayāt* ʿAbd al-Qādir, p. 27.

43. Muḥammad ʿAbd al-Jawād al-Qāyātī, *Nafḥat al-bashām fī riḥlat al-shām* (Cairo: Jarīdat al-Islām Press, 1901/2), pp. 4–6, 30, 145, 192–195. Qāyātī was among the exiled Egyptians. He left an account of his sojourn in Beirut and travels in Syria, including a visit to Damascus in the winter of 1885. Nikki R. Keddie, *Sayyid Jamāl al-Dīn "al-Afghānī"* (Berkeley: University of California Press, 1972), p. 187; Muḥammad al-Jazā'irī, *Tuḥfat al-zāhir,* pp. 625–626, 820, 827; Qāsimī, "Taʿṭīr al-mashām," unrevised copy, II, unnumbered pages, p. 7; Bīṭār, *Ḥilyat al-bashar,* 1:11.

44. Jamāl al-Dīn al-Afghānī and Muḥammad ʿAbduh, *al-ʿUrwah al-wuthqā* (Beirut: Dār

al-Kitāb al-ʿArabī, 1980); Muḥammad ʿAbduh, *Risālat al-tawḥīd* (Cairo: Dār al-Maʿārif, n.d.).

45. Afghānī and ʿAbduh, *al-ʿUrwah al-wuthqā,* pp. 50, 61, 68, 160–61, 175.

46. Jamāl al-Dīn al-Afghānī. Works listed in Iraj Afshar, *Majmūʿah-i asnād va madārik-i chap na-shudah dār barah-i Sayyid Jamāl al-Dīn mashhūr bi-Afghānī,* (Tehran, 1963), p. 43. Film copy of originals in Kitābkhānah-i Majlis, Tehran. University of California, Los Angeles.

47. ʿAbduh, *Risālat al-tawḥīd,* p. 24.

48. On ʿAbduh and Faraḥ Anṭūn, see Hourani, *Arabic Thought,* pp. 149–148, 254–258.

49. ʿAbduh, *Risālat al-tawḥīd,* pp. 30, 37.

Chapter 3

1. Malcolm Kerr, *Islamic Reform: The Political and Legal Theories of Muhammad ʿAbduh and Rashid Rida* (Berkeley: University of California Press, 1966); Charles Adams, *Islam and Modernism in Egypt* (London: Russell & Russell, 1933); Henri Laoust, "Le réformisme orthodoxe des 'salafiya' et les caractères généraux de son orientation actuelle," *Revue des Études Islamiques* 6 (1932): 175–232.

2. Munīr Mūsā, *al-Fikr al-ʿarabī fī al-ʿaṣr al-ḥadīth* (Beirut: Dār al-Ḥaqīqah, 1973), pp. 12, 25; Z. I. Livin, *al-Fikr al-ijtimāʿī wa al-siyāsī al-ḥadīth fī lubnān wa sūriyā wa miṣr* (Beirut: Dār Ibn Khaldūn, 1978), pp. 45, 97 n. 5.

3. John Voll, *Islam: Continuity and Change in the Modern World* (Boulder: Westview Press, 1982), pp. 37, 48.

4. On the early history of the Naqshbandiyyah, see Hamid Algar, "The Naqshbandi Order: A Preliminary Survey of Its History and Significance," *Studia Islamica* 44 (1976): 123–152; J. Spencer Trimingham, *The Sufi Orders in Islam* (London: Oxford University Press, 1971), pp. 62–64, 95; on the Murādīs, see Linda Schatkowski Schilcher, *Families in Politics: Damascene Factions and Estates of the 18th and 19th Centuries* (Stuttgart: Franz Steiner Verlag Wiesbaden GMBH, 1985), pp. 161–165.

5. On Shaykh Khālid, see ʿAbd al-Majīd al-Khānī, *al-Ḥadā'iq al-wardiyyah fī ḥaqā'iq ajillā' al-naqshbandiyyah* (Cairo: Dār al-Ṭibāʿah al-ʿĀmirah, 1890), pp. 229–258; ʿAbd al-Razzāq al-Bīṭār, *Ḥilyat al-bashar fī tārīkh al-qarn al-thālith ʿashar,* 3 vols. (Damascus: Majmaʿ al-Lughah al-ʿArabiyyah, 1961–1963), 1:570–587; Albert Hourani, "Shaykh Khalid and the Naqshbandi Order," in S. M. Stern, A. Hourani, and V. Brown, eds., *Islamic Philosophy and the Classical Tradition: Essays Presented to R. Walzer* (Columbia, SC: University of South Carolina Press, 1972), pp. 89–103. On the reformed Naqshbandiyyah's intolerance, see Juan R. Cole, "Imami Shi'ism from Iran to North India, 1722–1856: State, Society, and Clerical Ideology in Awadh," (Ph.D. dissertation, University of California, Los Angeles, 1984), p. 324; Butrus Abu-Manneh, "The Naqshbandiyya-Mujaddidiya in the Ottoman Lands in the Early 19th Century," *Die Welt des Islams* 22 (1982): 15.

6. Voll, *Islam,* pp. 37, 48; Jamāl al-Dīn al-Qāsimī, "Taʿṭīr al-mashām fī ma'āthīr dimashq al-shām," 4 vols. manuscript, Qāsimī library, Damascus, revised copy, 2:442.

7. On Muḥammad ibn ʿAbd Allah al-Khānī, see Khānī, *al-Ḥadā'iq al-wardiyyah,* pp. 262–276; Bīṭār, *Ḥilyat al-bashar,* 3:1210–1215; Muḥammad Salīm al-Jundī, *Tārīkh maʿarrat al-nuʿmān,* 3 vols. (Damascus: Wizārat al-Thaqāfah wa al-Siyāḥah wa al-Irshād al-Qawmī, 1963–1967), 2:171–172; Muḥammad Jamīl al-Shaṭṭī, *Aʿyān dimashq fī al-qarn al-thālith ʿashar wa nisf al-qarn al-rābiʿ ʿashar* (Damascus: Al-Maktab al-Islāmī, 1972), pp. 237–238.

8. Abu-Manneh, "The Naqshbandiyya-Mujaddidiyya," p. 35.

9. Bīṭār, *Ḥilyat al-bashar,* 2:1038; Khānī, *al-Ḥadā'iq al-wardiyyah,* pp. 267–268; on the

Naqshbandiyyah-Mujaddidiyyah's appeal to reformist bureaucrats in Istanbul, see Abu-Manneh, "The Naqshbandiyya-Mujaddidiyya," pp. 19–32.

10. Muḥammad ibn ʿAbd Allah al-Khānī, *Kitāb al-bahjah al-saniyah fī ādāb al-ṭarīqah al-ʿaliyah al-khālidiyyah al-naqshbandiyyah* (Cairo: Dhāt al-Taḥrīr Press, 1885).

11. Khānī, *al-Ḥadā'iq al-wardiyyah,* pp. 278–279.

12. Ibid., pp. 280, 288–290. The pagination in this work on pages 287–288 is mistakenly printed as pages 279–280, so the reference to page 288 is to the second printing of page 280. Khānī's marriage to Shaykh Khālid's daughter probably gave him an edge in his competition with two other aspirants to lead the order in Damascus; see Abu-Manneh, "The Naqshbandiyya-Mujaddidiya," pp. 34–35. On Khānī's property, see Center for Historical Documentation, Damascus, sijill 1151, pp. 180–182.

13. Bīṭār, *Ḥilyat al-bashar,* 1:184–185. Center for Historical Documentation, Damascus, sijill 500 no. 290, sijill 1183, pp. 1–2.

14. On ʿAbd al-Majīd's correspondence with ʿAbduh, see Muḥammad ʿAbd al-Jawād al-Qāyātī, *Nafḥat al-bashām fī riḥlat al-shām* (Cairo: Jarīdat al-Islām Press, 1901/2), pp. 186–191; Rashīd Riḍā, *Tārīkh al-ustādh al-imām al-shaykh Muḥammad ʿAbduh,* 2 vols. (Cairo: Al-Manār Press, 1931), pp. 611–613; on Khānī's caution in expressing his views, see Adham al-Jundī, *Aʿlām al-adab wa al-fann,* 2 vols. (Damascus: Majallat Ṣawt Sūriyah, 1954), 2:116; on his praise for the anti-Wahhābī essay, see ʿAṭā' al-Kasm, *al-Aqwāl al-murḍiyah fī al-radd ʿala al-wahhābiyyah* (Cairo: Al-ʿUmūmiyyah Press, 1901), p. 29; on his laudatory verse for Ottoman officials, see Iskandar Lūqā, *al-Ḥarakah al-adabiyyah fī dimashq* (Damascus: Alif Bā' Press, 1976), p. 127. On ʿAbd al-Majīd al-Khānī, see Bīṭār, *Ḥilyat al-bashar,* 2:1037–1040; Muḥammad Adīb Āl Taqī al-Dīn al-Ḥiṣnī, *Muntakhabāt al-tawārīkh li dimashq,* 3 vols. (Damascus: Al-Ḥadīthah Press, 1928), 2:749–750; Shaṭṭī, *Aʿyān,* p. 403.

15. Qāsimī, "Taʿṭīr al-mashām," unrevised copy, II, unnumbered pages, 7; Bīṭār, *Ḥilyat al-bashar,* 2:1038–1039.

16. Bīṭār, *Ḥilyat al-bashar,* 2:1038–1039.

17. On Muḥammad al-Khānī's appointment to the conscription council, see Kamāl al-Ṣalībī, "Lamaḥāt min tārīkh dimashq fī ʿahd al-tanẓīmāt," *al-Abḥāth* 21 (1968): 69; on ʿAbd al-Majīd al-Khānī's court post, see Jamāl al-Dīn al-Qāsimī, "Taʿṭīr al-mashām," unrevised copy, II, unnumbered pages, 7.

18. On Aḥmad al-Jazā'irī, see Ḥiṣnī, *Muntakhabāt,* 2:704–705; Shaṭṭī, *Aʿyān dimashq,* pp. 414–415; Aḥmad al-Jazā'irī, *Nathr al-durr wa basaṭuhu fī bayān kawn al-ʿilm nuqṭah* (Beirut: Al-Ahliyyah Press, 1906), pp. 2–3; Qāsimī, "Taʿṭīr al-masham," unrevised, II, unnumbered pages, 23–24.

19. Aḥmad al-Jazā'irī, *Nathr al-durr.*

20. Qāsimī, "Taʿṭīr al-mashām," unrevised, II, unnumbered pages, 23–24.

21. *Al-Manār* 17 (1914): 558. On ʿAbd al-Razzāq al-Bīṭār, see *Ḥilyat al-bashar,* introduction by Muḥammad Bahjat al-Bīṭār, pp. 9–20; Muḥammad Bahjat al-Bīṭār, "Tarjamat al-shaykh ʿAbd al-Razzāq al-Bīṭār," *al-Manār* 21 (1919): 317–324; Adham al-Jundī, *Aʿlām al-adab,* 1:220–222.

22. Bīṭār was called "thānī al-amīr"; Muḥammad Bahjat al-Bīṭār, "Tarjamat al-shaykh," 318.

23. Bīṭār, *Ḥilyat al-bashar,* 1:6–7. The Bīṭārs' ancestors had come from Algeria in the seventeenth century; Muḥammad Bahjat al-Bīṭār, *al-Riḥlah al-najdiyyah al-ḥijāziyyah: ṣuwar min ḥayāt al-bādiyah* (Damascus: Al-Jadīdah Press, 1967), p. 50.

24. On Ḥasan al-Bīṭār, see Bīṭār, *Ḥilyat al-bashar,* 1:463–475.

25. On patronage in Damascene quarters early in the twentieth century, see Philip S. Khoury, "Syrian Urban Politics in Transition: The Quarters of Damascus During the French Mandate," *International Journal of Middle East Studies* 16 (1984): 507–540.

26. On Ḥasan al-ʿAṭṭār and ʿĀrif Ḥikmet Pasha, see Peter Gran, *Islamic Roots of Capitalism: Egypt, 1760–1840* (Austin: University of Texas Press, 1979), pp. 107–108, 125–126.

27. ʿAbd al-Razzāq wrote that around 1851 Ottoman provincial officers offered Ḥasan al-Bīṭār the post of jurisconsult, but Bīṭār declined to assume it because he felt secure in his local post and would not feel so as jurisconsult; *Ḥilyat al-bashar,* 2:748. Ḥasan al-Bīṭār expressed his loyalty to the sultan in a treatise enjoining Muslims to fulfill the duty of jihad during the empire's war with Russia in the Crimea; Ḥasan al-Bīṭār, "Irshād al-ʿibād fī faḍl al-jihād," manuscript no. 7166, Ẓāhiriyyah Library, Damascus. On Muḥammad al-Bīṭār, see Shaṭṭī, *Aʿyān dimashq,* pp. 359–360; on Muḥammad al-Bīṭār's estate, see Center for Historical Documentation, Damascus, sijill 1040, 38–43.

28. On ʿAbd al-Ghanī al-Bīṭār, see *Ḥilyat al-bashar,* 2:873–881; on Bahā' al-Dīn al-Bīṭār, see ibid., 1:380–381; on Salīm al-Bīṭār, see Ḥiṣnī, *Muntakhabāt,* 2:859.

29. On Bīṭār's sermon and the Maydani notables' protection for Christians, see Bīṭār, *Ḥilyat al-bashar,* 1:263–265; Schilcher, *Families in Politics,* pp. 78, 97.

30. For Bīṭār's account of July 1860, see Bīṭār, *Ḥilyat al-bashar,* 1:261–276.

31. Qāyātī, *Nafḥat al-bashām,* pp. 145, 192–195; Bīṭār, *Ḥilyat al-bashar,* 1:11, 204–205.

32. On superstitious beliefs and amulets, see ibid., 2:725–727; on Bīṭār's kind words for later adversaries, see on Muḥammad al-Manīnī, 3:1183–1188, and on Badr al-Dīn al-Ḥasanī, 1:375. Bīṭār stopped working on *Ḥilyat* in 1896 when he suffered partial paralysis in his right hand; see Muḥammad Bahjat al-Bīṭār, "al-Mudarrisūn taḥt qubbat al-nasr," *Majallat al-majmaʿ al-ʿilmī al-ʿarabī* 24 (1949): 59.

33. Conversations with Dr. Muṭīʿ al-Ḥāfiẓ of the Arabic Language Academy, Damascus, and Mr. Samīḥ al-Ghabrah, grandson of Jamāl al-Dīn al-Qāsimī.

34. Bīṭār, *Ḥilyat al-bashar,* 3:1573, 2:669–673, 2:682–683, 2:736–746, 1:486–487, 1:439–450.

35. On ʿAbd al-Ghanī al-Ghunaymī, see Bīṭār, *Ḥilyat al-bashar,* 2:867–872; Shaṭṭī, *Aʿyān dimashq,* pp. 175–176; Ḥiṣnī, *Muntakhabāt,* 2:670; Muḥammad Saʿīd al-Bānī, *Tanwīr al-baṣā'ir bi sīrat al-shaykh Ṭāhir* (Damascus: Al-Ḥukūmah al-ʿArabiyyah al-Sūriyyah Press, 1920), pp. 73–74; Anonymous, *Ḥasr al-lithām ʿan nakabāt al-shām* (Cairo, 1895), p. 235.

36. Muḥammad al-Jazā'irī, *Tuḥfat al-zāhir fī tàrīkh al-jazā'ir wa al-amīr ʿAbd al-Qādir,* (Beirut: Dār al-Yaqẓah al-ʿArabiyyah Press, 1964), pp. 671–672.

37. On Ṣāliḥ al-Jazā'irī, see Bīṭār, *Ḥilyat al-bashar,* 2:733–734; Shaṭṭī, *Aʿyān dimashq,* pp. 149–150; Ḥiṣnī, *Muntakhabāt,* 2:664; ʿAdnān al-Khaṭīb, *al-Shaykh Ṭāhir al-Jazā'irī-rā'id-al-nahḍah al-ʿilmiyyah fī bilād al-shām, (Cairo: Maʿ*had al-Dirāsāt al-ʿArabiyyah, 1971), pp. 91–94; on his emigration to Damascus, see Ṭāhir al-Jazā'irī, "Tārīkh hijrat wālidihi wa baʿḍ masā'il," manuscript no. 11613, Ẓāhiriyyah Library, Damascus. On Ṭāhir's regard for Ghunaymī see Muḥammad Kurd ʿAlī, *al-Muʿāṣirūn* (Damascus: Majmaʿ al-Lughah al-ʿArabiyyah Press, 1980), p. 268.

38. On Ṭāhir al-Jazā'irī, see Khaṭīb, *al-Shaykh Ṭāhir;* Bānī, *Tanwīr al-baṣā'ir;* Kurd ʿAlī, *al-Muʿāṣirūn,* pp. 268–277; Anwar al-Jundī, *Tarājim al-aʿlām al-muʿāṣirīn fī al-ʿālam al-islāmī* (Cairo: Maktabat al-Anglo al-Miṣrī, 1970), pp. 164–173; Muḥammad Kurd ʿAlī, "al-Muʿāṣirūn, al-Shaykh Ṭāhir al-Jazā'irī," *Majallat al-majmaʿ al-ʿilmī al-ʿarabī* 8 (1928) 577–594, 667–677; ʿĪsā Iskandar al-Maʿlūf, "al-Shaykh Ṭāhir al-Jazā'irī," *al-Hilāl* 28 (1921): 451–456; for a critical appraisal of Jazā'irī, see Ṣāliḥ Mukhliṣ Riḍā's review of Bānī's *Tanwīr al-baṣā'ir* in *al-Manār* 22 (1921): 635–640.

39. For example, see Kurd ʿAlī, "al-Muʿāṣirūn," p. 578; Riḍā's review of Bānī, p. 638.

40. Khaṭīb, *al-Shaykh Ṭāhir,* pp. 94, 103–110; Saʿīd al-Karamī, "Dawr al-kutub wa fā'idatuhā," *Majallat al-majmaʿ al-ʿilmī al-ʿarabī* 1 (1921): 8–12.

41. Bānī, *Tanwīr al-baṣā'ir,* pp. 15–23; Qāyātī, *Nafḥat al-bashām,* pp. 113–114.

42. In 1897, Ṭāhir al-Jazā'irī listed twenty-two essays by Ibn Taymiyyah that he found at the Ẓāhiriyyah Library; the essays had been copied in 1802 by Aḥmad ibn Ḥusayn ibn Thuwaymar al-Qawwāmī al-Khaṭṭī for ʿAlī ibn Muḥammad ibn ʿAbd al-Wahhāb. Ṭāhir al-Jazā'irī, "Rasā'il Ibn Taymiyyah wa al-kutub allatī naqala ʿanhā fī badīʿ al-qur'ān ghayr mā ishtahar," manuscript no. 11726, Ẓāhiriyyah Library, Damascus.

43. Maʿlūf, "al-Shaykh Ṭāhir al-Jazā'irī," 452; Zakī Mujāhid, *al-Aʿlām al-sharqiyyah fī al-mi'ah al-rābiʿah ʿasharah al-hijriyyah,* 2 vols. (Cairo: Dār al-Ṭibāʿah al-Miṣriyyah al-Ḥadīthah, 1950), 2:114.

44. The best source on Qāsimī is Ẓāfir al-Qāsimī, *Jamāl al-Dīn al-Qāsimī wa ʿaṣruhu* (Damascus: Al-Hāshimiyyah Press, 1965); also Bīṭār, *Ḥilyat al-bashar,* 1:435–438; Rashīd Riḍā's obituary of Qāsimī in *al-Manār* 17 (1914): 558–560, 628–636; in western languages, Qāsimī has merited only brief mention in Henri Laoust, *Essai sur les doctrines sociales et politiques de Takī-al-Dīn Aḥmad ibn Taimiyyah* (Cairo: L'Institut Français d'Archéologie Orientale, 1939), pp. 535–536, as a disciple of Ibn Taymiyyah; in Laoust, "Le réformisme orthodoxe des 'salafiya,' " p. 191; and Abd al-Latif al-Tibawi, *A Modern History of Syria* (London: Macmillan and Co., 1969), p. 185.

45. On Qāsim al-Ḥallāq, see Shaṭṭī, *Aʿyān dimashq,* pp. 221–224; Bīṭār, *Ḥilyat al-bashar,* 2:725–727; Qāsimī, "Taʿṭīr al-mashām," revised copy, 2:443–445, 458–462; Muḥammad Saʿīd al-Qāsimī, "al-Thughr al-bāsim fī tarjamat al-shaykh Qāsim," manuscript, Qāsimī library, Damascus. ʿAbd al-Raḥmān al-Kuzbarī enjoyed prestige and wealth because of his family's stature in Damascus. He followed in the path of his father and grandfather as the foremost scholar of oral reports in Damascus, holding the teaching post at the Nasr Dome in the Umayyad mosque; Bīṭār, *Ḥilyat al-bashar,* 1:165–166, 2:833–836; Shaṭṭī, *Aʿyān dimashq,* pp. 160–162; on the Kuzbarīs' wealth, see Center for Historical Documentation, sijillāt 839, 138; 885, 146–147; 926, 134; 960, 134–136; 1035, 157–158; 1233, 101; 1340, 59–60; the Kuzbarīs held the Nasr Dome post from 1782 until 1913; Muḥammad Bahjat al-Bīṭār, "al-Mudarrisūn taḥt qubbat al-nasr," 224–226.

46. Qāsimī, "Taʿṭīr al-mashām," revised copy, 2:458.

47. Qāsim al-Ḥallāq belonged to the Qādirī, Rifāʿī, and Khālidī-Naqshbandī orders; Shaṭṭī, *Aʿyān dimashq,* p. 221. Muḥammad Saʿīd al-Qāsimī, "al-Thughr al-bāsim," p. 70; Qāsimī, "Taʿṭīr al-mashām," revised copy, 2:460.

48. Center for Historical Documentation, sijill 581, 109–110.

49. On Muḥammad Saʿīd al-Qāsimī, see Bīṭār, *Ḥilyat al-bashar,* 2:654–661; Muḥammad Saʿīd al-Qāsimī, *Qāmūs al-ṣināʿāt al-shāmiyyah* (Paris: Mouton & Le Haye, 1960), 1:8–10; Aḥmad ʿIzzat ʿAbd al-Karīm's introduction to Aḥmad al-Budayrī's *Ḥawādith dimashq al-yawmiyyah* (Cairo: Al-Jamʿiyyah al-Miṣriyyah li al-Dirāsāt al-Tārīkhiyyah, 1959), pp. 17–23; Qāsimī, "Taʿṭīr al-mashām," unrevised copy, 2:24–40; Jamāl al-Dīn al-Qāsimī, "Bayt al-qaṣīd fī tarjamat al-imām al-wālid al-saʿīd," manuscript, Qāsimī library, Damascus.

50. Center for Historical Documentation, sijill 581, 110. On Muḥammad Saʿīd al-Qāsimī's purchase of his brothers' shares, see Qāsimī, "Bayt al-qaṣīd," p. 8; on his retail trade, see *Qāmūs al-ṣināʿāt,* p. 8; Ẓāfir al-Qāsimī, *Jamāl al-Dīn al-Qāsimī*, p. 21; interview with Ẓāfir al-Qāsimī, July 1980; on the post at the Ḥassān mosque, see Qāsimī, "Bayt al-qaṣīd," p. 5.

51. Qāsimī, "Bayt al-qaṣīd," pp. 7–8.

52. Ibid., pp. 78–79, 82–83, 100–104.

53. Philip S. Khoury, *Urban Notables and Arab Nationalism: The Politics of Damascus, 1860–1920,* (Cambridge: Cambridge University Press, 1983), pp. 31–35.

54. Aḥmad ʿIzzat ʿAbd al-Karīm in al-Budayri, *Ḥawādith dimashq al-yawmiyyah,* p. 21.

55. On Jamāl al-Dīn al-Qāsimī's youth, see Ẓāfir al-Qāsimī, *Jamāl al-Dīn al-Qāsimī* (hereafter *JDQ*) pp. 23–30. Most of these pages consist of citations from Jamāl al-Dīn's

incomplete autobiography, "Tārīkh al-ustādh Jamāl al-Dīn al-Qāsimī," manuscript, Qāsimī library, Damascus, pp. 1–4. Though Ṭāhir al-Jazā'irī was teaching at the Ẓāhiriyyah school that year, Qāsimī did not have him as a teacher.

56. *JDQ,* pp. 26–29.

57. Qāsimī, "Taʿṭīr al-mashām," unrevised copy, II, unnumbered pages, 26; revised copy, 2:484–485; *JDQ,* p. 30.

58. Qāsimī "Taʿṭīr al-mashām," unrevised copy, II, unnumbered pages, 6; *JDQ,* pp. 383–384.

59. Jamāl al-Dīn al-Qāsimī, *Iṣlāḥ al-masājid min al-bidaʿ wa al-ʿawā'id* (Cairo: Al-Salafiyyah Press, 1923), pp. 262, 269.

60. Jamāl al-Dīn al-Qāsimī, *al-Nafḥah al-raḥmāniyyah, sharḥ matn al-maydāniyyah fī ʿilm al-tajwīd* (Damascus, 1905), p. 2–3.

61. *JDQ,* p. 42; Qāsimī, "Tārīkh al-ustādh Jamāl al-Dīn al-Qāsimī," p. 6. Qāsimī entitled his text "al-Kawkab al-munīr fī mawlid al-bashar al-nadhīr," *JDQ,* pp. 637–638.

62. *JDQ,* p. 637–638.

63. Ibid., p. 36; Jamāl al-Dīn al-Qāsimī, "Badhl al-himam fī mawʿiẓat ahl wādī al-ʿajam," manuscript, Qāsimī library, Damascus.

64. Aḥmad Taymūr, *Aʿlām al-fikr al-islāmī fī al-ʿaṣr al-ḥadīth* (Cairo: Lajnat Nashr al-Mu'allafāt al-Taymūriyyah, 1967), pp. 293–295; Muḥammad Saʿīd al-Bānī, *Majallat al-majmaʿ al-ʿilmī al-ʿarabī* 9 (1929): 742–749; *al-Manār* 29 (1928): 633–634.

65. Muḥammad Saʿīd al-Bānī, *ʿUmdat al-taḥqīq fī al-taqlīd wa al-talfīq* (Damascus: Ḥukūmat Dimashq Press, 1923), pp. 63–67.

66. Zakī Mujāhid, *al-Aʿlām al-sharqiyyah,* II, p. 119; *al-Manār* 8 (1905): 79–80.

67. Maḥmūd al-Arnā'ūṭ, Review of *al-Madkhal ila madhhab al-imām Aḥmad ibn Ḥanbal* by ʿAbd al-Qādir ibn Badrān, in *Majallat al-fayṣal* 7 (1983): 10–11; Mujāhid, *al-Aʿlām al-sharqiyyah,* pp. 128–130; ʿAbd al-Qādir ibn Badrān, *al-Madkhal ila madhhab al-imām Aḥmad ibn Ḥanbal* (Damascus: Dār Iḥyā' al-Turāth al-ʿArabī, n.d.), biographical note at end of the book, pages alif, bā', jīm; on Ibn Badrān's stipend for teaching at ʿAbd Allah al-ʿAẓm school, see Jundī, *Aʿlam al-adab,* p. 224.

68. Saʿīd al-Afghānī, "al-Shaykh Aḥmad al-Nuwaylātī," *al-Tamaddun al-islāmī* 4 (1938): 216–219; Kāmil al-Naṣrī, "al-Ustādh al-Nuwaylātī," *al-Tamaddun al-islāmī* 5 (1939): 166–167. I would like to thank Dr. Muṭīʿ al-Ḥāfiẓ of the Arabic Language Academy for drawing my attention to al-Nuwaylātī and for kindly lending me these two articles.

69. For sketches of these prestigious ulama families, see Schilcher, *Families in Politics,* pp. 156–211; Khoury, *Urban Notables,* pp. 31–35.

Chapter 4

1. The sole account of the incident comes from Qāsimī himself, who provided a wealth of detail but gave a one-sided description. See Ẓāfir al-Qāsimī, *Jamāl al-Dīn al-Qāsimī wa ʿaṣruhu* (Damascus: Al-Hāshimiyyah Press, 1965), pp. 48–69. Hereafter cited as *JDQ*.

2. On Salīm Samārah (1838/9–1913) see ʿAbd al-Razzāq al-Bīṭār, *Ḥilyat al-bashar fī tārīkh al-qarn al-thālith ʿashar,* 3 vols. (Damascus: Majmaʿ al-Lughah al-ʿArabiyyah, 1961–1963), 2:684–685; Samārah and Bīṭār knew each other since their childhoods, and they studied together.

3. On Muṣṭafā al-Ḥallāq (1860–1911) see Jamāl al-Dīn al-Qāsimī, "Taʿṭīr al-mashām fī ma'āthīr dimashq al-shām," manuscript, Qāsimī library, Damascus, unrevised copy, II, unnumbered pages, 37–41. Ḥallāq was Qāsimī's cousin. He gave religious lessons on Ḥanafī jurisprudence until he lost his source of patronage. He found official posts restricted to a few families, so he studied Ottoman civil law and became a lawyer. Muṣṭafā al-Ḥallāq became one of Qāsimī's best friends and a fellow reformer.

4. On Bakrī al-ʿAṭṭār (1834–1903) see Muḥammad Saʿīd al-Bānī, *al-Kawkab al-durrī al-munīr fī aḥkām al-dhahab wa al-fiḍḍah wa al-ḥarīr* (Damascus: Al-Mufīd Press, 1931), pp. 163–175; Muḥammad Jamīl al-Shaṭṭī, *Aʿyān dimashq fī al-qarn al-thālith ʿashar wa niṣf al-qarn al-rābiʿ ʿashar* (Damascus: Al-Maktab al-Islāmī, 1972), pp. 409–413.

5. ʿAbd al-Wahhāb al-Shaʿrānī, *Kashf al-ghummah ʿan jamīʿ al-ummah* (Cairo, n.d.). On Shaʿrānī's life and thought, see Michael Winter, *Society and Religion in Early Ottoman Egypt* (New Brunswick, NJ: Transaction Books, 1982). Jamāl al-Dīn al-Qāsimī, "Ghanīmat al-himmah fī kashf al-ghummah," incomplete manuscript, Qāsimī library, Damascus.

6. For details on the salafi claim to ijtihād, see Chapter 5; for an overview of the history of debate on ijtihād, see Wael B. Hallaq, "Was the Gate of Ijtihād Closed?" *International Journal of Middle East Studies* 16 (1984): 3–41.

7. *JDQ*, p. 52. On Badr al-Dīn al-Ḥasanī, who later became the salafis' adversary, see Chapter 8.

8. On Muḥammad al-Manīnī, see below Notes 12–13.

9. For details of the interrogation, see *JDQ*, pp. 54–63.

10. The essay's Arabic title is "Tanbīh al-ghamr fī radd shubuh ṭahārat al-khamr;" *JDQ*, p. 54.

11. On the dispute over succession to the jurisconsult's post following Maḥmūd al-Ḥamzāwī's death, see Bīṭār, *Ḥilyat al-bashar*, 1:311, where Bīṭār insinuated that Asʿad al-Ḥamzāwī was not fit to be mufti, and 3:1186, 1476; Great Britain, Public Record Office, Foreign Office, 195/1583/37: Dickson to White, 29 September 1887; no. 38 Dickson to White, 7 November 1887.

12. *JDQ*, p. 65; for a similar view of Manīnī, see ʿAbd al-Qādir ibn Badrān, *Munādamat al-aṭlāl wa musāmarat al-khayāl* (Damascus: Al-Maktab al-Islāmī, 1960), pp. 123–126; more sympathetic descriptions are in Bīṭār, *Ḥilyat al-bashar*, 3:1183–1188; Muḥammad Adīb Āl Taqī al-Dīn al-Ḥiṣnī, *Muntakhabāt al-tawārīkh li dimashq*, 3 vols. (Damascus: Al-Ḥadīthah Press, 1928), 2:788–790.

13. Kamāl Ṣalībī and ʿAbd Allah Abū Ḥabīb, "Lamaḥāt min tārīkh dimashq fī ʿahd al-tanẓīmāt," *al-Abḥāth* 21 (1968): 62, 70, 72–73. On Aḥmad ibn ʿAlī al-Manīnī (1678–1759) see Ḥiṣnī, *Muntakhabāt*, 2:617; Badrān, *Munādamat al-aṭlāl*, pp. 123–124; Bīṭār, *Ḥilyat al-bashar*, 3:1185–1187. On Manīnī's taking Ḥalabī's post after 1860, see Bīṭār, *Ḥilyat al-bashar*, 2:1010.

14. On Manīnī's reconciliation with the salafis, see *JDQ*, pp. 66–68.

15. Bīṭār, *Ḥilyat al-bashar*, 1:436.

16. *JDQ*, p. 71.

17. Qāsimī read Mālik's *al-Muwaṭṭa'* and the works of Muslim and Ibn Mājah between mid-June and early September 1898. Jamāl al-Dīn al-Qāsimī, *Qawāʿid al-taḥdīth min funūn muṣṭalaḥ al-ḥadīth* (Damascus: Ibn Zaydūn Press, 1931), p. 263.

18. On Sultan Abdülḥamīd, Abū al-Hudā al-Ṣayyādī, and the salafis, see *al-Manār* 1 (1897): 598–601, 665–667; Rashīd Riḍā, *Tārīkh al-ustādh al-imām al-shaykh Muḥammad ʿAbduh*, 2 vols. (Cairo: Al-Manār Press, 1931), 1:72–73, 84–90, 580–581, 1015; Muḥammad Bahjat al-Atharī, *Maḥmūd Shukrī al-Alūsī wa ārā'uhu al-lughawiyyah* (Cairo: Al-Kamāliyyah Press, 1958), pp. 8, 77–87; on Abū al-Hudā al-Ṣayyādī, see Butrus Abu-Manneh, "Sultan Abdülḥamīd II and Shaikh Abūlhudā al-Ṣayyādī," *Middle Eastern Studies* 15 (1979): 131–153; Muḥammad Salīm al-Jundī, *Tārīkh maʿarrat al-nuʿmān*, 3 vols. (Damascus: Wizārat al-Thaqāfah wa al-Siyāḥah wa al-Irshād al-Qawmī, 1967), 1:210, 214–215, 257–260, and 2:163, 215–229; Bīṭār, *Ḥilyat al-bashar*, 1:72–84.

19. On ʿAbd al-Ḥamīd al-Zahrāwī, see Bīṭār, *Ḥilyat al-bashar*, 2:791–796; Adham al-Jundī, *Shuhadā' al-ḥarb al-ʿālamiyyah al-kubrā* (Damascus: Al-ʿUrūbah Press, 1960), pp. 97–99; Qadrī Qalʿajī, *al-Sābiqūn* (Beirut: Dār al-ʿIlm li al-Malāyīn, 1954), pp. 31–38; Aḥmad

Nabhān al-Ḥumsī, "Tarjamat al-Sayyid ʿAbd al-Ḥamīd ibn al-Sayyid Muḥammad Shākir ibn al-Sayyid Ibrāhīm al-Zahrāwī," *al-Manār* 21 (1919): 150–153, 207–211; Rashīd Riḍā, "al-Sayyid ʿAbd al-Ḥamīd al-Zahrāwī," *al-Manār* 19 (1916): 169–178; for a critical, indeed hostile, portrait of Zahrāwī, see Muḥammad Kurd ʿAlī, *Mudhakkirāt*, 3 vols. (Damascus: Al-Taraqqī Press, 1947), 1:116–118.

20. Riḍā, "al-Sayyid ʿAbd al-Ḥamīd al-Zahrāwī," 169.

21. The newspaper's name was *al-Maʿlūmāt;* Riḍā, "al-Sayyid ʿAbd al-Ḥamīd al-Zahrāwī," 170. On the incident causing Zahrāwī's expulsion from Istanbul, see Ḥumsī, "Tarjamat al-Sayyid ʿAbd al-Ḥamīd," 151–152; FO 195/2097/80: Richards to O'Conor, 30 December 1901.

22. Riḍā, "al-Sayyid ʿAbd al-Ḥamīd al-Zahrāwī," 170–171; on the article "al-Imāmah wa shurūṭuhā," see Jundī, *Shuhadā'*, pp. 97–98.

23. ʿAbd al-Ḥamīd al-Zahrāwī, *al-Fiqh wa al-taṣawwuf* (Cairo: Al-ʿUmūmiyyah Press, 1901). Muḥammad Kurd ʿAlī related that he helped publish the essay in Cairo and that as a result he could not return to Damascus for a long time; see Muḥammad Kurd ʿAlī, *Mudhakkirāt*, 1:251. For accounts of the controversy over Zahrāwī's essay, see Bīṭār, *Ḥilyat al-bashar*, 2:791–792; Jundī, *Shuhadā'*, p. 98; Riḍā, "al-Sayyid ʿAbd al-Ḥamīd al-Zahrāwī," 170–171; FO 195/2097/80: Richards to O'Conor, 30 December 1901; no. 82 Richards to O'Conor, 31 December 1901.

24. *JDQ*, p. 205; Bīṭār, *Ḥilyat al-bashar*, 2:796; FO 195/2097 no. 80.

25. Zahrāwī, *Al-Fiqh wa al-taṣawwuf* (hereafter cited as *Fiqh*); the essay originated in an exchange of views between Zahrāwī and Riḍā in the summer of 1901. See *Fiqh*, pp. 2–10. Other reformers who wrote on the issue of disunity included ʿAbduh and Afghānī; they wrote in *al-ʿUrwah al-wuthqā* that Muslim solidarity began to decline during the Abbasid era early in the third Muslim century; see Jamāl al-Dīn al-Afghānī and Muḥammad ʿAbduh, *al-ʿUrwah al-wuthqā* (Beirut: Dār al-Kitāb al-ʿArabī, 1980), p. 74; ʿAbduh later traced splits in the Muslim community back to the murder of the third caliph ʿUthmān; see Muḥammad ʿAbduh *Risālat al-tawḥīd* (Cairo: Dār al-Maʿārif, n.d.), pp. 26–30; Rafīq al-ʿAẓm, a Damascene salafi expatriate writer in Cairo, also dated divisions among Muslims to the murder of ʿUthmān; see "al-Jāmiʿah al-islāmiyyah wa urūbā," in ʿUthmān al-ʿAẓm, ed., *Majmūʿat āthār Rafīq Bey al-ʿAẓm* (Cairo: Al-Manār Press, 1925), p. 49. On niẓām in the sense of constitution, see Ami Ayalon, *Language and Change in the Arab Middle East* (New York: Oxford University Press, 1987), p. 94.

26. For Qāsimī's and Bīṭār's positions on Sufism, see the section on Sufi Orders and Sufism in Chapter 6.

27. Bīṭār, *Ḥilyat al-bashar*, 2:792; Riḍā, "*al-Fiqh wa al-taṣawwuf*," *al-Manār* 4 (1902): 838–839.

28. The literary riddles were published as *al-Ṭā'ir al-maymūn fī ḥall lughz al-kanz al-madfūn* (Beirut: Thamārat al-Funūn Press, 1898); the Sunnah prayers are in *al-Awrād al-ma'thūrah* (Beirut: Thamārat al-Funūn Press, 1902); Qāsimī had published an article in Damascus's only newspaper of the time, "Tanwīr al-lubb fī maʿrifat al-qalb," *al-Shām*, no. 62, September 25, 1897.

29. Jamāl al-Dīn al-Qāsimī, *Muntakhab al-tawassulāt* (Damascus: Rawḍat al-Shām Press, 1901), pp. 3–4.

30. Manuscript, Qāsimī library, Damascus.

31. Jamāl al-Dīn al-Qāsimī, "Tārīkh al-ustādh Jamāl al-Dīn al-Qāsimī," manuscript, Qāsimī library, Damascus, p. 63. Qāsimī copied a number of letters he exchanged with ʿAbd al-Razzāq al-Bīṭār when the latter was in Istanbul in 1897; see ibid., pp. 69–80.

32. Ibid., p. 67.

33. For Jamāl al-Dīn al-Qāsimī's early correspondence with Moroccan salafis, see *JDQ*,

pp. 561–571 (letters from ʿAbd al-Raḥmān and ʿAbd al-Ḥayy al-Kattānī); Jamāl al-Dīn al-Qāsimī, *Dalā'il al-tawḥīd* (Damascus: Al-Fayḥā' Press, 1908), pp. 182–187 (letters from ulama in Java, the Sudan, and Tunisia). Qāsimī listed his contributions to such Syrian newspapers as *Ṭarāblus al-shām* and *al-Shām* in "T ārīkh," pp. 55–56, 86; to the Egyptian magazine *al-Muqtaṭaf* (1897), ibid., p. 85; and to the Beirut newspaper *Thamārat al-funūn* (1901–1902), ibid., pp. 85–86.

34. Jamāl al-Dīn al-Qāsimī, "Bayt al-qaṣīd fī tarjamat al-imām al-wālid al-saʿīd," manuscript, Qāsimī library, Damascus, pp. 8–10; *JDQ,* p. 37. The only printed source for Muḥammad Saʿīd al-Qāsimī's verse is Bīṭār, *Ḥilyat al-bashar,* 2:656, 660–661, where Qāsimī excoriated the wealthy for their indifference toward the hardships the poor suffered during winter.

35. Adīb Khuḍūr, *Al-Ṣiḥāfah al-sūriyyah; nash'atuhā, taṭawwuruhā, wa wāqiʿuhā al-rāhin* (Damascus: Dār al-Baʿth, 1972), p. 77; Donald J. Cioeta, "Ottoman Censorship in Lebanon and Syria, 1876–1908," *International Journal of Middle East Studies* 10 (1979): 179.

36. Jamāl al-Dīn al-Qāsimī alluded to the refuge Cairo afforded to Syrian intellectuals when he explained Ṭāhir al-Jazā'irī's emigration in 1907: "Attracting him [Jazā'irī] to reside in Egypt is the presence of a number of his friends there, such as Muḥammad Afandī Kurd ʿAlī, Maḥmūd Bāshā al-Jazā'irī, Rafīq Bey al-ʿAẓm, al-Shaykh Muṣṭafā al-Qabbānī, ʿAbd al-Ḥamīd al-Zahrāwī, and others. . . ." *JDQ,* p. 438. Kurd ʿAlī, ʿAẓm, and Zahrāwī, like Jazā'irī, advocated religious reform and favored the restoration of constitutional government. Ḥumsī, "Tarjamat al-Sayyid ʿAbd al-Ḥamīd," p. 153; *JDQ,* pp. 437–438; Walid Kazziha, "The Jarīdah-Ummah Group in Egyptian Politics," *Middle Eastern Studies* 13 (1977): 374–375. On Riḍā's emigration to Cairo to seek greater intellectual freedom, see his autobiography in Shakīb Arslān, *Al-Sayyid Rashīd Riḍā, aw ikhā' arbaʿīn sanah* (Damascus: Ibn Zaydūn Press, 1937), pp. 128–129.

37. On Qāsimī and Bīṭār's journey to Egypt, see *JDQ,* pp. 133–160.

38. Ibid., p. 134. Three years later electric lighting and a tramway came to Damascus; FO 195/2217/36: Devey to Barclay, 5 December 1906; 195/2245/2: Devey to Barclay 12 January 1907; no. 5, Devey to O'Conor, 11 February 1907; no. 6, Devey to O'Conor, 17 February 1907. Qāsimī wrote in his diary on 12 February 1907, "The tramway officially ran from in front of the courthouse to al-Salihiyyah . . . and a line was extended to illuminate Bab al-Sarijah with electricity. Civilization has burst in on Damascus and no wonder, for today is the age of electricity and steam." *JDQ,* p. 376.

39. Ibid., pp. 140, 142, 144, 147–148, 154–155. In all, Qāsimī attended ʿAbduh's lessons seven times, four of them his lesson on exegesis.

40. Ibid., p. 139. For details on Rafīq al-ʿAẓm, see the section on the senior circle in Chapter 7.

41. Qāsimī and Bīṭār met with the Shaykh al-Azhar but once; otherwise they went to al-Azhar only to attend ʿAbduh's lessons; ibid., p. 139. On the antagonism between ʿAbduh and al-Azhar, see A. B. de Guerville, *New Egypt* (London: William Heinemann, 1906), p. 141; Daniel Crecilius, "Nonideological Responses of the Egyptian Ulama to Modernization," in *Scholars, Saints, and Sufis,* Nikki R. Keddie, ed. (Berkeley: University of California Press, 1972), pp. 192–193; Albert Hourani, *Arabic Thought in the Liberal Age* (London: Oxford University Press, 1962), pp. 154–155.

42. *JDQ,* p. 157; Jamāl al-Dīn al-Qāsimī, *Mawʿiẓat al-mu'minīn min iḥyā' ʿulūm al-dīn* (Cairo: Al-Saʿādah Press, 1913).

43. *JDQ,* p. 159. Muḥammad ʿAbduh considered al-Shāṭibī's *al-Muwāfaqāt* the best work on legal theory; Riḍā, *Tārīkh al-ustādh al-imām Muḥammad ʿAbduh,* p. 516.

44. *JDQ,* pp. 148, 151. For Riḍā's review, see *al-Manār* 7 (1904); Jamāl al-Dīn al-Qāsimī, *Shadhrah min al-sīrah al-muḥammadiyyah* (Cairo: Al-Manār Press, 1904).

45. *JDQ*, pp. 206–209.

46. On Muḥammad Fawzī al-ʿAẓm, see Philip S. Khoury, *Urban Notables and Arab Nationalism* (Cambridge: Cambridge University Press, 1983), pp. 36–37, 62, 63, 65, 70.

47. On the restrictions on discussion set by convention at central mosques and freer discourse in lesser mosques and salons in Morocco, see Dale F. Eickelman, "The Art of Memory: Islamic Education and Its Social Reproduction," *Comparative Studies in Society and History* 20 (1978): 500–503.

Chapter 5

1. Jamāl al-Dīn al-Qāsimī, *al-Masḥ ʿala al-jawrabayn wa al-naʿlayn* (Damascus: Al-Taraqqī Press, 1914), p. 4.

2. ʿAdnān al-Khaṭīb, *al-Shaykh Ṭāhir al-Jazāʾirī* (Cairo: Maʿhad al-Dirāsāt al-ʿArabiyyah, 1971), pp. 23–25; Muḥammad Saʿīd al-Bānī, "Salīm al-Bukhārī," *Majallat al-majmaʿ al-ʿilmī al-ʿarabī* 9 (1929): 744; ʿAbd al-Qādir ibn Badrān, *Munādamat al-aṭlāl wa musāmarat al-khayāl* (Damascus: Al-Maktab al-Islāmī, 1960); *al-Madkhal ila madhhab al-imām Aḥmad ibn Ḥanbal* (Dār Iḥyāʾ al-Turāth al-ʿArabī, n.d.). For a list of Ibn Badrān's works still in manuscript, see Zakī Mujāhid, *al-Aʿlām al-sharqiyyah fī al-miʾah al-rābiʿah ʿasharah al-hijriyyah,* 2 vols. (Cairo: Dār al-Ṭibāʿah al-Miṣriyyah al-Ḥadīthah, 1950), 2:129–130.

3. Jamāl al-Dīn al-Qāsimī, *al-Faḍl al-mubīn ʿala ʿiqd al-jawhar al-thamīn* (Beirut: Dār al-Nafāʾis, 1983).

4. Qāsimī's most concise statement on reason and revelation is in "Taʿāruḍ al-ʿaql wa al-naql," *al-Manār* 13 (1910): 613–634.

5. For summary treatments of classical Muslim philosophers dealing with the reason-versus-revelation issue, see Majid Fakhry, *A History of Islamic Philosophy* (New York: Columbia University Press, 1970), on al-Kindī, pp. 84–85, 104–109; on al-Rāzī, pp. 115–124; on al-Fārābī, p. 134; on Ibn Sīnā, pp. 163–164; on the Brethren of Purity, pp. 200, 204; on al-Tawḥīdī, pp. 208–209; on al-Ashʿarī, p. 235; and on Ibn Rushd, pp. 308–316.

6. Jamāl al-Dīn al-Qāsimī, *Dalāʾil al-tawḥīd* (Damascus: Al-Fayḥāʾ Press, 1908), pp. 177–178; Qāsimī referred to the materialists variously as *al-dahriyyah, al-mulāḥidah,* and *al-zanādiqah,* thus showing the identity in his terms of materialists and atheists; ibid., p. 100; Ṭāhir al-Jazāʾirī also was concerned about young educated men abandoning Islam; Muḥammad Saʿīd al-Bānī, *Tanwīr al-baṣāʾir bi sīrat al-shaykh Ṭāhir* (Damascus: Al-Ḥukūmah al-ʿArabiyyah al-Sūriyyah Press, 1920), pp. 46, 89.

7. For a discussion of other works in this genre, see Fahmī Jadʿān, *Usus al-taqaddum ʿinda mufakkirī al-islām fī al-ʿālam al-ʿarabī al-ḥadīth* (Beirut: Al-Muʾassasah al-ʿArabiyyah li al-Dirāsāt wa al-Nashr, 1979), pp. 193–229. Jamāl al-Dīn al-Qāsimī, *Dalāʾil,* pp. 176, 182–187.

8. Jamāl al-Dīn al-Qāsimī, *Dalāʾil,* pp. 13–50; Ṭāhir al-Jazāʾiri is said to have given similar arguments to prove monotheism; Bānī, *Tanwīr,* p. 45. On the other hand, Rashīd Riḍā argued that religions spread because of "efficient organization rather than intrinsic truth." Juan Ricardo Cole, "Rashīd Riḍā on the Bahāʾī Faith: A Utilitarian Theory of the Spread of Religions," *Arab Studies Quarterly* 5 (1983): 276–291.

9. Jamāl al-Dīn al-Qāsimī, *Dalāʾil,* pp. 77–85, 103, 106; Bānī, *Tanwīr,* p. 90.

10. Jamāl al-Dīn al-Qāsimī, *Dalāʾil,* pp. 107, 115–117.

11. Ibid., p. 7.

12. Ibid., pp. 38, 40, 108–109, 118; Ṭāhir al-Jazāʾirī expressed the same opinion on reason and revelation; Bānī, *Tanwīr,* pp. 40–41.

13. Jamāl al-Dīn al-Qāsimī, "Taʿāruḍ," 621; *Sharḥ luqṭat al-ʿajlān* (Damascus: Ibn Zaydūn Press, 1934), pp. 115–117.

14. Jamāl al-Dīn al-Qāsimī, "Taʿāruḍ," 621; *Jawāmiʿ al-ādāb fī akhlāq al-anjāb* (Cairo:

Al-Sa'ādah Press, 1921), p. 5; for similar expressions on the need to combine knowledge and virtue, see Jamāl al-Dīn al-Qāsimī, *Qawā'id al-taḥdīth min fu nūn muṣṭalaḥ al-ḥadīth* (Damascus: Ibn Zaydūn Press, 1935), pp. 395–396.

15. Jamāl al-Dīn al-Qāsimī, "Ta'āruḍ," 622–626.

16. Jamāl al-Dīn al-Qāsimī, *Dalā'il,* p. 118.

17. Ṭāhir al-Jazā'irī also called for tolerance among sects and legal schools; Bānī, *Tanwīr,* pp. 78–79; Jamāl al-Dīn al-Qāsimī, *Risālah fī iqāmat al-ḥujjah* (Damascus: Al-Ṣadāqah Press, 1924), pp. 4–5; Jamāl al-Dīn al-Qāsimī, "Ta'āruḍ," 616–617.

18. Jamāl al-Dīn al-Qāsimī, *Mīzān al-jarḥ wa al-ta'dīl* (Cairo: Al-Manār Press, 1912), pp. 3, 9–13, 17, 29, 31–36; *Naqḍ al-naṣā'iḥ al-kāfiyah* (Damascus: Al-Fayḥā' Press, 1910), p. 31; *Tārīkh al-jahmiyyah wa al-mu'tazilah* (Cairo: Al-Manār Press, 1913), pp. 62–63, 65, 74–80; Bānī, *Tanwīr,* p. 47.

19. Jamāl al-Dīn al-Qāsimī, *Risālah fī iqāmat al-ḥujjah,* pp. 14, 49–50.

20. Khaṭīb, *al-Shaykh Ṭāhir,* p. 157; Jamāl al-Dīn al-Qāsimī, *Risālah fī iqāmat al-ḥujjah,* p. 60.

21. Untitled notebook in the hand of Shaykh Ḥāmid al-Taqī, pp. 20–21; Ḥamid al-Taqī, Jamāl al-Dīn al-Qāsimī's neighbor and disciple, copied Ḥamzāwī's fatwa in 1907 from a collection of papers belonging to Jamīl al-Shaṭṭī. Qāsimī library, Damascus.

22. Maḥmūd al-Ḥamzāwī, *al-Ṭarīqah al-wāḍiḥah ila al-bayyinah al-rājiḥah* (Damascus: Nahj al-Ṣawāb Press, 1883), pp. 2–3, 245–246. On Maḥmūd al-Ḥamzāwī, see Bīṭār, *Ḥilyat al-bashar fī tārīkh al-qarn al-thālith 'ashar,* 3:1467–1476.

23. Ẓāfir al-Qāsimī, *Jamāl al-Dīn al-Qāsimī wa 'aṣruhu* (Damascus: Al-Hāshimiyyah Press, 1965), p. 357.

24. Jamāl al-Dīn al-Qāsimī, *Qawā'id al-taḥdīth,* p. 52.

25. Ibid., p. 53; for similar passages also see pp. 90, 95, 353.

26. Ibid., p. 281.

27. Ibid., pp. 93, 323–336, 364; *al-Fatwā fī al-Islām* (Damascus: Al-Muqtabas Press, 1911), pp. 8–9. Qāsimī cited Shāh Walī Allah's *Ḥujjat Allah al-bālighah.* For a sample of this Indian thinker's writings on ijtihād, see Muhammad Daud Rahbar, "Shāh Walī Ullah and Ijtihād," *Muslim World* 45 (1955): 346–358.

28. Jamāl al-Dīn al-Qāsimī, *Iṣlāḥ al-masājid min al-bida' wa al-'awā'id* (Cairo: Al-Salafiyyah Press, 1923), pp. 94–95; *Mīzān,* p. 36; *Qawā'id al-taḥdīth,* p. 194.

29. Jamāl al-Dīn al-Qāsimī, *Qawā'id al-taḥdīth,* p. 357.

30. Ẓāfir al-Qāsimī, *Jamāl al-Dīn al-Qāsimī,* pp. 357–358.

31. Jamāl al-Dīn al-Qāsimī, *Dalā'il,* p. 106; *Tanbīh al-ṭālib ila ma'rifat al-farḍ wa al-wājib* (Cairo: Madrasat Wālidat 'Abbās al-Awwal Press, 1908), p. 53.

32. Jamāl al-Dīn al-Qāsimī, *Kitāb al-isti'nās li-taṣḥīḥ ankiḥat al-nās* (Damascus: Al-Taraqqī Press, 1914), p. 46.

33. Jamāl al-Dīn al-Qāsimī, *Qawā'id al-taḥdīth,* p. 390; the same passage is in *al-Ajwibah al-murḍiyah 'ammā awradahu Kamāl al-Dīn ibn al-Humām 'ala al-mustadillīn bi thubūt sunnat al-maghrib al-qibliyyah* (Damascus: Rawḍat al-Shām Press, 1908), p. 3.

34. Jamāl al-Dīn al-Qāsimī, *Sharḥ luqṭat al-'ajlān,* p. 60.

35. Jamāl al-Dīn al-Qāsimī, *Qawā'id al-taḥdīth,* p. 390.

36. Jamāl al-Dīn al-Qāsimī, *Awāmir muhimmah fī iṣlāḥ al-qaḍā' al-shar'ī,* (Damascus: Al-Taraqqī Press, 1913).

37. Ṭāhir al-Jazā'irī also favored practicing ijtihād; Bānī, *Tanwīr,* p. 133. On the history of ijtihād in Islamic legal theory and practical adaptation to new circumstances without invoking ijtihād, see Wael B. Hallaq, "Was the Gate of Ijtihād Closed?" *International Journal of Middle East Studies* 16 (1984): 30–32.

38. Jamāl al-Dīn al-Qāsimī, *Irshād al-khalq ila al-'amal bi khabar al-barq* (Damascus: Al-Muqtabas Press, 1911), p. 4.

39. Jamāl al-Dīn al-Qāsimī, *Irshād al-khalq,* p. 5; *Tanbīh al-ṭālib,* pp. 32, 48; "Taʿāruḍ," 630; Bānī, *Tanwīr,* p. 35.

40. Jamāl al-Dīn al-Qāsimī, *al-Ajwibah,* p. 37; *al-Fatwā,* p. 39; "Taʿāruḍ," 616; *Sharḥ luqṭat al-ʿajlān,* pp. 63, 119–120.

41. Jamāl al-Dīn al-Qāsimī, *al-Fatwā,* p. 64; *Mīzān,* p. 29; "Taʿāruḍ," 616.

42. Jamāl al-Dīn al-Qāsimī, *al-Ajwibah,* p. 3. The following summary of the essay is based on pp. 3–14, 20–25.

43. "Multaqaṭāt min ma'āthīr sayyidi al-ustādh imām waqtihi wa nābighat qaṭrihi al-kātib al-balīgh Qāsimī Zādah Shaykh Muḥammad Jamāl al-Dīn," manuscript, Qāsimī library, Damascus, pp. 109–110.

44. Muḥammad Abū al-Khayr al-Ṭabbāʿ, *Kitāb fatḥ al-aʿlām fī intiṣār li al-ʿallāmah al-muḥaqqiq Kamāl al-Dīn ibn al-Humām* (Damascus: Al-Iṣlāḥ Press, 1909). The following discussion is based on pp. 2, 4–7, 12–17, 21, 50.

45. For instance, Ṭabbāʿ took issue with the title of Qāsimī's essay, *The Pleasing Responses,* by asking to whom are they pleasing. Ibid., p. 3.

46. Rashīd Riḍā, "Ṭahārat al-aʿṭār dhāt al-kuḥūl wa al-radd ʿala dhī fuḍūl," *al-Manār* 4 (1902): 821–827.

47. Muḥammad al-Ṭabbāʿ, *Fatḥ al-aʿlām,* p. 22.

48. Jamāl al-Dīn al-Qāsimī, *Risālah fī iqāmat al-ḥujjah,* pp. 60–61.

49. On the meaning of ḥashwiyyah as interpolators, see Jamāl al-Dīn al-Qāsimī, *Tanbīh al-ṭālib,* p. 55; on its meaning nonsense, see *Sharḥ luqṭat al-ʿajlān,* pp. 144–147. *Iṣlāḥ al-masājid,* p. 243.

50. Jamāl al-Dīn al-Qāsimī, *Iṣlāḥ al-masājid,* pp. 173, 175; *al-Fatwā,* pp. 55–56.

51. Ẓāfir al-Qāsimī, *Jamāl al-Dīn al-Qāsimī,* pp. 248–249.

52. Jamāl al-Dīn al-Qāsimī, *Qawāʿid al-taḥdīth,* pp. 347, 350; *Iṣlāḥ al-masājid,* pp. 71–74, 149–150, 171–176, 199–200.

53. For a description of Ṭāhir al-Jazā'irī's scorn for incompetent ulama and his wish to have a chance to reform society by obtaining government posts, see Bānī, *Tanwīr,* pp. 81–84.

54. Jamāl al-Dīn al-Qāsimī, *Irshād al-khalq,* pp. 71–72.

Chapter 6

1. The clearest statement of Qāsimī's attitudes toward various social groups is in his work on manners and morals, *Jawāmiʿ al-ādāb fī akhlāq al-anjāb* (Cairo: Al-Saʿādah Press, 1921).

2. Jamāl al-Dīn al-Qāsimī, *Iṣlāḥ al-masājid min al-bidaʿ wa al-ʿawā'id* (Cairo: Al-Salafiyyah Press, 1923), pp. 11–14, 76, 102–113, 116.

3. Ibid., pp. 16–18, 22, 26.

4. Ibid., pp. 32–33, 112.

5. Ibid., pp. 196–197, 248–250. George Makdisi has debunked the notion that adherents of the Ḥanbalī legal school reject Sufism; he showed that many Ḥanbalīs criticized certain Sufi practices but embraced "correct" Sufism. George Makdisi, "The Ḥanbalī School and Sufism," *Humaniora Islamica* 2 (1974): 61–72. Makdisi also demonstrated that Ibn Taymiyyah belonged to a Sufi order. George Makdisi, "Ibn Taymiya: A Sufi of the Qādiriya Order," *American Journal of Arabic Studies* 1 (1977): 118–130.

6. Ẓāfir al-Qāsimī, *Jamāl al-Dīn al-Qāsimī wa ʿaṣruhu* (Damascus: Al-Hāshimiyyah Press, 1965), pp. 303–304.

7. Ibid., p. 353.

8. Jamāl al-Dīn al-Qāsimī, *Iṣlāḥ,* pp. 248, 250.

9. Copy of letter from Muṣṭafā al-Ghalāyīnī to Jamāl al-Dīn al-Qāsimī, 2 April 1907; "Multaqaṭāt min ma'āthīr sayyidī al-ustādh imām waqtihi wa nābighat qaṭrihi al-kātib al-

balīgh Qāsimī Zādah Shaykh Muḥammad Jamāl al-Dīn," manuscript, Qāsimī library, Damascus, p. 135. Muṣṭafā al-Ghalāyinī (1886–1945) was a salafi writer and journalist in Beirut; Fahmī Jadʿān, *Usus al-taqaddum ʿinda mufakkirī al-islām fī al-ʿālam al-ʿarabī al-ḥadī th* (Beirut: Al-Mu'assasah al-ʿArabiyyah li al-Dirāsāt wa al-Nashr, 1979), pp. 406–408, 445–448, 502–504, 571.

10. Jamāl al-Dīn al-Qāsimī, *Iṣlāḥ*, p. 249; "Taʿṭīr al-mashām fī ma'āthīr dimashq al-shām," 4 vols. manuscript, Qāsimī library, Damascus, unrevised copy, II, unnumbered pages, 23.

11. Ibn ʿArabī's tomb is in Damascus; on ʿAbd al-Qādir al-Jazā'irī's interest in Ibn ʿArabī, see Jamāl al-Dīn al-Qāsimī, "Taʿṭīr al-mashām," revised copy, 2:529; Muḥammad Jamīl al-Shaṭṭī, *Aʿyān dimashq fī al-qarn al-thālith ʿashar wa niṣf al-qarn al-rābiʿ ʿashar* (Damascus: Al-Maktab al-Islāmī, 1972), p. 178; on Muḥammad ʿAbduh's Sufi period, see Charles C. Adams, *Islam and Modernism in Egypt* (London: Russell & Russell, 1933), pp. 23–24, 31–32; on Rashīd Riḍā's involvement in Sufism and Sufi orders, see Shakīb Arslān, *Al-Sayyid Rashīd Riḍā aw ikhā' arbaʿīn sanah* (Damascus: Ibn Zaydūn Press, 1937), pp. 36–98; for a discussion of Riḍā's ideas on Sufism, see Albert Hourani, "Sufism and Modern Islam: Rashīd Riḍā," in *The Emergence of the Middle East,* (London: The Macmillan Press, 1981), pp. 90–102.

12. See the exchange between Yūsuf al-Nabahānī and Shukrī al-Alūsī for an example of the debate over tomb visits and saints' intercession; Yūsuf al-Nabahānī, *Shawāhid al-ḥaqq fī al-istighāthah bi sayyid al-khalq* (Cairo: Al-Yamaniyyah Press, 1905), and *al-Rā'iyah al-ṣughrā fī dhamm al-bidʿah wa madḥ al-sunnah al-gharrā'* (n.p., n.d.); Abū'l Maʿālī al-Ḥusaynī al-Salāmī [Maḥmūd Shukrī al-Alūsī] *Ghāyat al-amānī fī al-radd ʿala al-Nabahānī* (Cairo: Kurdistān al-Islāmiyyah Press, n.d.). Also see following, Chapter 9.

13. Ẓāfir al-Qāsimī, *Jamāl al-Dīn al-Qāsimī*, pp. 170, 604; Jamāl al-Dīn al-Qāsimī, *Iṣlāḥ,* pp. 131–132, 181–182, 219–228; *Jawāmiʿ*, p. 100.

14. Jamāl al-Dīn al-Qāsimī, *Jawāmiʿ*, pp. 9, 68–69.

15. Albert Hourani, *Arabic Thought in the Liberal Age, 1798–1939* (London: Oxford University Press, 1970), pp. 164–170; Charles D. Smith, *Islam and the Search for Social Order in Modern Egypt* (Albany: State University of New York Press, 1983), pp. 22–31; for a treatment of the debate in Egypt over women's status and the social context of the debate, see Juan Ricardo Cole, "Feminism, Class, and Islam in Turn-of-the-Century Egypt," *International Journal of Middle East Studies* 13 (1981): 387–407.

16. Iskandar Lūqā, *al-Ḥarakah al-adabiyyah fī dimashq, 1800–1918* (Damascus: Alif Bā' Press, 1976), pp. 282–284.

17. Gertrude Bell described the Circassian wife of the Ottoman governor of Syria, Nāẓim Pasha, around 1904; the Circassian woman marched out her children to recite French verse and play the piano, while she smoked cigarettes; Gertrude Bell, *Syria: The Desert and the Sown* (New York: E. P. Dutton and Company, 1907); reprint ed., (New York: Arno Press, 1973), p. 142.

18. Ẓāfir al-Qāsimī, *Jamāl al-Dīn al-Qāsimī,* pp. 297–298; Jamāl al-Dīn's comments on an article entitled "Woman in Islam" [*al-mar'ah fī al-islām*], which appeared in *al-Muqtabas* magazine in Cairo in 1907; "Multaqaṭāt," pp. 87–91.

19. Ẓāfir al-Qāsimī, *Jamāl al-Dīn al-Qāsimī,* pp. 254–255; excerpted from Jamāl al-Dīn al-Qāsimī, *Maḥāsin al-ta'wīl,* 17 vols. (Cairo: Dār Iḥyā' al-Kutub al-ʿArabiyyah, 1957), 7:2624.

20. Ẓāfir al-Qāsimī, *Jamāl al-Dīn al-Qāsimī,* p. 298; Jamāl al-Dīn al-Qāsimī, *Jawāmiʿ*, p. 35.

21. Jamāl al-Dīn al-Qāsimī, *Jawāmiʿ*, p. 37; *Iṣlāḥ*, pp. 250–252; Ẓāfir al-Qāsimī, *Jamāl al-Dīn al-Qāsimī,* p. 193, note 1.

22. Jamāl al-Dīn al-Qāsimī, *Jawāmiʿ*, p. 33, 36, 133; Muḥammad Saʿīd al-Qāsimī,

Qāmūs al-ṣināʿāt al-shāmiyyah, vol. 1 (Paris: Mouton & Co., 1960), pp. 157–158; Jamāl al-Dīn al-Qāsimī and Khalīl al-ʿAẓm, *Qāmūs al-ṣināʿāt al-shāmiyyah,* vol. 2 (Paris: Mouton & Co., 1960), pp. 224, 231;

23. ʿAbd al-Raḥmān Sāmī, *al-Qawl al-ḥaqq fī bayrūt wa dimashq* (Beirut: Dār al-Rā'id al-ʿArabī, 1981), p. 61; originally published as *Safar al-salām fī bilād al-shām* (Cairo: Al-Muqtaṭaf Press, 1892). On Aḥmad al-Shamʿah and Abū al-Hudā al-Ṣayyādī, see Foreign Office, 195/1940/49: Eyres to Currie, 1 December 1896. "Barnāmaj jamʿiyyat al-iḥsān al-islāmiyyah fī maḥallat al-kharāb bi al-shām," *al-ʿIrfān* 3 (1911/12): 311–312.

24. Jamāl al-Dīn al-Qāsimī, *Mīzān al-jarḥ wa al-taʿdīl* (Cairo: Al-Manār Press, 1912), pp. 4, 17; also *Qawāʿid al-taḥdīth min funūn muṣṭalaḥ al-ḥadīth* (Damascus: Ibn Zaydūn Press, 1935), pp. 194, 288.

25. Muḥammad ibn ʿAqīl's work is entitled *al-Naṣā'iḥ al-kāfiyah li man yatawallā Muʿāwiyah.* Ibn ʿAqīl wrote his essay to refute a fatwā by Riḍā against cursing Muʿāwiyah, see *al-Manār* 13 (1910): 152; Qāsimī wrote that Ibn ʿAqīl solicited his comments in *Naqḍ al-naṣā'iḥ al-kāfiyah li man yatawallā Muʿāwiyah* (Damascus: Al-Fayḥā' Press, 1910), p. 2. The copy of Ibn ʿAqīl's *al-Naṣā'iḥ al-kāfiyah* in the Qāsimī library contains Jamāl al-Dīn's notes on the margins. On the rough draft he sent to Ibn ʿAqīl and his friend in Jeddah, see letter from Qāsimī to Ibn ʿAqīl, 13 July 1910, in "Multaqaṭāt," pp. 131–133.

26. Jamāl al-Dīn al-Qāsimī, *Naqḍ al-naṣā'iḥ,* pp. 11–12, 17.

27. Jamāl al-Dīn al-Qāsimī, *Mīzān al-jarḥ,* pp. 17, 28. Qāsimī first published *Mīzān al-jarḥ wa al-taʿdīl* in serial form in *al-Manār* 15 (1912): 857–874, 912–940, and 16 (1913): 30–40; for the Shīʿī shaykh's letter, see *al-ʿIrfān* 4 (1912/13): 377–389.

28. Muḥammad al-Ḥusayn Āl Kāshif al-Ghiṭā', *ʿAyn al-mīzān* (Sidon: Al-ʿIrfān Press, 1912). He wrote and published this work after the first installment of *Mīzān al-jarḥ* in *al-Manār.* On Muḥammad Ḥusayn Āl Kāshif al-Ghiṭā', see his essay, *Aṣl al-shīʿah wa uṣūluhā* (Najaf: Al-Ḥaydariyyah Press, 1962), pp. 5–15.

29. Kāshif al-Ghiṭā', *ʿAyn al-mīzān,* pp. 4–7.

30. Muḥammad Bahjat al-Bīṭār, *Naqd ʿayn al-mīzān* (Damascus: Al-Taraqqī Press, 1913), pp. 4–21.

31. Jamāl al-Dīn al-Qāsimī, *Iṣlāḥ,* pp. 183–185; *Naqḍ al-naṣā'iḥ,* p. 9.

32. Muḥammad Saʿīd al-Qāsimī, *Qāmūs,* 1:27–28; interview with Ẓāfir al-Qāsimī, July 1980; Ẓāfir al-Qāsimī, *Jamāl al-Dīn al-Qāsimī,* p. 20.

33. Dominique Chevallier, "À Damas, production et société à la fin du XIXe siècle," *Annales* 19 (1964): 967–968.

34. Muḥammad Saʿīd al-Qāsimī, *Qāmūs,* 1:36, 92, 131, 140–141; Jamāl al-Dīn al-Qāsimī, *Qāmūs,* 2:164, 279, 424–425, 456–458.

35. Muḥammad Saʿīd al-Qāsimī, *Qāmūs,* 1:16, 20, 22–23, 43–45, 55–56, 146–147; Jamāl al-Dīn al-Qāsimī, *Qāmūs,* 2:240, 310, 320; *Jawāmiʿ,* p. 122.

36. Jamāl al-Dīn al-Qāsimī, "Taʿṭīr al-mashām," revised copy, III, insert between pages 245 and 246; *Jawāmiʿ,* pp. 126–128.

37. Jamāl al-Dīn al-Qāsimī, "Taʿṭīr al-mashām," revised copy, III, unnumbered pages following page 247; *Jawāmiʿ,* pp. 124–125.

38. See the section on *al-Ḥaqā'iq* magazine in Chapter 9 for conservative ulama's opposition to certain inventions.

39. On these feminist issues, Qāsimī agreed with Rashīd Riḍā; Cole, "Feminism, Class, and Islam," p. 403.

40. Jamāl al-Dīn al-Qāsimī, *Jawāmiʿ,* p. 108.

41. Alūsī wrote to Qāsimī:

I send blessings and congratulate you on the emergence of your pupil, the erudite shaykh al-Bīṭār [Muḥammad Bahjat al-Bīṭār]. God bless you and him. He has made

> the Rāfiḍī (Shīʿī) [Muḥammad al-Ḥusayn Āl Kāshif al-Ghiṭā'] swallow a stone and revealed all his faults. He [Muḥammad al-Ḥusayn] used to bring forth silver coated dung and whitewashed toilets; that is the sum of their learning from the first to the last of them. They speak only in distortions and errors. Many debates on various issues have taken place between me and the father of your wicked adversary, and they did no good. This cursed one's ancestors corrupted Iraq. . . . Their ancestor was nicknamed "Remover of the Cover" [*kāshif al-ghiṭā'*] for revealing the Rāfiḍīs' imperfections and defects. . . . [M]ay God fight this misguided sect for its intense hostility to Muslims.

Maḥmūd Shukrī al-Alūsī to Jamāl al-Dīn al-Qāsimī, 13 September 1913. Original correspondence in the possession of Mr. Samīḥ al-Ghabrah, Damascus. Photocopy of correspondence in author's possession.

Chapter 7

1. Zeine N. Zeine, *Arab–Turkish Relations and the Emergence of Arab Nationalism* (Beirut: Khayats, 1958). C. Ernest Dawn, *From Ottomanism to Arabism: Essays in the Origins of Arab Nationalism,* (Urbana, IL: University of Illinois Press, 1973); Philip S. Khoury, *Urban Notables and Arab Nationalism: The Politics of Damascus, 1860–1920* (Cambridge: Cambridge University Press, 1983); Rashid Khalidi, "Social Factors in the Rise of the Arab Movement in Syria," in Said Amir Arjomand, ed., *From Nationalism to Revolutionary Islam* (Albany: State University of New York Press, 1984), pp. 53–70. Arabist here does not refer to a specialist in Arabic nor to a supporter of Arab political causes.

2. Roderic H. Davison, *Reform in the Ottoman Empire, 1856–1876* (Princeton: Princeton University Press, 1963), p. 404.

3. On Żiyā Pasha's life and thought, see Şerif Mardin, *The Genesis of Young Ottoman Thought* (Princeton: Princeton University Press, 1962), pp. 337–359; for references to the points in this paragraph, see pp. 13, 32, 36–37, 41, 59–60, 115; for Nāmik Kemāl's thought as described in the following paragraph, see pp. 284–331.

4. On Żiyā Pasha's tenure as governor of Syria, see Max Gross, "Ottoman Rule in the Province of Damascus, 1860–1909" (Ph.D. dissertation, Georgetown University, 1979), pp. 226–227; ʿĪsā Iskandar Maʿlūf, "al-Shaykh Ṭāhir al-Jazā'irī," *al-Hilāl* 28 (1920): 452.

5. Gross, "Ottoman Rule," pp. 230–239.

6. Ibid., p. 241. Aḥmed Cevdet Pasha served the Tanzimat movement in numerous high civil posts, most notably in the field of judicial reform; see Richard L. Chambers, "Aḥmed Cevdet Paşa: The Formative Years of an Ottoman Transitional" (Ph.D. dissertation, Princeton University, 1968). Niyazi Berkes, *The Development of Secularism in Turkey* (Montreal: McGill University Press, 1964), p. 217.

7. Muḥammad Adīb Āl Taqī al-Dīn al-Ḥiṣnī, *Muntakhabāt al-tawārīkh li dimashq,* 3 vols. (Damascus: Al-Ḥadīthah Press, 1928), 2:271–272.

8. ʿAdnān al-Khaṭīb, *al-Shaykh Ṭāhir al-Jazā'irī* (Cairo: Maʿhad al-Dirāsāt al-ʿArabiyyah, 1971), pp. 136–137. On Midḥat Pasha, see ʿAlī Ḥaydar Midḥat Bey, *The Life of Midḥat Pasha* (London: John Murray, 1903), pp. 176–195. Maʿlūf, "al-Shaykh Ṭāhir," 452; Muḥibb al-Dīn al-Khaṭīb, "Rafīq al-ʿAẓm," *al-Zahrā'* 2 (1925): 225, note 2.

9. Khaṭīb, *al-Shaykh Ṭāhir,* p. 111. None of the sources mention exactly when Jazā'irī lost his post. In 1885, Qāyātī reported meeting Jazā'irī while he was still on the education council; the British consul listed the members of the education council in March 1887, and Ṭāhir was not among them. Muḥammad ʿAbd al-Jawād al-Qāyātī, *Nafḥat al-bashām fī riḥlat al-shām* (Cairo: Jarīdat al-Islām Press, 1901), pp. 113–114; Foreign Office, 195/1583/14:

Dickson to White, 21 March 1887. Jazā'irī recorded his receiving notification of his appointment on 17 August 1898; Ṭāhir al-Jazā'irī, "Tawārīkh siyāḥiyyah fī ba'ḍ al-bilād," manuscript no. 11631, Ẓāhiriyyah Library, Damascus, p. 16.

10. Muḥammad Saʿīd al-Bānī, *Tanwīr al-baṣā'ir bi sīrat al-shaykh Ṭāhir* (Damascus: Al-Ḥukūmah al-ʿArabiyyah al-Sūriyyah Press, 1920), p. 25–26; *al-Kawkab al-durrī al-munīr fī aḥkām al-dhahab wa al-fiḍḍah wa al-ḥarīr* (Damascus: Al-Mufīd, 1931), p. 168.

11. Maʿlūf, "al-Shaykh Ṭāhir," 452. Correspondence between Jamāl al-Dīn al-Qāsimī and Maḥmūd Shukrī al-Alūsī amply demonstrates their commitment to searching for rare manuscripts and publishing them. For published examples of Qāsimī's letters indicating his work on reviving the Arab-Islamic heritage by gathering information on the location of manuscripts, see Ẓāfir al-Qāsimī, *Jamāl al-Dīn al-Qāsimī wa ʿaṣruhu* (Damascus: Al-Hāshimiyyah Press, 1965), pp. 585–590, 608–610.

12. Muḥammad Kurd ʿAlī, "al-Muʿāṣirūn: al-Shaykh Ṭāhir al-Jazā'irī," *Majallat al-majmaʿ al-ʿilmī al-ʿarabī* 8 (1928): 595; Ẓāfir al-Qāsimī, *Jamāl al-Dīn al-Qāsimī* (hereafter cited *JDQ*), p. 434; Muḥammad Saʿīd al-Bānī, "Salīm al-Bukhārī," *Majallat al-majmaʿ al-ʿilmī al-ʿarabī* 9 (1929): 743–744; Aḥmad Taymūr, *Aʿlām al-fikr al-islāmī fī al-ʿaṣr al-ḥadīth* (Cairo: Lajnat Nashr al-Mu'allafāt al-Taymūriyyah, 1967), p. 294.

13. Jamāl al-Dīn al-Qāsimī, "Bayt al-qaṣīd fī tarjamat al-imām al-wālid al-saʿīd," manuscript, Qāsimī library, Damascus, p. 12; Ẓāfir al-Qāsimī, *JDQ*, pp. 426–435.

14. Ẓāfir al-Qāsimī, *JDQ*, pp. 437–438.

15. Maʿlūf, "al-Shaykh Ṭāhir," 454; F.O. 195/2122/94: Richards to O'Conor, 17 November 1902; Ẓāfir al-Qāsimī, *JDQ*, p. 438.

16. For Muḥibb al-Dīn al-Khaṭīb's description of the two reform camps, see ʿAdnān al-Khaṭīb, *al-Shaykh Ṭāhir*, p. 44. Authors who give importance to the salafis' influence on Arab nationalists include Luṭfī al-Ḥaffār, *Dhikriyyāt: Muntakhabāt min khuṭub wa aḥādīth wa maqālāt* (Damascus: Ibn Zaydūn Press, 1954), p. 8; Muṣṭafā al-Shihābī, *Muḥāḍarāt ʿan al-qawmiyyah al-ʿarabiyyah* (Cairo: Jāmiʿat al-Duwal al-ʿArabiyyah, 1958), pp. 49–53; Fakhrī al-Bārūdī, *Mudhakkirāt al-Bārūdī*, 2 vols. (Beirut: Dār al-Ḥayāt, 1951), 1:58–59, 79.

17. Bānī, "Salīm al-Bukhārī," 745–746.

18. On Rafīq al-ʿAẓm, see ʿAbd al-Razzāq al-Bīṭār, *Ḥilyat al-bashar fī tārīkh al-qarn al-thālith ʿashar*, 3 vols. (Damascus: Majmaʿ al-Lughah al-ʿArabiyyah, 1961–1963), 2:630–634; "Rafīq al-ʿAẓm: Wufātuhu wa tarjamatuhu," *al-Manār* 26 (1925): 288–289; Muḥibb al-Dīn al-Khaṭīb, "Rafīq l-ʿAẓm," *al-Zahrā'* 2 (1925): 224–234; introduction by Rashīd Riḍā to ʿUthmān al-ʿAẓm, ed., *Majmūʿat āthār Rafīq Bey al-ʿAẓm* (Cairo: Al-Manār Press, 1925), first nine pages numbered in Arabic letters bā' to kāf. Abdul-Karim Rafeq, *Province of Damascus, 1723–1783* (Beirut: Khayats, 1970), pp. 85–201, 285–319. On the ʿAẓms in the eighteenth and nineteenth centuries, see Linda Schatkowski Schilcher, *Families in Politics: Damascene Factions and Estates of the 18th and 19th Centuries* (Stuttgart: Franz Steiner Verlag Wiesbaden GMBH, 1985), pp. 136–144. On Maḥmūd al-ʿAẓm, see Bīṭār, *Ḥilyat al-bashar*, 3:1478–1481. ʿAẓm, known for his poetic talents, squandered his considerable patrimony. Bīṭār wrote that ʿAẓm became despondent over losing his wealth and then overcame despair when he joined the Shādhilī Sufi order. In his later years, he depended on subsidies from ʿAbd al-Qādir al-Jazā'irī.

19. Riḍā in ʿUthmān al-ʿAẓm, *Majmūʿat*, letter jīm; Bīṭār, *Ḥilyat al-bashar*, 2:631.

20. Riḍā in ʿUthmān al-ʿAẓm, *Majmūʿat*, letter jīm; Shihābī, *Muḥāḍarāt*, p. 51; "Rafīq al-ʿAẓm," *al-Manār*, 290; Muḥammad Kurd ʿAlī, *al-Muʿāṣirūn* (Damascus: Majmaʿ al-Lughah al-ʿArabiyyah Press, 1980), p. 225; Adham al-Jundī, *Aʿlām al-adab wa al-fann*, 2 vols. (Damascus: Majallat Ṣawt Sūriyah Press, 1954), 1:191.

21. Khayr al-Dīn al-Ziriklī, *al-Aʿlām: Qāmūs tarājim li ashhar al-rijāl wa al-nisā' min al-ʿarab wa al-mustaʿribīn wa al-mustashriqīn*, 8 vols. 4th ed. (Beirut: Dār al-ʿIlm li al-

Malāyīn, 1979), 3:172. Other sources on ʿAsalī include, Adham al-Jundī, *Shuhadā' al-ḥarb al-ʿālamiyyah al-kubrā* (Damascus: Al-ʿUrūbah Press, 1960), pp. 101–102; Ḥiṣnī, *Muntakhabāt,* 2:883, 893; on ʿAsalī's contributions to the development of modern Arabic fiction as a short story writer, see Iskandar Lūqā, *al-Ḥarakah al-adabiyyah fī dimashq* (Damascus: Alif Bā' Press, 1976), pp. 170–176, 183, note 63. A number of sources state that ʿAsalī was born in 1868 (Ziriklī, Lūqā), whereas others give 1878 as the year of his birth (Jundī). The accounts in Jundī and in ʿAdnān al-Khaṭīb's *al-Shaykh Ṭāhir al-Jazā'irī* suggest that ʿAsalī was ʿAbd al-Wahhāb al-Inklīzī's classmate and, therefore, that ʿAsalī was born in 1878. Khaṭīb, pp. 81–82. On Inklīzī, also see Ziriklī, *al-Aʿlām,* 4:182.

22. Shihābī, *Muḥāḍarāt,* p. 51; Bānī, *Tanwīr,* p. 129.

23. Muḥibb al-Dīn al-Khaṭīb, "Rafīq al-ʿAẓm," 227; on Rifʿat Bey and Jazā'irī, see Bānī, *Tanwīr,* pp. 128–129.

24. Both Ramsaur's account of the early Young Turks and Feroz Ahmad's profiles of prominent members of the CUP suggest that Istanbul's colleges were centers of recruitment for the constitutional movement. Ramsaur, *The Young Turks—Prelude to the Revolution of 1908,* 2nd ed. (New York: Russell & Russell, 1970), pp. 14–21; Feroz Ahmad, *The Young Turks: The Committee of Union and Progress in Turkish Politics, 1908–1914* (Oxford: Clarendon Press, 1969), pp. 166–181.

25. Ernest E. Ramsaur, *The Young Turks,* pp. 14–37.

26. Gross, "Ottoman Rule," p. 463; F.O. 195/1940/37: Eyres to Currie, 17 September 1896; F.O. 195/1984/10: Richards to Currie, 1 March 1897; F.O. 195/1984/37: Richards to Currie, 20 July 1897; no. 38: Richards to Currie, 23 July 1897.

27. Shihābī, *Muḥāḍarāt,* p. 53. The senior circle members were Shukrī al-ʿAsalī (b. 1878), ʿAbd al-Wahhāb al-Inklīzī (b. 1878), Salīm al-Jazā'irī (b. 1879), ʿAbd al-Raḥmān Shahbandar (b. 1880), Muḥammad Kurd ʿAlī (b. 1876), and Fāris al-Khūrī (b. 1877). The junior circle members were Ṣāliḥ Qanbāz (b. 1886), Ṣalāḥ al-Dīn al-Qāsimī (b. 1887), Muḥibb al-Dīn al-Khaṭīb (b. 1887), Luṭfī al-Ḥaffār (b. 1891), ʿĀrif al-Shihābī (b. 1889), and ʿUthmān Mardam-Beg.

28. "Al-Shahīd al-saʿīd: Ṣalīḥ Qanbāz, 1303–1344," *al-Zahrā'* 2 (1925): 419. Except where otherwise noted, the following information on Maktab ʿAnbar is from Fakhrī al-Bārūdī, *Mudhakkirāt,* 1:29–32, 55, 57.

29. Muḥibb al-Dīn al-Khaṭīb, ed., *al-Duktūr Ṣalāḥ al-Dīn al-Qāsimī, 1305–1334* (Cairo: Al-Salafiyyah Press, 1959), page letters alif and bā'. Hereafter this reference will be given as *SDQ*. Bārūdī, *Mudhakkirāt,* 1:31, 81.

30. This was Muḥibb al-Dīn al-Khaṭīb's description of the salafis' message; Khaṭīb, "Rafīq al-ʿAẓm," 226–227.

31. Shihābī, *Muḥāḍarāt,* p. 54.

32. The following account of the Arab Renaissance Society's establishment in Istanbul and Damascus is from Ṣalāḥ al-Dīn al-Qāsimī, "Kalimah fī tārīkh al-jamʿiyyah," in Khaṭīb, *SDQ,* pp. 5–7.

33. ʿAdnān al-Khaṭīb, *al-Shaykh Ṭāhir,* pp. 79–80. Scattered references to Salīm al-Jazā'irī are in Bānī, *Tanwīr,* p. 125; Shihābī, *Muḥāḍarāt,* pp. 51, 62, 69; Muḥammad ʿIzzat al-Darwaza, *Ḥawla al-ḥarakah al-ʿarabiyyah al-ḥadīthah,* 2 vols. (Sidon: Al-ʿAṣriyyah Press, 1950), 1:33; Rashīd Riḍā, "Riḥlat ṣāḥib *al-Manār* (fī sūriyah)," *al-Manār* 11 (1909): 948; Jundī, *Shuhadā',* p. 13.

34. Jundī, *Shuhadā',* p. 131.

35. On Ṣalāḥ al-Dīn al-Qāsimī, see Muḥibb al-Dīn al-Khaṭīb, *SDQ,* prefaces by Khaṭīb and Ẓāfir al-Qāsimī. This book is a collection of Ṣalāḥ al-Dīn al-Qāsimī's articles, lectures, essays, and poems.

36. Ẓāfir al-Qāsimī, *JDQ,* pp. 92–95.

37. For lists of the Arab Renaissance Society's members and the tendency for youn-

ger brothers, cousins, and classmates to join, see Muḥibb al-Dīn al-Khaṭīb, *SDQ*, pp. 8–9, 16.

38. Aḥmad al-Qadrī, *Mudhakkirātī ʿan al-thawrah al-ʿarabiyyah al-kubrā* (Damascus: Ibn Zaydūn Press, 1956), p. 7.

39. Ṣalāḥ al-Dīn al-Qāsimī, "Ḍarrā' al-ʿulamā'," in Khaṭīb, *SDQ*, pp. 258–273.

40. Ṣalāḥ al-Dīn al-Qāsimī, "al-Khiṭābah wa al-khuṭbah," in ibid., pp. 58–68.

41. Ibid., p. 67.

42. Ṣalāḥ al-Dīn al-Qāsimī, "al-ʿIlm wa al-ijtimāʿ," in ibid., pp. 19–21, 34–35.

43. Ṣalāḥ al-Dīn al-Qāsimī, "Samā' turkiyā," in ibid., p. 39.

44. Ibid., pp. 39–40.

45. Ṣalāḥ al-Dīn al-Qāsimī, "al-Mas'alah al-ʿarabiyyah wa nash'atuhā," in ibid., p. 74; "al-Qawmiyyah fī al-umam," p. 42; "al-Taʿlīm bi al-ʿarabiyyah," pp. 44–47.

46. Ṣalāḥ al-Dīn al-Qāsimī, "al-Thawrah al-faransiyyah," in ibid., pp. 48–57.

47. Ṣalāḥ al-Dīn al-Qāsimī, "Kalimah fī tārīkh al-jamʿiyyah," in ibid., pp. 4, 17–18, 105.

48. Ṣalāḥ al-Dīn al-Qāsimī, "al-ʿIlm wa al-ijtimāʿ," in ibid., p. 19.

49. Ibid., p. 21.

50. Ṣalāḥ al-Dīn al-Qāsimī, "al-Ḥashwiyyah wa al-wahhābiyyah," in ibid., p. 252.

51. Ibid., pp. 253–256.

52. Ẓāfir al-Qāsimī, *JDQ*, pp. 603–604.

53. ʿAlī al-Muḥāfaẓah, *al-Ittijāhāt al-fikriyyah ʿinda al-ʿarab fī ʿaṣr al-nahḍah, 1798–1914* (Beirut: Al-Ahliyyah li al-Nashr wa al-Tawzīʿ, 1980), p. 211.

Chapter 8

1. On ʿAbd al-Qādir al-Iskandarānī al-Kaylānī, see Muḥammad Adīb Āl Taqī al-Dīn al-Ḥiṣnī, *Muntakhabāt al-tawārīkh li-dimashq*, 3 vols. (Damascus: Al-Ḥadīthah Press, 1928), 2:826. On the Kaylānīs in the eighteenth and nineteenth centuries, see Linda Schatkowski Schilcher, *Families in Politics: Damascene Factions and Estates of the 18th and 19th Centuries* (Stuttgart: Franz Steiner Verlag Wiesbaden GMBH, 1985), pp. 194–196. All three anti-Wahhābī essays by Iskandarānī came out in 1922, and his name was given as ʿAbd al-Qādir al-Iskandarī. See *al-Nafḥah al-zakiyah fī al-radd ʿala shubuh al-firqah al-wahhābiyyah* (Damascus: Al-Fayḥā' Press, 1922); *al-Minḥah al-ilāhiyyah fī al-radd ʿala mazāʿim al-ṭā'ifah al-wahhābiyyah* (Damascus: Al-Fayḥā' Press, 1922); *al-Ḥujjah al-murḍiyah fī ithbāt al-waṣītah allatī nafatha al-firqah al-wahhābiyyah* (Damascus: Al-Fayḥā' Press, 1922).

2. On ʿArif al-Munayyir, see Ḥiṣnī, 2:757–759. Among the list of works by Munayyir cited in Ḥiṣnī, four of them very likely represented refutations of works by Jamāl al-Dīn al-Qāsimī; Jamāl al-Dīn al-Qāsimī, "Tārīkh al-ustādh Jamāl al-Dīn al-Qāsimī," manuscript, Qāsimī library, Damascus, pp. 75–80; Muḥammad Jamīl al-Shaṭṭī, *Aʿyān dimashq fī al-qarn al-thālith ʿashar wa nisf al-qarn al-rābiʿ ʿashar* (Damascus: Al-Maktab al-Islāmī, 1972), p. 361. For a translation of one of Munayyir's works, see Jacob Landau, *The Hijaz Railway and the Muslim Pilgrimage: A Case of Ottoman Political Propaganda* (Detroit: Wayne State University Press, 1971), p. 23.

3. ʿArif al-Munayyir, "al-Ḥaqq al-mubīn fī aḥādīth arbaʿīn fī man kharaja ʿan ṭāʿat amīr al-mu'minīn wa shaqq ʿaṣā al-muslimīn," manuscript, no. 8618, Ẓāhiriyyah Library, Damascus, pp. 3, 11.

4. On ʿAbd al-Qādir al-Khaṭīb's antisalafi agitation, see Chapter 10. On Hāshim al-Khaṭīb, ʿUmar Riḍā Kaḥḥālah, *Muʿjam al-mu'allifīn: Tarājim muṣannifī al-kutub al-ʿarabiyyah*, 15 vols. (Damascus: Al-Taraqqī Press, 1957), 12:86. *Al-Ḥaqā'iq* 2 (1911) 152–153.

5. Hāshim al-Khaṭīb and Maḥmūd al-ʿAṭṭār were students of Badr al-Dīn al-Ḥasanī, who wrote in *al-Ḥaqā'iq*. On Badr al-Dīn al-Ḥasanī, Muḥammad Riyāḍ al-Māliḥ, *ʿAlim al-ummah*

wa zāhid al-ʿaṣr al-ʿallāmah al-muḥaddith al-akbar Badr al-Dīn al-Ḥasanī (Damascus: Maktabat al-Fārābī, 1977); ʿAbd al-Qādir al-Maghribī, *Majallat al-majmaʿ al-ʿilmī al-ʿarabī* 13 (1933): 297–298, 351–352; Maḥmūd Yāsīn, "Khātimat al-muḥaddithīn," *al-Hidāyah al-islāmiyyah* 8 (1935): 17–23, 76–85, 264–269.

6. Muḥammad ibn Abd al-Qādir al-Jazā'irī, *Tuḥfat al-zāhir fī tārīkh al-jazā'ir wa al-amīr ʿAbd al-Qādir* (Beirut: Dār al-Yaqẓah al-ʿArabiyyah, 1964), pp. 609–615.

7. Muḥammad ʿAbd al-Jawād al-Qāyātī, *Nafḥat al-bashām fī riḥlat al-shām* (Cairo: Jarīdat al-Islām Press, 1901), p. 111; Khayr al-Dīn al-Ziriklī, *al-Aʿlām: Qāmūs tarājim li ashhar al-rijāl wa al-nisā' min al-ʿarab wa al-mustaʿribīn wa al-mustashriqīn*, 8 vols. 4th ed. (Beirut: Dār al-ʿIlm li al-Malāyīn, 1979), 8:33.

8. Foreign Office, 195/2097/80: Richards to O'Conor, 30 December 1901; Butrus Abu-Manneh, "The Naqshbandiyya-Mujaddidiya in the Ottoman Lands in the Early 19th Century," *Die Welt des Islams* 22 (1982): 35. For more information on Asʿad al-Ṣāḥib, see Ziriklī, *al-Aʿlām*, 1:301. Jamāl al-Dīn al-Qāsimī, "Taʿṭīr al-mashām fī ma'āthīr dimashq al-shām," manuscript, Qāsimī library, Damascus, unrevised copy, II, unnumbered pages, 9–11.

9. On Ṣāliḥ al-Sharīf al-Tūnisī, see Arnold Green, *The Tunisian Ulama, 1873–1915: Social Structure and Response to Ideological Currents* (Leiden: E. J. Brill, 1978), pp. 171, 181–184, 222–223, 286–287.

10. See Chapter 10, section entitled "The Conservative Reaction."

11. Amīn Saʿīd, *al-Thawrah al-ʿarabiyyah al-kubrā*, 3 vols. (Cairo: ʿĪsā al-Bānī al-Chalabī Press, 1934), 1:52–53.

12. *Al-Ḥaqā'iq*, 2 (1911): 87–96; Jamāl al-Dīn al-Qāsimī, "Bayt al-qaṣīd fī tarjamat al-imām al-wālid al-saʿīd," manuscript, Qāsimī library, Damascus, p. 5. On Muḥammad al-Qāsimī, also see Ḥiṣnī, *Muntakhabāt*, 2:795; interview with Muḥammad Saʿīd al-Qāsimī, Damascus, Syria, 20 January 1983.

13. Ḥiṣnī, *Muntakhabāt*, 2:795; Iskandar Lūqā, *al-Ḥarakah al-adabiyyah fī dimashq* (Damascus: Alif Bā' Press, 1976), p. 251; Rashīd Riḍā, "Riḥlat ṣāḥib *al-Manār* (fī sūriyah)," *al-Manār* 11 (1908): 951; "Ṭahārat al-aʿṭār dhāt al-kuḥūl wa al-radd ʿala dhī fuḍūl," *al-Manār* 4 (1902): 821–827.

14. Information on the wealth of ulama families is at the Center for Historical Documentation, Damascus. On the Kaylānīs, sijillāt 878: 87, 145; 1119: 60–67; 1183: 152–154, 180; 1233: 148–152; 1313: 15–18, 120–123; 1354: 21–23; 1533: 114–116. On ʿArif al-Munayyir's brother's wealth, see sijill 1203: 84–88. On the Usṭuwānīs, sijillāt 885: 87; 906: 147, 183; 1030: 177–178. On the Khaṭībs, sijillāt 1229: 153–155; 1490: 68–69. On Muḥammad al-Qāsimī, sijill 1508: 197–198.

15. Māliḥ, *ʿĀlim al-ummah*, pp. 211–212.

16. Niyazi Berkes, *The Development of Secularism in Turkey* (Montreal: McGill University Press, 1964), pp. 254–255. On the Young Turks' humble social origins and the obstacles these origins posed in the way of winning popular support, see Feroz Ahmad, *The Young Turks: The Committee of Union and Progress in Turkish Politics, 1908–1914*, (Oxford: Clarendon Press, 1969), pp. 16–18.

17. On Abū al-Hudā al-Ṣayyādī, see Muḥammad Salīm al-Jundī, *Tārīkh maʿarrat al-nuʿmān*, 3 vols. (Damascus: Wizārat al-Thaqāfah wa al-Siyāḥah wa al-Irshād al-Qawmī, 1963–1967), 1:210, 214, 257–260; 2:163, 215–228; ʿAbd al-Razzāq al-Bīṭār, *Ḥilyat al-bashar fī tārīkh al-qarn al-thālith ʿashar*, 3 vols. (Damascus: Majmaʿ al-Lughah al-ʿArabiyyah, 1961–1963), 1:72–79; ʿAbd al-Ḥafīẓ al-Fāsī, *Riyāḍ al-jannah aw al-mudhish al-muṭrib*, 2 vols. (Rabat: Al-Waṭaniyyah Press, 1932), 2:146–155; Rashīd Riḍā, Review of *al-Ḥaqīqah al-bāhirah fī asrār al-sharīʿah al-ṭāhirah* by Abū al-Hudā al-Ṣayyādī, in *al-Manār* 9 (1906): 309–311; Butrus Abu-Manneh, "Sultan Abdülḥamīd II and Shaikh Abūlhudā al-Ṣayyādī," *Middle Eastern Studies* 15 (1979): 131–153.

18. Abu-Manneh, "Shaikh Abūlhudā," 139; Jundī, *Tārīkh maʿarrat al-nuʿmān,* 2:163, 216, 225.

19. Abu-Manneh, "Shaikh Abūlhudā," 140–142.

20. Berkes, *Secularism in Turkey,* pp. 268–270.

21. Nikki R. Keddie, *Sayyid Jamāl al-Dīn "al-Afghānī": A Political Biography* (Berkeley: University of California Press, 1972), p. 383; Rashīd Riḍā, *Tārīkh al-ustādh al-imām al-shaykh Muḥammad ʿAbduh* (Cairo: Al-Manār Press, 1931), vol. 1, p. 88.

22. Şerif Mardin, "Libertarian Movements in the Ottoman Empire, 1878–1895," *Middle East Journal* 16 (1962): 172; ʿUthmān al-ʿAẓm, ed., *Majmūʿat āthār Rafīq Bey al-ʿAẓm* (Cairo: Al-Manār Press, 1925), p. 122; Anonymous, *Thawrat al-ʿarab* (Cairo: Al-Muqaṭṭam Press, 1916), p. 48.

23. Sylvia G. Haim, ed., *Arab Nationalism: An Anthology* (Berkeley: University of California Press, 1962), pp. 26–29.

24. Walid Kazziha, "The Jarīdah-Ummah Group in Egyptian Politics," *Middle Eastern Studies* 13 (1977): 373–374.

25. William Ochsenwald, *Religion, Society, and the State in Arabia: The Hijaz Under Ottoman Control, 1840–1908* (Columbus: Ohio University Press, 1984), p. 48; William R. Polk, *The Arab World* (Cambridge: Harvard University Press, 1980), p. 145; Jundī, *Tārīkh maʿarrat al-nuʿmān,* 2:219; Muḥammad Bahjat al-Atharī, *Maḥmūd Shukrī al-Alūsī wa ārāʾuhu al-lughawiyyah* (Cairo: Al-Kamāliyyah Press, 1958), p. 19.

26. John Baldry, "Imam Yaḥyā and the Yamani Uprising of 1904–1907," *Abr-Nahrain* 18 (1978–1979): 42, 47, 60, 63.

27. Rashīd Riḍā, "Muḥāribat al-wahm li al-ʿilm, aw taʾthīr al-saʿāyah fī al-dawlah al-ʿuthmāniyyah," *al-Manār* 8 (1905): 315–317; "Anbāʾ sūriyah al-muzʿijah–al-dawlah wa al-raʿīyah," *al-Manār* 8 (1905): 346–348; Foreign Office 195/2190/39: Drummond-Hay to O'Conor, 10 June 1905.

28. Riḍā, "Muḥāribat al-wahm," 317; Ibrāhīm al-ʿAdawī, *Rashīd Riḍā, al-imām al-mujāhid* (Cairo: Al-Muʾassasah al-Miṣriyyah al-ʿĀmmah li al-Taʾlīf wa al-Anbāʾ wa al-Nashr, 1964), p. 145; Riḍā, "Anbāʾ sūriyah," 346; F.O. 195/2190/50: Drummond-Hay to O'Conor, 5 August 1905.

29. The source for the following account of Badr al-Dīn al-Ḥasanī's charge against ʿAbd al-Razzāq al-Bīṭār and the uproar over Jamāl al-Dīn al-Qāsimī's essays on legal theory is an untitled manuscript with the first four pages missing. The manuscript is in the hand of Ḥāmid al-Taqī, Qāsimī's neighbor and disciple. Taqī apparently made a copy of Qāsimī's account because it is written in the first person by Qāsimī. Pages 5 through 21 are numbered. Unless otherwise noted, the information on the incidents of the fall of 1906 is from this manuscript.

30. Badr al-Dīn al-Ḥasanī indeed became the leading shaykh in Damascus by about 1915. See Māliḥ, *ʿĀlim al-ummah,* pp. 39–43, 70–71.

31. Muḥammad ʿAlī al-Maydānī showed the poem to Qāsimī, who advised the student to avoid satirical poetry in the future. Ẓāfir al-Qāsimī, *Jamāl al-Dīn al-Qāsimī wa ʿaṣruhu* (Damascus: Al-Hāshimiyyah Press, 1965), p. 337.

32. The deputy jurisconsult was Muḥsin al-Usṭuwānī; the shaykh was Salīm al-Kuzbarī; and the notable was Yaḥyā Tallū; Jamāl al-Dīn al-Qāsimī, untitled manuscript, Qāsimī library, Damascus, p. 8.

33. Jamāl al-Dīn al-Qāsimī, *Majmūʿ al-rasāʾil fī uṣūl al-fiqh* (Beirut: Al-Ahliyyah Press, 1906). Qāsimī's name does not appear on the title page; it shows up in the text on page 35. The four essays were Abū Bakr Muḥammad ibn al-Ḥusayn ibn Fawrak al-Iṣbahānī al-Shāfiʿī, "Muqaddimah fī nukat min uṣūl al-fiqh;" Muḥyi al-Dīn Muḥammad Ibn ʿArabī, "Risālah fī uṣūl al-fiqh;" Najm al-Dīn al-Ṭūfī al-Ḥanbalī, "Risālah fī al-maṣāliḥ al-mursalah;" and Jalāl

al-Dīn al-Suyūṭī, "Risālah fī uṣūl al-fiqh," from *Kitāb al-niqāyah.* Qāsimī also added a passage by Ibrāhīm al-Shāṭibī on legal theory from his *Kitāb al-muwāfaqāt.*

34. Copy of a letter from Jamāl al-Dīn al-Qāsimī to ʿAbd al-Raḥmān Nasīb, 13 September 1906; "Multaqaṭāt min ma'āthīr sayyidi al-ustādh imām waqtihi wa nābighat qaṭrihi al-kātib al-balīgh Qāsimī Zādah Shaykh Muḥammad Jamāl al-Dīn," manuscript, Qāsimī library, Damascus, pp. 24–25. Two days later Qāsimī wrote to a Moroccan salafi shaykh whose brother had visited Damascus the previous year and become acquainted with Qāsimī's circle. Jamāl al-Dīn mentioned that he intended to print three essays on legal theory and promised to send 100 copies to his friend in Fez and another set of 100 to Tunis. Copy of a letter from Jamāl al-Dīn al-Qāsimī to ʿAbd al-Raḥmān al-Kattānī, 15 September 1906; untitled notebook, Qāsimī library, Damascus.

35. Jamāl al-Dīn al-Qāsimī's brother-in-law lived in Lebanon near Zahle. Qāsimī had the custom of visiting this in-law just before Ramadan. Conversation with Muḥammad Saʿīd al-Qāsimī, January 1984. Written evidence of Qāsimī's pre-Ramadan travels is in an incomplete commentary on a work of Ḥanbalī jurisprudence, "Fiqh al-dīn li ʿāmmat al-mu'minīn: mukhtaṣar al-iqnāʿ wa sharḥ;" on the margins of the manuscript Qāsimī noted that he had worked on it between 1906 and 1909 in the month before Ramadan each year while in Lebanon; Qāsimī library, Damascus. Also see the untitled manuscript on the 1906 incidents, p. 12.

36. Ẓāfir al-Qāsimī, *Jamāl al-Dīn al-Qāsimī,* p. 393.

37. Ibid., p. 597.

38. Untitled manuscript on the 1906 incidents, p. 13.

39. Jamāl al-Dīn al-Qāsimī, *Majmūʿ al-rasā'il fī uṣūl al-fiqh,* pp. 31–34.

40. Ẓāfir al-Qāsimī, *Jamāl al-Dīn al-Qāsimī,* pp. 430–431; untitled manuscript on the 1906 incidents, p. 15.

41. Ẓāfir al-Qāsimī, *Jamāl al-Dīn al-Qāsimī,* pp. 385–386.

42. Ibid., p. 209.

43. Ibid., pp. 200–201. The work was *Dalā'il al-tawḥīd.*

Chapter 9

1. On Yūsuf al-Nabahānī see, Yūsuf al-Nabahānī, *Jāmiʿ karāmāt al-awliyā',* 2 vols. (Cairo: Dār al-Kutub al-ʿArabiyyah al-Kubrā, 1911), 2:52, 332, 390; ʿAbd al-Ḥafīẓ al-Fāsī, *Riyāḍ al-jannah aw al-mudhish al-muṭrib,* 2 vols. (Rabat: Al-Waṭaniyyah Press, 1932), 2:161–166; Rashīd Riḍā, "al-Radd ʿala aʿdā' al-iṣlāḥ al-islāmī," *al-Manār* 13 (1910): 796–798; Butrus Abu-Manneh, "Sultan Abdülḥamīd II and Shaikh Abūlhudā al-Ṣayyādī," *Middle Eastern Studies* 15 (1979): 147.

2. Nabahānī, *Jāmiʿ karāmāt,* 2:390.

3. Riḍā, "al-Radd ʿala aʿdā'," 797.

4. Ẓāfir al-Qāsimī, *Jamāl al-Dīn al-Qāsimī wa ʿaṣruhu* (Damascus: Al-Hāshimiyyah Press, 1965), p. 590.

5. Ibid., p. 170.

6. Yūsuf al-Nabahānī, *Shawāhid al-ḥaqq fī al-istighāthah bi sayyid al-khalq* (Cairo: Al-Yamaniyyah Press, 1905), pp. 4, 19, 154.

7. Yūsuf al-Nabahānī, *al-Rā'iyah al-ṣughrā fī dhamm al-bidʿah wa madḥ al-sunnah al-gharrā'* (n.p., n.d.), p. 7; Abū al-Maʿālī al-Ḥusaynī al-Salāmī [Maḥmūd Shukrī al-Alūsī] *Ghāyat al-amānī fī al-radd ʿala al-Nabahānī* (Cairo: Kurdistān al-ʿIlmiyyah Press, n.d.), pp. 45–46, 334–337; Sulaymān ibn Saḥmān al-Najdī, Muḥammad ibn Ḥasan al-Qaṭarī al-Marzuqī, and ʿAlī ibn Sulaymān ibn al-Tamīmī al-Yūsuf, *al-Dāhiyah al-kubrā ʿala al-rā'iyah al-ṣughrā* (Bombay: Al-Muṣṭafawiyyah Press, n.d.); Muḥammad Bahjat al-Bīṭār *al-Ṭāmma al-kubrā.* I have not been able to locate a copy of Bīṭār's essay.

8. *Al-Ḥaqā'iq* 1 (1910). The first number was dated 7 August 1910. For a description of *al-Ḥaqā'iq*, see Jūzuf Ilyās, "Taṭawwur al-ṣiḥāfah al-sūriyyah fī al-ʿahd al-ʿuthmānī" (Master's thesis, Lebanese University, 1972), pp. 175–176, 179–180.

9. "Fātiḥat al-sanah al-ūlā," *al-Ḥaqā'iq* 1 (1910): 2–3. All articles cited in this chapter are from *al-Ḥaqā'iq* unless otherwise noted.

10. "*Al-Ḥaqā'iq* wa al-sā'iḥ," 1 (1911): 389. On *al-Mufīd* newspaper, see Rashid I. Khalidi, "The Press as a Source for Modern Arab Political History: ʿAbd al-Ghanī al-ʿUraisī and *al-Mufīd*," *Arab Studies Quarterly* 3 (1981): 22–42. For Ṣāliḥ al-T ūnisī's speeches and legal opinions, see "Khiṭāb," 1 (1910): 180–190; "Naṣīhah li al-Yamaniyyīn," 1 (1911): 418–426; "Fatwā sharʿī fī adā' zakāt al-amwāl li iʿānat al-usṭūl al-ʿuthmānī," 2 (1911): 71–74. Among the contributors we mentioned in Chapter 8 are Hāshim al-Khaṭīb, Mukhtār al-Mu'ayyad al-ʿAẓm, Maḥmūd al-ʿAṭṭār, Muḥammad al-Qāsimī, Ḥasan al-Usṭuwānī, and ʿArif al-Munayyir.

11. "Al-ʿUlamā'," 1 (1910): 22; "al-Iṣlāḥ wa muntaḥilūhu wa daʿwah ila al-iṣlāḥ," 2 (1911): 8; "al-As'ilah wa al-ajwibah," 2 (1911): 66–67; "Dimashq wa zuʿamā'uhā aw naẓarah fī mā taḥtāj ilayhi," 2 (1912): 288.

12. "Naṣīhah li al-Yamaniyyīn," 418–426; "Ṭarāblus wa al-iʿānah fī dimashq," 2 (1911): 107; "Bi mā yunhaḍ al-muslimūn?" 2 (1912): 242; "al-Madāris al-ajnabiyyah," 2 (1912): 334.

13. "Al-ʿUlamā'," 21; "*al-Ḥaqā'iq* wa makānat al-dīn min al-raqī," 1 (1911): 300; "al-ʿUlamā' wa al-waẓā'if," 2 (1912): 245; "Waẓā'if al-ʿulamā'," 2 (1911): 42.

14. "Jarā'im al-kuttāb," 2 (1911): 75; "al-Iṣlāḥ wa muntaḥilūhu wa daʿwah ila al-iṣlāḥ," 10.

15. "Fatwā sharʿī fī adā' zakāt al-amwāl li iʿānat al-usṭūl al-ʿuthmānī," 73; "*al-Ḥaqā'iq* wa al-sā'iḥ," 390–391; "Kalimah fī al-fiqh wa al-fuqahā'," 1 (1910): 11; "al-Iṣlāh wa muntaḥilūhu wa daʿwah ila al-iṣlāḥ," 10.

16. "Kalimah fī al-fiqh wa al-fuqahā'," 12; "*al-Ḥaqā'iq* wa al-sā'iḥ," 391, 394; *al-Ḥaqā'iq* 2 (1911): 188.

17. "Ṭarāblus wa al-iʿānah fī dimashq," 2 (1911): 106; "Istiḥbāb al-qiyām ʿinda dhikr wilādatihi," 2 (1911): 201–212; "Taḥqīq al-kalām fī wujūb al-qiyām," 11,12 (1912): 409–427.

18. "Al-Iṣlāḥ wa muntaḥilūhu," 2 (1911): 235.

19. "Al-Iṣlāḥ wa muntaḥilūhu wa daʿwah ila al-iṣlāḥ," 2 (1911): 8–9; "Fātiḥat al-sanah al-ūlā," 1 (1910): 2; "al-ʿUlamā'," 1 (1910): 21; "al-Tafalsaf al-ḥadīth," 1 (1910): 86–89; "al-Muslimūn wa al-siyāsah al-dīniyyah," 2 (1911): 212–213.

20. "Ṣāḥib *al-Muqtabas* yaftarī ʿala ʿulamā al-dīn," 1 (1911): 369, 372. For other attacks on Kurd ʿAlī, see "Jināyat *al-Muqtabas* ʿala al-dawlah wa al-waṭan," 2 (1911): 118–120; "*al-Muqtabas* wa al-mūmisāt," 1 (1911): 496–480, in which Kurd ʿAlī is accused of favoring prostitution.

21. "Bushrā ʿilmiyyah wa khuṭwa qaḍā'iyyah," *al-Muqtabas* (Damascus), no. 500, 17 October 1910.

22. "Mas'alat al-talaghrāf wa khulāṣat al-qawl fīhā," 1 (1910): 171–182; ʿArif al-Munayyir, "Munāẓarah bayn ʿālimayn," 1 (1910): 211–216, 264–267; Mukhtār al-Mu'ayyad [al-ʿAẓm], "ʿAwd ʿala bud'," 310–313.

23. Jamāl al-Dīn al-Qāsimī, *Irshād al-khalq ila al-ʿamal bi khabar al-barq* (Damascus: Al-Muqtabas Press, 1911), pp. 44–48, 52.

24. "Riwāyat Zuhayr al-Andalusī," 2 (1911): 68–70; ʿArif al-Munayyir, "Ajwibat al-ʿulamā' ʿan al-tamthīl," 2 (1911): 85–87; Muḥammad al-Qāsimī al-Ḥallāq, "al-Jawāb al-thānī," 87–96.

25. Ilyās, "Taṭawwur al-ṣiḥāfah al-sūriyyah," p. 180; See note 1, Chapter 8 for Iskandarānī's essays. Other works included Muṣṭafā al-Karīmī, *Nūr al-yaqīn fī mabḥath al-talqīn*

(Cairo: Al-Miṣriyyah Press, 1927); Tawfīq ibn Najīb al-Sūqiyah, *al-Risālah al-ūlā: Tabyīn al-ḥaqq wa al-ṣawāb bi al-radd ʿala atbāʿ Ibn ʿAbd al-Wahhāb* (Damascus: Al-Fayḥā' Press, 1922); Ḥasan ibn Ḥasan Khazbak, *al-Maqālāt al-wufiyah fī al-radd ʿala al-wahhābiyyah* (Cairo: Al-Kamāl Press, 1928). Muḥammad Bahjat al-Bīṭār published an essay as Nāṣir al-Dīn al-Ḥijāzī al-Atharī, *Nafkhah ʿala al-nafḥah wa al-minḥah* (Damascus: Al-Taraqqī Press, 1922). This obviously was a refutation of Iskandarānī's essays published the same year. Bīṭār published another essay under the pseudonym Abū al-Yasār al-Dimashqī al-Maydānī, *Naẓarah fī al-nafḥah al-zakiyah fī al-radd ʿala al-firqah al-wahhābiyyah* (Damascus: Al-Taraqqī Press, 1922).

26. On these political developments, see Chapter 10.

Chapter 10

1. Rashid Khalidi, "Social Factors in the Rise of the Arab Movement in Syria," in *From Nationalism to Revolutionary Islam,* ed., Said Amir Arjomand (Albany: State University of New York Press, 1984), p. 55.

2. Alvin Gouldner, *The Future of Intellectuals and the Rise of the New Class* (New York: Oxford University Press, 1979), pp. 62–66.

3. Ẓāfir al-Qāsimī, *Jamāl al-Dīn al-Qāsimī wa ʿaṣruhu* (Damascus: Al-Hāshimiyyah Press, 1965), pp. 214–215. Hereafter this reference will be given as *JDQ*.

4. Jamāl al-Dīn al-Qāsimī, *Dalā'il al-tawḥīd* (Damascus: Al-Fayḥā' Press, 1908), p. 206.

5. Public Record Office, Foreign Office 195/2277/33: Devey to Lowther, 12 August 1908; Muḥibb al-Dīn al-Khaṭīb, ed., *Al-Duktūr Ṣalāḥ al-Dīn al-Qāsimī*, 1305–1334 (Cairo: Al-Salafiyyah Press, 1959), pp. 8, 36–40. Hereafter this reference will be given as *SDQ*. Luṭfī al-Ḥaffār, *Dhikriyyāt: Muntakhabāt min khuṭub wa aḥādīth wa maqālāt* (Damascus: Ibn Zaydūn Press, 1954), p. 8.

6. F.O. 195/1984/13: Richards to Currie, 13 March 1897; Fakhrī al-Bārūdī, *Mudhakkirāt al-Bārūdī*, 2 vols. (Beirut: Dār al-Ḥayāt, 1951), 1:63, 67.

7. *JDQ*, p. 216.

8. Ibid., p. 217–226.

9. Ibid., p. 221.

10. Ibid., p. 224.

11. Ibid., p. 224.

12. Ibid., pp. 231–233.

13. Muḥammad Saʿīd al-Bānī, *Tanwīr al-baṣā'ir bi sīrat al-shaykh Ṭāhir* (Damascus: Al-Ḥukūmah al-ʿArabiyyah al-Sūriyyah Press, 1920), pp. 116–117.

14. Rafīq al-ʿAẓm arrived in Damascus on 11 August, *JDQ*, p. 227; ʿAbd al-Ḥamīd al-Zahrāwī returned to Syria to run for the parliamentary seat of Homs; Rashid Khalidi, *British Policy Towards Syria and Palestine, 1906–1914* (London: Ithaca Press, 1980), p. 258.

15. Feroz Ahmad, *The Young Turks: The Committee of Union and Progress in Turkish Politics, 1908–1914* (Oxford: Clarendon Press, 1969), p. 18.

16. F.O. 195/2277/33: Devey to Lowther, 12 August 1908; F.O. 195/2277/51: Devey to Lowther, 1 October 1908; "Multaqaṭāt min ma'āthir sayyidi al-ustādh imām waqtihi wa nābighat qaṭrihi al-kātib al-balīgh Qāsimī Zādah Shaykh Muḥammad Jamāl al-Dīn," manuscript, Qāsimī library, Damascus, pp. 101–102.

17. F.O. 195/2277/51: Devey to Lowther, 1 October 1908.

18. Ibid.; Rashīd Riḍā, "Riḥlat ṣāḥib *al-Manār* (fī sūriyah)," *al-Manār* 11 (1908): 948–949; also see Philip S. Khoury, *Urban Notables and Arab Nationalism: The Politics of Damascus, 1860–1920* (Cambridge: Cambridge University Press, 1983), pp. 56–57.

19. F.O. 195/2277/42: Devey to Lowther, 9 September 1908.

20. Ibrāhīm al-ʿAdawī, *Rashīd Riḍā, al-imām al-mujāhid* (Cairo: Al-Mu'assasah al-Miṣriyyah al-ʿĀmmah li al-Ta'līf wa al-Anbā' wa al-Nashr, 1964), p. 225; *JDQ*, pp. 445–446; Riḍā, "Riḥlat," 940.

21. Riḍā, "Riḥlat," 949.

22. *JDQ*, p. 447. The main sources on the Ramadan incident are Riḍā, "Riḥlat;" Bārūdī, *Mudhakkirāt*, 1:71–73; "Ḥādithat dimashq," *al-Ittiḥād al-ʿuthmānī* (Beirut), 16 November 1908; *JDQ*, pp. 445–450.

23. Riḍā, "Riḥlat," 950; Bārūdī, *Mudhakkirāt*, 1:72.

24. *JDQ*, p. 449.

25. Bārūdī, *Mudhakkirāt*, 1:72–73; F.O. 195/2277/58: Devey to Lowther, 27 October 1908.

26. Riḍā, "Riḥlat," 947; *JDQ*, p. 449.

27. F.O. 195/2311/1: Devey to Lowther, 2 January 1909; Riḍā, "Riḥlat," 950; Bārūdī, *Mudhakkirāt*, 1:73.

28. *JDQ*, pp. 594–595.

29. Ibid., p. 451. Qāsimī's diary shows a slip of the pen. The correct date was 29 Ramadan.

30. Ibid., p. 462.

31. F.O. 195/2277/60: Devey to Lowther, 5 November 1908; Khalidi, *British Policy*, pp. 258–259.

32. *Al-Muqtabas* (Damascus), 18 December 1908.

33. The Society changed its name to Jamʿiyyat al-nahḍah al-sūriyyah in early November 1908. *Al-Ittiḥād al-ʿuthmānī* 6 November 1908. On the law forbidding public associations based on nationality, see Ahmad, *The Young Turks*, p. 62. *Al-Muqtabas*, 17 December 1908.

34. *SDQ*, pp. 8–10; Saʿīd al-Afghānī, "al-Shaykh Aḥmad al-Nuwaylātī," *al-Tamaddun al-islāmī* 4 (1938): 216–217.

35. Ahmad, *The Young Turks*, p. 40. On the Muḥammadan Union, see David Farhi, "The Şeriat as a Political Slogan—or the Incident of the 31st Mart," *Middle Eastern Studies* 7 (1971): 275–299; Victor R. Swenson, "The Military Rising in Istanbul, 1909," *Journal of Contemporary History* 5 (1970): 171–184. F.O. 195/2311/18: Devey to Lowther, 3 April 1909; Rashīd Riḍā, "al-Diyār al-sūriyyah fī ʿahd al-ḥukūmah al-dustūriyyah," *al-Manār* 12 (1909): 795; *JDQ*, p. 523.

36. Ahmad, *The Young Turks*, pp. 40–44; Swenson, "The Military Rising," 177–178; F.O. 195/2311/22: Devey to Lowther, 19 April 1909.

37. *JDQ*, p. 523.

38. F.O. 195/2311/25: Devey to Lowther, 29 April 1909; F.O. 195/2311/34: Devey to Lowther, 31 May 1909.

39. *JDQ*, p. 594.

40. Ibid., p. 595.

41. Zeine N. Zeine, *Arab–Turkish Relations and the Emergence of Arab Nationalism* (Beirut: Khayats, 1958).

42. Bānī, *Tanwīr*, pp. 110–111.

43. Copy of a letter from Jamāl al-Dīn al-Qāsimī to Rashīd Riḍā inserted in Jamāl al-Dīn al-Qāsimī, "Tārīkh al-ustādh Jamāl al-Dīn al-Qāsimī," manuscript, Qāsimī library, Damascus, between pp. 22–23.

44. *JDQ*, p. 205.

45. Ibid., pp. 205–210.

46. Ibid., p. 211.

47. Ibid., p. 228.

48. *SDQ*, pp. 157, 176–177.

49. Ṣalāḥ al-Dīn al-Qāsimī, "al-Mas'alah al-ʿarabiyyah wa nash'atuhā," *SDQ,* pp. 71–75.

50. *Al-Muqtabas,* 14 September 1909; for the consequences of the article, see "al-Saʿāyah wa al-khilāfah al-ʿarabiyyah fī dimashq," *al-Nibrās* 1 (1909–1910): 300–303. For the British consul's view of Kurd ʿAlī and the incident, see FO 195/2312/48: Devey to Lowther, 18 September 1909.

51. Rashīd Riḍā, "al-Diyār al-sūriyyah," 795.

52. "Al-Saʿāyah wa al-khilāfah," 302–303; for the following account of Qāsimī's and Bīṭār's interrogation, see *JDQ,* pp. 470–476.

53. Ibid., p. 472.

54. Ibid., p. 204; "Ahamm al-akhbār wa al-ārā'," *al-Nibrās* 2 (1910–1911): 35.

55. Adham al-Jundī, *Shuhadā' al-ḥarb al-ʿālamiyyah al-kubrā* (Damascus: Al-ʿUrūbah Press, 1960), p. 11; Ṣalāḥ al-Dīn al-Qāsimī, "ʿAqabāt fī ṭarīq al-jamʿiyyah," *SDQ,* pp. 11–16.

56. In the CUP camp, clients of Muḥammad Fawzī al-ʿAẓm ran for municipal office, whereas ʿAẓm himself, ʿAbd al-Muḥsin al-Usṭuwānī, Amīn al-Tarzī, and ʿAbd al-Raḥmān al-Yūsuf (who had broken with the salafis and Arabists) ran for parliament. In the Arabist camp, ʿUthmān al-ʿAẓm ran for municipal office, and ʿAbd al-Raḥmān Shahbandar and Shafīq al-Mu'ayyad al-ʿAẓm rallied support for the Liberal Entente. Ḥaqqī al-ʿAẓm, *Ḥaqā'iq al-intikhābāt al-niyābiyyah fī al-ʿirāq wa filasṭīn wa sūriyah* (Cairo: Al-Akhbār Press, 1912), pp. 10, 12, 15, 33–34, 39–40, 44–45. Salīm al-Bukhārī, a salafi and longtime supporter of the CUP, left the Committee to work for the Liberal Entente; Muḥammad Saʿīd al-Bānī, *Majallat al-majmaʿ al-ʿilmī al-ʿarabī* 9 (1929): 745. On the 1912 election in Syria, see Rashid Khalidi, "The 1912 Election Campaign in the Cities of *bilād al-Shām,*" *International Journal of Middle East Studies* 16 (1984): 461–474.

57. Ahmad, *The Young Turks,* p. 98. ʿAbd al-Ḥamīd al-Zahrāwī participated in founding the Liberal Entente and greeted its formation in the Arabic newspaper he published in Istanbul. He listed its founding members and the parliamentary deputies who joined, and he described its platform. Jawdat al-Rikābī and Jamīl Sulṭān, *al-Irth al-fikrī li al-muṣliḥ al-ijtimāʿī ʿAbd al-Ḥamīd al-Zahrāwī* (Damascus: Al-Hāshimiyyah Press, 1963), pp. 479–486.

58. ʿAẓm, *Ḥaqā'iq al-intikhābāt,* pp. 63–64.

59. The Party for Administrative Decentralization published its platform in "Bayān ḥizb al-lāmarkaziyyah al-idāriyyah al-ʿuthmānī," *al-Manār* 16 (1913): 226–231; for the party's charter and bylaws, see Anonymous, *Thawrat al-ʿarab* (Cairo: Al-Muqaṭṭam Press, 1916), pp. 57–62. Rashīd Riḍā, ʿAbd al-Ḥamīd al-Zahrāwī, and Rafīq al-ʿAẓm were among the party's founders; Rashid Khalidi, *British Policy Towards Syria and Palestine, 1906–1914,* pp. 285–286.

60. Members of the Arab Renaissance Society signed the petition: Ṣalāḥ al-Dīn al-Qāsimī, ʿArif al-Shihābī, Luṭfī al-Ḥaffār, Rushdī al-Ḥakīm, ʿUthmān Mardam-Beg, Adīb Mardam-Beg, Muḥammad Kurd ʿAlī, Aḥmad Kurd ʿAlī, and Maḥmūd Kurd ʿAlī; other Arabists included ʿAbd al-Raḥmān Shahbandar and ʿAbd al-Wahhāb al-Inklīzī; members of the salafi camp also signed: Ḥāmid al-Taqī, and Muḥammad ʿId al-Qāsimī (Jamāl al-Dīn's brother). Wajīh Kawtharānī, ed., *Wathā'iq al-mu'tamar al-ʿarabī al-awwal,* 1913 (Beirut: Dār al-Ḥadāthah, 1980), pp. 153–154.

61. Muḥammad Fawzī al-ʿAẓm and ʿAbd al-Raḥmān al-Yūsuf headed the list of opponents to the Congress. Ibid., pp. 88–89, 98.

62. Jundī, *Shuhadā',* pp. 94–102; Adnān al-Khaṭīb, *al-Shaykh Ṭāhir al-Jazā'irī* (Cairo: Maʿhad al-Dirāsāt al-ʿArabiyyah, 1971), pp. 55, 84; for Jamāl Pasha's side of the events, see *La vérité sur la question syrienne,* (Istanbul, 1916). On Bukhārī's and Bānī's exile, see Adham al-Jundī, *Aʿlām al-adab wa al-fann,* 2 vols. (Damascus: Majallat Ṣawt Sūriyah Press,

1954), 2:119; Bānī, *Tanwīr,* p. 125; Qadrī Qalʿajī, *al-Sābiqūn,* (Beirut: Dār al-ʿIlm li al-Malāyīn, 1954), p. 27. On Jamāl al-Dīn al-Qāsimī, see ʿAbd al-Razzāq al-Bīṭār, *Ḥilyat al-bashar fī tārīkh al-qarn al-thālith ʿashar,* 3 vols. (Damascus: Majmaʿ al-Lughah al-ʿArabiyyah, 1961–1963), 1:438; on his fatal bout of typhoid fever, personal correspondence from Mr. Samīḥ al-Ghabrah (Qāsimī's grandson), 11 February 1985; on ʿAbd al-Razzāq al-Bīṭār, see Muḥammad Bahjat al-Bīṭār, "Tarjamat al-shaykh ʿAbd al-Razzāq al-Bīṭār," *al-Manār,* 21 (1919): 317.

63. Djemāl Pasha, *Memories of a Turkish Statesman, 1913–1919* (London, n.d.), p. 59; Gouldner, *The Future of Intellectuals,* pp. 57–72.

64. The following citations are from Gouldner, *The Future of Intellectuals,* pp. 61–65.

65. Rashid Khalidi, "Social Factors in the Rise of the Arab Movement," pp. 55–57.

66. Khoury, *Urban Notables,* pp. 45–46.

Conclusion

1. In 1906, Jamāl al-Dīn al-Qāsimī told ʿAbd al-Razzāq al-Bīṭār that the days when ulama exercised power ended with the exile of ʿAbd Allah al-Ḥalabī following the 1860 massacre of Christians. Jamāl al-Dīn al-Qāsimī, untitled manuscript on the incidents of the autumn of 1906, Qāsimī library, Damascus.

2. Goran Therborn discusses the impact of changes in education and careers in terms of changes in the "subjection and qualification" of human subjects, and he relates those changes to ideological change. Goran Therborn, *The Ideology of Power and the Power of Ideology,* (London: Verso, 1980) pp. 46–48.

3. Gouldner, *The Future of Intellectuals and the Rise of the New Class* (New York: Oxford University Press, 1979), pp. 1–4.

APPENDIX

The Qāsimī Library

Several of the manuscripts that I frequently cite are located at the Qāsimī library in the home of Mr. Muḥammad Saʿīd al-Qāsimī, which is in the Muhajirin quarter of Damascus. The library consists of books, manuscripts, periodicals, and papers stacked on shelves lining three walls. The collection contains copies of Jamāl al-Dīn al-Qāsimī's published works, his unpublished manuscripts, and a portion of his own collection of books and manuscripts; the balance of Jamāl al-Dīn's personal collection was in the West Beirut home of the late Ẓāfir al-Qāsimī. As of July 1989 his home had not suffered any damages from the war in Lebanon, but I do not know if its materials have been moved to Damascus since Ẓāfir al-Qāsimī's demise.

At the Qāsimī library in Damascus, Jamāl al-Dīn's published works and manuscripts are kept together on shelves along one wall. Nearly all the manuscripts are bound; they vary in size, and the bindings are unlabeled and unnumbered. The paper of the manuscripts is in good condition, and the script's legibility ranges from fine to fair. Along the same wall are a few manuscript works by Jamāl al-Dīn's father, Muḥammad Saʿīd al-Qāsimī. Books and manuscripts gathered by family members beginning with Qāsim al-Ḥallāq line the upper shelves of the same wall.

The other two walls of shelves hold works collected for the most part by Jamāl al-Dīn's younger brothers and descendants. These works consist mostly of dictionaries, bound periodicals, and books on history and literature. Some of the periodicals date from the early years of the twentieth century. Finally, some boxes contain letters and loose papers.

The Qāsimī library's holdings are not numbered, but Muḥammad Saʿīd al-Qāsimī has so arranged them in a topical fashion that he can quickly find items on request. Mr. Qāsimī willingly loaned me published works from the collection; as for manuscripts, he keeps them in his home, where he allowed me to study them.

SELECT BIBLIOGRAPHY

Archival Sources

Great Britain (London): Public Record Office
Foreign Office General Correspondence (Turkey)
FO 78/2985 Damascus 1879
Foreign Office Consular Correspondence (Turkey)

FO 195/1448	Damascus	1883
/1480	Beirut	1884
/1583	Damascus	1887
/1940	Damascus	1896
/1984	Damascus	1897
/2024	Damascus	1898
/2097	Damascus	1901
/2122	Damascus	1902
/2165	Damascus	1904
/2190	Beirut	1905
/2217	Damascus	1906
/2245	Damascus	1907
/2277	Damascus	1908
/2311	Damascus	1909
/2312	Damascus	1909

Syria (Damascus): Mudīriyyat al-wathā'iqiyyah al-tārīkhiyyah, Markaz al-wathā'iq al-tārīkhiyyah (Directorate of Historical Documents, Center for Historical Documents)
Inheritance Documents:
Sijillāt 500, 581, 839, 878, 885, 906, 926, 960, 993, 1001, 1030, 1035, 1040, 1053, 1054, 1055, 1059, 1080, 1093, 1103, 1113, 1119, 1124, 1135, 1139, 1151, 1166, 1183, 1189, 1192, 1203, 1226, 1229, 1233, 1252, 1263, 1273, 1278, 1285, 1313, 1340, 1347, 1354, 1382, 1490, 1508, 1533.

Unpublished Manuscripts in the Qāsimī Library

al-Qāsimī, Jamāl al-Dīn. 1892. "Badhl al-himam fī maw'iẓat ahl wādī al-'ajam." An account of Qāsimī's Ramadan teaching tour of 1892.

______. 1901. "Bayt al-qaṣīd fī tarjamat al-imām al-wālid al-sa'īd." Biography of Muḥammad Sa'īd al-Qāsimī.

______. "Ghanīmat al-himmah fī kashf al-ghummah."

______. "Multaqaṭāt min ma'āthir sayyidi al-ustādh imām waqtihi wa nābighat qaṭrihi al-kātib al-balīgh Qāsimī Zādah Shaykh Muḥammad Jamāl al-Dīn." Compiled by Qāsimī's neighbor and student, Ḥāmid al-Taqī. Copies of Qāsimī's correspondence, comments on other writers and articles from periodicals, and diary entries.

———. "Tārīkh al-ustādh Jamāl al-Dīn al-Qāsimī." Qāsimī's incomplete autobiography, which goes up to 1905, and includes additions from 1909–1910.
———. "Taʿṭīr al-mashām fī ma'āthīr dimashq al-shām." 4 vols. The rough draft of Qāsimī's history of Damascus has several unnumbered inserted pages, including 44 on the biographies of ulama. Qāsimī completed the revised version in May 1901.
———. Untitled manuscript on the incidents of autumn, 1906. Apparently a copy of an original by Qāsimī, this manuscript is a first-person narration by him of those incidents. According to the colophon, it is in the hand of Ḥāmid al-Taqī.
———. Untitled notebook. Some of the entries are in Qāsimī's hand, most of them in Taqī's hand. It includes passages copied from books, newspapers, obituaries on Muḥammad ʿAbduh's death, letters, biographies of Taqī's ancestors, and stories about Badr al-Dī al-Ḥasanī.
al-Qāsimī, Muḥammad Saʿīd. "Al-Thughr al-bāsim fī tarjamat al-shaykh Qāsim." Biography of Qāsim al-Ḥallāq.
al-Taqī, Ḥāmid. Untitled notebook. Contains a legal decision by Maḥmūd al-Ḥamzāwī on emulation, which Ḥāmid al-Taqī copied from another shaykh's notes.

Unpublished Correspondence

Letters from Maḥmūd Shukrī al-Alūsī to Jamāl al-Dīn al-Qāsimī. Eighteen letters dated between 25 December 1908 and 27 November 1913. Original set bound together and in the possession of Mr. Samīḥ al-Ghabrah, Damascus. Photocopies of originals in the author's possession.
Letter from Mr. Samīḥ al-Ghabrah, 11 February 1985.

Manuscripts at the Ẓāhiriyyah Library

al-Bīṭār, Ḥasan. 1853. "Irshād al-ʿibād fī faḍl al-jihād." Number 7122.
al-Jazā'irī, Ṭāhir. 1897. "Rasā'il Ibn Taymiyyah wa al-kutub allatī naqala ʿanhā fī badīʿ al-qur'ān ghayr mā ishtahar." Number 11726.
———. 1899. "Tārīkh hijrat wālidihi wa baʿḍ masā'il." Number 11613.
———. 1898. "Tawārīkh siyāḥiyyah fī baʿḍ al-bilād." Number 11631.
al-Munayyir, Muḥammad ʿArif. 1901. "Al-Ḥaqq al-mubīn fī aḥādīth arbaʿīn fī man kharaja ʿan ṭāʿat amīr al-muminīn wa shaqq ʿasa al-muslimīn." Number 8618.

Published Works by Jamāl al-Dīn al-Qāsimī

Al-Ajwibah al-murḍiyah ʿammā awradahu Kamāl al-Dīn ibn al-Humām ʿala al-mustadillīn bi thubūt sunnat al-maghrib al-qibliyyah. Damascus: Rawḍat al-Shām Press, 1908.
Awāmir muhimmah fī iṣlāḥ al-qaḍā' al-sharʿī. Damascus: Al-Taraqqī Press, [1913].
Al-Awrād al-ma'thūrah. Beirut: Thamārat al-Funūn Press, 1902.
Dalā'il al-tawḥīd. Damascus: Al-Fayḥā' Press, 1908.
Al-Faḍl al-mubīn ʿala ʿiqd al-jawhar al-thamīn; sharḥ al-arbaʿīn al-ʿajlūniyyah. Beirut: Dār al-Nafā'is, 1983.
Al-Fatwā fī al-Islām. Damascus: Al-Muqtabas Press, 1911.
Irshād al-khalq ila al-ʿamal bi khabar al-barq. Damascus: Al-Muqtabas Press, 1911.
Iṣlāḥ al-masājid min al-bidaʿ wa al-ʿawā'id. Cairo: Al-Salafiyyah Press, 1923.
Jawāmiʿ al-ādāb fī akhlāq al-anjāb. Cairo: Al-Saʿādah Press, 1921.
Kitāb al-isti'nās li taṣḥīḥ ankiḥat al-nās. Damascus: Al-Taraqqī Press, 1914.

Maḥāsin al-ta'wīl. 17 vols. Cairo: Dār Iḥyā' al-Kutub al-ʿArabiyyah, 1957.
Majmūʿ al-rasā'il fī uṣūl al-fiqh. Beirut: Al-Ahliyyah Press, 1906.
Al-Masḥ ʿala al-jawrabayn wa al-naʿlayn. Damascus: Al-Taraqqī Press, 1914.
Mawʿiẓat al-mu'minīn min iḥyā' ʿulūm al-dīn. Cairo: Al-Saʿādah Press, 1913.
Mīzān al-jarḥ wa al-taʿdīl. Cairo: Al-Manār Press, 1912.
Muntakhab al-tawassulāt. Damascus: Rawḍat al-Shām Press, 1901.
Al-Nafḥah al-raḥmāniyyah; sharḥ matn al-maydāniyyah fī ʿilm al-tajwīd. Damascus, 1905.
Naqḍ al-naṣā'iḥ al-kāfiyah li man yatawallā Muʿāwiyah. Damascus: Al-Fayḥā' Press, 1910.
Qawāʿid al-taḥdīth min funūn muṣṭalaḥ al-ḥadīth. Damascus: Ibn Zaydūn Press, 1935.
Risālah fī iqāmat al-ḥujjah ʿala al-muṣalli jamāʿatan qabl al-imām al-rātib min al-kitāb wa al-sunnah wa aqwāl sā'ir a'immat al-madhāhib. Damascus: Al-Ṣadāqah Press, 1924.
Shadhrah min al-sīrah al-muḥammadiyyah. Cairo: Al-Manār Press, 1904.
Sharḥ luqṭat al-ʿajlān. Damascus: Ibn Zaydūn Press, 1934.
"Taʿāruḍ al-ʿaql wa al-naql." *Al-Manār* 13 (1910): 613–634.
Al-Ṭā'ir al-maymūn fī ḥall lughz al-kanz al-madfūn. Beirut: Thamārat al-Funūn Press, 1898.
Tanbīh al-ṭālib ila maʿrifat al-farḍ wa al-wājib. Cairo: Madrasat Wālidat ʿAbbās al-Awwal, 1908.
Tārīkh al-jahmiyyah wa al-muʿtazilah. Cairo: Al-Manār Press, 1913.
al-Qāsimī, Jamāl al-Dīn and al-ʿAẓm, Khalīl. *Qāmūs al-ṣināʿāt al-shāmiyyah*. Vol. 2. Paris: Mouton & Co., 1960.

Arabic Newspapers

Al-Ittiḥād al-ʿUthmāni. 1908 (Beirut).
Al-Muqtabas. 1908, 1910 (Damascus).

Articles from Arabic Periodicals (by Journal)

Al-Abḥāth (Beirut)
Ṣalībī, Kamāl and Abū Ḥabīb, ʿAbd Allah. "Lamaḥāt min tārīkh dimashq fī ʿahd al-tanẓīmat." 21 (1968): 57–78, 117–153; 22 (1969): 51–69.

Al-Hidāyah al-Islāmiyyah (Damascus)
Yāsīn, Maḥmūd. "Khātimat al-muḥaddithīn." 8 (1936): 17–23, 76–85, 264–269.

Al-Hilāl (Cairo)
Maʿlūf, ʿIsā Iskandar. "Al-Shaykh Ṭāhir al-Jazā'irī." 28 (1920): 451–456.

Al-ʿIrfān (Sidon)
"Barnāmaj jamʿiyyat al-iḥsān al-islāmiyyah fī maḥallat al-kharāb bi al-shām." 3 (1911): 311–312.
[Al Kāshif al-Ghiṭā', Muḥammad al-Ḥusayn]. "ʿAyn al-mīzān." 4 (1912): 377–389.

Majallat al-Fayṣal (Riyad)
Arnā'ūṭ, Maḥmūd. Review of *al-Madkhal ila madhhab al-imām Aḥmad ibn Ḥanbal*. 7 (1983): 10–11.

Majallat al-Majmaʿ al-ʿIlmī al-ʿArabī (Damascus)
al-Karamī, Saʿīd. "Dawr al-kutub wa fā'idatuhā." 1 (1921): 8–12.
"Majmūʿah makhṭūṭah." 5 (1925): 61–69.
Kurd ʿAlī, Muḥammad. "Al-Muʿāṣirūn: al-Shaykh Ṭāhir al-Jazā'irī." 8 (1928): 577–595, 667–677.
al-Bānī, Muḥammad Saʿīd. [On Salīm al-Bukhārī]. 9 (1929): 742–749.

al-Maghribī, ʿAbd al-Qādir. [On Badr al-Dīn al-Ḥasanī]. 13 (1935): 297–298, 351–352.
"Risālah tārīkhiyyah min al-Shaykh Ṣāliḥ Qaṭanā ila al-Sayyid ʿAlā' al-Dīn ʿĀbidīn—1279."
15 (1937): 231–240.
al-Bīṭār, Muḥammad Bahjat. "Al-Mudarrisūn taḥt qubbat al-nasr." 24 (1949): 59–72, 222–233.

Al-Majallah al-Tārīkhiyyah al-Miṣriyyah (Cairo)
al-ʿAqqād, Ṣalāḥ al-Dīn. "Daʿwah ḥarakat al-iṣlāḥ al-salafī." 7 (1958): 86–105.
Nawwār, ʿAbd al-ʿAzīz. "Mawāqif siyāsiyyah li Abī Thinā' Maḥmūd al-Alūsī." 14 (1968): 143–168.

Al-Manār (Cairo)
"Al-Ḥikmah al-sharʿiyyah fī muḥākamat al-qādiriyyah wa al-rifāʿiyyah." 1 (1897): 598–601.
"Jarā'id sūriyah al-mustaʿbadah." 1 (1897): 665.
"Ṭahārat al-aʿṭār dhāt al-kuḥūl wa al-radd ʿala dhī al-fuḍūl." 4 (1902): 821–827.
Review of *al-Fiqh wa al-taṣawwuf.* 4 (1902): 838.
"ʿAbd al-Bāqī al-Afghānī." 8 (1905): 79–80.
"Muḥāribat al-wahm li al-ʿilm, aw ta'thīr al-saʿāyah fī al-dawlah al-ʿuthmāniyyah." 8 (1905): 315–317.
"Anbā' sūriyah al-muzʿijah–al-dawlah wa al-raʿīyah." 8 (1905): 346–348.
Review of *al-Ḥaqīqah al-bāhirah fī asrār al-sharīʿah al-ṭāhirah.* 9 (1906): 309–310.
"Riḥlat ṣāḥib *al-Manār* (fī sūriyah)." 11 (1909): 936–950.
"Fitan ramaḍān fī dimashq al-shām." 12 (1909): 720.
"Al-Diyār al-sūriyyah fī ʿahd al-ḥukūmah al-dustūriyyah." 12 (1909): 793–799.
"Al-Radd ʿala aʿdā' al-iṣlāḥ al-islāmī." 13 (1910): 796–798.
"Bayān ḥizb al-lāmarkaziyyah al-idāriyyah al-ʿuthmānī." 16 (1913): 226–231.
[On Jamāl al-Dīn al-Qāsimī]. 17 (1914): 558–560, 628–636.
"Al-Sayyid ʿAbd al-Ḥamīd al-Zahrāwī." 19 (1916): 169–178.
al-Ḥumṣi, Aḥmad Nabhān. "Tarjamat al-Sayyid ʿAbd al-Ḥamīd ibn al-Sayyid Muḥammad Shākir ibn al-Sayyid Ibrāhīm al-Zahrāwī." 21 (1919): 150–153, 207–211.
al-Bīṭār, Muḥammad Bahjat. "Tarjamat al-Shaykh ʿAbd al-Razzāq al-Bīṭār." 21 (1919): 317–324.
Riḍā, Ṣāliḥ Mukhliṣ. Review of *Tanwīr al-baṣā' ir bi sīrat al-Shaykh Ṭāhir.* 22 (1921): 635–640.
"Rafīq al-ʿAẓm: Wufātuhu wa tarjamatuhu." 26 (1925): 288–299.
"Wufāt al-ʿallāmah al-jalīl al-Shaykh Salīm al-Bukhārī." 29 (1928): 633–634.

Al-Nibrās (Beirut)
"Al-Saʿāyah wa al-khilāfah al-ʿarabiyyah fī dimashq." 1 (1909): 300–304.
"Ahamm al-akhbār wa al-ārā'." 2 (1910): 35–40, 77.

Al-Tamaddun al-Islāmī (Damascus)
al-Afghānī, Saʿīd. "Al-Shaykh Aḥmad al-Nuwaylātī." 4 (1938): 216–219.
al-Naṣrī, Kāmil. "Al-Ustādh al-Nuwaylātī." 5 (1939): 166–167.

Al-Zahrā' (Cairo)
"Rafīq al-ʿAẓm." 2 (1925): 224–234.
"Al-Shahīd al-saʿīd: Ṣāliḥ Qanbāz, 1303–1344." 2 (1925): 419–420.

Works in Arabic

Anonymous. 1895. *Ḥasr al-lithām ʿan nakabāt al-shām.* Cairo: n.p.
———. 1916. *Thawrat al-ʿarab.* Cairo: Al-Muqaṭṭam Press.

ʿAbduh, Muḥammad. N.d. *Risālat al-tawḥīd*. Cairo: Dār al-Maʿārif.
al-ʿAdawī, Ibrāhīm. 1964. *Rashīd Riḍā, al-imām al-mujāhid*. Cairo: Al-Mu'assasah al-Miṣriyyah al-ʿĀmmah li al-Ta'līf wa al-Anbā' wa al-Nashr.
al-Afghānī, Jamāl al-Dīn. Works listed in Iraj Afshar. 1963. *Majmūʿah-i asnād va madārik-i chap na-shudah dār barah-i Sayyid Jamāl al-Dīn al-Afghānī*. Tehran. Film copy at University of California, Los Angeles. Originals in Kitābkhānah-i Majlis, Tehran.
al-Afghānī, Jamāl al-Dīn and ʿAbduh, Muḥammad. 1980. *Al-ʿUrwah al-wuthqā*. Beirut: Dār al-Kitāb al-ʿArabī.
Āl Kāshif al-Ghiṭā', Muḥammad al-Ḥusayn. 1962. *Aṣl al-shīʿah wa uṣūluhā*. Najaf: Al-Ḥaydariyyah Press.
______. *ʿAyn al-mīzān*. 1912. Sidon: Al-ʿIrfān Press.
al-Alūsī, Maḥmūd Shukrī [Abū al-Maʿālī al-Ḥusaynī al-Salāmī]. N.d. *Ghāyat al-amānī fī al-radd ʿala al-Nabahānī*. Cairo: Kurdistān al-ʿIlmiyyah Press.
al-Alūsī, Nuʿmān Khayr al-Dīn. 1881. *Jalā' al-ʿaynayn fī muḥākamat al-ahmadayn*. Cairo: Būlāq Press.
ʿAnūtī, Usāmah. 1971. *Al-Ḥarakah al-adabiyyah fī al-shām fī al-qarn al-thāmin ʿashar*. Beirut: St. Joseph University Press.
Arslān, Shakīb. 1937. *Al-Sayyid Rashīd Riḍā, aw ikha' arbaʿīn sanah*. Damascus: Ibn Zaydūn Press.
al-Atharī, Muḥammad Bahjat. 1926/7. *Aʿlām al-ʿirāq*. Cairo: Al-Salafiyyah Press.
______. 1958. *Maḥmūd Shukrī al-Alūsī wa ārā'uhu al-lughawiyyah*. Cairo: Al-Kamāliyyah Press.
ʿAwaḍ, ʿAbd al-ʿAzīz Muḥammad. 1969. *Al-Idārah al-ʿuthmāniyyah fī wilāyat sūriyah, 1864–1914*. Cairo: Dār al-Maʿārif.
al-ʿAẓm, Ḥaqqī. 1912. *Ḥaqā'iq ʿan al-intikhābāt al-niyābiyyah fī al-ʿirāq wa filasṭīn wa sūriyah*. Cairo: Al-Akhbār Press.
al-ʿAẓm, ʿUthmān. 1925. *Majmūʿat āthār Rafīq Bey al-ʿAẓm*. Cairo: Al-Manār Press.
al-ʿAzzāwī, ʿAbbās. 1958. *Dhikrā Abī Thinā' al-Alūsī*. Baghdad: Sharikat al-Tijārah wa al-Ṭibāʿah.
al-Bānī, Muḥammad Saʿīd. 1931. *Al-Kawkab al-durrī al-munīr fī aḥkām al-dhahab wa al-fiḍḍah wa al-ḥarīr*. Damascus: Al-Mufīd Press.
______. 1920. *Tanwīr al-baṣā'ir bi sīrat al-shaykh Ṭāhir*. Damascus: Al-Ḥukūmah al-ʿArabiyyah al-Sūriyyah Press.
______. 1923. *ʿUmdat al-taḥqīq fī al-taqlīd wa al-talfīq*. Damascus: Ḥukūmat Dimashq Press.
al-Bārūdī, Fakhrī. 1951. *Mudhakkirāt al-Bārūdī*. 2 vols. Beirut: Dār al-Ḥayāt Press.
al-Bīṭār, ʿAbd al-Razzāq. 1961–1963. *Ḥilyat al-bashar fī tārīkh al-qarn al-thālith ʿashar*. 3 vols. Damascus: Majmaʿ al-Lughah al-ʿArabiyyah.
al-Bīṭār, Muḥammad Bahjat
[Nāṣir al-Dīn al-Ḥijāzi al-Atharī]. 1922. *Al-Nafkhah ʿala al-nafḥah wa al-minḥah*. Damascus: Al-Taraqqī Press.
______. *Naqd ʿayn al-mīzān*. 1913. Damascus: Al-Taraqqī Press.
______. [Abū al-Yasār al-Dimashqī al-Maydānī]. 1922. *Naẓarah fī al-nafḥah al-zakiyah fī al-radd ʿala al-firqah al-wahhābiyyah*. Damascus: Al-Taraqqī Press.
______. 1967. *Al-Riḥlah al-najdiyyah al-ḥijāziyyah: ṣuwar min ḥayāt al-bādiyah*. Damascus: Al-Jadīdah Press.
al-Budayrī, Aḥmad. 1959. *Ḥawādith dimashq al-yawmiyyah*. Edited by Muḥammad Saʿīd al-Qāsimī. Cairo: Al-Jamʿiyyah al-Miṣriyyah li al-Dirāsāt al-Tārīkhiyyah.
Churchill, Charles Henry. 1971. *Ḥayāt ʿAbd al-Qādir: al-Sulṭān al-sābiq li ʿarab al-jazā'ir*. Tunis: Dār al-T ūnisiyyah li al-Nashr. Arabic translation by Abū al-Qāsim Saʿd Allah of

Charles Henry Churchill. 1867. *The Life of Abdel Kader, Ex-Sultan of the Arabs of Algeria*. London: Chapman & Hall.

al-Dahhān, Sāmī. 1955. *Muḥammad Kurd ʿAlī: Ḥayātuhu wa āthāruhu*. Damascus: al-Majmaʿ al-ʿIlm-i al-ʿArabī.

Darwazah, Muḥammad ʿIzzat. 1950. *Ḥawla al-ḥarakah al-ʿarabiyyah al-ḥadīthah*. 2. vols. Sidon: Al-ʿAṣriyyah Press.

al-Fāsī, ʿAbd al-Ḥafīẓ. 1932. *Riyāḍ al-jannah aw al-mudhish al-muṭrib*. Rabat: Al-Waṭaniyyah Press.

al-Ḥaffār, Luṭfī. 1954. *Dhikriyyāt: Muntakhabāt min khuṭub wa aḥādīth wa maqālāt*. Damascus: Ibn Zaydūn Press.

al-Ḥamzāwī, Maḥmūd. 1882/3. *Al-Ṭarīqah al-wāḍiḥah ila al-bayyinah al-rājiḥah*. Damascus: Nahj al-Ṣawāb Press.

al-Ḥiṣnī, Muḥammad Adīb Āl Taqī al-Dīn. 1928. *Muntakhabāt al-tawārīkh li dimashq*. 3 vols. Damascus: Al-Ḥadīthah Press.

Ibn Badrān, ʿAbd al-Qādir. N.d. *Al-Madkhal ila madhhab al-imām Aḥmad ibn Hanbal*. Damascus: Dār Iḥyā' al-Turāth al-ʿArabī.

______. 1960. *Munādamat al-aṭlāl wa musāmarat al-khayāl*. Damascus: Al-Maktab al-Islāmī li al-Ṭibāʿah wa al-Nashr.

Ilyās, Jūzuf. 1972. "Taṭawwur al-ṣiḥāfah al-sūriyyah fī al-ʿahd al-ʿuthmānī." Thesis, Lebanese University.

al-Iskandarī, ʿAbd al-Qādir. 1921/22. *Al-Ḥujjah al-murḍiyah fī ithbāt al-wasītah allatī nafatha al-firqah al-wahhābiyyah*. Damascus: Al-Fayḥā' Press.

______. 1921/22. *Al-Minḥah al-ilāhiyyah fī al-radd ʿala mazaʿim al-ṭā'ifah al-wahhābiyyah*. Damascus: Al-Fayḥā' Press.

______. 1921/22. *Al-Nafḥah al-zakiyah fī al-radd ʿala shubuh al-firqah al-wahhābiyyah*. Damascus: Al-Fayḥā' Press.

Jadʿān, Fahmī. 1979. *Usus al-taqaddum ʿinda mufakkirī al-islām fī al-ʿālam al-ʿarabī al-ḥadīth*. Beirut: Al-Mu'assasah al-ʿArabiyyah li al-Dirāsāt wa al-Nashr.

Jamʿiyyat al-Shabbān al-Muslimīn. 1935. *Dhikrā ḥujjat al-islām ṣāḥib al-Manār*. Baghdad.

al-Jazā'irī, ʿAbd al-Qādir. N.d. *Dhikrā al-ʿāqil wa tanbīh al-ghāfil*. N.p.

______. 1966. *Kitāb al-mawāqif fī al-taṣawwuf wa al-waʿẓ wa al-irshād*. 3 vols. Damascus, n.p.

______. N.d. *al-Miqrāḍ al-ḥādd li qaṭʿ lisān muntaqiṣ dīn al-islām bi al-bāṭil wa al-ilḥād*. Beirut: Dār Maktabat al-Ḥayāt.

al-Jazā'irī, Aḥmad. 1906. *Nathr al-durr wa basaṭuhu fī bayān kawn al-ʿilm nuqṭah*. Beirut: Al-Ahliyyah Press.

al-Jazā'irī, Muḥammad ibn ʿAbd al-Qādir. 1964. *Tuḥfat al-zāhir fī tārīkh al-jazā'ir wa al-amīr ʿAbd al-Qādir*. Beirut: Dār al-Yaqẓah al-ʿArabiyyah.

al-Jundī, Adham. 1954. *Aʿlām al-adab wa al-fann*. 2 vols. Damascus: Majallat Ṣawt Sūriyah Press.

______. 1960. *Shuhadā' al-ḥarb al-ʿālamiyyah al-kubrā*. Damascus: Al-ʿUrūbah Press.

al-Jundī, Anwar. 1970. *Tarājim al-aʿlām al-muʿāṣirīn fī al-ʿālam al-islāmī*. Cairo: Maktabat al-Anglo al-Miṣrī.

al-Jundī, Muḥammad Salīm. 1963–1967. *Tārīkh maʿarrat al-nuʿmān*. 3 vols. Damascus: Wizārat al-Thaqāfah wa al-Siyāḥah wa al-Irshād al-Qawmī.

Kaḥḥālah, ʿUmar. 1957. *Muʿjam al-mu'allifīn; tarājim muṣannifī al-kutub al-ʿarabiyyah*. 15 vols. Damascus: Al-Taraqqī Press.

Karīmī, Muṣṭafā. 1926/27. *Nūr al-yaqīn fī mabḥath al-talqīn*. Cairo: Al-Miṣriyyah Press.

al-Kasm, ʿAṭā'. 1901. *Al-Aqwāl al-murḍiyah fī al-radd ʿala al-wahhābiyyah*. Cairo: Al-ʿUmūmiyyah Press.

Kawtharānī, Wajīh. 1980. *Wathā'iq al-mu'tamar al-ʿarabī al-awwal, 1913*. Beirut: Dār al-Ḥadāthah.

al-Khānī, ʿAbd al-Majīd. 1890. *Al-Ḥadā'iq al-wardiyyah fī ḥaqā'iq ajillā' al-naqshbandiyyah*. Cairo: Dār al-Ṭibāʿah al-ʿĀmirah.

al-Khānī, Muḥammad ibn ʿAbd Allah. 1885–86. *Kitāb al-bahjah al-saniyah fī ādāb al-ṭarīqah al-ʿaliyah al-khālidiyyah al-naqshbandiyyah*. Cairo: Dhāt al-Taḥrīr Press.

al-Khaṭīb, Adnān. 1971. *Al-Shaykh Ṭāhir al-Jazā'irī, rā'id al-nahḍah al-ʿilmiyyah fī bilād al-shām*. Cairo: Maʿhad al-Dirāsāt al-ʿArabiyyah.

al-Khaṭīb, Muḥibb al-Dīn. 1959. *Al-Duktūr Ṣalāḥ al-Dīn al-Qāsimī, 1305–1334: Ṣafaḥāt min tārīkh al-nahḍah al-ʿarabiyyah fī awā'il al-qarn al-ʿishrīn*. Cairo: Al-Salafiyyah Press.

Khazbak, Ḥasan. 1928. *Al-Maqālāt al-wufiyah fī al-radd ʿala al-wahhābiyyah*. Cairo: Al-Kamāl Press.

Khuḍūr, Adīb. 1972. *Al-Ṣiḥāfah al-sūriyyah: Nash'atuhā, taṭawwaruhā, wa wāqiʿuhā al-rāhin*. Damascus: Dār al-Baʿth.

Kurd ʿAlī, Muḥammad. 1980. *Al-Muʿāṣirūn*. Damascus: Majmaʿ al-Lughah al-ʿArabiyyah.

______. 1947–1949. *Mudhakkirāt*. 3 vols. Damascus: Al-Taraqqī Press.

Livin, Z. I. 1978. *Al-Fikr al-ijtimāʿī wa al-siyāsī al-ḥadīth fī lubnān wa sūriyā wa miṣr*. Translated by Bashīr al-Sibāʿī. Beirut: Dār Ibn Khaldūn.

Lūqā, Iskandar. 1976. *Al-Ḥarakah al-adabiyyah fī dimashq, 1800–1918*. Damascus: Alif Bā' Press.

Maḥmūd, Manīʿ ʿAbd al-Ḥalīm. 1978. *Manāhij al-mufassirīn*. Cairo: Dār al-Kitāb al-Miṣrī.

al-Māliḥ, Muḥammad Riyāḍ. 1977. *ʿĀlim al-ummah wa zāhid al-ʿaṣr al-ʿallāmah al-muḥaddith al-akbar Badr al-Dīn al-Ḥasanī*. Damascus: Maktabat al-Fārābī.

Mudhakkirāt tārīkhiyyah ʿan ḥamlat Ibrāhīm Bāshā ʿala sūriyā. Edited by Aḥmad Ghassān Sbānū. N.d. Damascus: Dār Qutaybah.

al-Muḥāfaẓah, ʿAlī. 1980. *Al-Ittijāhāt al-fikriyyah ʿinda al-ʿarab fī ʿaṣr al-nahḍah, 1798–1914*. Beirut: Al-Ahliyyah li al-Nashr wa al-Tawzīʿ.

Mujāhid, Zakī Muḥammad. 1950. *Al-Aʿlām al-sharqiyyah fī al-mi'ah al-rābiʿah ʿasharah al-hijriyyah*. 2 vols. Cairo: Dār al-Ṭibāʿah al-Miṣriyyah al-Ḥadīthah.

Mūsā, Munīr. 1973. *Al-Fikr al-ʿarabī fī al-ʿaṣr al-ḥadīth*. Beirut: Dār al-Ḥaqīqah.

Al-Mu'tamar al-duwalī al-thānī li tārīkh bilād al-shām, 1516–1939. 1978. 2 vols. Damascus: Jāmiʿat Dimashq.

al-Nabahānī, Yūsuf. 1911. *Jāmiʿ karāmāt al-awliyā'*. 2 vols. Cairo: Dār al-Kutub al-ʿArabiyyah al-Kubrā.

______. N.d. *Al-Rā'iyah al-ṣughrā fī dhamm al-bidʿah wa madḥ al-sunnah al-gharrā'*. N.p.

______. 1905. *Shawāhid al-ḥaqq fī al-istighāthah bi sayyid al-khalq*. Cairo: Al-Yamaniyyah Press.

al-Najdī, Sulaymān ibn Saḥmān, al-Marzuqī, Muḥammad ibn Ḥasan al-Qaṭarī, al-Yūsuf, ʿAlī ibn Sulaymān. N.d. *Al-Dāhiyah al-kubrā ʿala al-rā'iyah al-ṣughrā*. Bombay: Al-Muṣṭafawiyyah Press.

al-Qadrī, Aḥmad. 1956. *Mudhakkirātī ʿan al-thawrah al-ʿarabiyyah al-kubrā*. Damascus: Ibn Zaydūn Press.

Qalʿajī, Qadrī. 1954. *Al-Sābiqūn*. Beirut: Dār al-ʿIlm li al-Malāyīn.

Qasāṭilī, Nuʿmān. 1879. *Al-Rawḍah al-ghannā' fī dimashq al-fayḥā'*. Beirut, n.p.

al-Qāsimī, Muḥammad Saʿīd. 1960. *Qāmūs al-ṣinā ʿāt al-shāmiyyah*. Vol. 1. Paris: Mouton & Le Haye.

al-Qāsimī, Ẓāfir. 1965. *Jamāl al-Dīn al-Qāsimī wa ʿaṣruhu*. Damascus: Al-Hāshimiyyah Press.

al-Qāyātī, Muḥammad ʿAbd al-Jawād. 1901. *Nafḥat al-bashām fī riḥlat al-shām*. Cairo: Jarīdat al-Islām Press.

Riḍā, Rashīd. 1931. *Tārīkh al-ustādh al-imām al-shaykh Muḥammad ʿAbduh.* 2 vols. Cairo: Al-Manār Press.

al-Rifāʿī, Shams al-Dīn. 1969. *Tārīkh al-ṣiḥāfah al-sūriyyah: al-ṣiḥāfah al-sūriyyah fī al-ʿahd al-ʿuthmānī, 1800–1918.* Cairo: Dār al-Maʿārif.

al-Rikābī, Jawdat, and Sulṭān, Jamīl. 1963. *Al-Irth al-fikrī li al-muṣliḥ al-ijtimaʿī, ʿAbd al-Ḥamīd al-Zahrāwī.* Damascus: Al-Hāshimiyyah Press.

Rustum, Asad, ed. 1940–1943. *Al-Maḥfūẓāt al-malikiyyah al-miṣriyyah: Bayān bi wathā'iq al-shām wa mā yusāʿid ʿala fahmihā wa yuwaḍḍiḥ maqāṣid Muḥammad ʿAlī Bāshā.* 4 vols. Beirut: American University of Beirut Press.

Ṣābāt, Khalīl. 1958. *Tārīkh al-ṭibāʿah fī al-sharq al-ʿarabī.* Cairo: Dār al-Maʿārif.

Saʿīd, Amīn. 1934. *Al-Thawrah al-ʿarabiyyah al-kubrā.* 3 vols. Cairo: ʿIsā al-Bānī al-Chalabī Press.

Sāmī, ʿAbd al-Raḥmān. 1892. *Safar al-salām fī bilād al-shām.* Cairo: Al-Muqtaṭaf Press; reprint ed., *al-Qawl al-ḥaqq fī bayrūt wa dimashq.* 1981. Beirut: Dār al-Rā'id al-ʿArabī.

al-Shaʿrānī, ʿAbd al-Wahhāb. N.d. *Kashf al-ghummah ʿan jamīʿ al-ummah.* Cairo: N.p.

al-Shaṭṭī, Ḥasan. 1932. *Aqrab al-masālik li bayān al-manāsik.* Damascus: Al-Taraqqī Press.

———. 1908. *Risālah fī al-taqlīd wa al-talfīq.* Damascus: Rawḍat al-Shām Press.

al-Shaṭṭī, Muḥammad Jamīl. 1972. *Aʿyān dimashq fī al-qarn al-thālith ʿashar wa niṣf al-qarn al-rābiʿ ʿashar.* 2nd edition. Damascus: Al-Maktab al-Islāmī.

———. 1921. *Mukhtaṣar al-ṭabaqāt al-ḥanābilah.* Damascus: Al-Taraqqī Press.

al-Shaṭṭī, Muṣṭafā. N.d. *Al-Nuqūl al-sharʿiyyah fī al-radd ʿala al-wahhābiyyah.* N.p.

al-Shihābī, Muṣṭafā. 1958. *Muḥāḍarāt ʿan al-qawmiyyah al-ʿarabiyyah: Tārīkhuhā wa qawāmuhā wa marāmīhā.* Cairo: Jāmiʿat al-Duwal al-ʿArabiyyah.

al-Ṣulḥ, ʿĀdil. 1966. *Suṭūr min al-risālah: Tārīkh ḥarakah istiqlāliyyah qāmat fī al-mashriq al-ʿarabī sanat 1877.* Beirut: Dār al-ʿIlm li al-Malāyīn.

al-Sūqiyah, Tawfīq. 1921/22. *Al-Risālah al-ūlā: Tabyīn al-ḥaqq wa al-ṣawāb bi al-radd ʿala atbāʿ Ibn ʿAbd al-Wahhāb.* Damascus: Al-Fayḥā' Press.

al-Ṭabbāʿ, Muḥammad Abū al-Khayr. 1909. *Kitāb fatḥ al-aʿlām fī intiṣār li al-ʿallāmah al-muḥaqqiq Kamāl al-Dīn ibn al-Humām min al-ustādh al-ʿallāmah al-shaykh Muḥammad Jamāl al-Dīn Afandī al-Qāsimī bi mā nāqashahu bi hi fī mas'alat al-rakʿatayn qabl al-maghrib.* Damascus: Al-Iṣlāḥ Press.

al-Tamīmī, ʿAbd al-Jalīl. "Wathā'iq jadīdah li al-amīr ʿAbd al-Qādir." *Revue d'histoire maghrebine* 6 (1979): 23–32.

Ṭarabayn, Aḥmad. "Al-Ḥayāt al-ʿilmiyyah fī bilād al-shām fī al-qarn al-thālith ʿashar al-hijrī min khilāl *Ḥilyat al-bashar fī tārīkh al-qarn al-thālith ʿashar* li al-shaykh ʿAbd al-Razzāq al-Biṭār." In *al-Mu'tamar al-duwalī al-thānī li tārīkh bilād al-shām, 1516–1939.* 2 vols. 1978. Damascus: Damascus University.

Ṭarrāzī, Philippe de. 1947–1951. *Khazā'in al-kutub al-ʿarabiyyah fī al-khāfiqayn.* Beirut: Dār al-Kutub.

Taymūr, Aḥmad. 1967. *Aʿlām al-fikr al-islāmī fī al-ʿaṣr al-ḥadīth.* Cairo: Lajnat Nashr al-Mu'allafāt al-Taymūriyyah.

Zabārah, Muḥammad ibn Muḥammad. 1929/30–1931/32. *Nayl al-waṭar min tarājim rijāl al-yaman fī al-qarn al-thālith ʿashar.* 2 vols. Cairo: Al-Salafiyyah Press.

al-Zahrāwī, ʿAbd al-Ḥamīd. 1901. *Al-Fiqh wa al-taṣawwuf.* Cairo: Al-ʿUmūmiyyah Press.

al-Zayāt, Ḥabīb. 1902. *Khazā'in al-kutub fī dimashq wa ḍawāḥīhā.* Cairo: Dār al-Maʿārif; reprint ed., 1982. Damascus: Alif Bā' Press.

al-Ziriklī, Khayr al-Dīn. 1979. *Al-Aʿlām; Qāmūs tarājim li ashhar al-rijāl wa al-nisā' min al-ʿarab wa al-mustaʿribīn wa al-mustashriqīn.* 8 vols. 4th edition. Beirut: Dār al-ʿIlm li al-Malāyīn.

Zukkār, Suhayl. 1982. *Bilād al-shām fī al-qarn al-tāsiʿ ʿashar.* Damascus: Dār Ḥassān.

Works in European Languages

Abu-Manneh, Butrus. "The Naqshbandiyya-Mujaddidiyya in the Ottoman Lands in the Early 19th Century." *Die Welt des Islams* 22 (1982): 1–36.

______. "Sultan Abdülḥamīd II and Shaikh Abūlhudā al-Ṣayyādī." *Middle Eastern Studies* 15 (1979): 131–153.

Abun-Nasr, Jamil. 1971. *A History of the Maghrib*. Cambridge: Cambridge University Press.

Adams, Charles. 1933. *Islam and Modernism in Egypt*. London: Russell & Russell.

Ageron, Charles-Robert. "Abd el-Kader souverain d'un royaume arabe d'orient." *Revue de l'Occident Musulman et de la Méditerranée*. Numéro Spécial, 1970: IIe Congrès International d'Études Nord-Africaines. Actes du Congrès, 15–30.

Ahmad, Feroz. 1969. *The Young Turks: The Committee of Union and Progress in Turkish Politics, 1908–1914*. Oxford: Clarendon Press.

Ahmad Khan, Mu'in al-Dīn. 1955. *History of the Fara'idi Movement in Bengal*. Karachi: Pakistan Historical Society.

Algar, Hamid. "The Naqshbandī Order: A Preliminary Survey of Its History and Significance." *Studia Islamica* 44 (1976): 123–152.

Ayalon, Ami. *Language and Change in the Arab Middle East*. New York: Oxford University Press, 1987.

Baer, Gabriel, ed. *The ʿUlama in Modern History. Asian and African Studies* 7 (1971).

Baldry, John. "Imam Yaḥyā and the Yamani Uprising of 1904–1907." *Abr-Nahrain* 18 (1978–1979): 33–73.

Barbir, Karl. 1980. *Ottoman Rule in Damascus*. Princeton: Princeton University Press.

Bell, Gertrude. 1907. *Syria: The Desert and the Sown*. New York: E.P. Dutton and Company; reprint ed., 1973. New York: Arno Press.

Berkes, Niyazi. 1964. *The Development of Secularism in Turkey*. Montreal: McGill University Press.

Braude, Benjamin and Bernard Lewis, eds. 1982. *Christians and Jews in the Ottoman Empire*. 2 vols. New York: Holmes & Meier. Vol. 2: *The Arabic-Speaking Lands*.

Bury, John P. T. 1964. *Napoleon III and the Second Empire*. London: English Universities Press.

Chambers, Richard L. 1968. "Aḥmed Cevdet Paşa: The Formative Years of an Ottoman Transitional." Ph.D. dissertation, Princeton University.

Chevallier, Dominique. "À Damas, production et société à la fin du XIXe siècle." *Annales* 19 (1964): 966–972.

Cioeta, Donald J. "Ottoman Censorship in Lebanon and Syria, 1876–1908." *International Journal of Middle East Studies* 10 (1979): 167–181.

Cole, Juan Ricardo. "Feminism, Class, and Islam in Turn-of-the-Century Egypt." *International Journal of Middle East Studies* 13 (1981): 387–407.

______. 1984. "Imāmī Shīʿism from Iran to North India, 1722–1856: State, Society, and Clerical Ideology in Awadh." Ph.D. dissertation, University of California, Los Angeles.

______. "Rashīd Riḍā on the Bahā'ī Faith: A Utilitarian Theory on the Spread of Religions." *Arab Studies Quarterly* 5 (1983): 276–291.

______. "Rifāʿa al-Ṭahṭāwī and the Revival of Practical Philosophy." *Muslim World* 70 (1980): 29–46.

Dabbagh, Salah M. "Agrarian Reform in Syria." *Middle East Economic Papers* (1962): 1–15.

Danziger, Raphael. 1977. *Abd al-Qādir and the Algerian Resistance to the French and Internal Consolidation*. New York: Holmes & Meier.

Davison, Roderic H. 1963. *Reform in the Ottoman Empire, 1856–1876*. Princeton: Princeton University Press.

Dawn, C. Ernest. 1973. *From Ottomanism to Arabism: Essays on the Origins of Arab Nationalism*. Urbana, IL: University of Illinois Press.

de Guerville, A. B. 1906. *New Egypt*. London: Heinemann.

Eickelman, Dale. "The Art of Memory: Islamic Education and Its Social Reproduction." *Comparative Studies in Society and History* 20 (1978): 485–516.

Emerit, Marcel. "La crise syrienne et l'expansion économique française en 1860." *La Revue Historique* 207 (1952): 211–232.

d'Estailleur-Chanteraine. 1959. *L'Emir magnanime Abd-El-Kader le croyant*. Paris: Librairie Arthème Fayard.

Fakhry, Majid. 1970. *A History of Islamic Philosophy.* New York: Columbia University Press.

Farhi, David. "The Şeriat as a Political Slogan—or the Incident of the 31st Mart." *Middle Eastern Studies* 7 (1971): 275–299.

Gerth, H. H. and C. Wright Mills. 1946. *From Max Weber: Essays in Sociology.* New York: Oxford University Press.

Gouldner, Alvin W. 1979. *The Future of Intellectuals and the Rise of the New Class*. New York: Oxford University Press.

Gran, Peter. 1979. *Islamic Roots of Capitalism*. Austin: University of Texas Press.

Green, Arnold. 1978. *The Tunisian Ulama, 1873–1915: Social Structure and Response to Ideological Currents*. Leiden: E. J. Brill.

Gross, Max. 1979. "Ottoman Rule in the Province of Damascus, 1860–1909." Ph.D. dissertation, Georgetown University.

Haim, Sylvia G., ed. 1962. *Arab Nationalism: An Anthology.* Berkeley: University of California Press.

Hallaq, Wael B. "Was the Gate of Ijtihād Closed?" *International Journal of Middle East Studies* 16 (1984): 3–41.

d'Hauterive, Ernest, ed. 1970. *The Second Empire and Its Downfall: The Correspondence of the Emperor Napoleon III and His Cousin Prince Napoleon*. Freeport, NY: Books for Libraries Press.

Heyd, Uriel. "The Ottoman 'Ulemā' and Westernization in the Time of Selīm III and Maḥmūd II," *Scripta Hierosolymitana,* Studies in Islamic History and Civilization. Jerusalem: Magnes Press, 1961.

Hiskett, Mervyn. "An Islamic Tradition of Reform in the Western Sudan from the Sixteenth to the Eighteenth Century." *Bulletin of the School of Oriental and African Studies* 25 (1962): 577–596.

Hourani, Albert. 1970. *Arabic Thought in the Liberal Age, 1798–1939*. London: Oxford University Press.

______. 1981. *The Emergence of the Middle East*. London: The Macmillan Press.

______. "Ottoman Reform and the Politics of the Notables." In *The Beginnings of Modernization in the Middle East: The Nineteenth Century,* pp. 41–68. Edited by William R. Polk and Richard L. Chambers. 1968. Chicago: University of Chicago Press.

______. "Shaykh Khalid and the Naqshbandi Order." In *Islamic Philosophy and the Classical Tradition: Essays Presented to R. Walzer,* pp. 89–103. Edited by S. M. Stern, A. Hourani, and V. Brown. 1972. Columbia, SC: University of South Carolina Press.

Issawi, Charles. "British Consular Views on Syria's Economy in the 1850s–1860s." In *American University of Beirut Festival Book,* pp. 103–120. Edited by Fu'ad Sarruf and Suha Tamin. 1967. Beirut: American University of Beirut Press.

______. "British Trade and the Rise of Beirut, 1830–1860." *International Journal of Middle East Studies* 8 (1977): 91–101.

Issawi, Charles, ed. 1966. *The Economic History of the Middle East*. Chicago: University of Chicago Press.

Kazziha, Walid. "The Jarīdah-Ummah Group in Egyptian Politics." *Middle Eastern Studies* 13 (1977): 373–385.

Keddie, Nikki R. 1972. *Sayyid Jamāl al-Dīn "al-Afghānī": A Political Biography.* Berkeley: University of California Press.

______, ed. 1972. *Scholars, Saints, and Sufis: Muslim Religious Institutions Since 1500.* Berkeley: University of California Press.

Kerr, Malcolm. 1966. *Islamic Reform: The Political and Legal Theories of Muhammad ʿAbduh and Rashīd Riḍā.* Berkeley: University of California Press.

Khalidi, Rashid I. 1980. *British Policy Towards Syria and Palestine, 1906–1914.* London: Ithaca Press.

______. "The Press as a Source for Modern Arab Political History: Abd al-Ghanī al-Uraisī and *al-Mufīd.*" *Arab Studies Quarterly* 3 (1981): 22–42.

______. "Social Factors in the Rise of the Arab Movement in Syria." In *From Nationalism to Revolutionary Islam,* pp. 53–70. Edited by Said Amir Arjomand. 1984. Albany: State University of New York Press.

______. "The 1912 Election Campaign in the Cities of *bilād al-Shām.*" *International Journal of Middle East Studies* 16 (1984): 461–474.

Khoury, Philip S. "Syrian Urban Politics in Transition: The Quarters of Damascus During the French Mandate." *International Journal of Middle East Studies* 16 (1984): 507–540.

______. 1983. *Urban Notables and Arab Nationalism: The Politics of Damascus, 1860–1920.* Cambridge: Cambridge University Press.

Koury, George. 1970. "The Province of Damascus, 1783–1832." Ph.D. dissertation, University of Michigan.

Landau, Jacob. 1971. *The Hijaz Railway and the Muslim Pilgrimage: A Case of Ottoman Political Propaganda.* Detroit: Wayne State University Press.

Laoust, Henri. 1939. *Essai sur les doctrines sociales et politiques de Takī-al-Dīn Aḥmad ibn Taimiya.* Cairo: L'Institut Français d'Archéologie Orientale.

______. "Le réformisme orthodoxe des ʿsalafiya' et les caractères généraux de son orientation actuelle." *Revue des Études Islamiques* 6 (1932): 175–224.

Lewis, Bernard. 1961. *The Emergence of Modern Turkey.* New York: Oxford University Press.

Makdisi, George. "The Ḥanbalī School and Sufism." *Humaniora Islamica* 2 (1974): 61–72.

______. "Ibn Taimiya: A Sufi of the Qādiriya Order." *American Journal of Arabic Studies* 1 (1973): 118–130.

Ma'oz, Moshe. "Communal Conflict in Ottoman Syria During the Reform Era: The Role of Political and Economic Factors." In *Christians and Jews in the Ottoman Empire: The Arabic-Speaking Lands,* pp. 91–105. Edited by Benjamin Braude and Bernard Lewis. 1982. New York: Holmes & Meier.

______. 1968. *Ottoman Reform in Syria and Palestine, 1840–1861.* Oxford: Clarendon Press.

______. "Syrian Urban Politics in the Tanzimat Period Between 1840–1861." *Bulletin of the School of Oriental and African Studies* 29 (1966): 277–301.

______. "The Ulama and the Process of Modernization in Syria During the mid-nineteenth Century." In *The ʿUlama in Modern History.* Edited by Gabriel Baer, *Asian and African Studies* 7 (1971): 77–88.

Mardin, Şerif. 1962. *The Genesis of Young Ottoman Thought.* Princeton: Princeton University Press.

______. "Libertarian Movements in the Ottoman Empire, 1878–1895." *Middle East Journal* 16 (1962): 169–182.

Mardin, Şerif. "Some Notes on an Early Phase in the Modernization of Communication in Turkey." *Comparative Studies in Society and History* 3 (1961): 250–271.

Metcalf, Barbara Daly. 1982. *Islamic Revival in British India: Deoband, 1860–1900*. Princeton: Princeton University Press.

Midḥat Bey, Alī Ḥaydar. 1903. *The Life of Midḥat Pasha*. London: John Murray.

Nadir, Ahmad. "Les ordres religieux et la conquête française." *Revue Algérienne des Sciences Juridiques* 9 (1972): 819–868.

Ochsenwald, William. 1984. *Religion, Society, and the State in Arabia: The Hijaz Under Ottoman Control, 1840–1908*. Columbus: Ohio University Press.

Owen, E. Roger. 1981. *The Middle East in the World Economy, 1800–1914*. London: Methuen.

Pasha, Djemāl. *La Vérité sur la question syrienne*. 1916. Istanbul.

______. N.d. *Memories of a Turkish Statesman, 1913–1919*. London, n.p.

Philby, Harry St. John Bridger. 1955. *Saudi Arabia*. New York: Praeger.

Polk, William R. 1980. *The Arab World*. Cambridge, MA: Harvard University Press.

Polk, William R. and Richard L. Chambers, eds. 1968. *The Beginnings of Modernization in the Middle East: The Nineteenth Century*. Chicago: University of Chicago Press.

Rafeq, Abdul-Karim. 1970. *Province of Damascus, 1723–1783*. Beirut: Khayats.

Rahbar, Muhammad Daud. "Shāh Walī Ullah and Ijtihād." *Muslim World* 45 (1955): 346–358.

Rahman, Fazlur. 1968. *Islam*. Garden City, NY: Doubleday & Co.

Ramsaur, E. E. 1957. *The Young Turks: Prelude to the Revolution of 1908*. Princeton: Princeton University Press; 2nd edition, 1970. New York: Russell & Russell.

Roded, Ruth. 1984. "Tradition and Change in Syria During the Last Decades of Ottoman Rule: The Urban Elite of Damascus, Aleppo, Homs, and Hama, 1876–1918." Ph.D. dissertation, University of Denver.

Salibi, Kamal S. "The 1860 Upheaval in Damascus as Seen by al-Sayyid Muḥammad Abū'l-Suʿūd al-Ḥasībī, Notable and Later *Naqīb al-Ashrāf* of the City." In *The Beginnings of Modernization in the Middle East,* pp. 185–202. Edited by William R. Polk and Richard L. Chambers. 1968. Chicago: University of Chicago Press.

Schilcher, Linda Schatkowski. 1985. *Families in Politics: Damascene Factions and Estates of the 18th and 19th Centuries*. Stuttgart: Franz Steiner Verlag Wiesbaden GMBH.

Shinar, Pessah. "ʿAbd al-Qādir and ʿAbd al-Krim: Religious Influences on Their Thought and Action." *Asian and African Studies* 1 (1965): 139–174.

Smith, Charles D. 1983. *Islam and the Search for Social Order in Modern Egypt*. Albany: State University of New York Press.

Smith, William H. C. 1972. *Napoleon III*. London: Wayland Ltd.

Stern, S. M., A. Hourani, and V. Brown, eds. 1972. *Islamic Philosophy and the Classical Tradition*. Columbia, SC: University of South Carolina Press.

Swenson, Victor R. "The Military Rising in Istanbul, 1909." *Journal of Contemporary History* 5 (1970): 171–184.

Therborn, Goran. 1980. *The Ideology of Power and the Power of Ideology.* London: Verso.

Tibawi, Abd al-Latif. 1969. *A Modern History of Syria, Including Lebanon and Palestine*. London: Macmillan and Co.

Trimingham, J. Spencer. 1971. *The Sufi Orders in Islam*. London: Oxford University Press.

Voll, John O. 1982. *Islam: Continuity and Change in the Modern World*. Boulder: Westview Press.

______. "The Non-Wahhābī Ḥanbalīs of Eighteenth-Century Syria." *Der Islam* 49 (1972): 277–291.

______. "Old Ulama Families and Ottoman Influence in Eighteenth-Century Damascus." *American Journal of Arabic Studies* 3 (1971): 48–59.

Williams, Raymond. 1981. *Culture*. Glasgow: Fontana.
Winter, Michael. 1982. *Society and Religion in Early Ottoman Egypt*. New Brunswick, NJ: Transaction Books.
Yacono, Xavier. "Abdelkader, franc-macon." *Humanisme* 57 (1966): 5–37.
Zeine, Zeine N. 1958. *Arab–Turkish Relations and the Emergence of Arab Nationalism*. Beirut: Khayats.

Other Published Works by Jamāl al-Dīn al-Qāsimī

Ḥayāt al-Bukhārī. Sidon: Al-ʿIrfān Press, 1912.
Kitāb al-isrā' wa al-miʿrāj. Damascus: Al-Fayḥā' Press, 1913.
Kitāb madhāhib al-aʿrāb wa falāsifat al-islām fī al-jinn. Damascus: Al-Muqtabas Press, 1910.
Majmūʿat khuṭab. Damascus: Muḥammad Hāshim al-Kutubī, 1907.
Majmūʿ al-rasā'il fī uṣūl al-tafsīr wa uṣūl al-fiqh. Damascus: Al-Fayḥā' Press, 1913.
Risālah fī al-shāy wa al-qahwah wa al-dukhkhān. Beirut: Thamārat al-Funūn Press, 1904.
Shadhrat al-bāhiyah fī alghāz naḥawiyyah wa adabiyyah. Damascus: Rawḍat al-Shām, 1904.
Sharaf al-asbāṭ. Damascus: Al-Taraqqī Press, 1913.
al-Qāsimī, Jamāl al-Dīn, ʿAbduh, Muḥammad, and Riḍā, Rashīd. *Fatāwā muhimmah fī al-sharīʿah al-islāmiyyah fī al-maḥākim al-ʿuthmāniyyah wa al-miṣriyyah*. Cairo: Al-Manār Press, 1913.

Interviews

Muṭīʿ al-Ḥāfiẓ (Damascus, June 1983).
Samīḥ al-Ghabrah (Damascus, June 1983).
Muḥammad Saʿīd al-Qāsimī (Damascus, 20 January 1983).
Ẓāfir al-Qāsimī (Beirut, July 1980).

Index

ʿAbd Allah al-ʿAẓm school, 15
ʿAbd al-ʿAzīz, Shāh, 35
ʿAbduh, Muḥammad, 30–33, 40, 48, 60–64, 81, 106, 107, 109, 110, 117, 118
Abdülḥamīd, Sultan, 55, 56, 60, 89, 90, 92, 94, 105, 107–110, 114–116, 120, 124, 126, 128, 133, 137, 142
Abdülmecīd, Sultan, 39
al-ʿĀbid, Aḥmad ʿIzzat, 17, 117, 129
al-Afghānī, ʿAbd al-Bāqī, 47, 55
al-Afghānī, ʿAbd al-Ḥakīm, 47
al-Afghānī, Jamāl al-Dīn, 31–33, 40, 67, 109, 117, 118
Agriculture, al-Qāsimī (Jamāl al-Dīn) on, 87
Ahl-i Ḥadīth, 25
Ahmad, Feroz, 128
Ibn Aḥmad, Ṭāhir, 26
Ibn ʿAlī, Ḥusayn, 85
Āl Kāshif al-Ghiṭā', Muḥammad al-Ḥusayn, 85, 88
al-Alūsī, Abū Thinā Shihāb al-Dīn, 24
al-Alūsī, ʿAlī ʿAlā al-Dīn, 25, 60
al-Alūsī, Maḥmūd Shukrī, 25–26, 88, 109, 117, 118
al-Alūsī, Nuʿmān Khayr al-Dīn, 24–25, 60, 118
Alūsī family, 24–26, 32
Amīn, Qāsim, 82
Anglo-Ottoman treaty of 1838, 11
Anṭūn, Faraḥ, 31
Ibn ʿAqīl, Muḥammad, 84
Arab Congress of 1913, 138
Ibn ʿArabī, Muḥyi al-Dīn, 81, 112, 113
Arabists, 89–103
  alienation from Committee for Union and Progress (CUP), 133–137
  Arab Renaissance Society, 96, 98, 101, 103, 125, 132
  constitutional restoration and, 124–125, 128
  departure from salafism, 98–102
  fundamental differences between salafis and, 143
  al-Jazā'irī (Ṭāhir) as link between Young Ottomans and, 89–95
  junior circle, 95–98
  political behavior of, 139–140
  political realignment by, 138
  Syrian Renaissance Society, 132, 135–137
"Arab Question and Its Origin, The" (Ṣalāḥ al-Dīn al-Qāsimī), 135
Arab Renaissance Society, 96, 98, 101, 103, 125, 132
ʿĀrif Ḥikmet Pasha, 39
al-ʿAsalī, Shukrī, 93, 94, 129
al-ʿAṭṭār, Bakrī, 50–52, 56
al-ʿAṭṭār, Ḥasan, 39
al-ʿAṭṭār, Muḥammad, 24, 39
al-Ayyūbī, Tawfiq, 52
al-ʿAẓm, ʿAbd Allah al-Mu'ayyad, 131
al-ʿAẓm, ʿAlī, 91
al-ʿAẓm, Ismāʿīl Pasha, 92
al-ʿAẓm, Khalīl, 86
al-ʿAẓm, Maḥmūd, 93
al-ʿAẓm, Muḥammad Fawzī, 62, 129
al-ʿAẓm, Mukhtār al-Mu'ayyad, 106–107
al-ʿAẓm, Rafīq, 61, 92–93, 109, 126, 128, 129
al-ʿAẓm, ʿUthmān, 92

Ibn Badrān, ʿAbd al-Qādir, 47, 65
Badrī Bey, 93
Bahā' Bey, 90, 91
"Basis of Laying Down the Constitution, The" (Jamāl al-Dīn al-Qāsimī), 127
al-Bīṭār, ʿAbd al-Ghanī, 39, 50
al-Bīṭār, ʿAbd al-Razzāq, 31, 38–40, 45, 48, 50, 56, 59–63, 65, 81, 109, 122, 129, 134–136, 138
  mujtahids incident and, 50, 53, 54
  persecution of, 110–114
al-Bīṭār, Bahā' al-Dīn, 39
al-Bīṭār, Ḥasan, 38–39
al-Bīṭār, Ibrahīm, 38
al-Bīṭār, Muḥammad, 39
al-Bīṭār, Muḥammad Bahjat, 40, 85, 118
al-Bīṭār, Salīm, 39, 111, 138
Bīṭār family, 38–40, 47–48
Blunt, Wilfred, 108–109
Book of Harmonies, The (al-Shāṭibī), 62
Book of Stations (ʿAbd al-Qādir al-Jazā'irī), 30
British rule in Egypt, 107, 109
al-Bukhārī, Maḥmūd Jalāl, 97
al-Bukhārī, Murād, 35
al-Bukhārī, Salīm, 9, 46, 56–57, 65, 69, 75, 91–93, 96, 129